# The Media Student's Book

## Fifth Edition

**GILL BRANSTON**
with
**ROY STAFFORD**

Routledge
Taylor & Francis Group

LONDON AND NEW YORK

First published 1996
by Routledge

Second edition first published 1999

Third edition first published 2003

Fourth edition first published 2006

This fifth edition first published 2010
by Routledge
2 Park Square, Milton Park, Abingdon, Oxon OX14 4RN

Simultaneously published in the USA and Canada
by Routledge
270 Madison Avenue, New York, NY 10016

*Routledge is an imprint of the Taylor & Francis Group, an informa business*

© 1996, 1999, 2003, 2006, 2010 Gill Branston and Roy Stafford

Designed and typeset in Veljovic and Gill
by Keystroke, Tettenhall, Wolverhampton

Printed and bound in Great Britain

*British Library Cataloguing in Publication Data*
A catalogue record for this book is available from the British Library

*Library of Congress Cataloging in Publication Data*
A catalog record for this book has been requested
Branston, Gill.
    The media student's book / Gill Branston with Roy Stafford. – 5th ed.
        p. cm.
    1. Mass media. I. Stafford, Roy. II. Title.
    P90.B6764 2010
    302.23–dc22                                                 2009049055

ISBN10: 0–415–55841–7 (hbk)
ISBN10: 0–415–55842–5 (pbk)
ISBN10: 0–203–85064–5 (ebk)

ISBN13: 978–0–415–55841–9 (hbk)
ISBN13: 978–0–415–55842–6 (pbk)
ISBN13: 978–0–203–85064–0 (ebk)

# Praise for previous editions

## Fourth edition

'The best introduction I know to media studies with an extraordinary range of examples and highly effective suggestions for student activity. Brilliantly updated, making great use of web resources, the new sections . . . show how cleverly the authors take the pulse of media culture.'

Christine Geraghty, *University of Glasgow, UK*

## Third edition

'Brilliantly conceived and executed, this is simply the best introduction to media studies we have.'

Toby Miller, *University of California at Riverside, USA*

'What is by now evident . . . is the authors' exceptional genius at modernising their text, examples and case studies... As a set text, this is now in a class of its own.'

David Lusted, *Southampton Solent University, UK*

## Second edition

'A book which no college or first year undergraduate student of media studies can afford to ignore . . . indispensable.'

Andrew Beck, *Coventry University, UK*

'Finally! A textbook especially designed for a critical introductory course in media studies . . . It is the perfect introduction to complex concepts and the authors do a wonderful job of explaining key critical theories in terms accessible to undergraduate students. I am a passionate fan of this book.'

Clemencia Rodriguez, *University of Texas, San Antonio, USA*

## First edition

'Imaginative, accessible, comprehensive and shrewd – all textbooks should be like this. No student could read it without coming away thoroughly prepared for the pleasures, pitfalls and challenges of media studies, and no teacher in the field could fail to find it a superb and timely source of ideas.'

Andy Medhurst, *University of Sussex, UK*

'An exemplary textbook for media studies . . . they write in a lively, engaging style . . . they offer a strong sense of argument, debating the ideas of referenced authorities by asserting their own sense of where their positions lie . . . They deal with the widest imaginable, exhaustive and enviable range of references . . . they are not frightened to explore the most difficult theories and they do so with enviable explanatory skill, constant references and exemplification . . . An extraordinary feat of writing for an audience at this educational level. I've no doubt future publications will be judged by the standard it sets.'

David Lusted, *English and Media Magazine*

# Guided tour

**Part I Key Concepts** provides an excellent toolbox of analytical approaches to indispensible terms and aspects of media analysis such as semiotics, narrative, representation, genre and discourse.

**Part II Debates** provides a comprehensive overview of current major media debates, many involving digital and social media, as well as approaches to teaching them.

**Part III**, with its dedicated chapter **Research: Skills and methods**, provides you with useful guidelines, from questions of approaching theory and individual research methods to the key issues of the reliability of internet sources and plagiarism.

**title pages**
Illustrated title pages for the three main parts of the textbook clearly outline the chapters and stand-alone case studies for ease of location.

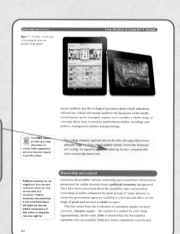

**yellow boxes**
Key concepts, biographies of major thinkers, discussion points, useful terms and worked examples offer clarity and further understanding.

**chapter menus**
A summary box indicates the main areas covered by the chapter.

**explore boxes**
A wide range of activities (some simple, others more complex) to encourage independent study and to aid learning. These explorations will help you to answer the probing questions that your media studies course will present you with.

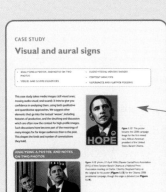

**case studies**
Stand-alone case studies provide in-depth analysis of contemporary and key issues. Shorter, embedded case studies (also highlighted in green for ease of reference) present a more condensed look at fascinating topics in the context of individual chapters.

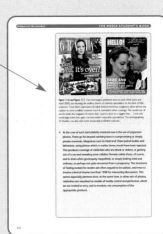

**marginal notes**
Key terms, theorists, questions, definitions, jokes, and links to further online viewing, reading and research are outlined here.

**online resources**
Links to the companion MSB5 website for new and updated material. All the web links from inside the book are also included on the website for ease of use (so there is no need to type them out!).

**references and further reading**
The book provides a wealth of references, both to print and internet sources. These are made doubly accessible by the combination of systematic further reading lists at the end of each chapter and case study, plus links to further material located in the marginal notes and yellow boxes within the text.

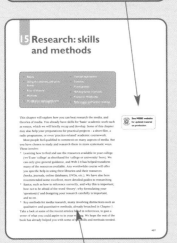

**research: skills and methods**
A dedicated chapter on research methods, skills and references will help you to prepare for essays and dissertations.

**glossary**
Key terms are highlighted in bold in the textbook when first used, and are collated here in a handy reference. The glossary has been designed to be used in conjunction with the index, contents list, chapter menus and MSB5 website to easily locate the information you are after.

# More praise for this new edition

'This is an excellent core text for first year undergraduates, offering breadth, balance and a wealth of guidance towards further reading and research.' Christa van Raalte, *Teesside University, UK*

'The fifth edition of *The Media Student's Book* is the best edition yet. Its reorganized and revised contents make the material more accessible and also provide valuable updated overviews of contemporary developments in both new and longer-standing forms of media. One of the book's major strengths is its combination of detailed up-to-date accounts of contemporary media forms together with a deeper historical and theoretical perspective. The widespread inclusion of discussions and case studies on media texts and genres which have emerged since the fourth edition also ensures the book's continuing ability to dialogue with media students and to provide a focused account of the contemporary media landscape.' Hilary Dannenberg, *University of Trier, Germany*

This book breaks down the discipline into concepts, then shows how each one links to others. It makes sense of the huge interdisciplinary area of media studies by providing clear definitions of key concepts, illustrated with up-to-date examples and a wealth of external links. The language is simple and direct without being patronising. As well as allowing students to understand different approaches within media studies, this book will be a useful tool in essay writing and other assessment projects. Perhaps most importantly, because of the range of examples used and its thought-provoking style, I think after reading this, students will apply what they read and through that at least begin to understand the media around them. I think both lecturers and students will find this interesting, stimulating and very useful.' Carole Fleming, *Nottingham Trent University, UK*

# Student feedback

'The new edition is great! It is accessible and easy to relate to. The use of normal everyday examples that a student will have come across instead of academic (probably unseen) ones makes understanding difficult theories and philosophies easy and straight-forward. It is like somebody your age is explaining it. I like how it acknowledges the change in the way people learn, with a greater reliance on the internet and absorbs this into its design and layout. The "Explore" sections are also really well put together as they make you aware of all the media things that saturate your day-to-day life that you have grown to ignore or take for granted, and they make you take a step back and critically analyse them.' Charlotte Dean, *media studies student at St Andrews University, UK*

'I think that the new edition is fantastic. It's very comprehensive and the examples used are very relevant to the topics discussed. I like the side information as it explains key concepts for readers who may not be aware of their meaning. Also, the extra websites and exercises I feel will enhance learning and allow the student to interact more with the topics covered. In the introduction, I like how readers can feedback to the authors directly by email. I think it displays two-way media and new media culture very well.' Anna Jordan, *media studies student at Stirling University, UK*

# Contents

# CONTENTS

# CONTENTS

# Illustrations

The images below have been reproduced with kind permission. Whilst every effort has been made to trace copyright holders and obtain permission, this has not been possible in all cases. Any omissions brought to our attention will be remedied in future editions.

# Acknowledgements

Thanks, for many different kinds of contribution, to Ralph Beliveau, Duncan Bloy, Jean Bool, Paul Bowman, Alison Charles, Simon Cottle, Cath Davies, Rian Evans, Bob Franklin, Jeremy Hawthorn, Val Hill, Anne Hubbard, Renee Lertzman, Jo Littler, Daniel Meadows, Glyn Mottershead, Paul Murschetz, Linda Pariser, Andres Schipani, Salvatore Scifo, Gillian Swanson, Tom Tyler, Richard Walker, Claire Wardle, Tana Wollen. From Roy, thanks to all the education staff and projectionists at the National Media Museum, Bradford, Cornerhouse Cinema, Manchester and other venues for help in understanding at least one media business.

To the usual mob, love and thanks from Gill for support and laughs through most stages of all of this: Lucy, Rob, Ruby and Lily Branston-Seago; Lauren, Alistair and Ben Bryan; and Alison and Paul O'Rourke. From Roy to Marion, heartfelt thanks for all your support.

To Natalie Foster, to Sarah Mabley, to Aileen Storry and to Moira Taylor (once more) many thanks, for patience, practicality and enthusiasm when it was needed – which was often, during such a complex production process. And for being generally a pleasure to work with during the many hours spent on images and design, a special thanks to Charlotte Wood.

Finally, and emphatically, yet again, none of this would have been possible without the help and questions of the students, teachers, researchers and media practitioners with whom we have worked over the years.

# Introduction

Previous editions of this book have always tried to work with the ways in which media studies *both*

- relates very intimately to the sharpest contemporary cultural pleasures, and
- draws on a range of sometimes difficult theories and approaches in order to explore, debate and locate these experiences.

Writing this edition we've been even more aware of huge recent changes in the media – and the other – worlds that we all navigate. But equally we're struck by the excitability and scale of recent claims made for media technologies themselves, for their impact on the world of work and business, and for the form which media studies has to take now because of this. These are respectively sometimes called Web 2.0 and Media Studies 2.0.

> As well as the internet, the impact of '9/11' has reshaped the world, and the uses of internet technologies, both for surveillance and for kinds of protest. We argue that awareness of such political contexts is key for study of media now.

## Modern media

You have most likely grown up in environments saturated with media experiences. In countries with reliable and widespread electricity supplies (and even broadband), as well as the provision of basic needs, including literacy, these experiences are interfused with everyday life itself, especially through the internet. One theorist wrote, decades ago, that 'TV now escorts children across the globe even before they have permission to cross the street' (Meyrowitz 1985: 238). This seems even truer today of global media which are 'always on' and instantaneous – for some. Portable and interactive media like 'mobiles' or cell phones can now keep children in touch with parents, and friends, and indeed the world, as they cross the street.

The familiarity and embeddedness of media, their easy pleasures, comforting habits and routines, as well as the terrors that they trade in, and inflict, create problems for any textbook. Interactive media compete for your attention. Colleges often have to forbid the use of mobile phones in classes, and the internet has transformed the activities of researching and writing at all levels.

*Figure 0.1* Interactive global media are a long way from the chained books of early print forms, which are here played with in a sculpture at the British Library in Wetherby. Our book explores some of the links to, as well as the differences from, this kind of print 'media'.

You are living through very interesting times. And you probably know that the saying 'May you live in interesting times' was an old Chinese curse.

*Figure 0.2* Web 2.0 has capacities for hoaxes, such as this, to be globally distributed. CGI (computer-generated images) can construct the new voyage of the cinematic *Starship Enterprise*, or a visual character assassination of a politician or celebrity.

For an outline of the Media Studies 2.0 approach see http://www.theory.org.uk/mediastudies2.htm and for discussion http://twopointzeroforum.blogspot.com/.

The name 'Twitter', like 'Wikipedia', signals the informality of many new media forms. The originators 'wanted to capture . . . the sensation that you're buzzing your friend's pocket . . . we . . . came across the word "twitter" . . . "a short burst of inconsequential information" and "chirps from birds" [which described] exactly what the product was'.

Our students are often surprised, in diary work, at the amount of media usage they discover they have made in an average week, from the personal soundtrack of music on their iPods, to TV viewing, to the hours that can vanish while surfing the internet and playing computer games. They certainly know more than we do about the use of some of these forms. We can't hope to compete (in either written or spoken appearances) with the vividness of the best educational TV or blog, or the sheer pleasure of discovering, let alone producing, a clip on YouTube,

or perhaps making a comment which is immediately circulated to global millions via a newsblog, or fanblog, or via Twitter. You may have quite sophisticated experience of interactive learning through computers, at home and at college, and 'smart' ways of working, through trial-and-error problem-solving, pattern recognition and strategic thinking, often honed in computer games.

Indeed some would argue that books are now an outdated way of 'delivering' the study of media. Writing the book this time it became clear that the design was always influenced by internet possibilities, especially the potential of the marginal material to entice readers into extras and by-ways to the main arguments. So we have reshaped the printed book to give it a closer relationship to the expanded accompanying website. Most of the production- and industry-related chapters in the last edition have now been moved there, where information can easily be kept up to date, along with other new material, and some popular case studies from previous editions. But there are advantages to a book, such as portability, independence from computer power sources, less eyestrain, and many would argue general ease of use.

What can such a book, and its website, offer in an age of Web 2.0? The so-called 'Media Studies 2.0' approach argues that you are empowered users (not audiences) of media, much more familiar with Web 2.0 forms than are your academic tutors, who simply 'add on' Web 2.0 material to books and textbooks. These are said to be based in 'broadcast' approaches (one to many), as are teaching methods such as lectures, rather than the interactivity of the internet now, with its deliberately informal and even frivolous-sounding names – 'tweeting' on 'Twitter' is apparently especially irritating for some people.

Our experience of students and teaching suggest that

a  this is something of a caricature of good media studies teaching, now and before Web 2.0;

b  students do not always feel like 'digital natives', a rather patronising term anyway for your assumed skills in the ways of interactive media. And another term, 'the digital generation' manages to squash together highly differentiated levels of skill and confidence, let alone age – are all 'young people' from thirteen (or five) to eighteen (or twenty) likely to have similar levels of digital skills and tastes?

c  one of the reasons why students enrol on media courses is therefore to explore broader frameworks for understanding and expansion of their uses of media, and perhaps to help to shape them, through their own productions and interventions;

d  the celebration of the business and political potential of the internet is often exaggerated. It fits with other 'neoliberal' pronouncements that 'big power' is gone, and we can all influence anything now, as 'wise crowds', etc. Meantime the capacity to win attention, to be listened to as well as to 'have a voice', is as unequally distributed as global incomes;

e  just as neoliberal cheerleading makes it harder to object to global inequalities, so it perhaps becomes difficult to state occasional boredom with some Web 2.0 forms, or a sense that voices are not being listened to, or perhaps that you'd simply like to know more about using some media;

f  'old' approaches to different sets of power still produce valuable ways of exploring media forms, for use in these times of unparalleled inequalities, of several kinds, and of dangers, as well as opportunities. Of course some of the founding theories originated several decades in the past, and we usually indicate this and try to update them here. But you will find it useful to know a little of the history of your chosen area of study, and perhaps to appreciate why these approaches have been important;

g  'old' and new combined can produce the most amazing campaigns, discussions, films and so on. See Chapter 12's account of the recent Trafigura case, which combined use of Twitter, a liberal British newspaper in print and internet forms, a principled MP, and a rhetorical appeal to an eighteenth-century radical's campaigning.

But enough of trying to summarise the book's arguments!

We hope you enjoy using this edition of a *book*. It has fewer chapters than the previous edition, but this has given us a chance to go into key concepts and debates in more detail. As we mentioned before, these are richly supplemented on the **MSB5 website**, along with other popular material from previous editions (a narrative study of *Psycho*, science

See the thoughtful report by Ranjana Das (2009), 'Researching Youthful Literacies' at http://personal.lse.ac.uk/dasr/DAS_POLIS_Summer_Report.pdf which gives voice, and attention, to some young people's difficulties and discontents with internet usage.

**Neoliberalism** is a term describing a socio-economic combination of privatisation and deregulation and an accompanying ideological celebration of 'free trade' and 'free markets'.

ONLINE @ RESOURCES

fiction, *Pulp Fiction*, including a debate around the term 'postmodernism', and a genre case study of the western), as well as brand new work (we're hoping to include a case study from New Zealand on the media treatment of 'swine flu' there, for example).

This edition is still designed not as a course or syllabus guide, with model essays, answers, learning outcomes and so on, but as, hopefully, a trusted and non-patronising guide to what are still key conceptual areas. Media studies is rich and exciting partly because it is interdisciplinary, drawing on social sciences, literary and visual approaches, computer studies, economics, communications theory of many kinds, cultural studies and so on. We hope to help you understand and apply what can sometimes feel like a jungle of theories, terms and approaches. Don't be surprised if you find things that aren't on your syllabus. Dip into them anyway – we hope you'll find that they increase your understanding of the key concepts (and they may well be required, or will be enriching for the next module or course you take).

We've suggested a wide range of 'EXPLORE' activities, some simple, others more complex. Most of these you can pursue on your own and there are no 'right answers', though the chapter will point you to relevant material for them. We hope they are enjoyable and worthwhile in their own right. Think of *The Media Student's Book* as a rather special toolbox. The Visual Preface demonstrates these pedagogical features and online resources, so you can familiarise yourselves with them before you start to read.

We've also developed further material from previous editions. There is an even greater emphasis on questions raised for media studies by environmental politics, as well as updated work on the changing business and other practices of media, the nature of 'new media', and the latest impacts of globalisation and of celebrity-related media forms. Newer debates, such as the moves to think of us always as 'users' rather than as 'audiences', are also broached. And we have occasionally floated metaphors of listening, which seem an interesting new way of thinking about some media activities, rather than the more usual 'giving people voices' emphasis, since voices only matter if those who can act on them are listening. Along with that goes an interest in: who has the power to remain 'silent', elusive, not having to answer or allow use of certain material?

The two of us 'combined' have worked, over the years, in both further and higher education, and in media education generally. We entered the area because we enjoyed popular culture in many forms, and recognised its cultural and even political importance and pleasures. We still feel that media studies should be challenging and fun. Whatever your interest, in

A third of people know that their communications devices consume more power now than they did two years ago. But fewer than four in ten consider the impact on the environment when buying devices. This is much lower than for 'white goods', for example, where more than half said the environment was a factor in their decision (summarised from Ofcom 2008 *Communications Market Report*).

'Mind Blowing Speculations about the Internet No. 569': previously it's been argued that 'forgetting' or 'tuning out' was a human norm for dealing with information flow, making decisions, etc. But Mayer-Schönberger (2009) argues that the internet 'remembers' everything, and this may give others, perhaps long in the future, informational power over you.

passing an exam or playing an informed part in the cultures you inhabit, we hope you enjoy reading and working with the book. Do let us know, by writing to the publishers about your ideas for improving it. Even better, email us direct with your comments: gill.branston@ntlworld.com and royitp@googlemail.com.

## References and further reading

Das, Ranjana (2009) *Researching Youthful Literacies: Concepts, Boundaries, Questions*, http://personal.lse.ac.uk/dasr/DAS_POLIS_Summer_Report.pdf.

Mayer-Schönberger, Viktor (2009) *Delete: The Virtue of Forgetting in the Digital Age*, Princeton: Princeton University Press.

Meyrowitz, Joshua (1985) *No Sense of Place: The Impact of Electronic Media on Social Behaviour*, New York: Oxford University Press.

# Part I
# Key concepts

Media scrum at Barcelona Football Club © Jordi Cotrina/El Periodico

# 1 Approaching media texts

- Semiotic approaches
- Structuralism, difference(s) and oppositions
- Denotation and connotation
- The social nature of signs

- Debates
- Content analysis
- Conclusion
- References and further reading

The media are not so much 'things' as places which most of us inhabit, which weave in and out of our lives. Their constant messages and pleasures seem to flow around and through us, and they immerse most of our waking lives. So there's usually little problem with immediate understanding or enjoyment of them. Yet precisely because of their taken-for-grantedness, many people have seen it as important, and enjoyable, to try to analyse the roles and consequences of this part of everyday lives. And because most of us have learnt their 'codes' so thoroughly, they can be hard to stand back from, to try to 'unpick'.

In this chapter we focus broadly on two examples of the two main approaches to media '**texts**': **qualitative** and **quantitative**, looking at **semiotic** and **content analysis** methods. As their names suggest, these are broadly interested, respectively, in:

- exploring the qualities of individual texts, and
- registering what can be discovered by counting repeated patterns or elements across groups or quantities of texts.

Some perceive an opposition between these approaches, and they are indeed different. But they can fruitfully be used together, and each of them is best used with an awareness of the other one as supplementing some of its own weaknesses.

**Note:** You will probably need to spend some time on all this. The terms you'll be trying out are now part of the bloodstream of much media study, and thus not *explicitly* used all the time, though they often structure many media scholars' work. Semiotic approaches (part of qualitative methods) have been hugely qualified and debated in recent years. Yet broadly semiotic approaches, with an awareness of how

*Figure 1.1* A famous image from the Second World War, urging the British to convert their gardens, flowerbeds, parks, etc. to vegetable growing resource (see *The Age of Stupid* case study). The interesting thing for this chapter is how few viewers perceive that there is only one leg shown – it is an 'impossible' image. But culturally formed habits of perception ignore this, perhaps because of the focus on the verbal message, the clouded skies, and the powerful combination of all three.

Part of the 'taken-for-grantedness' of broadly semiotic or constructionist approaches is media discussions of **spin**, or PR (public relations). News media often make minute interpretation of signs, debating what a celebrity's facial expression or a politician's choice of phrasing 'really' signifies. See Chapter 11.

meanings, images, etc. are 'constructed', are part not only of this subject area, but also of mainstream media. This is especially true in comment on fashion and politics. You may find you already know more about semiotic approaches than you at first imagine.

## EXPLORE 1.1

- When you have read this chapter, look through a few magazines and newspapers for discussion of fashions, politicians' or celebrities' dress, gestures and even speeches.
- How do such discussions relate to semiotic theories of 'signifying practices'?

### A note on the terms 'text' and 'readers'

The word 'text' originally referred to sacred writings, such as the Bible, and a written passage from them on which a sermon might be based. Then it came to specify the 'words on the page' as in 'the actual text' of a speech – or, more recently, of a 'text message'. But for semiotic and structuralist approaches, used in the study of media and culture, a text can be anything which is to be investigated – a haircut, hip-hop lyrics, a dance, a film.

The term comes from the Latin word meaning 'tissue'. Barthes emphasised that narrative texts were not one thing, but a weaving together of different strands and processes. Some of these are 'internal' to the story; others make connections to its 'outside' or the rest of the real; some refer to other texts in the process called '**intertextuality**'. This 'weave' approach can be usefully applied to all texts. It is the very opposite of the original sense of something with a single, sacred meaning which is to be carefully discovered.

Within semiotic analysis we, the audience, are called 'readers', partly as a way of emphasising that we are dealing with something learnt rather than 'natural' and partly to indicate the degree of activity needed to make sense of signs.

> **Roland Barthes** (1915–80) French literary theorist, critic and philosopher who applied semiotic analysis to cultural and media forms, famously in *Mythologies* (1972, originally published 1957), a collection of essays wittily working with ads, wrestling, Greta Garbo's face and so on.

> **Intertextuality**: the variety of ways in which media and other texts interact with each other, rather than being unique or distinct.

A major example of qualitative approaches seeking to relate texts to their surrounding social orders has been **semiotics** (now less often called 'semiology', Saussure's term). Content analysis, on the other hand, tries to explore what seem to be patterns or omissions across many of these 'texts', and is a prime quantitative method.

## Semiotic approaches

Media, especially news and factual media, have often been thought of as kinds of conveyor belts of meaning between 'the world' and audiences, producing images 'about' or 'from' this or that debate, event or place.

> **Ferdinand de Saussure** (1857–1913) French linguist who pioneered the semiotic study of language as a system of signs, organised in 'codes' and 'structures'. The Russian theorist Volosinov, however, suggested the term 'decoding' tends to treat language as a dead thing, rather than a living and changing *activity*.

The word 'media' comes from the Latin word 'medium' meaning 'middle'. 'Media' is the plural of this term.

Semiotics is a theory of signs, and how they work to produce meanings, or the study of how things come to have significance. This includes signs devised to convey meanings (language, badges) as well as 'symptoms' (as in 'that's the sign of swine flu').

You may find Daniel Chandler's glossary and discussion of key media studies terms useful here, at http://www.aber.ac.uk/media/ Documents/S4B/sem12.html.

**Structuralism**: an approach to critical analysis which emphasises universal structures underlying the surface differences and apparent randomness of cultures, stories, media texts, etc.

Sometimes this involves news, or the hidden secrets of celebrities. But it has often been assumed that the task of such communication is simply to tell 'the truth' about what it reports. Semiotics, however, does not assume that the media work as simple channels of communication, as 'windows on the world'. Instead they are seen as actually structuring the very realities which they seem to 'describe' or 'stand in for'. This disturbs powerful notions of 'a truth' to the complex worlds we inhabit which can be straightforwardly accessed and 'brought back'.

When the media were first seriously studied, in the late 1950s, existing methods from literary, social science and art criticism were routinely applied to them. Value was set on 'good dialogue', 'convincing characters', 'truthfulness' and 'beautiful compositions'. As well as comfortable assumptions about 'truth', high value was set on 'individuality' (usually of a very limited group of writers, artists). But it soon became clear that simply to discuss a film or television programme by such methods was not enough. People began to question the critical terms used and to ask: 'original' or 'truthful' or 'beautiful' according to what criteria? For whom? Experienced by whom?

At this same time semiotics and accompanying theories from **structuralism** were brought into play. They asked radical questions about how meanings are *constructed* in and by different languages and cultures. These approaches tried to 'hold off' questions of the value of different stories or images in order to explore the ways in which meanings are constructed. Some, though not all, developed these theories to insist that because meanings are constructed by humans, they can be changed, in progressive ways, by them.

Semiotics is defined as the study of signs, or of the social production of meanings and pleasures by sign systems, or the study of how things come to have significance. In later versions this social aspect was emphasised by calling such study 'social semiotics'. It draws largely on the work of the linguist Saussure, the logician Peirce and the literary theorist Barthes.

Saussure argued that a sign consists of a physical signifier (gesture, words on the page, music) and an immaterial signified (the idea associated with this gesture, words, etc.). He was a linguist, and thus mostly interested in language signs.

- First, Saussure argued that words, as verbal signifiers, have an arbitrary relation to their signifieds. They are sometimes marks on paper (R-O-S-E), sometimes sounds in the air (the spoken word 'rose'). There is nothing about actual roses which determines that the sound 'rose' or the equivalent marks on the page have to be used to name them. Any pronounceable combination of letters could have been originally decided on (as is clear if you know a language other than English). Hence different languages have different words for 'rose'. One reason many people find semiotics difficult is that languages have been learned over years, by individuals brought up in a community of users of the same language. Many years ago, somehow, 'rose' was settled on as an agreed signifier among this one group of language users.

*Figure 1.2* This photo signifies 'rose', as does the printed word, but in the case of the photo a specific rose (here a yellow one) has to be used – an iconic signifier. The printed or spoken word 'rose', however, as an *arbitrary* signifier, allows you to imagine your own signified 'rose'.

- Second, a sign refers to something other than itself. This is called the **signified** and it is important to grasp that it is a concept, not a real thing in the world. Though it's probably hard to separate the sound of the word 'rose', when you hear it, from your concept of a rose, semiotics emphasises that there is a distinction (see Peirce below).
- Third, semiotics emphasises that our perception of reality is itself constructed and shaped by the words and signs we use, in various social contexts. By having divided the world into imaginative categories, rather than simply labelling it, the language we inherit and use partly determines much of our sense of things, rather than it being the other way round, with 'the real' determining things in a simple way.

The most famous example of language giving imaginative access to the real is through conceptions of snow. English mostly uses only a few nouns – snow, slush, sleet – to differentiate snowy conditions. But the Inuit (Eskimos), living in a much closer and more crucial relationship to it, developed a language which made detailed distinctions between kinds of snow – 'light', 'soft', 'packed', 'waterlogged', 'shorefast', 'lying on surface', 'drifting on a surface' and so on. You may be able to think of examples from your own knowledge of different languages of how they 'divide up' or shape real experiences differently (see Hall 1997).

Arguably, thanks to the island climate, English has a rich set of words related to rain. Can you think of some? And of other areas of the world which have developed rich vocabularies out of their geographical location? Desert cultures and camels perhaps?

Saussure, then, was mostly interested in language, arguing it was a cultural creation rather than 'natural'. Peirce took the argument further. He suggested a third term, the **referent**, to emphasise that the 'signified' is itself a culturally shaped concept. The referent is what both the signifier and the signified refer to: real roses, in all their different colours and shapes, which inevitably differ from the single, rough and ready concept any one of us conjures up when we see or hear the word. Peirce also argued that there are three kinds of sign, **symbol, icon** and **index**, depending on the relation between the sign and what it stands for. Signs for which the relation is arbitrary (such as language) he called symbols. There is no necessary connection between the word 'rose' and real-life roses. Knowing other languages, where different words signify the same real-world referents, usually makes this clear. Also counting as arbitrary

**Charles Sanders Peirce** (1839–1914) American philosopher, logician and scientist. Usually quoted in semiotics for his distinctions between different kinds of sign – iconic, indexical, arbitrary and symbolic – and also for introducing the idea of the referent to Saussure's two-fold 'signifier–signified' concept of the sign.

Some students are confused by a more common use for the words 'icon' and 'iconic', which are now widespread terms for 'hugely famous'. This is a good example of the changing connotations or polysemy of a particular sign: the word icon.

signs would be the colours of traffic lights (why should amber signify 'get ready'?) or the design of many national flags (why red, white and blue?).

Iconic signs are those which resemble what they stand for, as in a drawing or photo or film of a rose – or perhaps those little expressions 'drawn' on text and typed messages :-0). One additional feature of iconic signifiers is that a picture of a rose always has to show a particular rose – or dog, or cup. Unlike the word 'rose' or 'dog' or 'cup', as arbitrary signs.

Another term you will come across here is 'motivated', which simply means there is some aspect of the signifier which corresponds to the signified, as in airport signs.

*Figure 1.3* Because of the number of people with different verbal languages using most airports, there is a need for clear non-verbal signifying systems – Peirce would say for iconic or motivated signs.

Go to www.portablefilm festival.com and watch *Airport*, a short film telling a story entirely via motivated signs from airports, with no verbal signifiers.

Finally, **indexical** signs are those in which there is a causal link between the sign and that for which it stands. A runny nose is usually the indexical sign of a cold; smoke is an indexical sign of fire; specialised detectives look for indexical signs of a murder in their forensic explorations. In practice of course these different kinds of signs are often combined, especially if we take 'language systems' to include gesture, clothing, architecture and so on. Barthes investigated some of these, using semiotic approaches, in his book *Mythologies* (1957/1972). This tried to relate visual codes to the broadly ideological connections of texts, though Barthes used the less political term 'myth' for this order of meaning.

## Discussion points on evidence and construction

Celluloid film stock was argued by André Bazin (see Chapters 8 and 13) to have a special 'reality effect' through its status as a kind of 'trace off' the real, like a 'death mask' as he once put it. He meant that there had to have been actual light falling on to celluloid for a photo or film shot to be made, hence the 'trace' or direct connection to the real.

See http://www.youtube.com/watch?v=R2bLNkCqpuY for a remarkable scene in US drama series *Mad Men* (2007–) set in the 1960s in the world of US advertising, where a 'pitch' for a slide projector pays powerful tribute to the links between memory, longing and photographs.

## EXPLORE 1.2

- Can you jot down in what sense this could be argued to make celluloid film shots both iconic and indexical signifiers?

**Discussion**: Viewers often assume that 'blurring' shows a photo or shot is 'truthful-because-not-polished-looking'. This is partly because pieces of photojournalism, including the kinds of shots taken by mobile phones at demonstrations, *are* necessarily sometimes blurred because they are occasionally snatched between the photographer avoiding injury, or even saving their own life, and taking the footage. There's an *indexical* as well as an *iconic* link between the event and the photo, if you like.

*Figure 1.4* A classic, recent example of an image 'snatched' and therefore not ideally composed, lit, clear, etc. – Ian Tomlinson just before his death at the G20 London demonstrations, 2009.

But this blur can be faked or constructed, as in several notorious (celluloid) examples of 'arranged' war footage, or, more recently, in film and TV codes such as the deliberately awkward, documentary 'snatched'-looking filming of *ER* or the *Bourne* series.

How do we read 'realist' codes? What do we take as (indexical) evidence that something 'really' happened? Digital media complicate this question, since they are infinitely changeable and do not have to be a 'trace off the real'. Games and SF films can create totally unreal but very convincing worlds. Here's a typical comment on cinema's current digital processes, from Dante Spinotti, cinematographer for *Public Enemies* (US 2009): 'You can go in and separate the layers, erase the grain, give more sharpness to a character who happens to be on the corner of your image.'

To some extent (and especially in an era when images can be faked by computers) we have to rely on evidence from outside the photo, or 'text', to answer these questions of 'realism'. For example, we rely on the trustworthiness of the institution which produced and circulated it (see Chapter 13 on documentary and 'reality TV').

Commutation is another term which has been loosely applied to media. In verbal language it refers to the substitution of one element for another, and the crucial change that can cause: 'the 'd' in 'dog' if replaced by 'f' to make 'fog' makes a whole change of meaning. Figure 1.6 is a publicity still of the Spanish film star Penélope Cruz in *Broken Embraces*. She is best known for her strong roles in the 'arthouse' films of Pedro Almodóvar, as well as for her lustrous dark hair and eyelashes, used in global advertising campaigns.

*Figure 1.5* An eloquent kind of *evidence* (both iconic and indexical) of numbers on one of the demonstrations against the 2001 US air strikes against Afghanistan.

- It is *constructed*: the angle and positioning of the camera, and choice of lens enables the huge scope of the image.
- But this construction was in order to provide *a kind of evidence* – of a visibly huge demonstration. We could almost say 'definite evidence' for institutional, as well as textual, reasons. A digital fake on this topic, with so much other evidence, elsewhere, of the size of the march, for the front page of a reliable newspaper, is highly unlikely.

*Figure 1.6*
Penélope Cruz in a
production still from
*Broken Embraces*
(Spain 2009).

*Figure 1.7*
Marilyn Monroe in
*The Misfits* (US 1962)

*Figure 1.8* Peroxide blonde signifies differently in this 1966 police shot of accomplice to child murder Myra Hindley (1946–2002). The dark roots, and brows, were used in the 'Other-ing' of Hindley as a particularly 'unnatural' killer, owing to her gender.

Several stars (e.g. Madonna) have played with the resonance of Monroe's glamour which was inextricably linked, in the 1950s, to the new technology of peroxide dyeing of hair. This was usually used by white female stars whose original hair colour was darker, as (indexically) signified by brows, and often skin tone. It comes as a slight shock to see the 'Latin' Cruz with this 'glamorous' hairstyle and colour, combined with the 'eyeball' earrings, evoking *Pan's Labyrinth* (Spain/Mexico/US 2006), a hit fantasy/horror film by a Mexican director.

The image can be usefully discussed via the loose concept of 'commutation'. The platinum blonde wig, perhaps styled to resemble Monroe's hair (figure 1.7) in *The Misfits* (US 1962), her last film, marks a crucial difference between the two stars. The wig, and Cruz's expression, may evoke 'Monroe: tragic and glamorous Hollywood star', so different in image to Cruz's own independent, Latina image. It may simply evoke 'showbiz glamour' of a kind not associated with 'arthouse' cinema. The white-blonde dyed hair has become much more widespread in such contexts, and in everyday life.

You may have experiences related to it, as a signifier, especially if you use it yourself.

## EXPLORE 1.3

- Look at the eight-minute film *Oracion* or *Prayer for Marilyn Monroe* (Cuba 1984); http://www.youtube.com/watch?v=C6pYZQBEHys. You may need to do this several times as it is a Spanish-language film with a rich image track, and varied connections between images and voice-over/soundtrack. It uses montage, where contrasting signs/images/shots are put together to produce new, and often surprising, sets of meaning. These are often political, but advertising also frequently now uses montage.
- How does *Oracion* use the sign 'Monroe'? Take three shots and say how their juxtaposition produces a surprising new set of associations for her image.
- Is 'commutation' applicable?
- Research who Ernesto Cardenal is. How, and why, does his poem work to try to re-anchor (see p. 24) the star-related film clips of Monroe?

## Structuralism, difference(s) and oppositions

So, semiotic theory argued that language and other signs, by which our perceptions of the world are organised, work by means of differences.

Another good example of this process is colours. Some colour categories, such as brown, do not exist in some cultures. Other cultures may have several signs with which to divide 'blue'. This is not because of faulty eyesight, but because a particular culture has not named that part of the spectrum, and thus, it is argued, that part is not perceived, because of the power of naming.

Structuralism is a name for a set of ideas and positions which flowed into parts of semiotics. These broadly emphasised two positions.

1  Firstly, important nineteenth-century thinkers argued that all human social order is determined by large social or psychological structures with their own irresistible logic, independent of human will or intention. Freud and Marx began to interpret the social world in this structured way. Freud argued that the human psyche (especially the unconscious mind) was one such structure. It makes us act in ways of which we're not aware, but which are glimpsed in the meanings of certain dreams, slips of the tongue and so on. Marx argued that economic life, and particularly people's relationship to the means of production (do they own them, or do they work for the owners of them?), was another, which shaped political sympathies and dominant power structures. Within both models, and structuralism more generally, there are often problems with thinking how change occurs; how can people make a difference if such huge impersonal structures actually determine everything?

2  Secondly, and later, structuralists argued that meanings can be understood only within systematic structures and the differences or distinctions which they generate. For example, structuralist anthropology might study how a culture organises its rules on food as a system:

   - by rules of exclusion (the English see eating frogs and snails as a barbaric French custom);
   - by signifying oppositions (savoury and sweet courses are not eaten together in most Western cuisine);
   - by rules of association (steak and chips followed by ice cream is OK; steak and ice cream followed by chips is not OK).

Only within such rules would particular combinations or menus be valued, or seen as 'wrong', or as rebellious, or eccentric. Lévi-Strauss was a structuralist anthropologist whose work greatly influenced semiotics. He emphasised the importance of structuring oppositions in myth systems and in language. These are sometimes called binary oppositions because the qualities can be grouped into pairs of opposites, and they produce key boundaries or differences within cultures, usually with unequal value attached to one side of the pairing.

**Sigmund Freud**
(1856–1939) hugely influential Austrian founder of psychoanalysis, a theory and practice of treating neuroses. Theories of 'normal' unconscious mental processes, revealed via dreams, etc., have been suggested from its procedures.

**Karl Marx** (1818–83) German philosopher, economist and journalist, analysing and seeking to overthrow, by revolutionary means, the emerging industrial capitalist order of nineteenth-century Europe. See Chapter 6.

**Claude Lévi-Strauss**
(1908–2009) French anthropologist (*not* the inventor of the jeans). Most active from the 1950s, studying myths, totems and kinship systems of tribal cultures in North and South America. One of his *Mythologiques* volume titles, translated as *The Raw and the Cooked* (1964), gives a sense of his work.

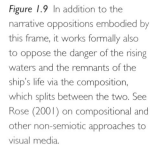

Feminists, for example, have argued that the 'feminine' side of such oppositions is often the devalued one, while it has been argued that Native Americans are the devalued part of such a set of oppositions in many westerns. See *The Western* on the **MSB5 website**.

Saussure applied this to the ways in which language produces meanings, often through defining terms as being the opposite of other terms: black/white; hot/cold; etc. We know that the word 'man', for example, means different things in different contexts. It can be opposed to 'boy' ('act like a man not a boy'), or to 'woman', or to 'god', or even to 'beast' ('are you a man or a mouse?'). So 'woman' is almost always defined in relation to 'man', and 'femininity' is usually defined through its perceived differences from 'masculinity'.

### Examples

**Example 1 : The film *Titanic* (US 1997)** Working with semiotic/structuralist approaches involves first trying to see which elements in any 'text' seem to be in systematic opposition. For example, the narrative of *Titanic* (US 1997) works partly by differences such as upper deck/lower deck; upper class/lower class; American/European. These are worked through in the signifiers of types of music, of degrees of formality, dance, dress, colours, sets and so on.

Using structuralist emphases we might explore the extent to which one side of a persistent opposition (or binary, as it's sometimes called) is always valued less than the other. In this case, the lively, egalitarian 'lower-deck/lower-class' passengers, represented by Jack/DiCaprio, are in contrast to the upper classes on the upper decks, but are valued more highly by the film's narrative in terms of characterisations, attitudes, responses to disaster and so on. This set of oppositions is part of why Rose/Winslet's development and decisions through the plot are given such weight. The

*Figure 1.9* In addition to the narrative oppositions embodied by this frame, it works formally also to oppose the danger of the rising waters and the remnants of the ship's life via the composition, which splits between the two. See Rose (2001) on compositional and other non-semiotic approaches to visual media.

character is constructed as throwing in her lot with a more democratic future through this system of difference.

**Example 2** concerns advertising campaigns. In planning meetings there will often be 'brainstorming' sessions where the valued qualities, which the campaign workers want to have attributed to the product (or celebrity, or campaign), are contrasted, in a classic list of binary oppositions, to qualities which are 'not-Levi's' or 'not-Mercedes'.

**Example 3** In news coverage of the 'Middle East' (an interesting verbal signifier all on its own), there is often a binary constructed between 'modern' and 'fundamentalist'. It came as a shock, to some, to have this binary cut across by those who talked of Islamic and Christian fundamentalisms, in the George W. Bush years. See Women Against Fundamentalism (www.womenagainst fundamentalism.org.uk) for a lucid discussion of how this term (or sign) is used.

> The terms through which geographical areas are signified are often 'dead' metaphors. Thus the 'Middle East' denotes an area which is east of Europe, but not so far east as other places. 'Western' has worked in a similar way, though now it has connotations of 'progresss', 'modernity': 'the West and the rest'. See Bennett et al. 2005: 372–4).

The structuralist emphasis on oppositions helps explain semiotics' insistence that signs are fully understood only by reference to their difference from other signs in their particular representing system or code.

One final point: this 'system' often ignores the ways in which signs are 'unstable', they have relationships among themselves, histories, as well as representing parts of the world. For example language is full of unnoticed dead metaphors – 'blind' marking; factory 'hands'; 'windfall' taxes – all severed from their original meanings, as language responds to users' use of it. Signs can be played with, they can 'float free' of meaning, and this is often part of the pleasure of some texts. Words can rhyme or be punned upon, often just for fun, as in limericks. Colours can be echoed (or 'rhymed') across a music video, an ad or a film (as red is in *Don't Look Now* (UK 1973)). Early semiotic theorists came out of language and literary studies, and focused on meaning. But we need to update some of these theories by the sense that pleasures and fun, as well as meanings, are produced by signs – including language.

## Denotation and connotation

Signs, then, signify or name or **denote** different aspects of our experience or of the world. The word 'red' denotes a certain part of the colour spectrum, differentiated by language from other parts (such as 'blue' or 'pink') within what is, in fact, a continuous spectrum, with colours merging into one another. But signs also **connote**, or link things. They may link things by repeated association with broader cultural concepts and values, as well as with meanings from personal history and experience. Let's explore this.

### Examples

The word 'red' denotes or classifies one part of the colour spectrum. Broadly (merging sometimes into pink, purple or orange) it denotes blood, fires, sunsets, blushing complexions. This perhaps indicates why, in certain cultures, the colour and the word have gathered connotations of fierceness, passion, danger.

1  In *Pretty Woman* (US 1990) there is a scene where Vivien/Julia Roberts wears a red, quite formal dress (after her multicoloured hooker's gear in the first scene, and before a black, more formal dress in a later scene). At this point in the film it could plausibly be argued that the red dress signifies or denotes a growing confidence and passion in her feelings for Edward/Richard Gere. But 'red' does this, for readers familiar with the codes, by several means:
   - its 'passionate' or 'heated' associations;
   - its deliberate difference from the colours of her other costumes in that film;
   - the cultural awareness of (competent) viewers that red is unlikely in this film to denote 'communism' or 'Manchester United' or 'danger' – as it might in other structures of meaning.

*Figure 1.10*  From title of *Mad Men*

2   A still from the title sequence of the US series *Mad Men*. This dealt
    with the apparently glamorous world of Madison Avenue advertising
    executives, their wives, secretaries and other women, in the 1960s. The
    title sequence is centred on an animated version of what turns out to be
    the central character, Don Draper, who walks slowly into, and then falls
    from, high up in a New York skyscraper office. The use of stylised
    animation (rather than film) means that the sequence's strong if
    ambiguous links with '9/11' are 'cooled' or distanced. The sight of people
    falling from the Towers was a terrible one, and at first only non-US
    magazines and news published photos of it. This particular connotation,
    or resonance, marked out *Mad Men* from the start as likely to be
    controversial and unconventional in the connections it made. It also
    deploys a certain kind of what is called 'modality', or relation to the real –
    here, via animation rather than live action.
3   Green is now a hugely connotative colour because of its association with
    environmental politics, sometimes simply called 'green' politics.
    White is also coming to signify in related ways, especially for car and
    computer ads (see Apple, Prius, Lexus ads). It draws on long Western
    traditions of signifying 'purity'.
    Find adverts or other widely circulated images which seem to draw on
    these, or other, kinds of colour connotation.

However, though these terms are useful for indicating the social
connections of signs, two criticisms can be made of them:

1   they suggest that the 'connotations' of any sign can be
    comprehensively listed, whereas a sign may have wildly different
    connotations for most people (depending on personal memories,
    sub-cultural knowledge and so on);
2   the internet has vastly increased this meaning potential, so the
    capacity for signs to have many attached values pretty much defies
    analysis and 'counting'. A broader cultural approach to the social
    existence of signs is needed.

## The social nature of signs

So signs, far from 'naturally' or simply 'labelling' the real world, are
socially constructed, and never as 'natural' as they seem. Semiotic
approaches rightly suggest there is no neat boundary between the real
and the imagined, indeed that they interpenetrate one another. In such
ways semiotics has been enormously useful in rethinking the key social

activity of meaning-making. But semiotic and post-structuralist emphases have often contributed to a crippling sense of powerlessness in the face of modern political and social developments. Language and representation have been emphasised as being *only* untrustworthy, slippery, and their relationship to the rest of the real world consistently downplayed.

It is worth emphasising the broad cultural or social agreement (or even force) which is needed for meaning to be produced, and reproduced, even though it remains arbitrary and slippery. Yes, we learn to read signs in relation to wider systems of meaning, to which the term 'codes' is often given. But these have to be broadly shared, as well as relying on 'difference'. The choice of 'green' for the traffic sign meaning 'GO' is arbitrary, and could indeed be replaced by 'pink', but only if that were the agreed colour for 'GO'. We learn to associate words, and media products, *with* each other, as well as to *differentiate* them.

Some post-structuralists argue that no shared meanings are possible because everything is understood only through difference. But it's also important to note that meaningful differences (e.g. black/white) differentiate things that also *share* certain qualities. Both 'black' and 'white' are parts of the colour spectrum, for example (see Andermahr *et al.* 2000). Later in this book we use more political words, such as 'ideologies' and 'discourses', to discuss important *struggles for meaning*. One of the dangers in using the word 'code' is that it can make communication sound like a conspiracy on the part of the mysterious 'encoders'. A couple of points to bear in mind:

a   signs are not fixed, or stable, but always polysemic, or capable of having several if not many meanings and associations. Control is attempted over the ambiguity of visual images, especially for news and advertising purposes, through the use of captions or voice-over commentary. Semiotics calls this **anchoring** – an image drawn from the way that an anchor tries to limit the movements of a boat or ship in the sea. It's less directly related to news 'anchors' (a newish signified for that word), though it's worth thinking of the power those figures have to frame or secure interpretations of news stories in some directions and not others, especially in the US;

b   signs are struggled over by those who have something to gain from anchoring, or re-anchoring, or resignifying them in particular ways. Signification is never 'secure' or fixed: many struggles can take place over signification, over how a sign is to be 'officially' or dominantly read.

Obscure joke to test how you're doing so far: Umberto Eco, semiotics professor, once said, 'I would still earn my living as a semiotician even if it was called something else.'

*Examples*

- In the 1960s the centuries-old negative connotations of the word 'black' in US culture were challenged by the US Civil Rights movement with the slogan 'Black is Beautiful'.
- Mahatma Gandhi (1869–1948), Indian political and spiritual leader during his country's struggle for independence from British rule, was once asked what he thought of Western civilisation. 'I think it would be a good idea,' he said, neatly resignifying the emphasis of the question to imply that Western *civilisation* did not yet exist.
- Fans will sometimes produce internet versions of favourite media products (such as *Lost* or *Dr Who*) which are wildly different from those officially circulated, and sometimes help shape the official product.
- Oppressed groups have often taken the derogatory verbal signs of their oppression and turned them into defiant signs of identity: gays began to call themselves 'queer' in the 1980s, for example.

## Debates

- A kind of scientific certainty is often implied by the tone and vocabulary of some semioticians' writing. 'Code', for example, with its roots in signals technologies, often seems to imply a much more traditional concept of communication. But how far can such slippery matters as 'interpretation' and 'meaning' be objectively and scientifically mapped? Better to say that 'texts' offer a meaning potential, not a fixed 'code' to be cracked once you've learnt it, like semaphore or traffic signs.

    We're now likely to have a more relaxed sense that 'textual analysis [is] an educated guess at some of the most likely interpretations that might be made of [a] text' (McKee 2001).
- Semiotics' heavy emphasis on 'meaning' ignores the pleasures and irrational play possible with, and within, texts, and the often mischievous misreadings of audiences, especially on the internet.
- Though semiotics is a textual approach, whose domain is not audience study, nevertheless it is striking *how* uninterested classic semiotic theorists have been in the ways in which real users actually engage with 'texts'.
- Semiotics uses an elaborate, even over-elaborate, terminology. Sometimes this can be confusing or even unnecessary (see Rose 2001: 97–8 for helpful comments).

- The idea of binary oppositions can be a very useful way into texts. But in assembling and numbering all the 'white/black' or 'male /female' oppositions in a text it can ignore ambivalences and shadings in texts, and by extension the world outside them.
- Along with this, the huge emphasis on 'difference' tends to corrode other, valuable concepts such as identification, or involvement, or solidarity.
- The necessary social 'agreement' needed for signs to work means we can never produce *completely* private languages of our own, however characteristic our individual language use will always be, in blogs or photos. To put it rather grandly, language (including media) is both constructed afresh, and also inherited by people using it within existing cultures.

Semiotic approaches spread partly through some vivid detailed readings of individual images (Barthes 1972; Williamson 1978) which were attractive to use in teaching and debate. But they raise questions about the representativeness and **replicability** of its analyses. How representative of ads in general are those chosen by Williamson, or Barthes? Would someone else necessarily have come up with the same conclusions? This is one place where quantitative analysis can be usefully combined with qualitative or textual approaches.

## Content analysis

This is a quantitative method, and as such does not offer the detailed interpretations of individual texts of semiotic and other textual approaches. They often look for 'hidden' meanings in texts, while content analysis (hereafter called CA) is based on counting the manifest or 'open', 'apparent' meanings in large numbers of texts. It tries to discover repeated processes of representation that might help structure beliefs and feelings. As such it offers ways to generalise and make a case about representations from the gathering and analysing of **empirical** evidence. Importantly it can sometimes affect policy and public opinion, since it has the weight of numbers behind it.

For you, on a smaller scale, it can also be a good way of checking out the 'hunches' which may be the starting point for your research (see Chapter 15 for more detail). Like any analytical method, it has drawbacks, and areas outside its scope, which we briefly outline.

CA is a major empirical method. It uses observable evidence or experience as its material, and seeks to avoid bias as far as possible. It works by counting the frequency of relevant elements in a clearly

**Empirical**: relying on observed experience as evidence. A controversial term, often caricatured to imply an approach opposed to any kind of theory, and said to rely on sense experience of simplistic 'quantity' of information and facts. 'Positivist' is sometimes used to mean almost the same.

defined sample of texts, and then analysing those frequencies (see Rose 2001: 56). You might want to explore, for example, how often the word 'immigrant' is used to mean the same as 'asylum seeker' in a sample of newspapers. Content analysis (perhaps using LexisNexis or SPSS software) could help you to do this. First, the selected quantities (of, say, newspapers or ads) must be 'coded'. This means a set of descriptive categories or labels are attached to them, such as 'headlines involving the words "asylum seeker" '. These should be unambiguous, such that 'different researchers at different times using the same categories would code the images in exactly the same way' (Rose 2001: 62). This is meant to make the process replicable.

It's a useful method because, as one set of researchers into magazine photos commented: 'It does allow . . . discovery of patterns that are too subtle to be visible on casual inspection and [also allows] protection against an unconscious search through the magazine for only those which confirm one's sense of what the photos say or do' (Lutz and Collins in Rose 2001: 89). Closer textual interpretation of individual texts is often needed at other stages of a research project, if there are enough resources, to explore or confirm or supplement the apparent findings. For example, counting will tell us whether one side in a conflict has been interviewed many more times than its opponents. But the tempting assumption is that this side has been advantaged. This needs to be checked: the style of the interviews might be generally hostile or sarcastic. Likewise the frequency with which words, or even systematic oppositions of words, are used will not give you the tone of their usage, or of their combination with photos, music, captions, for which textual analysis is needed.

> **Replicability**: the unambiguous quality of a research method, so that 'different researchers at different times using the same categories would [interpret] the images in exactly the same way' (Rose 2001: 62). It cannot be absolutely guaranteed, but it an important research ideal. See also Chapter 15.

## EXPLORE 1.4

- Conduct a simple content analysis research into TV car ads.
- Count how many car ads are there on any one or more TV channels on Friday or Saturday night between 8 p.m. and 10 p.m. (when large male audiences are assumed).
- How many of these take place in deserted, remote country roads?
- How many show gridlock, or traffic jams?
- Use textual approaches to suggest what is the tone of these ads – openly fantasising? Humorous, in ways which 'magic away' experiences of gridlock?
- Or are they very serious about the product, signified as 'hero' or as ultra-cool?

*Figure 1.11* The question 'what's missing?' is a key one when compiling or considering statistical data.

An important area for the method can even be the systematic *absence* of certain terms or topics in media discussions. Jay Katz (1999) reminds us that many news items fail to give the gender of actors in particular stories. By simply headlining 'school killers', news stories miss the chance to discuss the naturalised link between masculinity and violent behaviour. It is in fact overwhelmingly males who commit road rage offences, or school shootings in the US. And often, in more harshly male-dominated cultures, the overwhelmingly male presence in violent demonstrations goes unremarked.

Content analysis is popular partly because numbers, unlike languages, form a universal 'currency'. Such analysis is seen as more 'scientific', more full of 'hard facts', than other approaches. Though this is only partly true of CA, it does, as a result, operate as a powerful, often well-funded model of research into audiences.

The 'numbers game' here is notoriously unreliable. Rape statistics are shaped by the latest changes in definition of rape, in how far women are encouraged to report the crimes and so on. See also the excellent BBC4 programme *More or Less* (website or podcast) on general problems of statistical accuracy and clear current examples.

Many accounts of 'stranger danger' ignore the fact that 'the home' is the location of most violence and child abuse. Instead attention is focused on 'monster-ing' extreme cases (e.g. Josef Fritzl). The harder questions of unemployment, alcohol and other drug abuse in families are not seen as 'newsworthy'.

### Example: 'Violence and the media'

A dangerous jump is sometimes made from quantitative or content analysis research findings to media speculation about 'obvious' evidence of the supposed effects of the media.

The 'violence debate' is full of such 'countings'. Rightly concerned when horrible murders, apparently higher numbers of rapes and assault take place, campaigners then make the huge leap of arguing that these might be prevented by censoring 'violence in the media'. This often means countable acts of 'media violence' and ignores broader political and social questions, *as well as* closer textual ones. For example:

- The problem of defining the 'violence' that is to be counted. It may seem quite a simple thing to decide what to count as 'violence' or 'violent acts' in TV, rap music or computer games. Yet the question of what, in our culture, is *perceived* as 'violence' is a huge one, even outside media. Some kinds of activity are labelled 'violent' and others aren't. Gender expectations, and also 'invisible' official violence, help structure words and phrases like 'restraining' or 'keeping the peace' or 'boys will be boys'.

- The differences (qualitative) between the many *kinds* of media representations that are counted, and different audience perceptions of them. Is the 'violence' in a *Tom and Jerry* cartoon or a computer game the same as the violence in a news bulletin? Controversies over the possible effects of games imagery have been particularly sharp at times (see Dovey and Kennedy 2006 and Lister *et al.* 2009).

It is important to combine quantitative with qualitative issues, and indeed each of them often, already, includes a sense of the other. Barthes and others implicitly suggest their individual texts do have some kind of typicality, or relation to quantities of other such ads, posters, etc. And in CA the *quality* of the questions asked, and the conclusions drawn, is a key factor. These can be more complex for audio-visual forms than for printed ones. As with any media text, *the counting of elements that can be counted* can be a circular process. It sometimes ignores the ways codes and resonances of meaning are combined, let alone what 'readers' might be doing with 'texts'. In the case of film or television, for instance, research would have to combine the 'act of violence' with interpretative questions for individual texts such as:

- its place in the narrative;
- the stance that the audience is *invited* to take up in relation to it (by camera movement, narrative positioning, editing, costume, casting (is a sympathetic star involved?), lighting, set design, etc.);
- the likely audience which can be assumed from how the text is circulated (Sky Sports primetime? local campaign group leaflet?) and therefore likely interpretations for it;
- intertextual reference (is a joke being made about another text which somewhat changes the status of the 'act of violence', as can happen in *The Simpsons*?);
- the historical stage of its **genre** (e.g. is it a horror film/game, whose twenty-first-century audiences are likely to be blasé about special effects around violent death?);
- the full social context in which it 'plays' (e.g. are guns widely available and seen as normal possessions, as in the US?).

Research the British Board of Film Classification (BBFC) website(s) on how the Board takes decisions to request cuts to material involving easily imitable acts of violence, such as head butting. These involve quite detailed textual decisions on context, as well as research into possible effects.

Barker and Petley (2001) have some striking discussion around this area for UK contexts, though see Huesmann and Taylor (2008) for quite different views.

## EXPLORE 1.5

Take a recent film or television programme labelled 'violent'. Decide what genre it belongs to; a factor which mediates the violence. Go through the above list and decide:

- What would you say is its 'message' about violence?
- How precisely would you argue this? (use checklist above)
- How might this text seem to: (1) an audience experienced in its genre, (2) an audience not experienced in its genre? Research internet discussion, and say from which of these two groups the discussion seems to emerge.

Some vivid representations of violence may have not negative but positive effects in the revulsion they invite us to feel, for example at certain kinds of assault, or military power, or bullying. Content analysis of the prevalence of sanitised images of war and audiences' responses to them, whether in films or news, might back arguments that 'Western' viewers need to see *more* of the damage done to human bodies (and minds) by war if movements to try to stop wars are to flourish.

Some recent research on viewing revisits the qualitative/quantitative debate into broader social contexts for viewing, especially by young people, by assessing the empirical evidence of some effects on audiences (see Huesmann and Taylor 2003 and 2006, and internet discussion of their positions). Though moderated by the social context and influence, like gender and class, some experts suggest that such imagery is both a short- and a long-term 'health risk'. But this takes us into the material of Chapter 14 on Audiences.

## Conclusion

Media studies valuably emphasises that the meanings of representations are never 'given' but are always going to be socially constructed, slippery and contestable. This goes against both suggesting that meanings are 'natural' and 'obvious', and saying they can mean anything the audience wants them to. However slippery, and encrusted with different meanings for particular audience members, texts do have characteristics, and associations, which can sometimes rightly be called dominant.

We've presented two important approaches, which need to work more closely together. Even the most close-textured analysis of a single text needs to consider how typical that text is, and how else its users might engage with it. Equally, even the best-funded, largest content analysis needs to be aware of the complexities of the texts it is summarising, and the quality of its questions. Both need to bear in mind how users' possible responses complicate matters.

Bear these questions in mind as you test out these approaches. The rest of this book takes them into much wider arenas of power and battles to secure (or 'spin') one meaning or pleasure for a song, a flag, a slogan, over others. One of the challenges of this area is balance: a) appreciating some audiences' subversive, or simply 'knowing' interpretations, and b) exploring how texts themselves (textual *quality*), as well as easy availability (industry *quantity*) of some images, but not others, do encourage some meanings and pleasures, and try to cut off or marginalise others. The next chapter explores their classification into genres, as one powerful way of preparing us for such pleasures and habits.

## References and further reading

Andermahr, Sonya, Lovell, Terry, and Wolkowitz, Carol (2000) *A Glossary of Feminist Theory*, London and New York: Hodder Arnold.

Barker, Martin, and Petley, Julian (eds) (2001) *Ill Effects*, London: Routledge.

Barthes, Roland (1972) *Mythologies*, London: Paladin (originally published 1957).

Bennett, Tony, Grossberg, Lawrence, and Morris, Meaghan (eds) (2005) *New Keywords: A Revised Vocabulary of Culture and Society*, London and New York: Blackwell.

Dovey, Jon, and Kennedy, Helen (2006) *Game Cultures: Computer Games as New Media*, London and New York: Open University Press.

Eagleton, Terry (1983) *Literary Theory: An Introduction*, Oxford: Blackwell (esp. Chapter 3).

Hall, Stuart (ed.) (1997) *Representation: Cultural Representations and Signifying Practices*, London, Thousand Oaks and New Delhi: Sage.

Huesmann, Rowell, and Taylor, Laramie D. (2003) 'The Case against the Case against Media Violence', in Gentile, D. (ed) *Media Violence and Children*, Westport, CT: Greenwood Press, 107–30.

Huesmann, Rowell, and Taylor, Laramie D. (2006) 'The Role of Media Violence in Violent Behaviour', *Annual Review of Public Health*, 27: 393–415.

Katz, Jay (1999) *Tough Guise*, Amherst, MA: Media Education Foundation video, available on YouTube.

Kitzinger, Jenny (2004) 'Audience and Readership Research', in *The Sage Handbook of Media Studies*, London: Sage.

Lister, Martin, Dovey, Jon, Giddings, Seth, Grant, Iain, and Kelly, Kieran (2009) *New Media: A Critical Introduction*, 2nd edn, London and New York: Routledge.

McKee, Alan (2001) 'Introduction: Interpreting Interpretation', *Continuum: Journal of Media and Cultural Studies*, 15, 1.

Rose, Gillian (2001) *Visual Methodologies*, London: Sage.

Spinotti, Dante (2009) interviewed in *Sight and Sound*, April, p. 27.

Williamson, Judith (1978) *Decoding Advertisements: Ideology and Meaning in Advertising*, London: Marion Boyars.

# CASE STUDY

# Visual and aural signs

- ANALYSING A POSTER, AND NOTES ON TWO PHOTOS
- VOICES AND SOUND SIGNIFIERS
- AUDIO-VISUAL MOVING IMAGES
- CONTENT ANALYSIS
- REFERENCES AND FURTHER READING

This case study takes media images (still visual ones; moving audio-visual; and sound). It tries to give you confidence in analysing them, using both qualitative and quantitative approaches. We suggest other elements that go into the textual 'weave', including histories of production, and the sleuthing and discussion which are often now the context for high-profile images. Such discussions have become part of the meanings of many images for far larger audiences than in the past. This shapes the kinds and number of connotations they hold.

*Figure 1.13* This poster became the 2008 campaign image for the first mixed race, African-American president of the United States, Barack Obama.

## ANALYSING A POSTER, AND NOTES ON TWO PHOTOS

*Figure 1.12* photo, 27 April 2006 (Mannie Garcia/Press Association (PA)) of then-Senator Barack Obama at a National Press Association meeting on Darfur. Cited by Shephard Fairey as the original for his poster (**Figure 1.13**) for the Obama 2008 presidential campaign, though this origin is debated (see **Figure 1.14**).

*Figure 1.14* You may feel there is a mini-second difference here (argued via tiny differences in expression and angle of Obama's gaze). Fairey said he googled the photo in 2008, but Tom Gralish (in http://blogs.phillynews.com/inquirer/sceneonroad/2009/01/ found_again_ the_poster_source.html found another, differently framed original. Others have claimed the original was taken by Jim Young. See also http://community.livejournal.com/obey_giant/).

## Two discussion points

1 Such debates about origins may seem trivial, but they now form a fascinating part of how 'texts' circulate and what they mean in the age of 'Web 2.0' where comments on images are much easier to distribute. The issues of copyright, authorship and potential rights to a famous image are now a part of this poster's connotations for many.

2 Though such production details are not technically part of *textual* approaches, they can often form valuable confirmation of a 'reading'. When analysing photos (and many films) you will often have to guess at some production details: exactly what shutter speed or focal length has been used. You may be able to find out, especially with internet research of course. See http://www.flickr.com website for more, including the specifications (number of pixels, camera type, etc.) given on photos there.

   The date of the image, the context (celebrity or news photo?) and the overall 'look' may suggest whether significant digital alteration ('airbrushing') has taken place, especially on older photos – most images now go through Photoshop to fit them for their destination via cropping, etc. For though 'photoshopping' is sometimes used to mean 'significant airbrushing' of an image, it does not only signify that.

## EXPLORE 1.6

- Try the quiz 'Spot the fakes!' on the http://www.urbanlegends.about.com website.
- Note what your reasons were for assessing a hoax, or a 'real' shot, in this digital era – were they 'textual' or did they depend on 'contextual' knowledge? For, as Chapter 3 on Genres argues, we never encounter images in isolation, outside expectations and contexts.

The poster itself was designed by Shepard Fairey, a Los Angeles-based street artist. It resembles the 'silkscreen' process which Andy Warhol used for many of his celebrity portraits/posters in the 1960s. When you analyse photographic texts, consider the sets of 'codes' at play:

- lighting (here the context of a political meeting delivers artificial, easily legible lighting, for media coverage);
- use of colour or black and white. 'Natural' looking colour is used here. Deliberate use of black and white might suggest an evocation of nostalgia, of 'history' or of 'hard' realist codes such as were used in 1930s and 1940s documentary photography;

1   In cinema and photography, once colour stock became available the signifying potential of black and white film stock changed. Choosing to make a film in black and white, like *Schindler's List* (US 1993) or *Dead Man* (US 1995), was clearly a deliberate choice, not simply a necessity. It could signify 'pastness' or 'seriousness'.

2   Interesting, here, is the long time it took for the development of film stock which was sensitive to dark skin. This was part of the unequal allocation of high-status roles for black actors until quite recently, dependent as those roles are on close-up, specific lighting, and clearly perceptible facial gesture (see Dyer 1997).

- the kind of focus used. Here the priority seems to be on getting the face(s) in focus. Though the US flag is slightly blurred as a result, it is still visible, and the angle may have been determined by the desire to include it as background;
- production techniques which have exaggerated certain qualities of the image, by airbrushing of a digital image, for example. These seem not to have been used;
- framing decisions (also called cropping) including

camera angle, distance from the subject, what is included and excluded. Ask: why was *this* framing decision made, rather than others which were possible? Such selections are called paradigmatic choices by structuralist theory. In Figure 1.12 these involve celebrity codes of camera distance, etc., via the inclusion of George Clooney, who is lending his stardom to the event.

## EXPLORE 1.7

We've given two photo originals for the poster as they illustrate key decisions on framing.

**Q:** What difference does the second framing, of Obama alone, in a head shot, make to the image?

**A:** It shifts the effect of sharing the frame with George Clooney, which might suggest second 'celebrity' place to then-Senator Obama, within a paradigmatic choice of 'celebrity support for Darfur'. (The wider, first framing also allowed attention to drift towards whatever Obama is doing with the green wristband.)

For the poster consider these questions:

a   What elements of the photo which Fairey cited (Figure 1.12) have been heightened, and how?

b   What do the poster's chosen colours contribute to the image? What codes do they draw on?

c   What other codes, related to broad cultural and aesthetic frames of reference, are at play in the poster's style?

Suggested answers to the above questions:

a   The focus and frame is emphatically on Obama's face (though a badge has been added to his lapel). Fairey interpreted the upwards gaze as: 'He is gazing off into the future, saying, "I can guide you".' (*Washington Post* interview). Even though Fairey knew the denotation or simplest meaning of the image (Obama listening to a speaker), he chooses this much grander connotative meaning or association. The word 'Hope' anchors the image in this kind of meaning.

The 'code' of the upwards gaze has a long history in Western stained glass, painting and sculpture. It originates in religious views of the world, with 'heaven' (rather than just 'the sky') above it, from which the 'great man' or holy figure is assumed to gain inspiration.

b  The poster colours are often recalled as red, white and blue, and called 'patriotic'. In fact (and there *are* some simple facts in textual analysis) there are two shades of blue, and the 'white' is a kind of beige. But they serve to concentrate the image further (rather like the use of black and white in films, photos, etc.) than even the framing does.

c  The use of the 'silkscreen' style brings two artistic codes into play for those who may recognise them – or come to learn of them through the internet.

**Consider** firstly, that the celebrity portraits of Andy Warhol (1928–87), also often based on actual photos, used the simplified outlines of screen-printing, as well as the codes of comic books and advertising (celebrated by the movement known as 'Pop Art' in the 1960s). Interestingly though, his earlier work, like the famous multiple copies of a Marilyn Monroe silkscreen, following

on from his print of Campbell's soup can labels, are often taken to embody the 'mass-ness' of mass celebrity culture ('Monroe's image is in some ways churned out like that of a can of soup'). The typical slight flaws of printing in Figure 1.15 add to this – the colours look 'slipped', as happens in industrial mass processes, but not in individual paintings.

**Consider** secondly, posters from earlier workers' and revolutionary movements, and street posters. These often stylise and simplify their meanings, so as to be seen clearly from a distance, and because they were (are?) often addressing people with few literacy skills.

*Figure 1.16*  Cuban poster by Olivio Martinez, 1978, commemorating the death of Che Guevara in 1967. Though simplified in outline, like much Cuban campaigning art, the poster's sundrenched colours also seem to reference Western 'Pop Art' of the 1960s, such as that of Warhol and Roy Lichtenstein (1923–97).

*Figure 1.15*  Andy Warhol, *Marilyn*, 1967 © The Andy Warhol Foundation for the Visual Arts/Artists Rights Society (ARS), New York/DACS, London 2009.

**To summarise**: the 'Hope' poster weaves together several codes. It brought to the campaign of the little-known candidate:

- a memorable, clear image, which the artist made freely downloadable and was widely distributed via the internet;
- an image which was different to previous political imagery; it could be said both to 'modernise' Obama in the direction of 'cool' street posters and the now fashionable work of Andy Warhol, and to link it with previous reforming and radical social movements;
- an accompanying controversy about 'originating image', copyright, etc. which kept it in debate across the many 'new media'.

This poster was later imitated by Republican and other opponents of Obama, in a chain of signification and connotation. In particular a 'white face' image of Obama was used (see p. 174), disturbingly reminiscent of 'minstrel' performances, with the lipstick grin of Heath Ledger's Joker scrawled across it, all anchored by words such as 'Socialism'. This was in opposition to proposed healthcare and other reforms. The 'wolf in sheep's clothing' connotation is a particularly dangerous misrepresentation. See http://henryjenkins.org/2009/08/unmasking_the_joker.html for a good account of both the image and the mystery of its origins.

## VOICES AND SOUND SIGNIFIERS

Signifiers and 'images' need not always be visual. Sound is coded, and signifies in ways as complex as visual images, though, after decades of developed analysis, the visual image is more readily recognised as 'made up'. Sound is difficult to discuss: we can't offer you a sound 'text' on this page, for one thing, as we can a photo. Yet music, sound effects, etc. in the background can be key to how voices signify within films and television

## EXPLORE 1.8

- Try adding a sound effect 'behind' a recording of your own voice.
- Note how a particular 'soundtrack' on your iPod can 'interpret' your walk to work, or though a park, or a darkened urban landscape.
- Can this sometimes make you feel a bit as though you are 'starring' in your own film?

To ignore sound, for audio-visual media, can mean that a whole dimension is missing from analysis and appreciation (see Deacon *et al.* 2007, Chapters 12 and 13). Listen to a recording of someone's speaking voice. What does it signify for you?

- Pitch: is the voice 'high' or 'low'?
- Volume: 'loud' or 'quiet'?
- Texture: 'rough' or 'smooth', 'soft' or 'hard'?
- Shape: 'round' or 'flat'?

- Rhythm or cadence: does the voice rise and fall (or perhaps rise at the end of sentence, in a way which seems to have spread across much of the world from Australian soap operas)? Or does it keep a continuous or even monotonous pace and tone?

Other key components of voices will also be in play:

- accent, which usually refers to pronunciation (and often rhythm, cadence) and inflection. Every language has accents, but they are usually perceived very clearly by those within a larger culture – and perhaps less noticed by those close to them;
- dialect: everyone in the UK speaks a dialect, a sub-language. This differs from so-called 'standard English', also called 'received pronunciation' or 'BBC English', which is better described as the dialect of the southern English upper middle class. Dialects have differences of vocabulary ('wicked', 'nesh'), syntax and pronunciation.

### Voices: examples from popular film and music

1. From the 1930s to the 1950s many UK audiences had to endure the dominance of upper-class voices in most British films, perhaps most irritating when imitating the voices and accents of working-class people, coded as 'Cockney' or grotesque versions of 'Irish', 'Scottish' and 'Welsh' accents. This helps account for the perceived and popular 'classlessness' of US movies for UK audiences.

They were not classless, but the 'codings' of Bronx, posh New York, Deep South, etc. were much less familiar. **Note**: Hollywood too managed spectacularly careless accents, for example in *How Green Was My Valley* (US 1941).

2   As well as 'kitchen sink' social realist films of the 1960s, the Scottish accent and brusque delivery of lines by Sean Connery in his first appearance as James Bond in 1962 signified change. The 'modern' social world of 'Bond-as-scripted-and-performed-in-the-Broccoli-films' replaced the upper-class 'John-Buchan-type-hero-in-the-Cold-War' agent of Fleming's novels, and films of them. Connery's voice is arguably as important to this reinvention of Bond as his working-class, rugged physical presence. Connery's voice now is often gently mocked ('Shir Shean Connery'), perhaps as that ideal of masculinity gives way to different ones.

**Q:** How do you think the voice and star image of Daniel Craig alter the signification of the character? Who would you cast as 'the new James Bond'? Would voice be a part of this choice?

**Q:** Why do you think a particular voice-over for the British series of *Big Brother* was chosen (flat, male, north-east English accent, 'deadpan')? How did it try to 'anchor' that series' image in relation to gender, class, regional stereotypes?

Singing voices are different again, and always signify within a particular music genre, and, we could argue, in relation to speaking voices. Operatic singing would then be one extreme, and a singing which is as close as possible to kinds of everyday speech (of course, shaped by gender, age, class, region and ethnicity) another. For singers like Lily Allen the 'everydayness' of her lyrics is 'doubled' by the casual speech-like delivery of the singing and, for some, the emphatically English accent, as opposed to a 'mid-Atlantic' one. Others object to a 'mockney' quality of impersonation in it – internet comments often mention nepotism. It's at a far remove from opera but derives from forms such as reggae, ska and 'two tone'. Frank Sinatra, though working with very different lyrics, was also 'new' in the 1940s for performing with a casual, almost speech-like delivery and phrasing.

*Figure 1.17* Sean Bean in one of his most famous roles, Richard Sharpe. His Yorkshire accent was a key part of the signifed 'bluff honesty' of this role, as well as being his own original accent. He has since done advertising work where his very recognisable voice has been used to similar effect.

**EXPLORE 1.9**

- Listen to a track by your favourite singer.
- Try to describe their voice in terms of the discussions above.
- How do those qualities and their performance (phrasing, volume, emphasis, etc.) work with the instrumental parts of the track to produce your pleasure in it?
- Does knowledge of their social background shape your response, or anchor these signs, as happens, for some, with Lily Allen?

Unlike most of the voices we encounter at college or at home, the technical quality of voices in radio and music has been highly 'coded', even digitally shaped. What we hear is a reproduction of the original voice, dependent partly on ambience (the size of the studio, its acoustics: a room with hard, shiny surfaces will produce a harsh, 'bright' edge to the voice; one with absorbent surfaces will soften the voice), on technical codes, such as the choice of microphone, and on the engineer's processing of the signal, for example in an echo chamber, or a deliberately distorting process, when anonymity is needed.

Such institutional and technical codes can also shape the image of stations. Radio 5, for example, has a different mode of address to its listeners from Radio 4, partly through the voices of presenters and callers, especially those with distinctive regional accents. The ways in which voices are handled, especially in debates, can also characterise stations and programmes differently. The overlapping of voices, the amount of shouting permitted, sometimes to the point of being briefly inaudible, can signify 'realism'.

We hope that these brief ideas about a 'semiotics of sound' will help you think about voices and maybe also help you with choosing and recording voices for your own productions.

## AUDIO-VISUAL MOVING IMAGES

Watch www.youtube.com/watch?v=T-pzlZPRvx8 recording Beyoncé's performance of *At Last* at the 2009 Inaugural celebrations (here called a 'Neighbourhood Ball') for the new President Obama. Make notes on it, and repeat the screening – several times if you need to check details.

Figure 1.19  Beyoncé

Figure 1.18  Bourne poster

**Q:** Does this resemble the way the 'illegibility' of some fast-cut, shaky camera work in filmed action sequences can, for some, signify 'realistic'? (See http://flowtv.org/?p=1587 for John Cline's comments, and also David Bordwell's blog on *The Bourne Ultimatum*.)

### EXPLORE 1.10

- Jot down how this short sequence combines moving image and sound codes.
- Check if you agree with what we suggest here.

*Camera work:* several (at least three) cameras seem to be used, with well-rehearsed movements (give evidence, e.g. where they stop, what they seem to 'catch'). They range from an opening sweeping crane shot from behind Beyoncé towards the presidential couple, combined with a short dissolve to a long frontal shot of Beyoncé, poised, and another shot of the couple seeming nervous and giggling at their coming performance.

---

## EXPLORE 1.11

We'll stop here, but you could elaborate on the codes deployed, for example:

- How do the camera movements combine with framing choices, such as when to use close up, and for what purpose?
- What other camera style could have been used? Judging from the size of the audience there must be hundreds of very different, choppy, badly lit mobile camera films made of the event.

---

*The level of what is filmed*: for example, costume, lighting, set design, performance. For fiction films this would include casting. Here the choice of Beyoncé and the resonance of her star image is worth considering. Etta James was reported to be annoyed not to have been asked to perform the song associated with her (see below). Suggest other performers, and songs, which might shift the overall combination of codes here.

*Codes* of formality are embodied in the dress of the singer, and in that of Michelle Obama: formal but relaxed (the materials are soft, not stiff, or jewel-encrusted, other possible choices). Overall the combination of black and white outfits for the (mixed-race) President and his wife, Michelle, signifies a kind of elegance, and (expensive) simplicity, in such powerful figures.

The *setting* is striking, the darkness concealing hundreds of party-goers; the ceiling a bit like the sky, with small cameras flashing throughout; the presidential seal occasionally visible, and so on.

*Editing* (the choice of how shots are combined): this produces small surprises within what could be a repetitive text. An opening 'establishing shot' sets up

the space of the action, but the editing only later reveals the big screen of the whole performance.

*Performance*: movements, gestures as choreographed by editing, lighting, etc. Though clearly rehearsed, given that it is such an important event, all three central participants give impressively achieved performances. This may have been particularly tricky for the new 'First Couple' of the USA, who need both to perform a slow, formal dance, with a capacity for dignified ritual, and to display a kind of intimacy as a new 'celebrity' pair within twenty-first-century media cultures.

*Soundtrack*: finally, for this brief account, this 'anchors' the footage in a shifting way. The love song *At Last* was originally performed by Etta James (1938–), a great blues, soul and jazz singer and songwriter. For many in the audience that resonance alone would have evoked the days before the African-American Civil Rights movement (1955–68) aimed at outlawing racial discrimination and disenfranchisement in the US.

But the use of it here, and some of Beyoncé's gestures, as well as the audience's carefully orchestrated presence on the soundtrack, gives it a second meaning, a political one – '*at last* there is a non-white President for the USA'. The chorus of the audience at the end – 'O-ba-ma, O-ba-ma' – modulates the whole event into a political celebration.

---

This is the briefest example of moving image analysis. An excellent source of more detailed reflections on the form of films is David Bordwell's blog http://www.davidbordwell.net/blog. It is not, however, interested in theorising these in ways related to broader areas such as politics, which semiotics attempted.

---

## CONTENT ANALYSIS

Content analysis (CA) does not offer the detailed interpretations which semiotic and compositional approaches can, looking as they often do at 'hidden' meanings in texts. CA is a quantitative method, based on examining the manifest or 'open', 'apparent' meanings in large numbers of texts.

Figure 1.20 summarises the findings of one example, which you might try to apply to other areas.

Hunter Davies (2005), a writer on football, thought that the best football coverage was to be found in the broadsheet papers, not the tabloid press (or 'red-tops'). 'But have I made up this wisdom, based on . . . glimpses of one or two papers? Yeah, actually.' So, to check it, he employed a postgraduate, on work experience, to analyse every national newspaper's sports pages for a typical Monday, one with no big international match to skew the coverage. The question was: which devoted the most space to football?

As always with CA, what you find always partly depends on what you ask, and how aware you are of

its limitations. So Davies asks: 'What do you mean by space? Tabloid pages have fewer words, bigger pictures, bigger headlines than broadsheet pages . . . Pages also contain adverts, and sometimes a mixture of sports. So we had to count column inches.' They also counted how many first-person columns by players there were, and how much coverage of the Premiership as opposed to other leagues. But to supplement this quantitative work, they also give a qualitative, more subjective account of such aspects of coverage as:

- how opinionated different papers are: e.g. do they include abuse and 'rude quotations' such as 'the ref. was full of bull' (for you, such research could and should involve online responses and blogs);
- how witty and amusing the coverage is – a very subjective area!

*Figure 1.20*   National dailies

| Newspaper | Total number of pages | Number of sports pages | % of total devoted to sports | Number of football match reports | % of sports coverage devoted to football | Second most covered sport | Third most covered sport |
|---|---|---|---|---|---|---|---|
| The Guardian | 126 | 32 | 25 | 17 | 51 | racing (13%) | rugby union (11%) |
| Daily Star | 72 | 27 | 38 | 39 | 70 | racing (12%) | greyhounds (7%) |
| Daily Mail | 88 | 23 | 26 | 17 | 58 | rugby union (12%) | athletics (10%) |
| Sun | 88 | 41 | 47 | 38 | 85 | racing (4%) | cricket (4%) |
| Daily Mirror | 80 | 36 | 45 | 40 | 85 | racing (6%) | rugby union (3%) |
| The Times | 120 | 40 | 33 | 44 | 60 | rugby union (8%) | cricket (3%) |
| Daily Express | 80 | 20 | 25 | 23 | 59 | racing (10%) | rugby union (9%) |
| Independent | 108 | 22 | 20 | 12 | 60 | rugby union (13%) | racing (11%) |
| Daily Telegraph | 44 | 12 | 27 | 19 | 40 | rugby union (20%) | racing (10%) |

Source: Hunter Davies, 'The Fan', *New Statesman*, 14 February 2005, pp. 58–9

## EXPLORE 1.12

Although it is often suggested that there is a deadly enmity between qualitative and quantitative methods, the two can be combined, as above, and as in this activity.

1   Take four issues of your favourite magazine. Apply one of the content analysis methods outlined here to discover what proportions of it consist of:
   - adverts
   - celebrity coverage
   - a mix of those two, and
   - what the average of these kinds of content is across the magazine issues which you chose.
2   Assess (noting your textual methods) how many of the images are hostile or sympathetic towards the celebrities involved. This will involve qualitative approaches.

This is a very brief account of different kinds of textual analysis. Further chapters and the Further Reading section will give you more examples.

## REFERENCES AND FURTHER READING

Crisell, Andrew (1994) *Understanding Radio*, 2nd edn, London: Routledge.

Davies, Hunter (2005) 'The Fan', *New Statesman*, 14 February.

Deacon, David, Pickering, Michael, Golding, Peter, and Murdock, Graham (2007) *Researching Communications*, 2nd edn, London and New York: Hodder Arnold.

Dyer, Richard (1997) *White: Essays on Race and Culture*, London and New York: Routledge.

Fleming, Carole (2002) *The Radio Handbook*, London and New York: Routledge.

Hesmondhalgh, David (2006) 'Discourse Analysis and Content Analysis', in Gillespie, Marie, and Toynbee, Jason (eds) *Analysing Media Texts*, London and New York: Open University Press.

Rose, Gillian (2001) *Visual Methodologies*, London: Sage.

Wells, Liz (ed.) (2002) *Photography: A Critical Introduction*, 2nd edn, London and New York: Routledge.

# 2 Narratives

'Narrative' is a specialist term referring to the 'telling' of a sequence of events organised into a story. This shapes the events, characters, arrangement of time, etc., in very particular ways, so as to invite particular positions towards the 'story' on the part of audience members.

Think how you would respond if asked by a new friend about your childhood. Would you try to *connect* actions and events, rather than stringing together a set of impressions? How would you turn your life events so far into a narrative?

Bear these kinds of repetition and difference in mind, as well as the historical and industrial 'embeddedness' of different narratives. Read this chapter along with Chapter 3.

Making stories, or **narratives**, is a key way in which meanings and pleasures are organised, and made vivid both in and outside the media. Both factual and fiction forms are subject to this kind of shaping. Even the word 'history' comes from the Greek word for narrative: *historia*.

Most of us spend a great deal of time telling stories: gossiping about friends; telling jokes; 'day dreaming'; constructing blog characters as well as 'Second Lives' for ourselves on the internet. All cultures make stories, as involving ways to create sense and meanings. Indeed storytelling has been said to be one of the defining features of what it is to be human.

Two points about systematic study of narrative in modern media:

- Narrative theory suggests that stories, in whatever media and whatever culture, *share* certain features.
- But particular media and cultures are able or driven to 'tell' stories in *different* ways. This partly involves theories of **re-mediation**, of how older media forms (e.g. theatre) enter newer ones (e.g. cinema – see Chapters 8 and 14). It also involves the specific qualities of particular media forms – print or spoken language, TV or song, cinema and literature. And you will hardly ever encounter a story separate from expectations about it, usually about how it fits with **genres** and other forms of classification.

## General theories of narrative

This chapter explores the main narrative theories used in media studies. They offer explorations of the devices and conventions governing how stories (fictional or factual) are organised into sequence, and the invitations these may make to audiences to become involved in some ways, but not others. Such study suggests that these quite ordinary activities are usually so taken for granted that they stay unexamined. It's also interested in how media narratives are often connected to dominant sets of values and feelings.

Most of media studies is not involved in trying to create stories – a wildly unpredictable process, hard to reduce to a formula. Instead it has tried to understand critically the possible social roles of stories, which includes their pleasures, fantasy structures and so on. A good definition of narrative for these purposes (which applies to both fiction and non-fiction forms) is given by Branigan, who argues it is 'a way of organising spatial and temporal data into a cause-effect chain of events with a beginning, a middle and end *that embodies a judgement about the nature of those events*' (1992: 3 emphasis added).

> Like most semiotic approaches, these isolate texts from their context and use, for the purpose of analysis. In fact very few of us see a film or TV story without any knowledge of its genre or star, or the expectations set up by reviews.

## EXPLORE 2.1

Think of the structure of the last 'single' or 'closed' (i.e. not serial) story you experienced.

● How did the ending reflect back on to your feelings and understanding of the rest of the narrative? Genre will play a part here, with the ending of a thriller expected, by audiences, to be more surprising than that of a romantic comedy or a war movie. This in turn shapes what the makers assume they can do.

Important theorists have included Propp, Barthes, Todorov and Lévi-Strauss, who often worked with myths, novels and folk tales to explore how narrative *structures or shapings* act within particular cultures. Here are the bare bones of these influential **structuralist** approaches to narrative.

Propp, in the 1920s, examined hundreds of examples of one kind of folk tale to see whether they shared any structures. He argued that whatever the surface differences (i.e. whether the stories dealt with poor woodcutters or princes) it was possible to group its characters and actions into:

● eight character roles (or 'spheres of action' as he called them, to indicate how inseparable are character and action);

> **Vladimir Propp**
> (1895–1970) Russian critic and folklorist whose influential book on narrative, translated as *Morphology of the Folk Tale*, was first published in 1928.

---

**EXPLORE 2.2**

Think about this. How much of what you know of the 'character' of friends have you learned *apart from* through their 'actions'?

---

- thirty-one functions (such as 'a prohibition or ban is imposed on the hero' or 'the villain learns something about his victim') which move the story along, often in a highly predictable order. For example, 'the punishment of the villain' always occurs at the end of a story. And what is apparently the same act can function in different ways for different narratives. The 'prince' may build a castle (or a spaceship) as:
  - preparation for a war
  - defiance of a prohibition
  - solution of a task.

Roles or spheres of action, Propp argued, made sense of the ways in which many different figures (witch, woodcutter, monster, etc.) in the tales he studied could be reduced to eight character roles – not the same as the actual characters since one character can occupy several roles or 'spheres of action'. These are:

1 the *villain*
2 the *hero*, or character who seeks something, usually motivated by an initial lack – of money, or a mother, for example
3 the *donor*, who provides an object with some magic property
4 the *helper*, who aids the hero
5 the *princess*, reward for the hero (though see margin) and often object of the villain's schemes
6 her *father*, who rewards the hero
7 the *dispatcher*, who sends the hero on his way
8 the *false* hero.

> The very terms 'prince' and 'princess' are much more than job descriptions. They come to us loaded with narrative expectations and connotations. The same is true of 'a man on horseback' as echoing much older (often medieval, but then 'cowboy') figures of 'heroes'.

**Notes on Propp's terms now**

l   Propp's approach tried to uncover structures beneath the apparently haphazard differences of widely circulated, popular forms. It reminds us that, though characters may seem very 'real', especially in forms such as cinema and in some computer games, they must be understood as *constructed characters*. These can be pretty rudimentary, in 'shooter' games, for example. But even so, these games often structure the various tests of gaming skill into a kind of narrative, rather than simply organising them like a sports event, or an exam.

In films characters are played by actors (real or virtual), cast and visually 'designed' to resemble perceptions of their character ('princess-like' or 'wise' or 'villainous' looking). But they have *roles to play for the sake of the story* and often are perceived very quickly, if unconsciously, by audiences, in these roles – as 'hero', 'villain', 'helper' and so on. We tend to feel it very sharply when the person we thought was the hero or helper turns out to be the villain, as in *The Usual Suspects* (US 1995) or in *Psycho* (US 1960) where, to the shock of its first audiences, the female hero (and star) is killed off a third of the way through the film, and the shy young man who seemed to be a helper turns out to be something very different.

2   Such narrative theories are inevitably bound up with the times which produce them and their study object. Propp's original study worked with fairy tales, told in times when many women died in childbirth. Thus the role of stepmother could be a shared reference point for audiences, and 'wicked' ones a thrilling asset to a narrative. The longstanding Cinderella story draws on this. The related figure of 'the witch' is alive and well in enjoyable Western Hallowe'en parties and rituals.

3   'Hero' is one of those terms that does not mean the same within narrative theory as it does in life outside, where 'hero' usually refers to a male, and 'heroic' has moral connotations of 'admirable' or 'good'. Here the words are closer to describing someone who actively carries the events of a story, whether that's Bella Swan or Bart Simpson.

Today the 'hero' can often be an active female character like Lara Croft, or Noora in the Islamic superheroes story *The 99*. Such use of 'hero' can sound awkward (as 'actor' sounds to those who call a female actor an 'actress'). But the word 'heroine' is inadequate, signifying as it often does a character who hangs around looking decorative until the hero sweeps her away (as in Propp's 'princess' role).

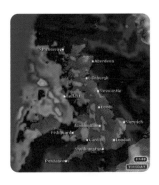

*Figure 2.1* Language can construct narrative 'roles' and thus 'characters' even in weather forecasts. Watch for the isobars which are 'to blame' for 'bad weather' or the warm front 'coming to the rescue' – even though both might be better understood as part of a disturbing global warming 'narrative'.

The title of *Heroes* (2006–) announces its play with several, equally prominent central characters, rather than one 'hero'. The twist is that they themselves do not, at the outset, realise their 'superhero' powers or the 'end of days' narrative they are part of.

*Figure 2.2* The distributors describe this as 'Noora: a superhero inspired by Islam'. See http://news.bbc.co.uk/1/hi/world/middle_east/8127699.stm for an account of the aspirations of this series, soon to be an animated film. The writer says he wanted to 'take back' Islam from militants who had taken it hostage.

Figure 2.2

*Figure 2.3* A controversial re-mediation of the Cinderella story, with a prostitute as 'hero'. Can you identify the Wicked Sisters, Helper and Prince roles – and the Magic Slipper equivalent? Are any extra 'roles' added?

*Figure 2.4* This poster for *Om Shanti Om* (India 2007), a much-loved Bollywood blockbuster, gives an idea of the narrative priorities of musicals, Eastern and Western.

**Tzvetan Todorov** (b. 1939) Bulgarian structuralist linguist, publishing influential work on narrative from the 1960s onwards.

For specialists: the five codes are the action or proairetic; the enigma or hermeneutic; the semic; the symbolic; and the cultural or referential code. See http://www.aber.ac.uk/media/Documents/S4B/semiotic.html for a useful guide.

Fairy tales, or versions of them, are still familiar, whether the immensely profitable Disney animated versions (*Cinderella*, *Snow White*, etc.) or more broadly the narratives of the *Star Wars* series, *Harry Potter* or *The Lord of the Rings* books and films, with their stories of male initiation, good versus evil, and so on. The *Shrek* films commented neatly on Disney, and fairy-tale conventions more generally, as well as on the ways these flow into contemporary 'beauty cultures'. Other stories, from real life, are regularly given fairy-tale shapings – think of celebrity 'rags to riches' tales, and many news stories (see Chapter 12).

Some narrative forms (the Mahabharata from Indian culture; Western musicals and 'women's films') take pleasure in much less action-driven or puzzle-driven narratives. Instead they use convoluted patterns (often circular) and several climaxes. Spectacle and fantasy are given real narrative weight – for example, in musical and 'Bollywood' forms, other events are sidelined to allow them to take place.

**Todorov**, another structuralist, argued that all stories begin with an 'equilibrium' where any potentially opposing forces are 'in an opening balance' – the 'once upon a time' moment. (It is not the same as a 'quiet' state; indeed it could be in the middle of a war. This is one of the ways in which the language of narrative theory differs from everyday usage, where equilibrium denotes a perfect balance.) This is disrupted by some event, setting in train a series of other events, to close with a second, but different 'equilibrium' or status quo.

His theory may sound just like the cliché that every story has a beginning, a middle and an end. But it's more interesting. 'Equilibrium' labels a state of affairs, a status quo, and how this is 'set up' in certain ways, and not others. How, where and when *else* any story (especially a news story) could have begun are always good questions to ask. What difference would it make, for example, to include the devastating recent history of Somalia as starting point for a news story covering 'pirates' around its coast?

Barthes suggested that narrative works with five different **codes** which activate the reader to make sense of it. This is an intricate theory, using deliberately unfamiliar terms, and Barthes is not at pains to make it accessible. We have opened it out a little to apply it to *CSI: Miami* in the case study. Particularly interesting is his suggestion that an 'enigma code' works to keep setting up little puzzles to be solved (and not only at the beginning of the story) so as to delay the story's ending pleasurably. In *Twilight*, for example, how will Robert Pattinson's character get out of *this* predicament? Have characters x and y been in love all along?

An action code will be read by means of accumulated details (looks, significant words) which invoke (and reinforce) our knowledge of what are often highly conventional '**scripts**' of such actions as 'beginning to fall in love' or 'first being tempted into a robbery'. Barthes is a key figure in both audience studies and textual studies for this early attempt at building the possible involvement of readers and their culturally formed expectations into a model of how narratives 'work' textually. Though very text based, his model does try to explore not just how the narrative works 'internally' but also how it evokes for its 'reader' connections to the world outside the text, via cultural references and so on.

Narrative involvements still matter, however much may be given away in media publicity (and some trailers do make you feel you don't need actually to see the film). But the urgent notices about 'spoilers' in some articles ('WARNING: STORY AND PLOT REVEALED'), and the convention that even serious discussion and reviewing should not reveal the ending of a film, book or TV programme, ignore the fact that serious discussion of the construction of any narrative has to consider how the ending 'closes' or 'ends' it (rather than it simply 'stopping').

> 'Scripts', in this specialist context, are 'shared expectations about what will happen in certain contexts, and what is desirable and undesirable in terms of outcome' (Durkin 1985: 126). See Chapter 4 for more discussion.

## EXPLORE 2.3

- Take your favourite recent film or TV drama. Survey a few reviews of it to see if/how the ending has been treated.
- Draft your own brief review of it,
  - first without any reference to the ending,
  - then feeling free to discuss the ending.
- What does discussing the ending allow you to engage with in the rest of the narrative?
- How does *not* mentioning it limit what you can discuss in the narrative?

Such structuralist approaches have been applied not just to individual fictions but also to non-fiction forms such as major news stories, to see whether narrative drives 'set up' certain expectations and puzzles, or look for (and in fact construct) tidy 'beginnings' and 'endings', etc. This widespread process can mean that complex historical and political explanations are structured out of news storytelling.

'During the Iraq War, there was a civil servant at the Foreign Office whose official title – you could ask for him by it at the switchboard – was head of story development.' (Hyde 2009).

For bitingly funny satire of the narrative and other 'taken-for-granted' habits of ordinary, as well as extraordinary, news reporting of 'stories', see BBC's *Charlie Brooker's Newswipe*, extracts available on YouTube.

## CASE STUDY: APPLYING TODOROV AND LÉVI-STRAUSS TO WAR NEWS

Important events such as wars finish. But narratives don't just come to a halt, or stop – they *end*, or *close*, in a way which 'rounds things off', assigns blame and praise, etc. (so as to form the 'new equilibrium'). The news media have often structured the end of wars so as to leave out stubborn elements that don't stop, but go on happening: soldiers' and civilians' injuries and post-traumatic stress syndrome; the continuing arms trade, which feeds wars and terror; corrupt regimes left in power after 'democratising' invasions. So deep are the satisfactions of 'an ending' or 'closure' that newsrooms, and many of those involved, will try hard to find signifiers which suggest a return to normality – very like the 'and so they all lived happily ever after' of the fairy tale.

Sometimes it may take the shape of a correspondent making his way into the now-said-to-be-liberated war zone, like the BBC's John Simpson entering Kabul in November 2001. Sometimes it will be footage like that of the tumbling of the statue of Saddam Hussein in 2003, with reporters

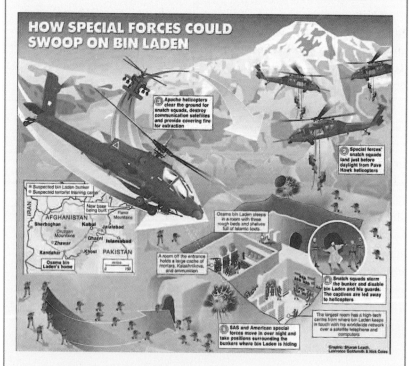

*Figure 2.5* In the days immediately after '9/11' in 2001, news images such as this drawing were used to offer a comforting narrative into which the event might be fitted.

commenting, 'It is absolutely, without doubt, a vindication of the strategy', and 'This war has been a major success', as though the Iraq 'problem' had been 'solved' and was now finished. In this particular case the image echoed older but hugely resonant 1989 footage of the Berlin Wall coming down as Eastern bloc state socialist regimes began to fall. A kind of re-mediation?

In the past, the 'happy' conclusion of war has typically been signified by ships sailing back home; soldiers talking of their pride at a job well done; and eventually the welcome home by 'women and children'. This last sign strongly genders such stories, via repeated imagery of an all-male armed force and 'waiting' women, even where many women are serving in armed forces, or may not be 'waiting'. This sense of an ending is much more difficult to achieve for such a nebulous and far-flung process as the 'global war on terror', especially when some strategists suggest it will go on for decades. The sad spectacle of soldiers' coffins carried to funerals when they arrive 'home' is very far from functioning as a 'happy ending'.

See http//www.information clearinghouse.info/article 2842.htm on the probable faking of the statue incident. It has nevertheless become a powerful signifier of 'democracy coming to Iraq'.

**Lévi-Strauss**, another structuralist, argued that an abiding structure of *all* meaning-making, not just narratives, was a dependence on binary oppositions, or a conflict between two qualities or terms. Usually one of these terms is much less valued than its opposite. He was less interested in the order in which events were arranged in the plot (called its syntagmatic relations) than in looking 'beneath' them for deeper or paradigmatic arrangements of themes. Though this theory can be applied to individual stories and can act as a useful 'way in', strictly speaking it should be applied to *sets* of narratives, across a number of news stories on the same theme – or in genres. Westerns and their narratives, for example, are still hugely influential on how the US imagines itself. The different sheriffs, cowboys, schoolmarms, Native Americans and so on in hundreds of westerns can be analysed through Propp's terms – 'white hats' and black hats'; Native Americans as thrilling villains, their motives often withheld.

Syntagm: an element which follows another in a particular sequence. A much used example: imagine choosing from a menu. Paradigmatic elements are those from which you choose (starters, main courses, desserts, and within those maybe soup, risotto, chocolate pudding). The syntagm is the sequence

> Some celebrity chefs are famous for 'scandalously' mixing these borders, as with Heston Blumenthal's bacon and egg ice cream.

into which they are arranged. It is not usual in the UK, for example, to have dessert before the main course.

Sometimes these structuring patterns in narratives are treated as 'horizontal' (across time – the syntagmatic) and 'vertical' (along values – the paradigmatic) aspects of narratives.

They could also be seen as organised, over time, according to systematic oppositions, including, among others:

 See the Classic Case Study *The Western* on the **MSB5 website**.

| | |
|---|---|
| homesteaders | Native Americans |
| Christian | pagan |
| domestic | savage |
| weak | strong |
| feminine | masculine |
| garden | wilderness |
| inside society | outside society |

> See Branston (2006) on how the story of the 'capture and rescue' of Private Jessica Lynch in Iraq, 2003, was handled, including gender assumptions about female soldiers and links to (re-mediations of?) powerful US myths of 'the US frontier' and of 'Red Indian' abductions of 'white women' or 'maidens'.

Interestingly some of this same structure, with its complex construction of an 'Other' whom those in the favoured list must often be prepared to destroy, is perceptible in modern wars, and in the construction of some figures in media panics. For media coverage of recent wars in Afghanistan and Iraq, for example, structuring oppositions include:

| East | West |
|---|---|
| barbarism | civilisation |
| feudal | modern |
| despotism | democracy |
| fundamentalism | freedom |
| (2001) backward 'dirty' weapons | modern 'clean' weapons ('surgical strikes') |
| chaotic terrorism | 'shock and awe' tactics (Iraq 2003–) |
| 'backward' cultures, especially via women wearing the burka | 'modern' cultures, often signified through women wearing 'Western' dress |
| evil | good |

---

**EXPLORE 2.4**

- Research current coverage of Middle Eastern wars and decide whether any or all of these binaries still apply.
- Has the long-running-ness and assumed global spread of these wars shaped the ways news narratives can 'tell' them? Do they seem less clearly structured than previously?

---

## Narration, story and plot

The term **narration** describes *how* stories are told, how their material is selected and arranged in order to achieve particular effects with their audiences. This partly involves how much knowledge we are allowed to have – think of the importance of 'secrets' in soap operas. The narrative theory term '**restricted narration**' refers to how information about events and characters is distributed – withheld or supplied for the sake of the story. More on this later.

The distinction which narrative theory makes between **plot** and **story** is key here. 'Story' is defined by Bordwell and Thompson (2008: 76) as consisting of 'all the events in a narrative, both the ones explicitly presented and those the viewer infers'. The plot, on the other hand, is 'everything visibly and audibly present in the film before us', including all the story events directly depicted.

There is one special aspect to this in audio-visual fictions (cinema, TV, some games) which can be useful in analysing sound. These kinds of fiction usually include elements related to what's called the **diegesis**, a term for the world of the story, which can include music (say in a biopic of a rock star). But in the plot, the film on screen, there will often be non-diegetic music. The soaring crescendo as characters reach the top of a mountain is not usually made by an orchestra waiting there for them.

Think of the story as something you are able to assemble once you have experienced the end of the narrative. It would imply routine events, like waking up in the morning, which we assume carry on happening during many stories, but would be a tedious part of the plot. It may also include material we find out only at the very end of the story, having been busy trying to piece things together throughout, such as the identity of a key figure in *The Usual Suspects* (US 1995). Figure 2.7 provides a helpful graph.

*Figure 2.6* The comedy-drama TV series *Desperate Housewives* (US 2004–) is constructed emphatically around secrets, gossip and power struggles. Music often playfully alerts viewers to a potential secret. Repeated imagery of immaculate front doors came to signify concealed secrets, crimes and despair.

A useful distinction was developed by Russian theorists in the 1920s between *syuzhet* (**plot**) and *fabula* (**story**). The Russian words are often used, partly because the meanings of the two English terms are often slippery and became confused with one another.

*Figure 2.7* Wuthering Heights graph

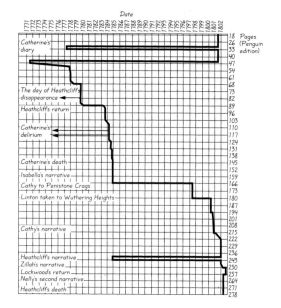

This graph indicates the complicated narrative structure of the novel *Wuthering Heights* (1847). The pages of the book, representing the flow of the final, plotted narrative, are listed on the right. The dates of events in the 'story', which we are able to piece together by the end, are listed along the top. (You would substitute minutes of the action on the right-hand side if applying this to a film or TV narrative. A less precise equivalent could use DVD 'chapters'.)

Our sympathies towards characters can be moved not only by their actions, and comments on them, but also by plot. For example, at a time towards the end of the plotted narrative (c.1800) when Heathcliff seems almost monstrous, the book goes into flashback via accounts of his childhood as a poor and bullied orphan. Readers' knowledge of this period has been restricted until now by the limited narrative information released .Their sympathies are likely to swing towards him, complicating an otherwise simple sense of his 'villainy' at this stage.

## EXPLORE 2.5

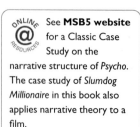

See **MSB5 website** for a Classic Case Study on the narrative structure of *Psycho*. The case study of *Slumdog Millionaire* in this book also applies narrative theory to a film.

- Note how any recent version (TV, film) of this novel, or perhaps of another novel you enjoyed, has arranged its events for the sake of narrative pleasures.
- Take a classic film employing flashback, such as *Psycho* or, less dramatically, *Saving Private Ryan* (US 1998). Imagine how its narrative would work if told without flashbacks.
- In the case of *Psycho*, what genre would it fit? Biography of troubled young male?
- What kinds of pleasures would be lost in a 'straightforward' telling?

Other writers have explored this area in terms of the knowledge which the 'reader' has, compared with that of the characters: is it the same or more? When more, when less? How much more? How has this been contrived? For example, we should feel at the end of a good detective story or thriller that we have been enjoyably puzzled, so that the 'solution', our piecing together of the story in its proper order out of the evidence offered by the plot, will come as a pleasure. We should not feel that the plot has cheated; that parts of the story have suddenly been revealed which we couldn't possibly have guessed. The apparently innocent secretary cannot, at the last minute, suddenly be revealed to be a top-class poisons expert.

*Figure 2.8* Michael Jackson's turn to camera at the end of the *Thriller* video is a classic ending to such a narrative, revealing something which changes our sense of the set of events before it.

### The special case of suspense, and the thriller

'Thrillers' are said to be broadly distinguished from 'horror' films by displaying:

- less emphasis on gory or 'bodily extreme' special effects;
- an overlap with crime films;
- 'thrilling' or suspenseful qualities which are possible in moving images, especially via editing in combination with music.

Thrillers often play with narrative knowledge, putting the audience in the (enjoyably) agonising position of knowing what perils and time constraints face the hero. In this sense the thriller is a pleasurably **masochistic** genre for audiences. This is perhaps present in the slogan in the woods which Jodie Foster runs through in the opening scene of *The Silence of the Lambs* 'Hurt – Agony – Pain – Love it'. Charles Derry argues that this kind of suspense is not necessarily related to the solving of narrative puzzles or the 'vague question of

Entertaining 'cheats' are possible. *Sunset Boulevard* (US 1950) and *Desperate Housewives* (US 2004–) told their stories through a first-person narrator who is dead in the plot's 'present', and only gives some of their knowledge to the viewer. *The Usual Suspects* (US 1995) relied for its surprise on a long, misleading flashback.

**Masochism**: broadly, a medical/psychoanalytic term for the pleasure or gratification of having pain inflicted, or of being controlled. In film theory it has been explored to explain some of the perverse pleasures of cinema.

*Figure 2.9* From the opening scene of *The Silence of the Lambs* (US 1991) – a knowing wink towards the audience about the masochistic pleasures they hope for in a horror-thriller?

what will happen next' (Derry 1988: 31). It depends on the expectation that a specific action *might* take place.

> During those moments when suspense is operative, time seems to extend itself, and each second provides a kind of torture for a spectator who is anxious to have his or her anticipation foiled or justified. (p. 32)

If you like thrillers, you like this agonising torture.

---

## EXPLORE 2.6

- Can you think of any scenes from recent films, or other media, where this kind of enjoyable 'torture' of the viewer takes place?
- How exactly is it managed, in terms of manipulation of time and of narrative point of view?
- Does it apply at all to games?

---

Explore how the unavoidable use of mobile phones (cellphones) in many narratives has altered how they must be shaped. *The Departed* (US 2006) is a striking film example of how the phones are used a) without ruining a thriller-shaped plot and b) so as to relate to one of the film's key themes, the disappearance of an earlier form of masculine 'community' in Boston.

The opening captions to Terry Gilliam's film *The Adventures of Baron Munchausen* (1988) play with this convention. They begin: 'The late eighteenth century, The Age of Reason, Wednesday.'

Another part of the construction of narratives, and of restricted narration, involves the 'voice' telling the story. A first-person narration will use 'I' as the voice of the teller, and should not give the reader access to events which that 'I' could not have witnessed or known of – a kind of enjoyable restriction. A third-person or impersonal narration, however, refers to a story which seems to 'get itself told', as in 'Once upon a time there was a prince . . .' It's often called the voice of the omniscient narrator, since it knows everything to do with the story. Though cinema and many television or video narratives begin with a literal 'voice-over' telling the story from a personal point of view, they usually settle into the mode of impersonal narration – no voice-over, just seeming to unfold before us.

The voice-over is often by one of the *characters* in a story, an underestimated area of narrative study. Characters 'work' on the basis of appearance, clothing, gestures, star image, etc. and often embody 'typical' traits, especially if they are only needed for background actions. Corrigan and White point out how, although movies aim to create broadly realistic characters, most of them are a blend of ordinary and extraordinary features (rather like stars). This makes for characters who are 'recognisable in terms of our experiences and exceptional in ways

that make us interested in them . . . Even [with] . . . characters [like] the
. . . heroine of *Alien* (1979) understanding them means appreciating how
that balance between the ordinary and extraordinary is achieved'
(Corrigan and White 2004: 224).

---

### EXPLORE 2.7

- Try out these theories by looking at how ads work, with their short, easily
  followed narratives. (Non-narrative ads do exist. They often consist simply of a
  set of claims about a product – a supermarket listing its best prices – or a car
  setting up a glamorous aura around itself by various mood shots.)
- Classify the next few ads you view into narrative and non-narrative kinds.

To revise: if using narrative form, an ad will

- group its events in cause and effect order;
- even in a few seconds, create a sense of characters, action and perhaps enigma
  codes through economical use of signs and typifying traits – blonde hair, certain
  glances, etc.

Ads work as Propp suggests: the same traits both build a sense of characters, being
like 'real people', and are also crucial for the action, the furthering of the plot.
There will be a discernible 'hero' who carries the plot along, though often the
'hero' is the product – solving the problems of the main characters. There will
be, as Todorov suggests, some sense of an initial situation, which is disrupted or
altered and then happily resolved – usually, of course, through the 'magical'
intervention of the product being sold.

   You will also probably be able to distinguish the *story* as you can reassemble it,
having gone through a narrative, and the *plot* which seeks to involve you. Even if
flashback is not used, try to imagine the same events told differently, from the
point of view of another character, for example, or with different amounts of
time, and therefore emphasis, given to different parts of the narrative.

"...but what happened to the iceberg?"

*Figure 2.10* Of course, audience
members will make different sense
of narratives, depending partly on
how far they feel they resemble or
identify with certain characters.

---

### Scripts and narratives

If you are on a scriptwriting course, focused on production rather than
analysis, you may know other ways of thinking about the telling and writing
of stories. A few names frequently come up. Joseph Campbell was a US
anthropologist interested in myths, or ancient stories which can be argued to
be shared across cultures. His book *Hero with a Thousand Faces* (1949)
argued that 'eternal' myths or stories are shared by all cultures. He is said by

**Joseph Campbell**
(1904–87) was influenced by
Carl G. Jung (1875–1961)
who argued that certain
myths and symbols represent
'archetypal' patterns which
have been central to human
existence (e.g. the anima or
'feminine' side of men, etc.).

film-makers like George Lucas to be a key influence on films such as the *Star Wars* series.

Some have suggested his fashionable theories:

- flatten differences between the ways myths and stories work within varied cultures;
- are used to give high cultural and quasi-religious meanings to commercially powerful products (e.g. the *Star Trek* or *Star Wars* series); and
- conveniently avoid offending lucrative global audiences by not being too specific about exactly which 'god' or religion is being invoked.

(Hollywood loves to give 'universal' explanations for the global success of its products, rather than outlining how they avoid 'offence' by too much specific reference; or by having the power to be massively distributed and marketed.)

Campbell's theories influenced such scriptwriting 'gurus' as Syd Field and Robert McKee (1941–), who has made his career via the book *Story Substance, Structure, Style and the Principles of Screenwriting* (1st edn 1999) and worldwide public seminars based on it. Some writers describe his 'perfect blueprint' (involving 'universal values' and 'archetypes') for scripts as being most valuable for studios who want a smooth production line from writers. This is similar to other 'Fordist' production methods, rooted in the 1920s. when the Ford motor company produced cheap, reliable, standardised cars via a production line, a method later applied by McDonalds and others. Mark Ravenhill (2007) comments:

> I've read it . . . and learned some valuable things from it . . . But now . . . writer delivers script, goes in for meeting. 'I'm missing the initiating incident on page 23' is a note you're likely to hear in our *Story*-centred world. Rarely 'Why are we making this?'

> Charlie Kaufmann's film *Adaptation* (2002) included a character called 'Donald Kaufmann', who is writing a formulaic serial-killer movie, based on McKee's theories, for which he is paid a huge sum. McKee has few film-writing credits, but the character is assumed to be based on him (see Ravenhill 2007).

## EXPLORE 2.8

- Research the theories of McKee (or Field, if your course uses him) and compare them with older Western theories of drama, including that of a 'three-act structure', as pioneered by the Greek writer Aristotle (384–322 BC).
- Explore how far these theorists of film scripts:
  a  take account of other audience pleasures in films (e.g. stars, context, etc.);
  b  focus heavily on the writer as author.

> - Do they avoid much account of the rest of the key processes in making films, such as the role of direction, design, casting, product placement, marketing and generally Hollywood's power to get certain stories shown, and publicised?

> 'Once upon a time it was a small gathering of people around a fire listening to the storyteller with his tales of magic and fantasy. And now it's the whole world . . . It's not "domination" by American cinema. It's just the magic of storytelling, and it unites the world' (Steven Spielberg, *Variety*, 7 December 1993, p. 62). A classic statement of Hollywood's myth of itself.

## Narratives in different media

As we said at the beginning, narrative theory suggests that stories, in whatever media and whatever culture, *share* certain features, but particular media and cultures are able or driven to 'tell' stories in *different* ways. This is worth bearing in mind if you're involved in a project which asks you to *choose* a medium in which to make a story. You will be asking: what can *x* medium do (strip cartoon, say, or radio) that *y* cannot, and vice versa? These differences are partly due to the nature of different media and technologies ('re-mediation') as well as the different audiences who use and enjoy them. We'll quickly summarise a few of them.

### Stories in words

There's no space to deal with literary or other verbal narratives, though this brief application highlights their capacities, compared with audio-visual or other forms.

---

**EXPLORE 2.9**

- See if you can storyboard this sentence, for adaptation to film or TV. How can you convey in images and sound what is put here in words?

  *'In years to come, Harry would never quite remember how he had managed to get through his exams when he half expected Voldemort to come bursting through the door at any moment.'*
  (from *Harry Potter and the Philosopher's Stone*, J.K. Rowling, 1997, p. 191)

- What questions does it raise about adaptations from words to screen in general?

### Photography

This might seem an odd example of a narrative form, since it deals in frozen moments of time (like stained-glass windows or drawings). But often the impact of a powerful news or advertising photo lies in what it invites us to imagine has gone before or is about to happen, or both. Narrative is often signalled by angle, visual information given, construction of imagined characters – and whether or not black and white film stock is involved (often signalling 'pastness' in a story). You can find more on all this in the case study for Chapter 1.

See Liz Wells' guides to this area (Wells 2002).

There is debate among some feminists as to whether people who have been raped should be called 'victims' or 'survivors'. Part of what's at stake is a very different sense of the ongoing 'narratives' these terms seem to be part of.
Q: How might this work through photos?

**EXPLORE 2.10**

*Figure 2.11* Cover of Wells (2002). Each of the four parts of this single photo seems to suggest a different character and even a narrative. How would you describe them?

### Comic strips and animation

Comic strips (and by extension animation films and serials) tell their stories by a compelling combination of

- words (including thought bubbles);
- line drawings. These can streamline and exaggerate characters and events more than even the highest-budget movie. You never have to worry about spots on the star's face or problems with lighting in comic strip and animation;
- flashpoint illustrations of key moments involving extreme angles and exaggerations.

Animation often represents worlds which differ from our own: as in the four-fingered, yellow-skinned inhabitants of *The Simpsons*, with their unlikely 'local media', babies that never grow up, far-flung storylines and pain-free violence. But most viewers relish this exaggeration/difference, which partly allows the series its 'double address' to both child and adult viewers. They also may enjoy the ways that characters and storylines (and particular lines of dialogue) do relate to 'our' world, with bitingly satirical comments on real-life political or cultural issues, relatively unlimited by budget constraints.

**Figure 2.12** The extreme and stylised dynamism of comic books and graphic novels has been re-mediated during the past forty years by the makers of audio-visual forms such as movies. This is a 1986 Frank Miller comic image from *Batman: The Dark Knight Returns* © 1986 DC Comics. All Rights Reserved. Used with permission.

**Figure 2.13** In a controversial move, 'Marge' 'appeared' on the cover of *Playboy* in 2009.

See the debate summarised in Churchwell (2009) around whether *The Simpsons* was escalating its satire or selling out. The character of Lisa in particular has long been seen as a 'feminist role model'.

What would she say?

### Radio

Radio uses sounds and silence (in particular the signifying capacities of voices), and this affects the way it can handle narrative. It has to construct the illusion of space between characters, and time between segments, through the use of voices, noises, sound effects and silence. It will not devote much time to features on which cinema might want to linger, as visual evidence of how the movie has spent its resources (say, the display of special effects (FX) or costumes).

Characters cannot stay silent for long periods of time (like the Tim Roth character, mostly silent, dying 'onstage' in *Reservoir Dogs* (US 1992)), since they would seem to have 'disappeared'. Since radio's signifiers are relatively cheap and easy to produce, it is free to construct the most bizarre and exotic stories, from time travel to a play about memories flashing through the head of a drowning woman.

### Cinema

Like video and audio recordings, this is a 'time-based' medium, manipulating time and space via camera movement and editing, as well as by images or words. The average feature film length of two hours, if audiences view it all at one sitting, can give it some of the intensity of a short story. With DVDs some choose to replicate this experience with 'special' DVD screenings at home and even box set 'power viewings' of series before the next comes along. Large-screen TVs (often sold by the same corporations) seem to be strengthening this tendency. It involves an experience different from that of more open-ended fictions, like soaps, serials or novels, read or viewed over days, weeks, even years, woven into our lives while we do other things in between.

For more detailed discussion of film texts, see Chapter 1 case study, Chapter 13, and the Chapter 6 case study on *The Age of Stupid*.

## Long-running 'open' narratives

So, differences between the ways stories are told in different media, or re-mediated, are partly to do with the material (sound, celluloid, digital media, line drawings, spoken or written words alone) of that medium. But they are also to do with *institutional* or *industrial* demands.

Soaps can be defined as open-ended, multi-strand serial forms, broadcast across fifty-two weeks of the year. They developed first on US radio in the 1930s as a cheap way of involving housewives, whose buying choices the detergent manufacturers (and other businesses) wanted to influence. It seemed an ideal form both for commercial television in the 1960s, keen to sell the promise of audiences' regular attention to advertisers, and for the BBC to revive in 1985 with *EastEnders*, wanting to boost its early evening audiences. This was partly in the hope that they would stay with the channel all evening, and also to help the BBC produce evidence of large audience numbers when making its arguments for the level of the next licence fee.

Major soaps have acted like big news programmes, and major serials as 'flagship programmes', which can help to **brand** channels. Though 'soap opera' is one of the most familiar and discussed forms of media, it is not just 'one thing'. Even on British terrestrial television there are Australian, US, Welsh, Scottish and other soaps, made within different kinds of broadcasting institutions (**public service broadcasting**, commercially funded, etc.).

These in turn divide into high- and low-budget products, and have different relationships to documentary forms, to sitcom, **romance**, regional identities, and to different audiences.

> Branding seeks to associate products with certain desirable meanings and emotions, and to establish something called a **USP** or Unique Selling Proposition for them. (See Chapter 11.)

---

The director of *The Wire*, in various interviews, suggested (2009) strategies to maximise audience impact/pull and build a sense of almost **ethnographic** realism/insight, etc. in the narrative of this much-praised serial:

1  don't explain anything to the audience. Let the characters engage with each other in their real idiom and the audience will find the thread and enjoy putting it together;

2  let some characters behave in unexpected ways, 'out of character', enhancing a sense of human complexity; and

3  every now and then insert a tiny insight/gem that only real people living in those conditions/contexts would know. But don't ever explain anything!

(Thanks to Simon Cottle for this).

---

Nevertheless, we can generalise. One of British soap's attractions for its producers has been that costs can be kept down, partly because narrative can be centred on a few key or 'nodal' locations (e.g. the hotel, pub, launderette or café). These are meeting places, one of the staples of the narrative, and also key to soaps' economies and production needs. Since soaps usually air on two or three nights a week, many storylines are necessary. Particular ones can swing in and out of prominence, allowing:

- time for rehearsals, and for actors' holidays, pantomime contracts, pregnancies, illnesses;
- a wide appeal, through several stories happening at once so as to involve different sections of the audience. If you're impatient with one 'strand', you know that another, which interests you more, will

probably be along in a minute or so. The 'nodal' meeting places give a chance for storylines to meet and switch, but also coherence and the feeling of 'community' so central to soap's pleasures. These have been extended recently through viewers' ability to contact the programme makers, through blogs and so on, with suggestions, queries, etc. Soap narratives may also change as a result of attempts to shift the composition of their audiences – and advertisers. Over the past few years several UK soaps have moved 'upmarket' in terms of their sets, costumes, situations and some character types, as part of the attempt to sell more expensive ad slots addressing more affluent audiences. After the success of *Brookside*, other soaps tried to attract male audiences to this traditionally female form, as happened with hospital series, which became tougher through gory special FX and certain storylines. The characters and storylines of *The Bill*, for example, fall between soap (continuous production, never a 'closed' ending to an episode) and series (self-contained storylines each week, as in *ER*). Serials (including 'classic' serials) and 'mini-series' (often a pilot project) are other narrative forms which are longer than a single narrative, but not 'open ended' as soaps are.

Soaps have also often covered controversial themes in order to aggregate audiences. A quick look at the website list of charities consulted by *EastEnders* for such storylines suggests the care that is often taken (see Chapter 4). It also seems that soap's very long-running narrative has advantages over more prestigious drama forms in treating traumatic happenings. The long-term, often invisible consequences of dramatic 'social issues' (such as rape, child abuse, the trauma of serving in a war) can be dealt with, and resurface for a particular character, over many years – as they do in real life.

*The Royle Family* (BBC 1998–2008) series, unlike soaps, was in one sense very 'realistic': in its representation of TV viewing. Wikipedia warns 'Not to be confused with the Royal Family.'

Of course soap opera has limitations to its 'realism'. When have you ever heard characters in a soap discussing real-life political campaigns or figures, the news, or even rival television soaps, as most of us do?

Explore why these absences occur.

Radio soaps, because cheaper to produce, can work slightly differently. *The Archers* is well known for the up-to-date-ness of its agricultural storylines, able to respond swiftly to real-world farming events. Foot and mouth disease, in 2001, with its devastating consequences for farming, was mentioned by the end of the first week in which it was reported.

**Q:** Why exactly might this have been more difficult for a TV soap to achieve?

## Conclusion

'Narrative' has long been a key theory helping us understand the workings of media forms, both 'factual' and fiction, both pre-modern media and in some, but only some, Web 2.0 interactive forms. We discuss later (Chapter 6) its expanding uses, for example into a kind of substitute for ideological position, as in 'the management narrative in the postal strike is that . . .'

A final example may focus this area of media theory, which for so long has been based in very textual approaches, using narratives assumed to be 'told to' audiences. Though some computer games use aspects of stories – characters, 'chained actions' and endings – the 'reader' or rather user should feel right in the middle of them, immersed. And a 'given' ending does not operate in the ways we've suggested for single narratives. For example, the player may have met challenges which halt or even stop the game/narrative.

It is hard to generalise about games, firstly since there are so many kinds (sports games, racing games, MMPORGs (massively multiplayer online role-play games), single-player fantasy adventure RPGs (role-playing games), first-person shooters and so on. Secondly, in their detailed setting, and often the 'blockbuster' genres they stay with (war films and action adventure especially), the narrative-related ones can seem like a more immersive version of cinema. But they tend to operate differently, with such narrative pleasures as taking on a character role, or performing a skilled task. Indeed, the question of how far narrative theory applies to them is controversial (see Dovey and Kennedy 2006).

Such 'immersive' cultural forms, like all media, are best understood by a range of theories, especially those of play and of gaming. In multiplayer online games the forking-path narrative structure, where player choices continually direct the narrative, is obviously much more extreme and open-ended.

> Study of theories of play is called **ludology**, from the Latin word for game or play 'ludus'. See *Charlie Brooker's Gameswipe* (BBC4 2009) on the BBC i-player for an entertaining and refreshingly unpatronising account of games.

> See Chapter 8 for much more discussion of 'new media' and how they invite us to rethink, as well as replay existing theories.

**EXPLORE 2.11**

- List your four favourite games.
- How many of them are narrative related, i.e. their appeal is partly the 'narrative' or character that a player may hope to be immersed in, but also *active* within?
- How would you describe your involvement with, and distance from, any **avatars**?
- Are characters important? Sound effects (as ever a highly neglected area of media analysis)? The visual representation of avatars?
- For those involving narrative play, how far do you agree with this statement by Sarah Roberts (1995, in Dovey and Kennedy 2006: 48): 'the illusion that goes along with interactivity is a kind of democracy . . . that the artist is sharing the power of choice with the viewer, when actually the artist has planned every option that can happen . . . it's a great deal more complex than if you [the user] hadn't had a sort of choice, but it's all planned.'

This takes us to Chapter 3 'Genres and other classifications', and how narrative expectations are prepared, and played with, in classifications known as genres.

## References and further reading

Barthes, Roland (1977) *Introduction to the Structural Analysis of Narratives*, London: Fontana.

Bordwell, David, and Thompson, Kirstin (2008) *Film Art: An Introduction*, 8th edn, New York: McGraw-Hill.

Branigan, Edward (1992) *Narrative Comprehension and Film*, London: Routledge.

Branston, Gill (2006) 'Understanding Genre', in Gillespie, Marie, and Toynbee, Jason (eds) *Analysing Media Texts*, London: Open University Press, pp. 75–6.

Campbell, Joseph (1949) *The Hero with a Thousand Faces*, new edition, Fontana, 1993.

Churchwell, Sarah (2009) 'What Would Lisa Think?' *The Guardian*, 24 October.

Corrigan, Timothy, and White, Patricia (2004) *The Film Experience: An Introduction*, Basingstoke: Palgrave Macmillan.

Derry, Charles (1988) *The Suspense Thriller: Films in the Shadow of Alfred Hitchcock*, Jefferson, NC: McFarland.

Dovey, Jon, and Kennedy, Helen W. (2006) *Game Cultures*, London and
    New York: Open University Press.

Durkin, Kevin (1985) *Television, Sex Roles and Children*, Milton Keynes:
    Open University Press.

Field, Syd (1994) *Four Screenplays: Studies in the American Screenplay*,
    New York: Dell.

Hyde, Marina (2009) 'Cameron's West Wing Plans Take us Closer to
    Government by Box Set', *The Guardian*, 4 July.

Lévi-Strauss, Claude (1972) 'The Structural Study of Myth', in De George,
    R. and F. (eds) *The Structuralists from Marx to Lévi-Strauss*, New York:
    Doubleday Anchor.

McKee, Robert (1999) *Story Substance, Structure, Style and the Principles of
    Screenwriting*, New York: HarperCollins.

Propp, Vladimir (1975) *The Morphology of the Folk Tale*, Austin:
    University of Texas Press.

Ravenhill, Mark (2007) 'The Cult of Story is Destroying our Culture from
    Within: It's Time to Start Fighting Back', *The Guardian*, 25 June.

Todorov, Tzvetan (1977) *The Poetics of Prose*, Oxford: Blackwell.

Wells, Liz (2002) *The Photography Reader*, London and New York:
    Routledge.

# CASE STUDY

# *CSI: Miami* and crime fiction

- THE CLASSIFICATION 'CRIME FICTION'
- PLOT/STORY
- APPLYING TODOROV
- APPLYING PROPP

- APPLYING BARTHES
- APPLYING LÉVI-STRAUSS
- NARRATIVES, INSTITUTIONS, IDEOLOGIES
- REFERENCES AND FURTHER READING

Stories centring on crimes and how they are solved are a good way into narrative since they have at their very centre the painstaking reconstruction of 'another story' – 'what really happened' – deducted from the evidence of the plot. This reconstructing involves the same kinds of speculation which 'readers' usually carry out on the detective stories and, indeed, on many fictions: attempts to assess character and motivation, likely actions and unlikely ones, and 'the evidence' for these.

Here we will:

- apply the main theories of narrative to the very first episode of *CSI: Miami*;
- update them for audio-visual forms with internet connections;
- suggest how such crime narratives might relate to dominant values.

## THE CLASSIFICATION 'CRIME FICTION'

We focus on the very first episode of the hugely successful CBS series *CSI: Miami*, one of the *CSI* (Crime Scene Investigation) series which are separately located in New York, Miami and Las Vegas. Though we're focusing on narrative, genre expectations play along with those for most audiences.

## EXPLORE 2.12

- Research how genre classifications operate in publicity, casting and opening sequences of these series.
- List what seem to be fans' pleasures and focus, on the official CBS site.

The group classified as 'crime fiction' most often deals with the *solving* of crimes. One further division could be into the 'whodunnit', the 'how-dunnit' and even the 'why-dunnit'. Rather unusually, the longest-running US TV crime series, *Law and Order* (US 1990–), divides episodes into the investigation of a crime, and then its legal prosecution. But usually:

1 the focus will be on solving rather than exploring crimes; their broader social causes, or the experience of committing them, or of being tried and punished for them, are examples of related areas usually broached in detail by other genres: 'the prison film', horror, the drama-documentary, the biopic, or the courtroom drama;

2 arguably the objects of investigation are not the crimes of the most powerful, which often belong to investigative journalism, and are often not defined as crimes.

Let's consider crime narratives in more detail. Most of them deal with detection. It doesn't take a Sherlock Holmes to deduce that 'detective fiction' usually involves a detective, but it also often involves a junior detective, and an enjoyment of the relationship between them, often as great as the crime they have to solve. There may also be a fascination with the place where the detectives are based, whether foggy nineteenth-century London, Miami, or the Chicago of V.I. Warshawski.

The most common narrative focuses on a single detective. Though these are all 'heroes' in Propp's sense, the pleasure for many fans lies in their different ways of operating in that role, in moving image fictions, their 'style'. There are two major roots for this genre's 'heroes':

1  the first is focused on the English 'gentleman' detective character, from Sherlock Holmes to Inspector Morse, or Peter Kingdom (with some involving 'gentlewomen' detectives such as Miss Marple);

2  the other strand, from the 1920s, was centred on a more 'hard-boiled' US detective, great with 'one-liners', not a gentleman, often an ex-police officer, more vulnerable than the Holmes figure, especially to the sexually available women he encountered. He often used dubious methods, and could voice telling criticisms of an unjust social order. The complex narratives took this 'man who is not himself mean' down the 'mean streets' of corrupt US cities.

## EXPLORE 2.13

- Can you see any traces of these two traditions in the detectives in *CSI: Miami*?
- Since they are usually male, this can involve a sense of masculinity, of 'cool' in the role.
- See YouTube on the 'greatest one-liners' of Horatio in *CSI: Miami*, including his use of his sunglasses in their delivery, and the sense among fans that this sometimes tips, enjoyably, into self-parody.
- Have you encountered any 'cool' women detective characters? How is their style constructed? Does it have the same authority as that of Horatio, or Grissom in *CSI: New York*?

The other increasingly popular strand within 'detective fiction' is the 'police procedural', involving a team of police, and focused on the working processes of solving

One of the narrative pleasures of earlier forms, like the Sherlock Holmes stories (written between 1887 and 1893) or TV's *Inspector Morse* (1987–2000), is that though we can never be as brilliant as Holmes/Morse, we can catch up the twisting story through Dr Watson/Lewis – and also enjoy the satisfaction of feeling that we will never be as 'slow' as the latter.

This narrative area involves both construction of intriguing central characters, and also 'delivery' of the plot and story.

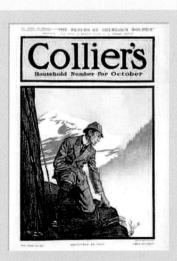

*Figure 2.14*  The aloof, 'above the world' image of Sherlock Holmes, his 'deerstalker' hat, as well as his Baker Street address, suggesting an upper-class identity. Often it is the foggy streets of other parts of Victorian London which challenge his 'stalking' capacities. The resonant imagery of fog often takes his stories to the border of the horror genre. In such a setting, Holmes worked like a 'beacon of intelligence' or 'a doctor who will cure the ills of society' and safely take us through the maze of streets.

crimes in methodical, often weary and footslogging ways. In the case of *CSI*, the frustrating work of investigation is replaced by a reliance on an almost magical high-tech scientific method, often referred to in specialised language and acronyms. The terminology itself has a special section in the *CSI* website.

**Q:** How far are the relationships between the members of the team still of interest for you in this kind of detective story?

## PLOT/STORY

We'll summarise the *plot* of 'The Golden Parachute', the first episode of *CSI: Miami*, and then consider how this has been arranged, so as to differ from the *story*, which we can reconstruct by the end.

**Note**: the word 'synopsis' often refers to a trailer-like teasing summary of the beginning of the narrative. A true synopsis summarises *all* the happenings in a text, and has to give away endings or use 'spoilers'. This is the only way to understand and discuss the whole narrative, for which the ending is crucial (see Chapter 2, on reviews).

### Synopsis: 'The Golden Parachute'

*Pre-title sequence*: two men fishing in swampland witness a plane crash. The Miami CSI team arrive, Horatio Caine in charge, with his junior, Eric. There is a question as to which section of the police force is in charge of the investigation. They find a body from the crash. Eric thinks it is alive, Horatio tells him it is not.

*Title sequence*: spectacular shots of the Florida Everglades and stylised 'hi-tech' montages of images of the main characters at work.

- Megan Donner, once boss of the team, arrives, returning after a six-month absence following the death of her husband. There's a brief argument between her and Horatio about who has jurisdiction in this case – the 'Feds' or CSI. Different approaches to detection arise, which resurface throughout the episode.

- A small entry wound is found in the upper torso of the first body, that of the pilot. The two 'fishermen' are interviewed and ask for a reward. The team discover substitute parts in the plane; they decide they need to find whoever shot the pilot. They find an empty briefcase and, surviving, Sommer, the head of the insurance firm whose managers were on the plane. They take Sommer to hospital.

- A woman's body is found five miles away. It's that of Christina, senior accountant of the firm, and the second passenger out of her seat (deduced from absence of seat-belt burn on the body). Her hands are hurt: first of several swift flashbacks to the possible scene of her death. Horatio visits her mother and discovers Christina 'battled depression' in high school and was 'so good at keeping secrets'.

- Horatio reveals to colleagues that the management team were going to Washington to appear before the SEC (Security and Exchange Commission) on charges of fraud. Calleigh discovers that the door opened in flight. Other research shows the exit door pins were tampered with.

- They find the (Hispanic) worker who filed down the pins, but, deducing that the door was opened from the inside, they release him.

- Sommer is interviewed in hospital. He claims not to recall anything, then says that he was in his seat (though has no seat-belt burns) and that Christina had been drinking and behaving oddly. He seems puzzled at a mention of gunshot. They fingerprint him and make tests on Christina's hair which reveal that she used anti-depressants and tried to kill herself six months ago. The aircraft's black boxes seem to be missing. Sommer's fingerprints are all over the aircraft door. Horatio and Megan decide there was a struggle, with Christina hanging on to the door. Sommer is discovered to have checked himself out of hospital.

- Eric and Tim ask the fishermen/poachers for items they accuse them of looting from the crash site. They retrieve the black box from a tank of baby alligators. The box gives them the last few moments of cockpit

## EXPLORE 2.14

Summaries take a long time! But hopefully it showed how the arrangement of the plot(ting) differed from the *story*, which we are able to reconstruct by the end. Revise the graph in Chapter 2. See if you can replicate it here.

**Q** When is the earliest story event?

**A** Christina's suicide attempt (revealed via analysis of a piece of her hair in the plot) six months before, as she wrestled with her feelings around revealing the fraud.

**Q** What other events are deliberately 'delayed' or altered for the sake of narrative pleasure?

**A** The delay in finding the black box keeps us speculating, in the absence of 'firm' evidence.

- The discovered briefcase could have been full of revealing documents.
- Christina's body could have been found first, along with trails to this full knowledge.
- The team look for a gunman for much of the episode, which turns out to be a false trail of speculation for viewers and characters.
- So does the quarrel about who is in charge of the investigation, CSI or 'the Feds' (though this contributes to 'character', another narrative pleasure).

This *plot* offers pleasures which the same events in a straightforwardly told *story* (A–Z) could not have done. And as a long-running TV narrative (unlike the ones Propp, Lévi-Strauss and Barthes were studying) it introduces story strands, debates and characters which can be picked up in later episodes.

---

sounds. These are manipulated to discover seventeen seconds of struggle, but no sound of a bullet fired.

- They search Christina's apartment. Ballistics expert Calleigh has discovered there was no bullet but that a substandard bolt killed the pilot. Horatio notices the fire extinguisher is missing and speculates that Sommer used it to force Christina off the plane.
- The team discovers that the plane's door had substandard parts. Copies of subpoenas reveal that the plane was taking insurance company executives to an SEC hearing over fraud allegations. The woman whose body was found miles from the crash was a whistleblower (exposing corruption in the company). The company chief is later found hanged.
- Horatio talks again with Christina's mother. He reads out the beginning of a letter she had written exposing the fraud, over shots of the team working. The episode ends with Horatio thinking of the whistleblower woman, and mentally 'saluting' her.

Her words 'without the truth we ourselves are powerless' act as final voice-over.

### APPLYING TODOROV

Todorov's theory can be applied here. But the 'once upon a time' moment, when opposing forces are 'in balance', is disrupted very fast, indeed hardly lasts the length of the title sequence. We've dealt above with the question 'where else it could have started?'

To have Christina's mental struggle, as she decides to 'blow the whistle', as the 'disruption' would place events in a different genre or group of fictions. It might signal the start of a corporate crime thriller, or 'issue' drama, or biopic, with a strong interest in corruption.

**Q** Are any values confirmed in the final equilibrium? Does it 'close' rather than simply 'stop'?

**A** Though the issue of corporate corruption is raised, it is narrativised so as to be 'at the side' of the investigation. And the suicide of the 'villain' softens the verdict on those misdeeds – much more than an arrest would have done.

## APPLYING PROPP

Propp's broad theory, around much earlier narratives, can still be applied. The characters here do indeed fall into certain character roles (hero, helper), though to a limited extent, and there is indeed 'solution of a task' which, along with 'punishment of the villain', coincides with narrative closure. But you may argue that suicide as 'punishment' softens the character to such an extent that we're not really invited to think of him as a villain. And the 'hero' sometimes seems like the whole team, even if Horatio is clearly in charge and picked out for narrative interest.

## APPLYING BARTHES

Barthes argued (in 1970) that a narrative text (from the Latin word meaning 'tissue') was not one thing, but a weaving together of different strands and processes, some of them 'internal' to the story, some making connections to its 'outside' or the rest of the real. Few now would find the theory as striking as it seemed when first published, but it is still useful in considering the different ways readers are given access to stories.

Barthes suggested that narrative works with five codes, which together 'activate' the 'reader'. The two codes which are 'internal' to the text are:

- The 'enigma (or hermeneutic) code', which sets up and usually solves major puzzles. Here the main one occurs at the start: why did this plane crash? At least two kinds of pleasure are involved: it can be as enjoyable to come to 'know' the answers as it is to have that prediction upset by the twists and surprises of the narrative.
- The action (or 'proairetic') code, which makes complex actions 'readable' through small details so we don't need to have everything spelt out. Here the sight of the stretcher with Sommer on it signals a

whole sequence of 'taking into hospital', so it is no surprise we next see him in a bed.

Then there are codes that point outwards from a story, and relate it to the rest of the culture:

- The semic code, which involves all the connotations built up around the characters and their actions. These stem from culturally recognisable discourses and patterns of meaning, such as those around 'powerful professional women' for *CSI: Miami*. Barthes and other deconstructive writers were relatively uninterested in the questions of 'character'. But these matter for online fans of this series. They conduct heated debates around Horatio. Is he a 'super-cool' deliverer of one-liners, or is he too infallible, controlled, impassive to be satisfying as a 'character', for whom flaws and a personal life are required?
- The symbolic code, which embodies the substitution of a small or concrete thing for a bigger, abstract one. The unrealistic darkness of the team's labs perhaps works in a symbolic way, as in *film noir*, to suggest the *moral* darkness of the world into which they're throwing the *light* of scientific investigation – echoes of Sherlock Holmes.
- The cultural or referential code, which anchors the text in its historical context, and points out of it towards that. In this episode there are lines like 'Most whistleblowers are women', signalling a contemporary fact, as well as using a contemporary term for someone who exposes corruption. 'The Dolphins' is a more 'local' reference to a Miami football team. And there is much audio-visual footage of the contemporary Florida setting, familiar both to those who live there and to those worldwide who watch US fictions. This is not available to a radio or print version of the same story.

## APPLYING LÉVI-STRAUSS

Lévi-Strauss is less interested in the chronological plotting of a single story (though that is how his 'syntagmatic' group has come to be used) than in repeated elements and their systematic relationship, usually across many stories. He called these the 'paradigmatic' aspect of myths. Nevertheless, the 'binary oppositions' into which they can sometimes be arranged are often applied to individual stories.

A Lévi-Straussian approach to the *CSI* series overall might locate it within the abiding binary 'crime/law and order' and ask:

Q: How does it embody this binary – through contrasts of characters, settings, actions?

Q: How does it fit into changing US TV and film treatments of that binary, which tend to blur a clear opposition?

## EXPLORE 2.15

If you've seen the US TV serial *Dexter* (2006–), also set in Miami, make notes on how it:

a plays with the narrative positioning, casting and characterisation of the hero as a police forensics expert;

b plays with the villain (who here is often the same figure as the hero: what does this do to binaries?);

c relates to the surrounding culture, including the huge success of the *CSI* series and their construction of 'hi-tech' science as 'saviour'.

It's also worth exploring how the different detection methods of Megan and Horatio (she insisting on staying strictly with the evidence, he often citing a 'gut feeling' for an idea) are consistently opposed. This relates to a broader gendered contrast in many crime fictions. *The X Files* (US 1993–2002) played with a reversal of gendered stereotyping (a reliance on supposedly female 'intuition' versus supposedly male 'reliance on evidence'). *Medium* (US 2005–) seems to take the opposite route in its clairvoyant female investigator.

## EXPLORE 2.16

- Consider *The Mentalist* (US 2008–), *Lie to Me* (US 2009–), and *Law and Order: Criminal Intent.* How does the figure of the hyperintuitive or even 'damaged genius' male detective work in their narratives? Are there any female equivalents?

- Compare them with series such as BBC1's *Criminal Justice* (especially the 2009 series) as ways of exploring 'criminality' and its detection.

## NARRATIVES, INSTITUTIONS, IDEOLOGIES

Branigan's (1992: 3) formulation of narrative as 'a way of organising spatial and temporal data into a cause-effect chain of events with a beginning, a middle and end that embodies a judgement about the nature of events' sums up much of what we've explored here.

But *CSI: Miami* is also a specific TV series, or rather franchise, in a hugely competitive market, not a novel or a single film. This shapes how it tells its stories. For

*Figure 2.15* One part of 'Miami' is this beach, a visual pleasure as well as segue to 'ad break'; another is the Everglades, with more sinister connotations. Both are rather different in their signifying potential to the *CSI* settings in New York or Las Vegas, let alone Sherlock Holmes' foggy nineteenth-century London.

example, it is shown mostly on advertising-funded TV channels, so you probably noticed that parts of it suddenly include a few seconds of spectacular aerial views, unmotivated by the story's needs. These offer themselves to the purchasing network as pleasurable in themselves, but also as possible 'ad breaks', allowing people a few seconds to return from the ads back to the narrative. Equally the episode can be watched without these sections interrupting things, as in DVD boxed sets and also for sales to TV regulatory regimes where ads do not interrupt programmes as often as on some US networks, and with ad-skipping recorders such as TiVo.

The show deploys audio-visual narrativity: it tells the tale differently from verbal language forms. For example, the opening sequence is an excitingly choreographed combination of music, cutting and the plane crash, which smoothly and shockingly culminates in the fuselage hitting the water, almost as the fishermen's lines do. As well as opening the narrative, it promises *how* it will be told – smartly, smoothly, slickly, but also so as to provide thrills, an exotic locale and clever choice of music.

Though it's mostly the Florida Everglades setting that is used here, in other episodes 'Florida' offers:

- a potentially big Hispanic audience;
- narratives centring on border-crossings, smuggling, drugs, refugees, etc.;
- a circling round the seedy, glamorous and bizarre aspects of its often sordid 'entertainment industries';
- audience genre knowledge of 'gangsters going south for the sun';
- the 'wet heat' atmosphere of fetid swamps, with their moral connotations (see the film *Wild Things* (US 1998), especially the title sequence, for similar resonances). In fact the series was shot in LA; the non-laboratory settings are often anonymous hotel rooms (especially the now generically horror-laden bathroom) or the sprawling housing of the Miami suburbs.

The use of CGI (computer-generated imagery) and ingenious 'body' effects for some of the laboratory scenes likewise form a kind of spectacular visual 'pleasure', offered in especially vivid ways by film, TV and computer games. The science-related CGI effects in many ways substitute, for the audience, for the 'Dr Watson' function – the 'helper' character who nevertheless needs fairly simple things explained. Here, the visuals will do that explaining. In narratives where the emphasis of the puzzle has shifted away from actually 'catching the bad guy' to 'what happened', the effects seem to substitute for the excitement of the now missing chase.

It has also been suggested that this flashy hi-tech science is the hero or star of the show, literally the 'light in the darkness' of many scenes. But it produces the

## EXPLORE 2.17

*Figure 2.16 CSI's high-tech science, its bright lights and dark surrounding space.*

- Might these lights signify detection as the 'beacon of enlightenment'?
- Compare the ways in which the UK series *Crimewatch* (factual) and *Waking the Dead* (fiction) narrativise and light their reconstructions and narratives. Is quite the same 'magic' of hi-tech being constructed?

problems of impoverished characterisation, which many fans complain of. The characters (especially Horatio) are said rarely to make mistakes and to show little emotion. The little speeches of the forensic surgeon to each corpse, 'Hello you . . .', seem the licensed space where some emotion can be expressed.

This blankness could be argued to be part of the hard-boiled tradition, and Horatio's manner is softened in the discussions with Christina's mother and in his mental 'salute' to the whistleblower at the end. Overall, however, time spent on developing such interiority, or doubts, is generally limited, partly because the team spend so much more time 'dishing out exposition' to explain the technical terms, than showing emotion or having complex lives, or indeed, arguing about the broader issues (here, capitalist corruption) raised by particular crimes.

The exaltation of hi-tech science as that which will save us, with its supposedly infallible accuracy and enlightenment, may be one reason for *CSI*'s popularity. McLean (2005) speculates that one reason was that it is 'very black and white – the evidence never lies – it was comforting in a grey world'. But this means that the series lacks a whole aspect of real-life crime investigations – failure to conclude a case, or even the making of mistakes, with horrendous results for those convicted. These parts of the representation and narrativisation of science in *CSI: Miami* are among the most ideologically powerful, and limiting, parts of its workings.

## REFERENCES AND FURTHER READING

Branigan, Edward (1992) *Narrative Comprehension and Film*, London: Routledge.

Cooke, Les (2001) 'The Police Series', in Creeber, Glen (ed.) *The Television Genre Book*, London: BFI, pp. 19–23.

McLean, Gareth (2005) 'CSI: Tarantino', *The Guardian*, 11 July.

Tasker, Yvonne (2009 unpublished), 'Smoke and Mirrors: "Psychic" Cops, Pseudo-Science and Male Intuition in Crime Television', part of the Salford University *Screens and Mediations* seminars.

# 3 Genres and other classifications

- Classifying films: *Thelma and Louise* (US 1991)
- Repetition and difference
- Case study: Formats and genres
- Repertoires of elements
- Status and genres 1: 'escapism', gender and verisimilitude
- Status and genres 2: the cultural context
- Formal classifications
- Conclusion
- References and further reading

All media output is classified, in various ways, by:

- its makers
- its marketers, reviewers, and official classifiers or censors
- its 'consumers' or users.

These classifications (emo or grunge? horror or thriller?) have material effects on the ways we encounter, enter into and understand media. They shape:

- the status of works;
- their ability to get made in the first place, and then how they are circulated;
- their ability to withstand marginalisation and even censorship;
- how their invitations are taken up, resisted or otherwise shaped by audiences, or users.

This chapter focuses on the concept of 'genre' and links it to other ways of grouping or **framing** texts.

'**Genre**' is simply a French word for type or kind. Some writers emphasise its similarity to biological classifications of plants and animals (vegetables or fruit? reptiles or mammals?). This assumes the 'naturalness' of genre. Such images may be useful in helping us think about how genres change, mutate and produce hybrids or 'in-betweens' – rather like species. But they are only metaphors. You can get into tricky territory using the image to argue that particular genres (such as the western) are 'extinct', only to find their major elements replayed in, say, *Brokeback Mountain*, or the TV series *Deadwood*.

Genre can usefully be understood as one of many forms of **classification**, rather like *maps*. Different maps (road, geological, consumer research) always have to leave out many features, and to emphasise only some parts of an area, in order to be useful, usable. Similarly gardeners and farmers may classify plants into 'weeds' and 'proper plants'/'crops'. Using another system of classification, asking other questions of them, all of these are simply 'plants' rather than, say, 'animals'. Classifying systems like this often use a binary 'either/or' division, when we might think in terms of a spectrum of varieties.

In media studies 'genre' is often taken to refer to cut and dried, simple boundaries: 'just another' gangster film, or hip-hop track. 'Once you've seen one, you've seen them all.' But in fact there is always both repetition and difference at play in genre products. An example: a lightbulb joke depends on the same kinds of familiarity and therefore expectations for its audience as any genre product. Unless you've *never* heard one before, when you hear the question you know that a joke is involved (a genre aiming to produce laughter) and are therefore likely to begin thinking in certain, potentially comic directions rather than other, more serious ones for the answer.

> The anthropologist Mary Douglas studied the ways some substances are classified as 'dirt', which she called 'matter out of place'. This usefully highlights the extent to which a notion of 'dirt' is partly based on taboo or classification systems.

> Or 'repetition with difference' as some say, to emphasise that the two cannot be separated. See Corrigan and White (2004).

> See http://www.lightbulb jokes.com for 'generic principles' and many more examples of these jokes.

Q: How many thought police does it take to screw in a light bulb?
A: None . . . There never 'was' any light bulb, don't you remember?
Q: How many Real Men does it take to change a lightbulb?
A: Real Men aren't afraid of the dark.
And so on.

In other words you, the participant, operate a kind of classification or framing of it – as *not* being a serious question, as *likely* to involve certain kinds of play. If you enjoy lightbulb jokes, part of your pleasure is that you both sort-of-know and don't-quite-know what to expect from it. In other words, a *system of expectation* is set up around it, involving both repetition and difference, and depending on you knowing this particular classification ('a kind of joke'). What's repeated is a bare framework of elements: a lightbulb, a group of people about which certain stereotypes exist, a number which relates the two amusingly. What's different is *how* the particular connections between those elements will be made *this* time. As the genre becomes established, play can be made with its conventions. Part of the pleasure here is often in over-the-top references to well-known stereotypes.

> **'Framing'** refers to a) the size and position of the subject of a photo, painting, shot, etc.; b) the power of media to shape and set limits to how audiences are invited to perceive certain groups, issues, genres.

## Classifying films: *Thelma and Louise* (US 1991)

*Figure 3.1* Geena Davies and Susan Sarandon in *Thelma and Louise* (US 1991)

1 Credits: in this book we have chosen to classify films by giving their title, then the main country of production ('US' here), then year of production. This is to give our examples a historical and global location. Other writers, using perhaps an authorship approach, often give the director's surname (here 'Scott') and date, and omit country of production. TV channels often give just film titles on screen. All are kinds of classification, helping to shape expectations.

2 Generically this film has been argued as primarily a road movie/a chick flick/a buddy movie/a women's film. But there are many other ways of classifying it, for different purposes, at different times.

- IMDb gives four main generic definitions (adventure, drama, crime, thriller), but if you click 'more', up pop sixty more terms (including 'tragedy', 'hair-dryer', 'feminism', 'orgasm' and so on).
- In terms of star classifications it would be seen by some viewers as a Susan Sarandon, Geena Davies, Brad Pitt and/or Harvey Keitel movie.
- Classic authorship classifications emphasise it as a Ridley Scott-directed movie. It's less usual to identify it by the writer's name, as with other Scott films like *Bladerunner* (often identified as a 'Philip K Dick' movie adaptation, after the celebrated SF writer). But there was some discussion of the fact that this film, which won an Oscar for Best Screenplay, had a female writer, Callie Khouri, as well as input from the two female stars.
- Increasingly *awards* are important as classifiers, not only for foreign language or low budget films, helping them to circulate in particular networks such as 'art cinemas' or special multiplex screens, but as a key part of descriptions on Amazon.

The wonderful film *Visions of Light* (US 1993), about Hollywood cinematography, credits all the film extracts used not by the director's name, but by the cinematographer's.

When Marge Simpson snapped into road rage frustration she was sent on holiday alone. Among her treats were hot fudge sundaes and drinking tequila in a bubble bath, while watching *Thelma and Louise*.

- Formal ratings (see imbd) ranged from France U, Netherlands 12, to USA R and UK 18.
- The Parents' Guide warned of the film's 'sex and nudity', 'violence and gore', 'profanity', 'alcohol/drugs/smoking', and warned, under 'Frightening/intense scenes', that 'The rape scene can be considered intense' and 'The ending is also quite intense.'

As Altman (1999: 102) writes: 'Who speaks each generic term? To whom? For what purposes? . . . Why are the same films sometimes described generically and at other times covered by an entirely different terminology? Only by asking questions like these can we hope to discover how (and why) genres are used.'

### A related example

In 2009 Cheryl Gascoigne published her account of her twelve-year marriage to the footballer Paul Gascoigne (*Stronger: My Life Surviving Gazza*), which involved vivid accounts of his alcoholism and abuse of her. The book was published in a completely plain wrapper. She said she did not want abused women's violent partners to identify what they were reading. A very striking use (or attempted avoidance) of 'classification' practices.

## Repetition and difference

Audiences understandably seek the pleasures of the familiar. We enjoy the ritual and reassurance involved in knowing *broadly* what 'might happen' in a particular media text, or even daily situation. The term *convention* is usually understood in a negative way, as a set of rules which will simply reinforce and repeat dominant (or 'normative') values. But conventions, precisely in order to survive, need to be able to adapt and shift. And if any story, or video game, or melody, were *utterly* different from all others, we would have no means by which to understand it.

> Even an apparently repetitious form – the 'cover' version, where an artist makes his/her 'repeat' of a well-known song – sells precisely on its blend of the familiar *and the new*.

**EXPLORE 3.1**

- Think of two everyday rituals you've been involved in – a birthday celebration or an introduction to someone new. What pleasures are involved in the ritual of repetition? How was the ritual framework used for innovation or difference – perhaps a jokiness?
- A related point: the very constraint of certain conventions or limits can be a source of pleasure for users and makers of media forms. Those who enjoy the challenge of making a message on Twitter (a 'tweet') often like having to keep within the limit of 140 'letters' or strikes of the keyboard. Have you experienced this pleasure with Twitter, or any other media form?

Yet genre products are not all the same. For one, generic media output is not like other industrial production. You may hope that your computer will be exactly as good as, the same as, all the others in that batch. But you probably don't want absolute repetition in the 'texts' it will deliver.

Rick Altman (1999), using film as example, broadens the links between 'genres' and theories of language and communication more generally. He argues that genres are classified by what he calls 'semantic' elements and 'syntactic' structures. Some writers identify film genres by (semantic) elements: music, character types, familiar objects or settings (e.g. guns, fang-like incisor teeth). Others recognise a genre because a group of films organises these 'building blocks' in a particular way (syntactic) via plot structure, character relationships and so on. Altman suggests both approaches can be operated together, and points to the western, the horror film and the musical as genres which maintain a high degree of both semantic and syntactic consistency over decades (Altman 1999: 90). He later goes on to add what he calls 'pragmatic' elements, or those contributed by audiences, fans, very specific situations in production and so on. We will deal with these in the case study Horror as Popular Art.

**EXPLORE 3.2**

- Take one of the three genres Altman cites above and try to identify its semantic and syntactic elements.
- How does a favourite recent example of your own from one of the genres (perhaps *Twilight*) mutate or play with these?

## EXPLORE 3.3

- Zap through some TV or radio channels
- How quickly are you able to tell what kind of programme is on offer? In seconds?
- How were you able to tell? What kinds of differences are signalled, for TV, through music, colours, kinds of dialogue, voices, pace of editing, costume, lighting, etc.?

## EXPLORE 3.4

- Try turning down the sound on the title sequence of a TV programme and substituting another kind of music.
- What difference does this make to its generic identity?
- What connotations does the music add to, or confirm for, the genre?

Industrially, 'genre' describes the ways that companies producing and trading in media 'texts' try to minimise risk by grouping, marketing and distributing their products via well-established expectations. Economically this helps to predict expenditure within costly and volatile media businesses, which all require some **standardisation** of production, in both senses of the term. Of course it requires difference too. This was true of the 'production line' in the Hollywood studio system (from around 1925 to 1950) and, in different ways, of many TV productions now. TV companies, whether 'independent', state or public service, need predictable annual income, whether from the licence fee (BBC) or selling advertising space, or selling ad space plus charging subscription fees (cable and satellite companies).

If output can be settled into *broadly* familiar groupings, then economies of scale can operate in production but also, importantly, in marketing and distribution. Broadly similar sets, script writers, key actors, advertising spaces, etc. can be profitably booked or reused, rather than made or searched for afresh each time. And advertisers can be assured they have access to certain audiences at particular times and on certain channels. Traditionally, British soap operas, such as *EastEnders* and *Coronation Street*, have promised large audiences, key to building a channel's 'audience share' in the early evening.

Standardisation has a double meaning. It can signify 'sameness', but also the maintenance of standards, in the sense of 'quality'. Worth bearing in mind in the debates around 'sameness' and 'difference' in media.

Economies of scale are the cost advantages which expansion, or scale, brings to a business. Average costs per unit fall as more units are produced. Arguably, however, increased 'marginal' revenue is key in marketing (relatively cheap) digital media.

 See **MSB5 website** section on industries.

The long-running *Coronation Street*'s capacity to attract large audiences made it worth Granada building a permanent set and employing a serial historian to avoid embarrassing mistakes in the storyline for loyal viewers.

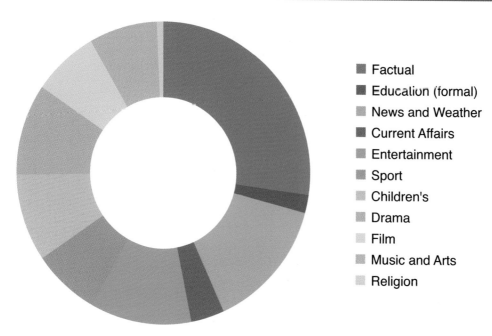

- ■ Factual
- ■ Education (formal)
- ■ News and Weather
- ■ Current Affairs
- ■ Entertainment
- ■ Sport
- ■ Children's
- ■ Drama
- ■ Film
- ■ Music and Arts
- ■ Religion

*Figure 3.2* The BBC divides up its output into a set of broad genres. Where are the overlaps? Why these classifications?

Several developments have shifted these apparent certainties, even before the recession of 2008 onwards. In cinema, since the breakup of the Hollywood studio system, and in UK broadcasting there have been huge changes. The founding of Channel 4 in 1982 was followed by cable and satellite broadcasting, and now Web 2.0 viewing, on computers and elsewhere, at whatever times are selected by the user. The 'audience' has to some extent been fragmented, which has led to attempts to target ever more specialised, small audience segments or **niches** of potential audience. The term 'narrowcasting' distinguishes these advertising-led developments from an older media ecology, where fewer channels (just BBC and ITV for UK television) had the power to 'broadcast' to larger audiences.

'Niche' originally meant a little nest or recess in a wall; niche marketing now refers to attempts to reach specialised but highly profitable groups of potential consumers, via particular media products or aspects of products.

## CASE STUDY: FORMATS AND GENRES

*Figure 3.3* A now-obsolete logo for the soon-to-be-obsolete UK *Big Brother*.

A new kind of difference/standardisation balance can be seen to operate in **format** TV productions, such as those of Endemol, an independent company, operating 'multi-platform' (i.e. mostly on TV and Web 2.0). It deals in formats, a category which overlaps with 'genre'.

Formats are concepts, or set-ups, which can be sold globally and then varied locally. A format can include everything from the presenting links, type of set, lighting, music, even the senior producer, who may be included as part of the contract. Simon Cowell is estimated to be worth £120 million as a result of his work as 'talent judge' and consequent ownership and management of TV formats. See Brown (2009).

Currently popular is the *genre* of the talent show, with such different *formats* as *Britain's Got Talent, Pop Idol, American Idol, The X Factor*.

- What characterises the talent show in these formats?
- Would you argue that BBC's *The Apprentice* is a version of the talent show?

Two key genres: both *The Weakest Link* and *Who Wants to Be a Millionaire?* belong to the genre 'quiz show' (an entertainment form centred around a quizmaster, contestants and prizes), though their formats or set-ups differ (the way the questions are asked, the set, prizes and penalties delivered, etc.).

*Big Brother* and others like it are 'game shows': an entertainment form centred around teams or individuals who are usually in competition with each other for a big prize, via 'games' or 'tasks' involving various degrees of playfulness, embarrassment, danger, difficulty.

The formats or set-ups obviously differ in terms of the activities demanded, the setting (desert island? jungle?), the prizes and penalties, etc. *Big Brother* as a genre/format operates a loose 'repertoire of elements' which can be played with both globally and over time. It combines:

1  'reality television' (it is unrehearsed, unscripted, and uses surveillance camera work, though the setting is usually highly lit 'entertainment');

2  game show (innovatively, it has both teams *and* the individuals within them set to compete against each other; and it uses highly selected contestants, increasingly willing to perform and often seeing the show as the route to a kind of celebrity, and fortune);
   *along with a third key element*

3  audience involvement via hugely profitable interactive technology, including blogs and phone votes on the fate of 'characters' and live web broadcasts not shown on TV.

See Chapter 13 for more on 'reality TV'.

**Hybridity**: term originally used with reference to the crossbreeding of plants. Here it signals media products mixing different sets of cultural values, technologies and/or formal properties so as to produce something new, e.g. 'cross-over hits' in pop music, comedy-drama (*Desperate Housewives*).

Media forms have consequently become more and more cross-generic or **hybrid** or 'mashed', as advertisers seek to attract more and more small segments of what used to be called 'the audience'. Makers and audiences draw on varied repertoires of pleasure and knowledge such that many different media forms now routinely clash and mix: cyber-punk,

**Intertextuality**: the variety of ways in which media and other texts interact with each other, rather than being unique or distinct. It is broader than 'hybrid', and it arguably benefits from not being linked, as 'hybrid' is, to a biological metaphor (hybrid plant and animal breeding) which suggests that the elements being combined are themselves unchanging.

drama-documentary, the comedy and 'reality' documentary mix of *The Office* (BBC 2002–3) and so on. This phenomenon is sometimes known by the broader term **intertextuality**, or the many ways in which media and other texts interact with each other, rather than being unique or distinct – including quotation, adaptation, re-mediation, etc.

Though such mixings are sometimes loosely labelled 'postmodern', most media forms have *always* involved some kind of 'hybridity' and were never 'pure' romantic songs/novels/films or horror films/books/comics, etc. Hollywood (and earlier nineteenth-century cultural forms) always tried to attract as many audience segments as possible – often by lacing a 'male' genre with a romance element, as in *Casablanca* (US 1942).

Another useful category is the 'sub-genre' which defines a specific version of a genre such as 'spaghetti western' or, for fans, gangster films which fall into the 'bank robbery' and 'crime syndicate' sub-genres. These are distinguished from hybrid genres, produced by the interaction of different genres to produce fusions: romantic comedies, musical horror films. Finally, to complicate matters further, the term 'cycle' describes brief but fairly intense periods of production within a genre, when individual films, say, seem to share a particular approach – as in the Dracula 'cycles' of the horror film. This process of mixing and

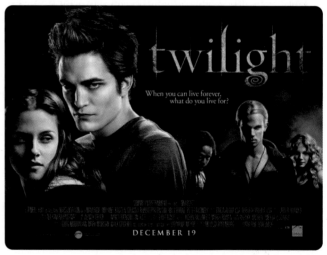

*Figure 3.4 and 3.5* Vampire-horror-action-comedy-teen-school series: the hybrids that are *Buffy the Vampire Slayer* and the film *Twilight* (US 2008). See below, and also this chapter's case study on Horror as popular art.

'mashing' has accelerated and increased in recent years, especially via the internet, and owing to advertisers' eagerness to contact more and more specialised groups. Try to take from all this a sense of the fluidity of 'genres'.

Figure 3.6 A striking shot from the 'spaghetti western' *The Good, the Bad, and the Ugly* (Italy 1966). See Corrigan and White (2004: 297) for a useful discussion of 'sub-genre' and 'hybrid genre'.

## Repertoires of elements

An important development in thinking about entertainment genres has been to put them into more pragmatic contexts, especially the varied understandings and activities of producers and audiences or media users. Genres are seen no longer as sets of fixed elements, constantly repeated and occasionally innovated within, but as working with '**repertoires of elements**', fluid systems of learnt conventions and expectations. These are shared by makers and audiences, who are *both* active on *both* sides of meaning-making. The maker can rely on certain kinds of audience familiarity to play with, and the audience looks forward to play within these stabilities. Increasingly they communicate with the producing institution about their preferences, enthusiasms, disappointments, rage, etc. The conventions, and the expectations they can invoke, include, for film, TV, games, etc., the areas of:

- *narrative* – how the stories in a genre usually begin and conclude; what kinds of characters are at the centre of the fiction, etc.;
- *audio-visual codes* (for which the term iconography is sometimes used), which include settings (the western's classic landscape; the hi-tech arena of SF), costumes, lighting and so on;
- *a relationship to the rest of the real world*, including perceptions of how realistic the genre is, how it handles the ideological values of the area it covers (e.g. war, romance, crime) and sometimes how its values have shifted over time.

Let's take the genre called romance, or 'chick flick', and the sub-genre 'romcom'. Like many much-used commercial and theoretical terms, these mix different elements. Romance originally referred to medieval tales of knights, honour, battle – and the (often adulterous) love of characters like Lancelot and Guinevere. 'Romantic' as we now understand it inherits feelings (of longing, of unrequited or troubled love, etc.) from the love strands in these earlier literary romances. A romance *narrative* will often start with the arrival into the life of the female 'hero' or central figure of a male who interests her romantically. This sets in play situations involving the nature of intimate or sexualised relations, in the teen years, or as a single woman aged thirty, or one trying to combine work and marriage, and perhaps children. The narrative will often proceed by means of intimate conversations and encounters,

'Prankster cinema – [a] combination of documentary, performance art, slapstick and satire – is scarcely out of its infancy, yet it commands our attention right now like no other genre.' Ryan Gilbey (2009) coins a new genre title. See Chapter 13.

**Iconography**: a term from art history, originally referring to fifteenth- and sixteenth-century guides to artists on the 'correct' colours, gestures, facial expressions, etc. with which to image Christian doctrine. Since media usually work with *moving, audio-visual* images, the term 'signification' (see Chapter 1) is more useful.

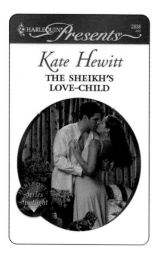

*Figure 3.7* Though labelled 'modern' this Mills and Boon cover centres around a dark mysterious man (forerunner of Mr Big? but with the mystery/threat/exoticism of being 'a sheik'?) taller than the woman, who seems 'swept away' by his embrace. Familiar?

coincidences, mistakes and so on, delaying and thus intensifying the audience's desire for the couple(s) to 'get it together' (though often desire is prolonged by this not happening).

> The character of Edward Cullen in the hugely successful *Twilight* franchise of books and films (2003–) is constructed so as to take these 'inaccessible' longings to an extreme. The blend of vampire and romance is ingeniously worked to deliver this masochistic pleasure.

## EXPLORE 3.5

For the controversy as to how far these books and films seem to be strongly shaped by Mormon religious doctrine, see http://writetools.wordpress.com and other sites.

*Ideologically* it is suggested (see La Place 1987) that the particularly close and caring attention paid to the woman by the hero provides female readers and viewers with a fantasy escape from the often inattentive men they are actually involved with. This figure is sometimes called the 'maternal male'. It may come as a surprise that if you look again at apparently classic macho figures like Rhett Butler/Clark Gable in *Gone with the Wind* (US 1939) as well as characters like Edward Cullen, they often act out these feelings at points in the script. Such intimacy was signalled in some of the *audio-visual conventions* of 'women's films': less use of fetishised shots of women's bodies than in male-centred genres; much use of close-ups, especially focused on the eyes, of both male and female actors; certain styles of intimate acting, voice and dialogue; and a particular kind of music – sweeping chords, piano and string sections of the orchestra – amplifying the key romantic moments (though see **'verisimilitude'** p. 86). Also often deployed were lavish or fashionable clothes and 'utopian' domestic settings, often with 'tie-ins' to clothing and household advertising – see the parody of such marketing in *The Truman Show* (US 1998) and interesting references to it in *Mad Men*.

*Figure 3.8* Two 'professionals', framed and dressed to emphasise their similarity, coolly assess each other, within a contemporary romance setting of a luxury hotel bedroom.

A recent variant, the romantic thriller *Duplicity* (US 2009), is an extreme contrast to the *Twilight* model, for older audiences? The director, Tony Gilroy wrote:

> '. . . the one idea . . . was . . . How would two people who don't trust anything, or are completely untrustworthy, fall in love? The film is purely about the idea of romance. Nobody's worried about getting married, nobody's worried about communicating and nobody's biological clock is ticking. It's elemental. Can I trust you? Can you trust me?' (Tony Gilroy quoted in Waters 2009).

*Figure 3.9* *Gone with the Wind* (US 1939): one aspect of Rhett as 'maternal male'.

*Figure 3.10* *Knocked Up* (US 2007): a comic rendering of contemporary problems around unexpected pregnancies and some decidedly un-maternal males.

Figures 3.9 and 3.10 show two very different images of the 'romance' male figure as parent. Rhett Butler/Clark Gable is here literally 'the maternal male'. His 'maternal' relating to Scarlett/Vivien Leigh involves a special and endlessly sympathetic understanding of her (often unsympathetic) nature – such as mothers are traditionally supposed to have for their children. It goes along with a sexualised attraction to her. The figures in the still from the 2007 romcom *Knocked Up* (Fig. 3.10) signify a very different relationship, characteristic of a stream of recent comedies which play with the idea of 'taming' the successful professional woman into a relationship with a 'lovable' but inept and inarticulate male.

## Status and genres I: 'escapism', gender and verisimilitude

When Jonathan Ross left his BBC film reviewing programme in 2010 it was almost taken for granted that a male reviewer would follow him, despite a persuasive campaign to have Anne Billson fill the post (see her film column in *The Guardian*).

'Male' genres have traditionally had higher status than romance, in terms of budgets, marketing and critical esteem. This status often operates through notions of 'escapism'. Male forms have been perceived and marketed as:

- more 'realistic', via references to 'the real world', e.g. battles, uniforms, generals' names, the training undertaken by actors, etc. in combat films;
- less emotional (though in fact they deal with *different kinds* of emotion);
- not 'escapist': it is usually more traditional 'feminine' genres (romance, musical) which are *classified* as 'escapist'.

Though all stories and entertainments are imaginary, are not 'real life' in one sense, they are a material part of most of our real lives in several others. We pay money to experience them, directly or indirectly; we spend time and imaginative energy 'playing' and fantasising roles in their worlds; and increasingly entertainment forms find themselves part of news programmes.

Moreover, we are never completely 'blissed out' in enjoying entertainment. Even the 'frothiest' or goriest kinds of 'escape' make connections to real-life questions. The term **verisimilitude** is useful here, with its marking of different links to the perceived 'real', 'probable', 'likely' in media forms. It has two main connections: cultural verisimilitude, or the connections of genres to the social order or culture around them, and formal verisimilitude, or the conventions audiences have grown so used to that they seem 'realistic' or even invisible. An example of formal verisimilitude is the CGI dinosaurs which seem so visually 'real' in *Jurassic Park* (US 1993). They can eat people but also, improbably, move neatly around a kitchen, open a door, and even tap their claws in apparent impatience. But they do not speak English –

*Figure 3.11* The kitchen-savvy monsters of *Jurassic Park* (US 1993) test the limits of verisimilitude.

because that would be 'unlikely' according to the rules of 'how creatures behave in science fiction'.

One of the ways in which gangster or war films (like other male-dominated genres) laid claim to higher status than, say, the musical (assumed to be a 'woman's genre') was by making a more explicit reference to public or political events from the world outside the film – cultural verisimilitude. So they used newspaper headlines, named real-life politicians, generals or criminals, and even made stars of ex-gangsters like George Raft. Until relatively recently gangster films made little use of the flamboyant colours, camera angles and movements enjoyed by fans of the musical ('unrealistic'). One of the innovations of Michael Mann's direction of the 1980s TV series *Miami Vice* was the use of flamboyant camera movements and pastel-coloured costumes for the male leads.

War films often allow their audiences fantasy escapes from the complication, the perceived mundaneness of the everyday, or of depressing news stories. It's also rarely that the emotional aspect of combat films is discussed. This means there is little space given to some of its central emotional pleasures: expressions of male bonding and closeness in a 'unit' made up of soldiers of very mixed backgrounds, as well as its expression of justifiable fears, around physical fragility and the conditions of survival and trauma in war.

Often popular media forms have been seen as 'escapist', and therefore inferior to 'true art', because they were industrially produced and aimed at non-elite audiences. Hollywood's early products, for example, were aimed at entertaining working-class audiences for an evening between one day's work and the next, rather than to be experienced at elite gatherings, such as opera houses. In addition, certain snobberies about America as inferior to Europe meant that the US was assumed for years to be incapable of producing anything worthy of serious cultural attention. And, as with romance forms, lower status often involved female audiences. Such positions have far less power now, though there are still traces in some film and TV reviews.

To return to romance, William Paul has argued that recent 'romcom' takes account of real-world events (operates cultural verisimilitude) in different ways. Women's increasing participation in work and other activities outside the home, more easily available contraception and changes in some men's sense of how they want to 'be a man' have shifted romantic comedy. Further, in terms of formal and cultural verisimilitude, such films now have to relate to another group of films aiming at younger audiences: 'gross out' or 'animal' comedies, like the *American Pie* series with their raunchiness and 'bad taste'.

*Figure 3.12* A rare example of a successful female Hollywood director, Kathryn Bigelow, directing an action adventure war film, *The Hurt Locker* (US 2009) in Jordan. Controversially the film suggests that the central character is addicted to the testosterone-fuelled crucible of war.

Marsha Kinder argued that the choreography of performers like Jackie Chan, Chow Yun Fat and Jet Li demonstrates the 'difference' of the Hong Kong action film, with the musical as a structuring device: Jackie Chan as a physical performer in the mould of Gene Kelly (Kinder 2001: 89).

In the 1920s, however, 'Hollywood' tried hard to attract middle-class (white) audiences to big city 'picture palaces', the names, design and lavishness of which, including orchestras and uniformed attendants, made striking claims to cultural prestige, rather like opera houses. See Branston (2000).

Contrast the sympathetic treatment of the theme in *Dirty Dancing* (US 1987).

Such changes have impacted on the language and extremity of the situations in new 'romcom' (see *There's Something about Mary* (US 1998) and its notorious semen-hair gel scene). But other kinds of realism, or social verisimilitude, are avoided because of their potentially polarising effects on audiences, and therefore box office. For example, there is hardly any reasoned discussion of the pros and cons of abortion, or of AIDS and condom use, in *Knocked Up* (US 2007), or even *Juno* (US/Canada 2007).

## Status and genres 2: the cultural context

**Pierre Bourdieu** (1930–2002) began ethnographic work after being conscripted into the French army during the Algerian war of 1958. *Distinction: A Social Critique of the Judgement of Taste* (1984) explored how the supposedly 'natural' 'universal' quality of 'taste' was shaped along class, cultural and educational lines in France in the early 1980s.

The French Marxist sociologist Pierre Bourdieu, in his hugely influential work on French taste culture patterns *Distinction* (1984), pioneered the term 'cultural capital' (meaning a familiarity with 'high' cultural forms such as opera, theatre, classical music). This was to draw attention to the ability of privileged groups (in twentieth-century France) to define their cultural forms and favoured genres as superior to those of the 'lower' classes. He argued this was itself a kind of asset or advantage.

### Gender and cultural competences

This theory was later applied to TV, and to women's soaps and magazines, assumed to be inferior media forms, which anyone could understand but which would only interest a rather stupid or trivial-minded audience. Feminist work (see Brunsdon 1981) suggested that the pleasures offered to women by the soap opera genre required particular 'feminine' skills and competences, such as reading the signs of 'emotional turmoil' or understanding the complexities of familiar relationships. These were learnt from outside the text through years of informal training for presumed future roles as nurturing mothers; or as carers in jobs like nursing or teaching; or through their confinement to the home, except in periods of high male unemployment. Women were more likely to realise the significance of certain kinds of looks between characters, small-scale gestures, silences and so on. Their involvement in the skills of domestic labour meant that they were competent to pick up on key parts of soaps' narratives, carried by intimate gesture and talk.

Women are argued to have access to such competences. We're not arguing that no male viewers ever come upon, or develop, the competences to enjoy romances or soaps, or that no women are irritated by those forms. But informal gender training from early on means that certain responses to some genres (like the sad-ending romance) are made unacceptable for some groups ('big boys don't cry') and natural seeming for others. From the male side of gendered competences it has been argued that boys are socialised into acting tough in the face of certain videos, computer games and horror films, which they sometimes find hard to 'stomach'. Our culture still expects men, in the end, to differentiate themselves from women along the lines of 'toughness'. Young men are encouraged not to cry, not to explore feelings and to try to appear as decisive and hard as the heroes of action adventures. Fortunately they do not all follow this encouragement.

Other 'cultural competence'-related work has suggested the reasons for young women's reluctance to use computers. This work suggests not that young women are incapable of using machines or technology, but that they resist, or feel ill at ease in, the world of the 'computer virtuosos', the 'geeks' and 'techno-heads'. These are often young men who seem to be involved in an intimate relationship with their machines, one which is often strongly competitive and macho – 'mine's bigger and faster than yours' – centred on very masculine games genres, such as action adventure and science fiction, and valuing the skill of swift, automatic decisiveness. Attempts are being made to counter such perceptions, both in media and in education more broadly. A very real fear is that the predicted 'information-rich' and 'information-poor' distinction will work along the lines not simply of class and a north–south divide, but also of gender.

## EXPLORE 3.6

- Does this outline correspond to your experience of
  a  genres (especially soaps and 'tough' genres) and their typical skilled viewers; or
  b  'computer cultures' and the assumed competences of male and female users?
- Do social networking websites such as Facebook seem to be free of such divides?

Tony Bennett and others recently explored how far this class-centred and specifically French model still applied, for Britain, in the twenty-first century. They concluded that though cultural class distinctions still operated, gender, ethnicity and age also need to be considered in the ways that certain 'tastes' or preferences are given, or denied, status. They also developed the idea of 'omnivorous' taste. This follows theorists of cult forms (such as 'trash television') who suggested that some fans have the privilege of 'double access' to both 'naive' enjoyment of the form 'for itself' (a low-status competence) and a knowing humour at its codes (higher-status). Further, they suggest that this, rather than older familiarities with 'high culture' such as Shakespeare or opera, is the form which cultural privilege or 'capital' now takes.

Consider this passage from Bennett *et al.* (2009) about their survey of recent British taste cultures:

> [The] dominant expression of cultural capital in Britain [now] is perhaps the adoption of an omnivorous orientation . . . [However] this is not always genuinely a taste for everything, for there are limits to its range. It is predominantly Anglophone, British and American cultural forms that are browsed. Within cultural fields key cultural divides are rarely crossed. For example, in the area of music, many people range across rock, heavy metal, electronic and world music, but rarely stray into classical music (and vice versa). There are particular stigmatised tastes (for country and western music, for example) which are avoided by nearly all except (working-class) enthusiasts . . .

Where are today's cultural boundaries? Working-class men baulk at the suggestion of going to opera or classical concerts. Professionals find it hard to admit to reading the *News of the World*, watching a lot of television, liking 'reality TV', 'merely' being entertained, or enjoying country and western music.

How fair do you consider this estimate of the 'country and western' genre?
What artists and range of music do you take it to include?

In 2009 some cinemas began screening live performances of 'elite' texts such as operas, and National Theatre plays like *Phèdre*. A new hybrid form – theatre-cinema? (Although this also happened in the early days of broadcast TV.)

## EXPLORE 3.7

Consider the genres which make up your own 'field' of media use.
- Are the boundaries mentioned here ones which you recognise from your own genre preferences and avoidance?
- Do you ever 'confess' to enjoying a genre which you know is low status – e.g. *The X Factor*? *Wife Swap*? 'Country and western' music?
- Do you ever hesitate to say you have enjoyed some 'higher-status' product, such as classical music?
- Or are you 'omnivorous', i.e. do you think you consume 'most things', in terms of media/culture/genres?
- Are terms like 'lowbrow', 'highbrow', 'middlebrow' used by you and your friends to classify products? If so, how, and for which media genres?

Bourdieu's emphasis on the importance of 'cultural capital' may not have the power it once did. But it still seems that to successfully to claim the status of 'art' for a piece of work is often a key seal of approval, signifying 'quality' and 'seriousness' and, commercially, involving the important power of copyright. Pragmatically, if a genre text can claim 'artistic' or fully 'authored' status for itself, then it may well occupy special media spaces. This is partly still true of the foreign language films (see this chapter's case study) though their classification as 'arthouse' is complicated now by the easy availability of DVD and downloaded films.

Another example, from the level of reception. There is controversy over whether the BBFC makes different classification decisions (e.g. about representing sexual activity) depending on whether the text is considered 'art' and is therefore assumed to circulate in 'safer' environments, such as arthouse cinemas, with more middle-class audiences than in big multiplex cinema screens. A key marker of 'art' status is of course the presence of an 'artist', whether director, singer or writer. This sometimes has to be argued, and marketed for.

> **BBFC**: The British Board of Film Classification, formerly the British Board of Film Censors, is an independent, non-governmental body, which has exercised responsibilities over cinema since 1913, over video since 1985, and now over some DVD products and games. See its excellent website(s) at http://www.bbfc.org.uk.

### Two case studies around 'horror'

1   The status of different genres can be shown by the work put into getting *The Silence of the Lambs* (US 1991) considered as a thriller rather than a 'simple' horror film. Textually it clearly fits into the cycle of 'slasher' horror films. The figures of psychiatrist and serial killer, separated in the horror genre from *Psycho* (US 1960) onwards, are fused in the 'fascinating' figure of Hannibal Lecter.

Jodie Foster plays a version of what the theorist Carol Clover (1992) called 'the final girl' of earlier, lower-status slasher-horror films. Clover emphasised that the series of attacks on women in them are avenged, not by a man, but by 'the final girl' to be attacked by the killer.

Institutionally, the timing of the film's first release, Valentine's Day 1991, fitted the 'watching horror together' slot sanctioned as an excuse for physical contact for teenage couples. As *Premiere* magazine put it: 'If it is a choice between this and chocolates for Valentine's Day, the bon bons might be a better choice, but then again, *The Silence* promises to be so terrifying, you're bound to end up in your sweetheart's arms.' Much publicity, however, classified it as a 'thriller' or 'psychological thriller', a term which easily invites the highly prestigious adjective 'Hitchcock-ian', a mix of authorship and generic status. Though *Silence* could be said to fall between the two categories, publicity for it tried to replace associations of 'horror'

> Interestingly the book of *Psycho* was greeted with revulsion by studio executives ('too repulsive for films', wrote a script reader) and the film had mixed reviews – but huge box office returns. This prompted positive re-reviews and eventually two Oscar nominations.

> This use of romance-centred marketing ploys for the horror genre (apparently its opposite) is a good example of Altman's emphasis on the pragmatic ways that genres are, in practice, used and classified.

by adjectives which produced a sense of ambivalence about the film: it is 'terrifying', 'brutally real', 'macabre', 'dark'.

Casting used prestigious actors. Clarice Starling, FBI agent, may arguably be one of the slasher-horror cycle's 'final girls'. But she is played by the Oscar-winning actor, Yale graduate, feminist Jodie Foster, in a much praised high-status 'Method' performance, researched via a week at FBI HQ, cited as an effort towards 'realism'. The film also made *restrained* use of violence, and colour, and avoided voyeurism, or the goriest of special effects (see Jancovich 2000). Judging by the latest description on IMDb this higher status of the film has been held: it is classified there as 'crime/thriller'.

## EXPLORE 3.8

*The Silence of the Lambs* came out some time ago.

- Do you think that the low status of the horror genre is changing, along with the importance of younger audiences, internet comment, knowledge of FX and easier availability of foreign language films?
- Is the BBFC right in suggesting the genre appeals to very knowledgeable (i.e. unshockable) fan or 'cult' audiences, and therefore does not deserve so many cuts?

2  Another example of the ways that status still works in classification. Reviews of Mel Gibson's *The Passion of the Christ* (2004) mostly took it very seriously. They classified it as a film dealing in a realistic and weighty way with a high-status subject (the last hours of the life of Jesus Christ). The signifiers for this were not only the subject matter, but also the use of subtitles for the 'authentic' Latin and Aramaic dialogue (these usually being associated with foreign language or 'arthouse' cinema), the sonorous music and the film's slow pace.

Only a few critics focused on its emphatic and prolonged use of hugely gory special effects around the crucifixion (classified by some as 'realism'), and the ways it was discussed as a kind of test of viewing endurance or toughness (as had parts of Gibson's previous film *Braveheart* (US 1995) and later *Apocalypto* (2006), also using foreign language dialogue). All this suggested that it might be considered as a kind of horror film. But this was a scandalous label, because of the low or even playful status of the horror genre and its often young, fan audiences, as opposed to the high status of the story of the last hours of Christ.

Fewer critics pointed to ways in which the film stayed within the familiar boundaries of 'biblical epics'. Christ (born in Palestine) and his family are played by fair-skinned actors (years of Eurocentric tradition here) rather than (more realistic) by darker-skinned actors. Only certain parts of his teachings are focused on, certainly not those which would encourage radical social change on behalf of the poor, which are highlighted in Pasolini's *The Gospel According to St Matthew* (Italy 1964) and in the work of liberation theologians.

*Figure 3.13* Pasolini's images of Christ, 1964. A related quote: 'When I give food to the poor they call me a saint. When I ask why the poor have no food, they call me a communist.' Dom Helder Camara, Catholic liberation theologian (1972).

## Formal classifications

Genre is not the only kind of classifying which positions or 'frames' media products for us, setting up expectations in some directions and not others. It can shade into censorship, as part of a *spectrum of activities*:

- everyday: we all self-censor what we say or write before committing to it;
- everyday: processes of news shaping by 'official sources', self-censorship as a 'good professional', etc.;
- formal classifications: these do not ban directly, but might put controversial programmes on at 'post-watershed' times, or strongly suggest that some films or DVDs should be shown to some age groups but not others;

For UK TV one key classification has been the timing of a programme ('before or after 9 p.m.?'), within the 'Family Viewing Policy'. This tries to ensure that material unsuitable for children is not transmitted at times when large numbers of children may be expected to be watching: 9 p.m. is normally fixed as the point up to which TV companies should see themselves as responsible for ensuring that nothing unsuitable for children is broadcast. After that, it is seen as the parents' responsibility.

This is based on, and helps to reinforce, a particular conception of the 'usual' household and 'usual' viewing patterns (gathered around a TV screen), which may now be quite outdated.

---

### EXPLORE 3.9

Make notes on the following:

- What has been your experience of 'family viewing' and of this classification policy?
- Do you have younger brothers or sisters? Do you feel it should apply to them? If so, how? Which genres do you think are key?
- How do technological changes such as online viewing, and bedrooms with computers in them, affect this area?

---

- censorship or decisive acts of forbidding or preventing distribution of media products, or parts of products. This can range from cutting off internet accesss, as has happened in China and Burma, or, much less frequent now, forbidding circulation of certain texts.

A formal classification system is operated in the UK for film, videos and DVDs and some other digital material (e.g. games) by the BBFC. This Board has no regulatory powers, but it is often called 'film censorship', it is although better understood as a classificatory body. It decides the audiences for which a product is presumed to be suitable, and sometimes suggests to the film-makers cuts or changes which will fit the presumed nature of this audience, especially if it believes harm to children is at stake.

The Board is responsible for checking that material is not in breach of criminal laws (e.g. on cruelty to animals or children; on incitement to racial hatred, blasphemy, etc.). Only very rarely will it deny a film a rating, although that happened in 2009 with the Japanese movie *Grotesque*, which the BBFC felt featured sexual sadism for its own sake (see BBFC website). Final powers on film remain with local councils, which can overrule any of the BBFC's decisions, though this rarely happens. In cinema, as well as age, the categories include 'accompanied by a parent' and 'only when over 18'. For DVDs the advice might be, for example, 'contains moderate sex references and one hard drug reference'.

Old joke about classification: 'If I like it, it's erotic; if I don't, it's porn.' The term 'propaganda' can be used for an equally deadly effect on discussion – see Chapter 6 and case study on *The Age of Stupid*.

## EXPLORE 3.10

Q: Sometimes ratings are said to work, not as censorship, but as advertising. Discuss.

A: Potential audiences may be attracted, as well as put off by different ratings labels.

*Parents* want to know which films might frighten their children, and broadly whether they contain images of violence, hard drug use, or might encourage head-butting and other easily imitatable forms of violence.

Equally, *younger audiences* often want to feel 'cool' by getting to see something which is in the next age range up from their actual age.

*Film-makers* often negotiate with classification boards, such as the BBFC, to achieve their desired classification. They will sometimes refuse to take out certain sections in order to gain a higher rating, especially for horror. Classification is a pragmatic, not a rigid process.

Unusually, in July 2009, Universal Pictures UK released a specially edited '15' certificate version of *Brüno* (knowingly titled *Brüno: Snipped*) 'to prevent growing disappointment among younger fans and to maximise revenues. UK cinemas had reported turning away large numbers of under-18s keen to see the film.' The '15' version is 1 minute and 50 seconds shorter than the original. Though this is said to be unprecedented, a letter to *Screen International* (14 July) reported that in 1979 Paramount edited *Saturday Night Fever* (US 1977) down from an X (18) to an A (PG) for a re-release timed to coincide with the school holidays, losing some ten minutes of footage in the process.

> Traditional methods of censorship still operate. The Ukrainian Ministry of Culture banned any screenings of *Brüno* (US 2009) in its territory, arguing that it 'contains unjustified showing of genital organs' and depicts 'homosexual perversions' in an 'explicitly realist manner'.

## Conclusion

This chapter has tried to place genres within broader systems of classification and framing, both formal and informal. These processes often exist along a spectrum, whether of genre forms or of kinds of classification, of a perceived relationship to the rest of the real, or of cultural status.

We have argued that genres require and indeed produce a certain amount of innovation, as well as the pleasures of repetition. Genre texts are themselves increasingly shaped by the producers' images of audiences, and now, much more, by the activities of audiences and fans, both on and off the internet. A cultural approach to genres may celebrate some of the expansion of users' presence, and suggest it is making for substantial innovation. But it may ask too whether some 'obvious' generic elements (the sense of what constitutes a 'happy ending', or of what cannot be mentioned) may still be perpetuating some oppressive identities or imaginings, and excluding others.

More examples are given in the following case study, which explores films that are 'classified' partly by their circulation as authorship, as 'foreign language', as genre and sometimes as 'arthouse' texts.

## References and further reading

Altman, Rick (1999) *Film/Genre*, London: BFI.

Bennett, Tony, Savage, Mike, Silva, Elizabeth Bortolaia, Warde, Alan, Gayo-Cal, Modesto, and Wright, David (2009) *Class, Culture, Distinction*, London and New York: Routledge.

Bourdieu, Pierre (1984) *Distinction: A Social Critique of the Judgment of Taste*, London: Routledge.

Branston, Gill (2000) *Cinema and Cultural Modernity*, London and New York: Open University Press.

Brown, Maggie (2009) 'Can Cowell Back a Global Winner?' *The Guardian*, 29 June.

Brunsdon, Charlotte (1981) 'Crossroads: Notes on Soap Opera', *Screen*, 22, 5: 52–7.

Clover, Carol (1992) *Men, Women and Chainsaws: Gender in the Modern Horror Film*, Princeton: Princeton University Press.

Cook, Samantha (2006) *The Rough Guide to Chick Flicks*, London: Rough Guides.

Corrigan, Timothy, and White, Patricia (2004) *The Film Experience: An Introduction*, Boston: Bedford/St Martin's.

Gilbey, Ryan (2009) 'Jokers to the Left, Jokers to the Right', *The Guardian*, 17 July.

Gledhill, Christine (ed.) (1987) *Home is Where the Heart is*, London: BFI.

Gomery, Douglas (1992) *Shared Pleasures: History of Movie Presentation in the United States*, London: BFI.

Jancovich, Mark (2000) ' "A Real Shocker": Authenticity, Genre and the Struggle for Distinction', *Continuum: Journal of Media and Cultural Studies*, 14, 1: 23–35.

Kinder, Marsha (2001) 'Violence American Style: The Narrative Orchestration of Violent Attractions', in Slocum, David J. (ed) *Violence and American Cinema*, London and New York: Routledge.

Krutnik, Frank (2002) 'Conforming Passions?: Contemporary Romantic Comedy', in Neale (2002).

La Place, Maria (1987) 'Producing and Consuming the Woman's film', in

Gledhill, Christine (ed.) *Home is Where the Heart is*, London and New York: Arnold.

Lovell, Alan, and Sergi, Gianluca (2009) *Cinema Entertainment*, London and New York: Open University Press.

Neale, Steve (2000) *Genre and Hollywood*, London: Routledge.

Neale, Steve (ed.) (2002) *Genre and Contemporary Hollywood*, London: BFI.

Paul, William (2002) 'The Impossibility of Romance: Hollywood Comedy 1978–1999', in Neale (2002).

Waters, Florence (2009) 'Duplicity: Tony Gilroy Interview', *Daily Telegraph*, 20 March.

# CASE STUDY

# Horror as popular art

- THE CHILD IN THE HORROR FILM
- GLOBAL AND LOCAL AUDIENCES
- STYLE AND THE GOTHIC: DIFFERENT REPERTOIRES
- AUTHORSHIP AND PROMOTION

- DISTRIBUTION STRATEGIES
- CONCLUSION
- REFERENCES AND FURTHER READING

Here we explore two films that use horror and other repertoires in interesting ways. Both have proved popular with audiences and critics around the world, challenging the low status sometimes ascribed to the genre.

Horror is one of the most endurable genres in film history, constantly evolving, often through distinct cycles of films. An important recent **cycle** was associated with the impact of East Asian ghost stories in global cinema. (See the J-horror case study on the **MSB5 website**.) That cycle has now run its course, but in its wake have come other notable films sharing elements of the same **repertoires** and which have in some ways benefited from audience awareness and industrial experience of the earlier films. *El orfanato* (*The Orphanage*, Spain/Mexico 2007) and *Låt den rätte komma in* (*Let the Right One In*, Sweden 2008) are quite different in terms of their narratives, characterisation and visual style, but they have been seen as referring to different sub-genres of the horror film and have been distributed and received by audiences in similar ways. In Rick Altman's (1999) terminology, we recognise them as horror in the inclusive, semantic sense, but they are respectively a ghost story and a vampire story (although we will problematise both classifications) in the exclusive or syntactic sense. Later we will ask some pragmatic questions about how they were distributed.

To make full use of this case study and the references, you should watch both films (preferably more than once). The films both depend on suspense and narrative surprises, so if you haven't seen the films yet, beware that what follows contains spoilers.

## THE CHILD IN THE HORROR FILM

In *The Orphanage*, Laura, with her husband and adopted son, returns to the orphanage on the coast of northern Spain where she lived as a child. She intends to reopen it as a school for children with learning difficulties. Her son is around the same age (seven or eight) that she was when she left the orphanage and he soon makes contact with the ghosts of the children who died after she left. Gradually, Laura becomes aware of her son's behaviour and when he disappears, she begins to suspect that there is something or someone in the house who is responsible.

This scenario immediately calls up an earlier Spanish film, *The Others* (Spain/US 2001), which in turn referred to a classic ghost story, *The Turn of the Screw* (1898) by Henry James and its adaptation as the film *The Innocents* (UK 1961).

*Figure 3.14* One of the original orphans.

## EXPLORE 3.10   WHY CHILDREN?

Jot down any films you know which feature children in potential horror scenarios.

- What kinds of 'play' do you remember around the ideas of 'innocence' and 'evil'?
- Are there relationships between parents and children, especially mothers (and surrogate mothers)?
- Are there any 'universal' experiences of childhood that you recognise?

*Let the Right One In* deals with children on the cusp of adolescence. A lonely 12-year-old boy, Oskar, is bullied at school. He finds a new friend when a man and a girl move in next door in his apartment building in a Stockholm suburb. The girl's arrival coincides with a series of grisly murders and eventually Oskar realises that she is a vampire – but also that he is emotionally attached to her. The character of Eli, 12 but going on 200, is just one of the ways in which this film creates 'difference' while at the same time repeating many of the conventions of the familiar vampire movie. The film's title appeals immediately to the horror fan who knows that a vampire must always be invited into a house. We've seen demonic children many times before, but rarely as 'humanised' as Eli. In a way, the difference of Eli stands out in sharper focus because of the success

of older teenage vampires and vampire hunters in such TV, novel and film franchises as *Buffy* and *Twilight*.

In this focus on the child, we can see how two films from different cultural backgrounds draw on the same broad repertoire and also how they are distinguished in syntactical ways.

### GLOBAL AND LOCAL AUDIENCES

*The Orphanage* was an international production. Mainly Spanish it also involved film and TV companies owned by conglomerates from France (Canal+) and Hollywood (Warner Bros) and was 'presented' by Guillermo del Toro, well known for films made in Spain and the US as well as Mexico. This production context helped the film's promotion in the international market.

*Let the Right One In* was produced by a group of Swedish film and TV companies. Popular films from Sweden usually circulate in a limited way in Sweden, Norway, Finland and Denmark. Only occasionally do they obtain exposure in the larger global market. *Let the Right One In* is one of three recent Swedish films/TV programmes to gain wider distribution. All are adaptations of popular genre novels. The massively popular 'Inspector Wallander' crime novels (rivalling Harry Potter in German sales) were first adapted for a Swedish TV series in 2005 and later shown in the UK in 2008 (when a British adaptation also began). The first film adaptation of Stieg Larsson's thriller novels, *The Girl with the Dragon Tattoo* (Sweden/Denmark/Germany 2009), swiftly became the biggest-selling 'local film' and then 'European film' at a time when the novels were bestsellers in the UK and around the world.

Both *The Orphanage* and *Let the Right One In* were seemingly guaranteed local and perhaps regional success, but their wider distribution involved careful marketing strategies, including appearances at various film festivals. This is explored later; here we consider what made the local impact of the films distinctive.

Genre study offers a useful means of exploring other media concepts, including representation. Because of repetition, audiences tend to find genre narratives are easily accessible. The same or similar characters are presented in familiar stories over long periods. Because of the **verisimilitude** of many genres, it then becomes interesting to see how these presentations change over time. What kinds of men become gangsters; how do their family backgrounds change over time? In this sense, genre films are 'porous'. They absorb aspects of what is happening in the real world and it is not unusual to see claims that horror film cycles have a direct relationship with changes in society. The ghosts of the East Asian cycle used 'new technologies' to manifest themselves via television and video, mobile phones and internet connections, and the characters themselves often came from single-parent or dysfunctional families, a relatively new phenomenon in East Asian cultures.

Horror films have the potential to act as metaphors for what is happening in the real world.

This was important in the reception of *El orfanato* in Spain. The film's release in autumn 2007 coincided with the introduction of a 'Law of Historical Memory' which promised to heal the wounds of losses incurred up to seventy years earlier by families during the Spanish Civil War and its aftermath. It allowed families to apply for exhumations from mass graves of thousands of civilian victims of Franco's Nationalist forces. They can now be reburied in family plots. *El orfanato* offers a powerful metaphor for this as Laura discovers the fate of her childhood friends. It also offers a metaphor about 'believing' in the past and coming to terms with what it means, represented here by Laura's husband who is first sceptical of the 'ghost story' but comes to accept that his wife and son have died. (Assuming that the film is set in Spain in 2005–6, the deaths of the children would have taken place around thirty years earlier – soon after Franco's death in 1975.)

References to the Civil War are still common in Spanish films, including the two Guillermo del Toro films *The Devil's Backbone* (Spain/Mexico 2001) and *Pan's Labyrinth* (Spain/Mexico/US 2006) and the earlier classic films *The Spirit of the Beehive* (Spain 1973) and *Raise Ravens* (Spain 1976). Both these films are metaphors about Spain under Franco and feature children (played by child star Ana Torrent) who have fantasy relationships. In *Raise Ravens*, the child's (ghost) mother was played by Geraldine Chaplin, who reappears as the medium in *The Orphanage*. Child stars and child-centred narratives were a feature of Spanish cinema under Franco (see Stone 2002). The outcome of all of these 'intertextualities' and historical resonances was that *El orfanato* was the biggest box office film in Spain in 2007. When the film travelled abroad it was a success as a universally accessible horror film, but not on quite the same scale.

The setting of *Let the Right One In* is perhaps less significant. But it is given precisely. The source novel even uses the correct dates for the events of the story, including the first sighting of a Soviet submarine in

Swedish waters on 27 October 1981. In the twentieth century, Sweden maintained its neutrality in both world wars and during the Cold War. A Russian submarine (with suspected nuclear weapons) was an unusual intruder and remained an issue in the Swedish media over the course of the next year. In the film there is a radio broadcast mentioning the Soviet leader Leonid Brezhnev. What do we make of this realist detail? Is it metaphorical in its introduction of a potentially threatening uninvited visitor? Or does it signal a different kind of horror film with documentary detail? This detail will mean more to Swedish audiences, but because of the universality of the repertoire, the global audience will easily pick up the connection between vampires and 'strangers' coming into our midst (perhaps bringing with them diseases?). It is noticeable that in the crime genre novels of Henning Mankell, contemporary Sweden is often portrayed as a once 'social democratic' country disturbed not only by the reaction to the arrival of refugees, but also by the importation of forms of criminal activity with global connections such as sex trafficking and the drugs trade.

Does it negate these ideas if we discover that the reason for setting the story in 1981 is that this was when the author (and adapter) was himself 12 years old?

## EXPLORE 3.11 THE VAMPIRE REPERTOIRE

Research the different versions of the Dracula story.

- Where has Dracula come from?
- How does he arrive in Western Europe?
- What kinds of threat does he pose to the community?
- How are Dracula or similar vampires portrayed in stories set in modern times?
- Refer to the 'character-functions' in Chapter 2 – what happens to the character-functions in the Dracula story in *Let the Right One In*?

## STYLE AND THE GOTHIC: DIFFERENT REPERTOIRES

The two case study films are recognisably horror films, both with a focus on children. They derive story ideas from the 'Gothic romances' of eighteenth- and nineteenth-century literature. The term 'Gothic' usually signals that a narrative will focus on what Wikipedia usefully describes as 'emotional extremes and dark themes'. Gothic stories are often set in inhospitable places, in dark and brooding castles and great houses, with action set at night or in extreme weather. *The Orphanage* is a 'dark house' on the coast of Asturias – a land of rain and mists. Stockholm in winter is dark and cold. The setting is in one sense commonplace and drab, but the freeze puts characters into extreme situations.

Over time, the Gothic has moved location, so that we now accept an 'urban Gothic' as well as one associated with wildness and isolation. The repertoire has expanded. But using Altman's syntactic approach, we can distinguish the two case study films by the way in which elements are combined in the narrative structure. In *The Orphanage*, the emphasis is on melodrama, long associated with the Gothic. The narrative is female-centred, with concerns about the mental and physical state of the mother – is she responsible for the death of her son? There is also a sense of *family* melodrama – how will the search for her son affect Laura's relationship with her husband? Does she see herself as some kind of surrogate mother – first for the children she hopes to enrol in her school and then later for the ghosts of the children she left behind? We can also see references to what was once known as 'the woman's film' – especially in the 1940s with films such as *Gaslight* (US 1944) in which Ingrid Bergman plays a woman being driven mad in the house where her aunt was murdered.

On the DVD the director and crew are quite clear about the melodrama they are creating – even though the term is not one favoured in the film industry (perhaps it is more used in Spain than in the UK?). In general discourse it is a pejorative term implying

*Figure 3.15 a, b & c* Three posters for *El orfanato*'s release in Spain.

'excessive' or 'over the top' plotting and performance. In critical terms melodrama is indeed about 'excess', in music, *mise en scène*, performance, etc., but these should be carefully orchestrated in the service of the genre. Melodrama and horror share many aspects of visual and aural style, but the former may appeal more to older audiences or to audiences expecting more in terms of metaphor than the thrill of action and the frisson of disgust/terror that some horror films promise.

 It is worth looking carefully at some of the poster material for the film from Spain and the US/UK presented here and on the **MSB5 website**.

---

## EXPLORE 3.12 MELODRAMA AND HORROR

In what ways do the posters for *El orfanato* suggest the different repertoires of horror and melodrama?

- Draw on your understanding from Chapter 1 in analysing how the posters create meaning.
- Can you distinguish references to different repertoires and an appeal to different audiences?

---

The other repertoires referenced in *Let the Right One In* are the 'coming-of-age romance' and what could be termed the 'social problem' film. In addition, there is a suggestion that this is a 'children's film'. This latter designation seems strange in a UK/US context, yet in some European film cultures, quite challenging narratives are considered appropriate for children's films. Noting that the film comes from a 'children's novel', a Cineuropa website profile describes it as 'in essence a sweet prepubescent love story that just happens to be disguised as an anti-bullying pamphlet with supernatural overtones' (Boyd van Hoeij, 16 December 2008).

Romance is part of the Gothic inheritance, but usually adult romance. The 'social' aspect of the film refers to the bullying theme as well as to the overall representation of the depressing atmosphere of the suburb. The 'victims' include members of a drinking group who are mainly unemployed, and the narrative touches on the problems of dysfunctional family relationships and Oskar's own obsession with violent murders as reported in the press. (The novel also includes other teen characters into glue-sniffing, etc.)

The romance and the social detail are important for fans of the film who compare it favourably with the

*Figure 3.16* Oskar, staying in after school to learn about Morse code.

more mainstream *Twilight* on the Facebook site for the Swedish film. An interesting comment on the combination of the real and the fantastic is contained in this extract from an interview with the director:

> The style of the screenplay was rather severe, there was truly very little dialogue, and what there was was very poetic. We were convinced that the film should be told through images. The older man who takes care of Eli was obviously a paedophile in the book. I think that today the subject of paedophilia is too often used to give stories an emotional special effect, without being thoroughly explored. I didn't want such a complex, strong and disconcerting subject to have a disturbing effect on the love story between the two main characters.
>
> (Cineuropa website)

There is one tiny gesture in the film that hints at the relationship between Eli and Håkan, but, as in *The Orphanage*, it is the careful mixing of repertoires in a controlled way that makes *Let the Right One In* so effective. Some realistic detail enhances the Gothic feel – too much of the wrong kind would destroy it.

## EXPLORE 3.13  A REALIST VAMPIRE STORY?

- How does the realist social detail of *Let the Right One In* distinguish the film from Hollywood vampire films?
- What does the casting of the film contribute to the realist effect?
- How do you read the ending? What do you think Oskar is doing now, thirty years on?

## AUTHORSHIP AND PROMOTION

*The Orphanage* was heavily promoted in the UK as 'presented by Guillermo del Toro'. Although del Toro enthusiastically endorsed the film and did his bit to help the production and promote it, he was in no way the 'author' of the film. The references may have set up false expectations about the film, which apart from the possible Civil War allusions, shares little of the repertoires utilised in *Pan's Labyrinth*. The UK DVD announces 'The new *Pan's Labyrinth*. Excellent – *The Guardian*'. *Time Out*, more helpfully and more accurately, suggests 'The most frightening ghost story since *The Others*.' Part of the problem for the distributor and for the critics is that subtitled films outside the mainstream don't usually have stars known to the general audience, so an *auteur* name or a hit film reference is essential. *El orfanato* had no such problem in Spain where Belén Rueda is well known for her television and film work (which includes international exposure). The massive Spanish success of the film suggests that without the language barrier (and with the local cultural knowledge) *El orfanato* is a mainstream genre film, not a specialised film.

*Let the Right One In* is slightly different. Director Tomas Alfredson has worked entirely within the Swedish film and television industry. The film has no stars as such and was the first feature film production of a small independent company with a background in advertising and TV entertainment shows. In another interview posted on Cineuropa, producer John Nordling discusses the difficulties created by classification which means that a story about a 12-year-old boy will in most countries be seen only by older audiences. In Sweden the film was released 'wide' (and although successful, was affected by film piracy). Outside Sweden, sales were handled by an experienced German sales agent.

In Sweden *Let the Right One In* sold to some extent on the profile of the original novel (first published in 2004). The English translation was not published in paperback until January 2009. This meant that the only promotional material available to the sales agent was the genre identification and what could be achieved by talking up the film around the festival circuit. Promotion purely as a horror genre offering was unlikely to appeal to international art cinema audiences, so it was important that the look and the tone of the film, combining the cinematography of Hoyte Van Hoytema and the slow pacing and use of music and sound, worked well through the trailers and the artwork for posters.

IMDb lists more than fifty awards to *Let the Right One In* at festivals during 2008 and 2009. These ranged across specialised horror/fantasy festivals and more general festivals in Europe, North America and East Asia. Awards went to the film, the director, writer, cinematographer and to the child actors. The feedback from the festivals fed into the array of different trailers, posters and web-based material produced for different territories. The Swedish and British websites made excellent use of Flash videos to present the look and tone (fade-ins and -outs with snow falling against mainly static scenes), whereas the trailers emphasised the action and shocks. The British trailer, which placed the ecstatic critical notices between shots, was more successful in presenting the tone than the American trailer, which pushed all the quotes to the end (giving the impression of a fast-paced horror film).

## DISTRIBUTION STRATEGIES

Since the early 1990s, when the international film industry began to recover after long years of decline in many territories, distribution practices have become associated with new forms of classification. Most major film industries have always had 'peak periods' for film releases at specific holiday times – Chinese New Year in Hong Kong, Eid and Diwali in South Asia, Thanksgiving in the US, etc. The threat of piracy has pushed Hollywood into 'day and date' releases of blockbuster films which now open in many territories across the world simultaneously. Some local holidays remain important, but overall, especially since the international market is now bigger than that in North America alone, film releases are being internationalised. This means that certain kinds of films can be classified in terms of when they are likely to be released.

Perhaps the best-known classification of this kind (apart from the 'summer blockbuster') is the 'awards film', released in the US, often on just a few prints, in time to qualify for Oscar nominations at the end of December and then heavily promoted during the nomination period in January and towards the ceremony in February. In these two months, when there is relatively little competition from blockbusters, which don't generally appear until May, the film will also be released in many overseas territories.

How does the horror film fit into distribution planning? Hallowe'en week at the end of October is important for the teen-oriented horror film. It falls between the summer and Thanksgiving peak periods, and horror, because of its reliable teen audience, offers the chance of making money in normally slack periods. Releasing a film in October/November and January–April for older audiences requires careful planning. In March 2000, Universal claimed a huge box office success for *Erin Brockovich*, a film in which Julia Roberts played outside her star image as a romantic comedy figure. In 2005, the same studio chose to release *The Interpreter* (UK/US/France 2005) with Nicole Kidman and Sean Penn a few weeks later in April, and in 2006 they repeated the trick with *Inside Man* starring Denzel Washington and Jodie Foster. These latter two films didn't match the more than $100 million take of *Erin Brockovich,* but they did well and prompted industry comment that the studio had seen them as 'smart, adult movies' with a genre feel that could flourish outside the blockbuster season (and away from the 'awards films').

*The Orphanage* and *Let the Right One In* are not Hollywood films and they were both released first in their home markets, gaining an international profile through film festival appearances, often being in contention for prizes. When they finally arrived in the UK they both had reputations and in a sense a kind of 'institutional classification'. Because they are both subtitled, they automatically became 'specialised films' in the UK. Usually this would mean being confined to small independent cinemas on a limited release. However, given the success in November/December 2006 of Guillermo del Toro's *Pan's Labyrinth*, the distributors of both films were prepared to gamble that the films would play successfully in selected multiplexes as well as specialised cinemas and that a wider release was possible. Both films were trailed carefully without subtitled dialogue (but with evidence of their festival success). *The Orphanage* was released by Optimum on seventy-four screens in late March 2008. *Let the Right One In* was released by Metrodome on sixty-eight screens in early April 2009.

Both films attracted larger audiences than most subtitled films in the UK. Perhaps inevitably both films are also scheduled for American remakes. This has already angered fans on the grounds that the original version will always be the 'authentic' one. Both proposals have in 2009 been announced with participation by the original producers. This didn't prevent a fan and critical backlash for Nakata Hideo when he remade his own Japanese *Ring 2* for a Hollywood studio. Perhaps it would be worth rereading this case study and trying to work out what the major issues might be in translating these two 'properties' into scripts for American films?

## CONCLUSION

Our application of aspects of genre theory helps to develop richer readings of these films and demonstrates the fluidity and dynamism of the concept of genre repertoires. Such analysis of popular films and their circulation and reception enables us to undertake the kind of pragmatic approach suggested by Altman which complements our semantic/syntactic knowledge. *The Orphanage* is a more conventional film than the interesting reinvention of the vampire story offered by *Let the Right One In*, but both challenge the classification of 'art' and 'popular'.

## REFERENCES AND FURTHER READING

Altman, Rick (1999) *Film/Genre,* London: BFI Publishing.
Cherry, Brigid (2009) *Horror*, London: Routledge.
Delgado, Maria (2008) 'The Young and the Damned', *Sight and Sound*, April (also online at: http://www.bfi.org.uk/sightandsound/review/4275).
Stone, Rob (2002) *Spanish Cinema*, Harlow: Longman.
http://cineuropa.org/ffocus.aspx?lang=en&treeID=1665
http://www.facebook.com/pages/Lat-den-ratte-komma-in-aka-Let-the-right-one-in/27543047841?ref=ts

The **MSB5 website** has supplementary material on this case study, plus an earlier case study on 'J-horror and the *Ring* cycle'.

# 4 Representations

## 'Representation' now

One of the key terms of media studies has always been 'representation', a rich concept, with several aspects to it.

1   It emphasises that, however realistic or compelling some media images seem, they never simply *present* the world direct. They are always a construction, a *re*-presentation, rather than a mirror, or a clear 'window on to the real'.

2   The term has the capacity to suggest that some media *re*-present, over and over again, certain images, stories, situations. This can make them seem 'natural' or familiar – and thereby marginalise or even exclude other images, making those *un*familiar or even threatening. The question of who has the power to make these familiarities, and their accompanying black holes of representation, can be evoked by this emphasis.

3   This prompts the question: if some groups, situations, etc. are *routinely* represented in oppressive or limited ways, how does this relate to public understandings, and to how some groups are treated by others – in the street, in the interview situation? Many relate this to the world of political *representatives*: people who 'stand in' for us, take crucial decisions with real consequences – as union or school or government representatives.

Two more recent connections for 'representation' have been:

4 the increased possibilities for 'self-representation' in digital forms, all the way from choice of email address, through to blogs, social networking sites, games and simulations like *Second Life*; and

5 recent cynicism about 'official' politics and how 'we' are represented in them. These have arguably weakened the political understandings of media representations. Equally, though, new forms of politics have made imaginative and impactful use of new media forms.

> a Have you ever played with self-representation through different email addresses?
> b For grouped representations, see, for example, the Cardiff young people's website *www.thesprout.co.uk*.

## Complications of 'representation' now

'Representation' has been an important concept for 'realistic' media forms such as documentary, news, etc. It works less well with fantasy or so-called 'immersive' forms, such as computer games. These arguably seek to involve the user in an experience rather than to 'present' a view of the world. Comedy forms also present some challenges to the theory (see Medhurst 2007).

But we've always argued against a simplistic application of 'representation', as can occur with 'stereotypes', or in metaphors like 'holding the mirror up to reality'. We'll come back to this, but for now let's explore the concepts of 'refraction' and **'re-mediation'**.

> See *The Age of Stupid* case study in Chapter 6, involving film, premiere 'stunts', website, lively emailings and other kinds of digital activism. And 2009 saw some remarkable 'Twitter'-related campaigns. See Introduction.

## EXPLORE 4.1

- Research the term 'refraction'. It comes from the study of light waves. When they travel from air to water, for example (such as in a sunny swimming pool) they give misleading images of the body which is in the water.

  'The real', or perceptions of it, are usually part of most media forms, even fantasy and comic ones (recall 'verisimilitude' and its role for genres). But this is 'bent' or refracted by the conventions and demands of those forms. Comedy needs to produce laughs, horror needs shocks and often the shiver of an 'Other' as 'villain'. Even news likes to tell a story and construct characters, suspense, etc.

- Jot down how 'refraction' might apply to your favourite media form or text.

- Can you say how it might develop the idea of 'representation'?

- When you've done this, explore how it might apply to 'realist' media forms, such as news.

*Figure 4.1* An example of visual refraction. The body is visible, is 'represented', in the water, but not as in a mirror. Like the media, the water cannot be a simple 'window' on to the real.

Some writers emphasise 're-mediation' as another useful concept (see Lister *et al.* 2009). It suggests that all media, when they are new, adapt previously existing media. So, cinema adapted theatre and literature, and computer games could be said to 're-mediate' forms of cinema (see Chapter 8). These involve further kinds of refraction, rather than a simple, mirror-like 'representation' of the world, or simple repetition of an earlier form. Some of these debates have been broached before, in discussions of adaptations, though 're-mediation' spreads it, as an emphasis, to include new media.

## Stereotyping and 'scripts'

Stereotype comes from Greek *stereo*, meaning 'solid'. It is a printer's term for solid blocks of type used to represent something which would otherwise need a great deal of work with individual pieces of type to show fine detail. Arguably it is now dated. Terms like 'scripts' and different 'stories' try for more fluidity in the idea of 'representation'.

Let's return to mainstream debates on 'representation'. The media give us ways of imagining particular groups, identities and situations. When these relate to *people* they are sometimes called stereotypes or types; when they offer images of *situations* or *processes*, the term 'script' is sometimes used, with the implication that we grow familiar with these and often know how to 'perform' them in our own lives, often to the exclusion of other ways of being. These imaginings can have material effects on how people expect the world to be, and then experience it.

Stereotyping has been a key concept in media studies, and is now often too taken for granted. Mistakes are easily made in using the term. It does *not* describe actual people or characters. Brad Pitt is not a stereotype. But the way his image is constructed does carry some, and not other, stereotypical assumptions about 'masculinity', 'toughness-with-tenderness', etc. Stereotypes are widely circulated *ideas* or *assumptions* about particular groups. They are often assumed to be 'lies' that need to be 'done away with' so we can all 'get rid of our prejudices' and meet as equals. The term is more derogatory than 'type' or even 'archetype' (which mean very similar things but which have higher status as terms).

Stereotypes have the following characteristics:

1   they involve both a categorising and an evaluation of the group being stereotyped;

2   they usually emphasise some easily grasped or perceived feature(s) of the group in question and then suggest that these are the *cause* of the group's position;

3   the evaluation of the group is often, though not always, a negative one; and

4   stereotypes often try to insist on absolute differences and boundaries

(between 'us' and 'others') whereas the idea of a spectrum of differences, which applies to many of us, is more appropriate. Let's explore this in a little more detail. Stereotyping is a process of categorisation or framing. This is necessary to make sense of the world, and the flood of information and impressions we receive minute by minute. We all have to be 'prejudiced', in its root sense of 'pre-judging', in order to make our way through any situation. We make mental maps of our worlds and the people we meet in order to navigate our way through them. And maps only ever represent parts of the real world, at a distance, and in particular ways.

So most of us employ stereotypes in certain situations. For example, on first meeting someone we might apply a sense of 'type', often on the basis of tiny pieces of evidence – a hairstyle, the length of a hem, an accent. In turn, we all belong to groups that can be typified, and stereotyped in this way – as students, lecturers, Londoners, etc. We often make sense of the people we meet on the basis of small signifiers related to gender, religion, sexuality, etc. and the expectations or 'scripts' these may produce. This process often resembles the ways we make sense of characters in the media.

> **Framing** refers both to a) how an image is literally 'framed' to select certain features for emphasis but also to b) the power of media to 'frame' or shape and set the limits to how audiences are invited to perceive certain groups, issues, stories, especially in news forms.

## EXPLORE 4.2

- Consider the points above. When did you last meet a stranger and apply 'typification' to his/her dress, accent, etc.? What were the key signifiers for you?
- Why did you interpret them as you did? Because of any media images?
- Were you proved right in your estimate?
- Final, tricky question: how do you know?

> In stories there is often not enough space or time (a kind of 'refraction') to amplify, or give a 'back story' to every figure that appears – hence the shorthand use of 'types' to mean background characters. They are often highly stereotyped, and often understood as such.

Moving to characteristic (2): stereotypes work by taking *some* easily grasped features *presumed* to belong to a group. These are often circulated by dominant discourses and relate to powerful ideological assumptions in the culture where they move (see Chapter 6). Stereotyping puts these at the centre of the imaginary figure ('Arabs', 'teenagers') and then imply that *all* members of the group *always* have those features. The next step is to suggest that these characteristics (often the result of historical processes) are themselves the *cause* of the group's position. One of the seductions of stereotypes is that they can point to features that apparently do have 'a grain of truth'. But they then repeat, across a whole range of media, jokes, etc., that this characteristic

> See the late Tessa Perkins' important pioneering work on this concept.

is, and has always been, *the central truth* about that group and the *cause* of its situation.

## CASE STUDY 1: US PLANTATION STEREOTYPING

Let's take an example. For many years, in Hollywood cinema and other discourses, black African slaves, traded as commodities, and working on cotton plantations before the American Civil War of 1861–5, were stereotyped through such signifiers as:

- a shuffling walk;
- musical rhythm, and a tendency to burst into song and dance readily; and
- (in characterisations of female house slaves) bodily fatness, uneducated foolishness and childlike qualities – see 'Mammy' and Prissy in *Gone With the Wind* (US 1939).

*Figure 4.2* Hattie McDaniel as 'Mammy' in *Gone With the Wind* (US 1939), playing a character rooted in a familiar oppressive stereotype of the older black plantation woman. The actor was one of the very few black performers ever to win an Oscar, here for her supporting role. See Shohat and Stam (1994) for an excellent discussion of such performances.

To say that these demeaning stereotypes embody a grain of truth may seem insulting. But consider the following:

- Slaves on the Southern plantations had their calf muscles cut if they tried to run away from slavery (the 'shuffling gait' of the stereotype).
- Slaves were given hardly any educational opportunities. The results of this surface in hostile stereotypes. These demean slaves' efforts to make music

and dance out of the very basic resources to hand. Instead they attribute 'rhythm' to primitive, animal qualities, thus justifying slave-owners' prejudices – 'slaves couldn't benefit from education anyway'.

- The women were often treated as little more than breeding stock by the slave-owners. Once they had given birth to numbers of new slaves, their bodies perhaps enlarged by repeated pregnancies with little medical care, they were often moved into the main house and used as nursemaids to the white children. Again, hostile use of the stereotype invites us to account for Mammy's size in terms of her physical laziness or ignorance rather than her exploitation at the hands of the brutal slave system.

Though historically oppressed groups have been heavily stereotyped by the dominant order, this usually happens through more than one stereotype. As the title of a famous book on racism and Hollywood (*Toms, Coons, Mulattoes, Mammies and Bucks* (Bogle 2003)) suggests there were always several heavily used figures of black Americans. Each stereotype itself changes over time, and relates to broader, changing historical discourses, such as those of colonialism or patriarchal values. As Bogle points out, some of the terms in his title were neutral ('coon' referred to rural whites until around 1848) until broader historical changes turned them into racist slurs. Some are used sympathetically, as in black Civil Rights reformist propaganda, or the broadly sympathetic if sentimental use of Irishness in *Titanic* (US 1997).

## 'Race' and ethnicity

**Racism** doesn't necessarily mean a hatred of non-white groups. More accurately it involves *any* account of the world which argues that:

1   People can be divided into 'races', usually via observable differences in appearance. Some accounts are obsessed with 'colour, hair and bone' difference, which are used to argue for an absolute difference between 'black' and 'white'. Some such differences do exist, but in far subtler, mixed ways than the relatively few 'races' (Negro, Aryan, etc.) listed by racists.

The next steps of the racist position imply that:

2   these supposed simple groupings (by 'blood' or 'race') give fundamental explanations for behaviour and character, indeed, that they account for more than any other factor, such as class, upbringing (including religion and education), gender;

3   that some 'races' are inferior to others, and 'innately' prone to certain kinds of behaviour.

> See the excellent www.racialicious.com, a US blog 'about the intersection of race and pop culture'.

> See the NUJ (National Union of Journalists) website for guidelines on UK race reporting.

Racism resembles stereotyping in the way it takes broadly observable features of a group, puts them at the centre of any account of that group, exaggerates them and (usually) gives them a negative value. Sometimes, as with Nazi ideology, a positive, even superior, valuation is given – to the 'white' or Aryan 'race'. Racism has been well summarised as 'the stigmatising of difference along the lines of "racial" characteristics in order to justify advantage or abuse of power, whether economic, political, cultural or psychological' (Shohat and Stam 1994).

**Ethnic** difference (**ethnicity**) usually signifies non-biological, broadly cultural distinctiveness and identities, produced through such activities as language and religion, as well as geographical location. As such it does not, like race-based divisions, collapse historical human differences into supposedly fundamental 'racial' divisions – white/black or Aryan, Caucasian, Semitic and so on.

A final characteristic of stereotypes is that they often insist on absolute boundaries, whereas in reality there exist spectrums of differences, and some steep, less easily movable rankings of inequality. But this idea of 'spectrums' is not usually how stereotypes are resisted. Usually, anti-stereotype arguments involve one of the dominant values of Western culture: that we are all unique individuals, not types.

In some ways this is true, though it ignores the social structuring we're all shaped by, differences which involve *shared* and *changing historical* structures, within particular social orders. Many experiences are typical, or held in common with others. And arguably our real differences are due not to 'unique essences' but to the particular ways in which very big, shared social forces (such as class, gender, ethnicity) have intersected and mixed in your or my unique instance (along with genetic elements and personal histories). This model, rather than the racist one, broadens the opportunities for understanding both other people's uniqueness, and our capacity to act together to change unjust social structures.

## Example

This is an extract from http://www.racialicious.com prompted by ads for a
Fisher Price toy 'Tickle Hands', based on *Sesame Street* characters, and for
a US context.

*Figure 4.3* Advertisement for Elmo Tickle Hands

'So let's trace the evolution of the gangster meme*

1   Government policy strips urban centers of resources, jobs leave . . .
    housing prices fall and the poor become concentrated . . . people turn to
    "underground" economies. With only the "underclass" left, politicians . . .
    continue policies that disinvest in urban communities of color. Say
    "goodbye" to things like nice parks and excellent fire protection.
2   In a world where obeying the rules gets you nowhere fast, violence
    flourishes.
3   The suffering and resourcefulness of young black, Latino, and Asian men in
    these communities appeals to a (mostly) white "mainstream" America for
    whom depictions of men of color doing violence confirms their beliefs
    about white superiority and advanced "civilization." Hip hop and rap music
    becomes a huge money maker for music studios and producers (and a
    handful of men of color).
4   As [these] become commodified, they are depoliticized . . .
5   Now depoliticized, being "hard" and "urban" becomes synonymous with
    being "cool". Everyone wants to be cool.
6   Being "gangster" is appropriated by white suburban youth.
7   Stripped of any meaning, it filters down to younger and younger kids.'

**Discuss**, from your experiences of gangster forms, including music, any uses
of the term 'urban' to mean black which you have came across.

* meme – see Wikipedia on this controversial term.

## EXPLORE 4.3

- Think of the 'cut-off points' at which age categories or named skin colours are classified as having shaded into their opposite (black/white; childhood/adulthood; old/young).
- Say how you have experienced one such important boundary – child/adult maybe?

A high-profile example: the Dutch 13-year-old Laura Dekker was temporarily made a ward of court in 2009 when she declared her desire to become the youngest person to sail single-handed round the globe. Her parents supported her wish.

How were the issues at stake represented (traceable in blog trails on news articles)?

## 'Scripts' and performances

A useful definition of **scripts**: 'shared expectations about what will happen in certain contexts, and what is desirable and undesirable in terms of outcome' (Durkin 1985: 126).

Shappi Khorsandi is a secular, Iranian-born, British-raised comedian.

The title of her book *A Beginner's Guide to Acting English* uses the idea of performing an identity which is partly real and partly 'performed'. See her comedy on YouTube.

Another powerful way of approaching the influence of repeated representations, this time of *events* and *situations* rather than constructed characters, is to think of the media as circulating dominant 'scripts'. These shared expectations are 'performed' with hugely different degrees of commitment, or subversion, by us, the 'actors' (see Durkin 1985; Goffman 1959). They involve important images of how life may be lived, how to behave with others in particular situations, and so on. The highly conventionalised ways in which romantic encounters are often portrayed may make you feel you will know when 'true love' 'hits' you because you've seen its stages 'scripted' so many times. Maybe you have even rehearsed your possible performance of it in private, fantasy moments.

Equally you may have tried to copy the ways in which 'being a proper man' is framed and 'scripted' by repeated media imagery, often involving notions of 'toughness' (see Katz 2006 on Youtube). These scripts include a sense of when is the appropriate time to resort to violence (demarcated in endless 'face-offs' in westerns, gangster films), how you do or do not express emotion, etc. They differ depending especially on ethnicity and class. Katz suggests the scripts for American black and Chinese young men, never plentiful, are structured towards violent notions of masculinity since they are refracted mostly through gangster and kung fu genres.

## EXPLORE 4.4

- Can you think of any other 'scripts' you've learnt from the media? In films, songs, games, soap operas?
- What sorts of situations are most often 'scripted' for you in computer games, or song lyrics?
- Have you ever been in a situation for which you had not previously come across some kind of media 'script'? What was it? How did you deal with it?

According to one researcher, disaster movies 'script' most people's responses to disasters wrongly: '9.9 times out of 10 people don't turn into crazed individuals but behave quite rationally. They tend to help each other too' (Ed Galea 2010, see www.guardian.co.uk/education/2010/mar/16/disaster-planning-research).

## CASE STUDY 2: REPRESENTATIONS AND GENDER

The distinction between sex and gender is a key one, even though the two terms may be used in different ways. Sex, in this context, is not the same as sexuality, which refers to people's sexual orientation, activities and imaginings. *Sex difference* refers here to the classification of people into male and female, depending on physical characteristics: sex organs, hormonal make-up and so on.

To put it another way, sex says 'It's a boy'; gender says 'Oh, good' and buys the blue greetings cards, gets out the blue baby clothes, later, the toy guns, and a whole set of assumptions (adapted from Branston 1984).

## EXPLORE 4.5

- How can you tell which of these very simply drawn characters is male and which female? Which lines on the drawing told you?

*Figure 4.4* Bruna cartoon

- Try to find other, similar examples in birthday cards, children's comics and cartoon characters. (A quick colour survey of 'new baby' greeting cards can also be striking as signifying gender difference.)
- What does this suggest about the sheer ease with which assumptions of gender difference circulate in our culture?

'When I was 3 or 4 my mother was already teaching me to see dust and other people's feelings' (woman interviewed by Shere Hite (1998)). The skills produced by such socialisation are said to be 'natural' and to 'suit' women to certain kinds of employment – a self-fulfilling prophecy.

See Jacqui Oatley's blog for fascinating observations on UK football, and research her career through online sources.

In April 2007 the Internet Watch Foundation reported, contrary to the usually invoked images of paedophilia, that 80 per cent of the children abused on the internet are girls.

Other categories also go unmarked, with oppressive consequences. While 'black on black' gun crime is often discussed, as Paul Gilroy once commented 'nobody said the Camden town bin bag murders [were] an example of "white on white" crime' (*The Guardian*, 8 January 2003).

*Gender differences* are culturally formed, and performed. Though they exist on the basis of biological classification, 'the body', they build a huge system of differentiation over and above it. So whereas your sex will determine broadly whether or not you can bear a child (though even this is not a universal truth), some gendered positions have taken a huge second step. They insist that *because* women bear children, they should be the ones to stay at home and bring them up. 'It's only natural,' says a whole social system of laws, tax and work arrangements, childcare – and media discourses.

Feminist studies of gender roles seem to show *both* that there have been huge changes in attitudes to gender difference, and that these co-exist alongside longstanding cultural discourses and stereotypes. Media changes might include the attitudes to sexuality, gender, ethnicity and disability revealed, or perhaps performed, in popular programmes such as *Big Brother* (Channel 4 2000–) and their accompanying blogs. The *Big Brother* victory, in 2004, of a transsexual called Nadia, of Portuguese origin, suggested public attitude changes, at least in the viewers of that series. Perhaps as important, for the first time ever a woman, Jacqui Oatley, commentated on male soccer matches on UK TV in 2007.

But such advances co-exist with limited representation of women in the most prestigious levels of news. For example, in election reporting (see Ross 2004), a woman has yet to run the key General Election night coverage on a major UK channel. Employment (and redundancy) statistics within the media remain stubbornly and unevenly gendered. 'Hollywood', despite its liberal image, and its importance as a source of gendered global imagery and media practices, shows huge gender employment imbalance. In 2008, women comprised 16 per cent of all directors, executive producers, producers, writers, cinematographers and editors working on the top 250 domestic grossing films. This represents a decline of 3 per cent from 2001, and an increase of just 1 per cent from 2007 (see Lauzen 2009).

One fascinating area of representation is: where and when is a category ignored? This can be particularly revealing in the area of gender. Katz (2006) points to newspaper accounts of US school massacres, or road rage incidents – overwhelmingly committed by males, but the stories are overwhelmingly ungendered. Often they simply speak of 'the Columbine killers' or 'road rage drivers', thus ignoring discussion of violent masculinities, and thereby naturalising them. Another example: in the past few years there has been media anxiety about some boys' exam results not matching girls' – but hardly any comment for all the years when the reverse was often the case. Gender then was not seen as an issue, it went 'unmarked'.

Gendered representation also works with taken-for-granted textual habits. Especially powerful within audio-visual media is 'the look'. The ground-breaking work of John Berger (1972), Erving Goffman (1979) and Laura Mulvey (1975) suggested that women have learned to see themselves as being 'looked at'. This has accumulated through, and outside, countless cultural forms and power structures, from classical art forms to Hollywood cinema and beyond. Men, however, have been represented as mostly the ones who do the active looking, along with other kinds of socially valued and purposeful action.

Mulvey's work explored this for certain Hollywood films of the 1950s and 1960s, mostly male-centred ones. She argued that three interlocking system of looks in cinema can be seen as 'male', and as constructing women characters as 'to be looked at' instead of the subject of the action. These looks go

- from camera to characters;
- between the characters on screen;
- between viewers and screen.

Much has changed since then, including Mulvey's own views on 'the look'. She later (1981) wrote of having ignored both lesbian desire in viewers, and also films which centred on women.

Other theorists have explored the changing relations of men to 'the look' (see During 2005). From the 1980s onwards, advertisers, seeking to expand consumption, sought to make men feel they should take an interest in appearance-related consumer goods (from stylish clothes to haircare) previously defined as 'feminine'. In order to do this, ads needed to display desirable male bodies, an increased display which has arguably legitimised not only women looking with desire, but also male-on-male looking and same-sex desire.

> See Chapter 3 for an account of Hollywood and other 'romance' forms, often assuming largely female audiences, and operating a different set of 'looks' (more focus on the face, eyes, and less on the sexualised body) as well as central rather than secondary narrative roles for women characters and stars.

## EXPLORE 4.6

Interestingly it was reported in 2009 that the men's magazine *FHM* UK sales had been overtaken by those of *Men's Health* magazine.

*Men's Fitness* is a similar magazine. Analyse the latest cover, taking Mulvey's suggestions as guide.

- How is the look given, and received by the model?
- Is the male a 'sex object' in the same ways that some female pin-ups are?
- What does this involve – pose? look to camera? sexualised bodily display?

*Figure 4.5* *Men's Fitness* magazine

'The pink cotton T-shirt's lettering reads: "So many boys, so little time." . . . But . . . this T-shirt is a "5–6 years" size . . . What about the thong for 7 year olds . . . or the padded bra for a 9-year old?' (Christina Odone, 'Sexy Kids', *New Statesman*, 15 July 2002). See http://www.pinkstinks.co.uk.

*Figure 4.6* A 2009 controversial shot of 20-year-old model Lizzie Miller, said to be 'overweight' because of the small roll of fat round her middle. She had hundreds of messages of support, and of relief at seeing a 'normal' body in such contexts.

**I'll be a post-feminist in post-patriarchy**

*Figure 4.7* A relevant Leeds postcard. Some would argue that we are now living in 'neopatriarchy', in both Arab and Western societies. Google the term, and see if you agree.

Whatever approach we take to current gender imagery, it appears hugely contradictory. As Ros Gill (2006) suggests:

- 'confident' expressions of 'girl power' (pole dancing?) are displayed alongside reports of 'epidemic' levels of anorexia and body dysmorphia;
- graphic tabloid reports of rape are placed alongside adverts for lap-dancing clubs and phone sex lines;
- the ages at which young girls are addressed as sexual beings, who need to be aware of their appearance and dress, seems to get ever younger;
- the re-sexualisation of women's bodies, often displayed in public space, and in near-soft-porn forms, goes comparatively unremarked – except by those from other, less 'liberated' cultures.

Many women feel that the balance of representation has tilted back, towards sexist images and language, and that this is not 'liberation' but **'retro-sexism'**. The 'alibi' use of irony ('I was only joking. No sense of humour?'); the 'laddishness' of music radio (including some female presenters), or magazines like *FHM*; the use of women in traditionally 'sex object' poses with 'playful' captions – all seem to point to this.

The term '*post-feminism*' suggests that women are now 'beyond' the need to struggle for gender equality: 'postmodern' playfulness or irony is said to be the proper response to all that. Young women are said to take for granted equal pay, contraception and the other freedoms struggled for by earlier feminists. 'Freedoms' are now defined differently, in consumerist terms – 'post-feminists love shopping/have plastic surgery/go binge drinking like the men'. Meanwhile persistent inequalities of pay and job opportunities, as well as women's anxieties about their body shapes, are ignored.

### EXPLORE 4.7

Q: Have you come across the term '*post-feminism*'? How adequate do you find it to describe women's experiences now? Might '*retro-sexism*' be a better term?

Q: How far can such images of women always be read ironically?

Q: Research and discuss the arguments around what has been called 'the pinkification' of young girls' dress, shops and culture in recent years. You could start with www.pinkstinks.co.uk.

## Stages of change, and 'positive/negative' debates

We've suggested how history shapes and changes some scripts and stereotypes. Once an oppressed group, such as people of colour, perceives its political and social oppression, it begins to try to change that oppression. This occurs *at the level of representation as well as at other levels*. Those seeking to change imagery have argued, first, simply for more images of a particular group, using a simple 'reflection' model. Then, in the early stage of 'getting a voice', they may try to achieve more stories which centre sympathetically on their group, as opposed to ones where they often feature as villainous or untrustworthy 'types'. These may be the result of violent historical processes, including wars or colonialism, which have left a legacy of hate-filled, insulting or trivialising images. There are long histories to this kind of stereotyping of ethnic 'others' – Mexicans or Native Americans in westerns, Arabs and Muslims in contemporary Hollywood.

Once such visibility is achieved, it is often argued that more 'positive' portrayals are needed. But how to replace 'negative' with 'positive' images? It sounds simple, but raises complex issues, involving:

- how to define the 'community' being represented – usually huge and complex 'communities' such as 'women'(?) 'Muslims'(?);
- what are to count, for whom, as 'positive' representations; and
- the effect of employment practices such as discrimination.

Let's take the last point first. Groups that are negatively stereotyped (as 'problems' or even 'potential terrorists') are likely to have less access to influential positions in the media or to other kinds of power. This can set up a vicious circle of unemployment, and of lack of pressure on news rooms, etc. from inside to represent certain issues. In the case of asylum seekers it may even be the case that they dare not be photographed or quoted by name, for fear of reprisals (see case study to this chapter). When images of the group do begin to be produced, they have to bear what has been called the **burden of representation**. This involves questions such as:

- What is *assumed to be* the reality of the group which is demanding adequate representation? Most groups large enough to make such demands are not homogeneous (think of the differences clumped together under the term 'students'). Which group members have the power to define what is positive and what is negative about an image? The success of the BBC series *Goodness Gracious Me* (UK 1998–2001; see the 'Let's go for an English' sketch on *YouTube*) and its spin-offs can be seen as part of a claim of younger British Asians to define their own group(s), sometimes in opposition to the 'better-behaved' images of an older, more threatened generation.

Such stages are not neatly gone through, and done with. They often co-exist with later kinds of representation. Lesbians have remained relatively invisible within popular cultural forms, despite apparently 'ground-breaking' series such as *Ellen* (US 1994–98) and *Xena: Warrior Princess* (US 1995–2001).

'. . . negative behavior by any member of the oppressed community is instantly generalized as typical . . . Representations of dominant groups [however] are seen not as allegorical but as "naturally" diverse . . . A corrupt white politician is not seen as an "embarrassment to the race" . . .' (Shohat and Stam 1994: 183).

- How to construct characters belonging to the group (particularly visible in the case of skin colour) if they have been relatively absent from media images previously? This can mean that when they do appear they are read as 'representing' the whole community, with the huge expectation they will help make it respectable. This is a real burden to those trying to construct new images and stories/scripts.

For many years there were very few images of 'black British' people on television, and those images which did exist were of 'blacks' as 'problems' or (more sympathetic, if patronising) as 'victims'. When black characters *did* appear, they were often felt to need to 'stand in for' or *represent* the whole of their particular 'community'. These 'positive' images often consisted of strict parents, noble teachers, respectable corner-shop keepers and so on – clearly a narrowing of the range of representation compared with the roles available to white characters. As a result, some members of such groups felt that, paradoxically, being represented in various and ordinary, even 'negative', ways might be a positive step.

> 'Pictures of perfection make me sick and wicked' (Jane Austen, novelist, in a letter, 1817).

> According to BARB, the UK audience ratings body, *EastEnders* is the third most popular series among ethnic minorities, behind *The X Factor* and *Britain's Got Talent*.

*EastEnders'* variety of non-white characters has often been controversial – some involved in petty crime, some coping with family difficulties and so on – and argued to be a kind of advance in representation.

The first Muslim family was introduced from 1987 to 1990, followed by another, much criticised family, the Ferreiras (2003–5). Prior to 2007, *EastEnders* had been heavily criticised by the Commission for Racial Equality (CRE) for not representing the East End's real 'ethnic make-up'. It was suggested that the average proportion of visible minority faces on *EastEnders* was substantially lower than the actual ethnic minority population in East London boroughs, reflecting the East End of the 1960s, not the East End of the 2000s. A production team member on *EastEnders* writes: 'The previous Asian family, the Ferreiras, were criticised as boring and unrealistic – their first names were a mixture of Muslim and Hindu, their surname was Portuguese . . . We played safe with them and didn't give them good storylines . . .' (Khan 2009).

Yet there will often be a tug of war between the requirements of a character and the ways that characters always have a 'socially representative' aspect. This latter aspect is keenly watched by groups (sometimes globally, and via internet comment) who may feel they are being misrepresented. In 2008, for example, a Muslim character, Masood, was shown eating during the

Ramadan fasting hours. Around a hundred viewers complained. The BBC argued that 'although Masood is a practising Muslim, he is not intended to be representative of the British Muslim experience. He's a fictional character who realises he has let himself down in a moment of weakness.' More recently the soap has run a romantic storyline centred on a Muslim character who has discovered his gayness, a risk for the serial, though not for its ratings: the soap's first gay Muslim kiss attracted 7.9 million viewers (see Holmwood 2009). In the same family a 2009 storyline featured Zainab (the Masoods' mother and a small businesswoman). In her mid-forties, with three children, two grown-up, she stated her wish not to continue with an unexpected pregnancy, shocking her husband and herself, since Islam does not support a woman's right to choose to have an abortion.

To summarise: 'negative' images are not always best opposed by (someone's idea of) 'positive', but by the availability of a range of fuller ways of being imagined, both by others and within the group itself.

> See the *EastEnders* website which has a special section devoted to the charities which have been consulted and often involved in various storylines: one way to think about social 'representation' and individualised characters.

There is another, quite different attitude towards 'positive' and 'negative'. Members of some groups may have good grounds for surliness, and for lack of co-operation with a social system or situation, such as that of slaves in US plantation conditions pre-1870. What if they are represented 'positively', as always smiling and whistling contentedly at their lot? They may well wonder whether this image is 'positive' only for those who want to be reassured that all is well with an unjust set-up.

Sometimes members of heavily stereotyped groups have responded by taking on the denigrated identity that an abusive nickname gives them. Examples would be black people calling themselves 'niggers', or gays calling themselves 'queens' and 'sissies', 'dykes' and 'fems'.

> For the importance of such representations consider this: 'I know of gay men who have been murdered in "honour killings" – in fact, the police often contact our sexual health organisation if there is an unexplained death of a young Muslim man to check if he is on our database' (Ibrahim, charity worker: Holmwood 2009).

> 'I like the sissy [stereotype of gay men]. Is it used in "negative" ways? Yeah. But my view has always been: visibility at any cost. Negative is better than nothing' (Harvey Fierstein in Russo 1981).

## EXPLORE 4.8

There is heated debate about whether people outside such groups have the right to apply derogatory labels.

- Explore Sacha Baron Cohen's various impersonations of the extreme characteristics often attributed to certain groups (and see Chapter 13).
- Do you think, as often claimed, he is 'really' satirising bigoted responses to these groups? What evidence would you draw on in your debate/reply?

> 'What I want is a film which is a gay love story where the love and not the gayness is the point. And where one or other person in the relationship does not have to die or be punished by the narrative.' Paul Burston, gay editor of *Time Out*, at Cardiff Iris event, 10 October 2009. See his writings in *Time Out*.

There is no such thing as the '100 per cent right-on' text or 'positive image' which is guaranteed to challenge hostile audiences all on its own. We have to understand images within particular histories, both of the media and more broadly, as well as through the complicated 'refractions' of different media forms.

The call for 'realism' arises when the media are assumed to reflect society, like a mirror, rather than re-present, let alone 'refract' it. Some degree of accuracy is understandably demanded by groups which have previously been invisible, or violently misrepresented. But how successful the call for more realism will be depends very much on, firstly, the power of the group seeking it, or seeking to avoid it. The case study to this chapter deals with one of the least powerful groups in most societies, and some ways in which they are often 'unrepresentable'.

But for groups such as the richest in society, invisibility and privacy is a key privilege. Paparazzi live off this set-up, and some celebrities collaborate with it. In 2009 it was striking how elusive and relatively invisible were, for example, the private arrangements, residences, etc. of top bankers, whose actions were a major contributory cause of global recession and unemployment. The story slipped off the front pages relatively quickly, and was replaced by stories of the shocking, but much smaller corruption of some MPs. The hounding of a so-called 'underclass' of 'chavs' and so on continued as usual, and seems now routine in some British media (see Chapter 6).

Representations are also shaped by the kinds or genres of media in which groups are *likely* to feature. This raises questions such as:

a How do different genres affect the demand for 'realism'? What of the needs of exaggerated character types for comedy or fantasy, for example?

b Are stereotypes replayed and used in exaggerated ways as they become familiar, so that they do not necessarily work to hostile ends but 'fly free' of the referent for the sake of comic pleasures?

c How does this process combine with older, less humorous and more limiting ways of imagining the group, which can suddenly resurface?

A simple call for 'realism' may ignore the fact that media texts do not have a straightforward relationship to the rest of the real. They may belong to a form (e.g. computer games) which is not experienced by audiences in the same way as, say, news or current affairs. Indeed some would argue that the need for games to 'immerse' their players in a world means issues such as how characters are 'represented' do not arise. Users' degrees of familiarity with a form's conventions will influence its 'reality effect' for them, and what they take for granted,

Asylum seekers often need to hide their identity, which makes adequate self-representation difficult. People from outside such groups will sometimes work with, and on behalf of, those denied representation, in both politics and media. See the 1950s and 1960s US Civil Rights movement for earlier examples of important calls for realism.

indeed, want to play with in order to obtain its pleasures. Equally, the skilled performance of a game itself can be part of a self-representation. See Dovey and Kennedy (2006: 119) on the pleasure taken by female players in mastery of some games, seen as requiring skills which are 'masculine'.

## Comedy, fantasy and questions of representation

The idea of images as *reflecting* reality is far too straightforward and mirror-like, especially for comedy and fantasy forms. It suggests there is a fairly simple thing called 'reality' to be 'reflected' in a one-to-one, undistorted glass.

Comedy also seems to *depend* on the exaggerations of stereotyping, understood playfully by audiences, and not always as a 'reflection' of 'the real' (see Medhurst 2007). Dafydd ('I'm the only gay in the village') in *Little Britain* (BBC 2003–4), for example, is a complex combination of ludicrous pouting presence and rubber costume, and a readiness to take offence. The character's 'failure' to realise how acceptable or indeed common it is to be gay now is the heart of the joke. The whole character, like many others in the series, such as the delinquent teenager 'Vicky Pollard' ('No but yeah but yeah but yeah but no . . .') seems to assume an audience which will feel superior to supposedly 'outmoded' prejudice about such figures. For some this will shade into a less attractive self-congratulation at the show's own knowingness, or a feeling that the sketch is premature in suggesting the death of homophobia – 'all in Dafydd's mind' – or of contempt for some working-class women (see Chapter 6).

> Explore how *Gavin and Stacey* (BBC 2007–10) works with stereotypes of Welshness, for example via the 'refraction' of the OTT performance of Ruth Jones as Nessa, and the twist that the lustfulness, for once, belongs to a female working-class Welsh character.

Or take the joke form. When the late Les Dawson delivered the line: 'I knew it was the mother-in-law 'cause when they heard her coming, the mice started throwing themselves on the traps' there were several pleasures on offer:

- his delivery, gravelly northern voice and timing, especially as contrasted with
- the verbal surprise of the exaggeration – the image of those mice!
- the verbal elegance of a concise, well-crafted joke, well delivered.

However, the joke's elegance also works because a quickly recognisable stereotype is in play (the 'mother-in-law'). This offers speedy recognition, but also involves, through this 'community' of shared laughter, a feeling of 'we'-ness and a 'them'-ness for a moment. It's worth pausing to consider:

Q: From whose point of view is it being told? Whose is excluded? Who is the 'them' or 'her' outside this cosy community?

Q: How is the group on the receiving end of the joke treated in the rest of the media? Does that change the experience of the joke?

To make this last point clearer: in the case of mothers-in-law, we may feel OK to laugh, since this is rather an outdated target. Changes in family structures have eroded the power of mothers-in-law of many working-class couples, who had to live in 'her' home for the first few years of married life. Maybe the degree of exaggeration itself signals the joke's distance from reality. To put it in semiotic language: pleasure is more from the play of the signifiers than from agreement with the way the sign signifies or represents its referent. It's a good example of the *refraction* which occurs in such forms.

However, you might feel differently if you were an older woman, and the object of many contemptuous jokes and comedy sketches. Or you might not, if age were only a relatively unimportant one of your several identities. But when jokes centre on groups who are being abused on the street, or in the home, for whom there may be fewer alternative 'communities of feeling' or media images to enter into, it becomes a much less easy thing to laugh along with them.

> An even older resonance: Propp's study worked with fairy tales from hundreds of years ago when many women would die in childbirth, and the role of ('wicked'?) stepmothers could therefore be a shared reference point for audiences. See Chapter 2.

## EXPLORE 4.9

- Can you think of a recent joke to which you might apply the same analysis?
- Are there any circumstances in which you would feel you should not laugh at a joke you found 'funny'? Can you apply to it the approach to Les Dawson used above? How might you relate the film *Brüno* to this debate?

The internet has made a difference to many kinds of oppression. Paul Burston of *Time Out* cited a young relative living in a fairly remote rural village where he dare not come out as gay – and might have never done so twenty years ago.

But now he can join groups of shared interest on Facebook and other sites.

## Historical and institutional processes

Debates over representation cannot be restricted simply to the level of textual analysis. They need to understand contexts such as media institutions, and their different processes and relationships to the rest of the real world. Historical changes widen (or narrow) imaginings, and struggles over media images are a key part of this.

- One of the achievements of the US black Civil Rights struggles in the 1950s and 1960s, or of environmental movements now, is to have put on the agenda different images of US ethnicity, and of 'lifestyle scripts' which are less consumerism-centred than dominant ones.

- The needs of capitalist entertainment industries to make profits in ever more fragmented markets inevitably lead to constant and unpredictable changes in the images offered to groups for self-representation, especially in internet forms. It remains true, though, that this is often within the limits of assumed purchasing power. The 'pink pound' was a key factor in persuading advertisers that they could target some affluent gay audiences, and thereby, eventually, shift images of gay identities. For poorer groups (such as long-term unemployed or asylum seekers) the prospects for changing images have to lie elsewhere, sometimes in alliances with sympathetic members of dominant groups.

- Changes to employment patterns in media industries, often as a result of affirmative action or equal opportunities policies, mean that, wherever possible, people from particular groups (defined through ethnicity, or gender, or perhaps disability, for example) are appointed to jobs *if their suitability is more or less equivalent to that of other candidates*. These can be 'positive' in helping to produce expectations and role models other than the (perhaps unspoken) conviction that 'women or working-class northerners can't do that work because I've never seen one doing it'.

  Affirmative action may also open up a newsroom or a drama unit to workplace discussions and experiences which may be remote from its usual experience. If people with disabilities work in a newsroom, it makes it harder to resort to the stereotype that 'disabled people are always helpless victims'. Several 'Black British' journalists have commented that racist headlines in 'red-top' papers would be harder to justify in the newsroom if there were more non-white British journalists employed there. The same may not be as true of internet forms.

> Imagery and employment are interestingly linked by Ben Stephenson, BBC Controller of Drama Commissioning (Khan 2009): 'The more on-screen we can do with minorities, the more those groups will feel like television is a realistic part of their experience and therefore a career option for them.'

*Figure 4.8* Cerrie Burnell

### Images of disabilities

Research from Cardiff University in 2009 found that, in a year's worth of programmes, an average of only 6.5 people a week with facial disfigurements were shown on TV.

However, there have been some striking developments in other areas of disability. The BBC's use of Frank Gardner, badly injured in a gun attack in Saudi Arabia in 2004, is a fine example of how to deploy such an expert foreign correspondent. Cutaway shots to him in his wheelchair, after one of his lucid analyses, often come as a shock to those who first see them.

Signing, on some TV programmes, already addresses deaf viewers. CBeebies' presenter Cerrie Burnell was born with one arm. She was subjected to letters from a small but vocal minority of viewers objecting to having their children 'scared' by her image, though one writer said how pleased his son was to see someone resembling himself on TV.

- Broadening of access to Web 2.0, and older, dissenting mechanisms has also been important. News forms have always had power to circulate hostile images of groups and individuals. Those targeted have had far less power to circulate their replies, or position them prominently. They have often been discredited by unfounded allegations, without access to expensive lawyers.

But there were huge internet protests in 2009 against the *Daily Mail* article by Jan Moir, calling the death of Stephen Gately, a singer with Boyzone, 'unnatural' and linking it to his sexuality. These protests were largely co-ordinated by Twitter messaging, and meant the Press Complaints Commission site crashed under a record number of complaints. See Charlie Brooker's angry, funny and brilliant reply to Moir at http://www.guardian.co.uk/commentisfree/2009/oct/16/stephen-gately-jan-moir.

*Figure 4.9* Stephen Gately (1976–2009)

### Conclusion

There are many examples of the media systematically narrowing imagery of particular groups, even of deliberately misrepresenting or under-representing them, especially in fiction forms. The concepts of discourse (discussed more fully in Chapters 6 and 15) and of scripts, stories and stereotyping are useful here.

But we have argued against the suggestion that the media have huge powers *all on their own*, simply at the textual level, to socialise people into beliefs, roles and behaviour. We have also questioned simple uses of 'representation', suggesting that 'refraction' and 're-mediation' usefully enrich the concept. And we suggest that rigid uses of the term 'stereotype' need to be avoided.

We hope you will find all these approaches more useful than ones which tend to automatically distrust, and thus simplify, the richness as well as the power of media representations.

## References and further reading

Antler, Joyce (2007) *You Never Call, You Never Write!*, Oxford: Oxford University Press.

Berger, John (1972) *Ways of Seeing*, Harmondsworth: Penguin.

Bignell, Jonathan (2004) *An Introduction to Television Studies*, London: Routledge.

Bogle, Donald (2003, anniversary edition) *Toms, Coons, Mulattoes, Mammies and Bucks: An Interpretative History of Blacks in American Films*, New York: Continuum.

Branston, Gill (1984) *Film and Gender*, London: Film Education.

Briggs, Adam, and Cobley, Paul (eds) (2002) *The Media: An Introduction*, 2nd edn, Harlow: Longman.

Campbell, Duncan (2001) 'Hollywood Still Prefers Men', *The Guardian*, 5 December.

Deacon, David, Pickering, Michael, Golding, Peter, and Murdock, Graham (2007) *Researching Communications: A Practical Guide to Media and Cultural Analysis*, 2nd edn, London: Arnold.

Dovey, Jan, and Kennedy, Helen W. (2006) *Game Cultures*, London and New York: Open University Press.

During, Simon (2005) 'Feminism's Aftermath: Gender Today', in *Cultural Studies: A Critical Introduction*, London: Routledge, Chapter 6.

Durkin, Kevin (1985) *Television, Sex Roles and Children*, Milton Keynes: Open University Press.

Gill, Ros (2006) *Gender and the Media*, Cambridge: Polity Press.

Goffman, Erving (1959) *The Presentation of Self in Everyday Life*, Garden City, NY: Doubleday.

Goffman, Erving (1979) *Gender Advertising*, London: Macmillan.

Hite, Shere (1998) *The Hite Report on Women and Love: A Cultural Revolution in Progress*, London: Viking.

Holmwood, Leigh (2009) 'TV Ratings: Gay Kiss Lifts EastEnders to Nearly 8m', *The Guardian*, 22 June.

Katz, Jackson (2006) *Violence, Media and the Crisis in Masculinity*, MEF Amherst, available through *YouTube*.

Khan, Yasmeen (2009) 'The Right Ethnic Mix', *MediaGuardian*, 22 June.

Lauzen, Martha (2009) 'The Celluloid Ceiling in 2008: Behind-the-Scenes Employment of Women in the Top 250 Films of 2008', http://www.womenarts.org.

Lister, Martin, Dovey, Jon, Giddings, Seth, Grant, Iain, and Kelly, Kieran (2009) *New Media: A Critical Introduction*, 2nd edn, London and New York: Routledge.

Medhurst, Andy (2007) *A National Joke: Popular Comedy and English Cultural Identities*, London and New York: Routledge.

Medhurst, Andy, and Munt, Sally R. (eds) (1997) *Lesbian and Gay Studies: A Critical Introduction*, London and Hendon: Cassell.

Mulvey, Laura (1975) 'Visual Pleasure and Narrative Cinema', reprinted in Mulvey, Laura (1989) *Visual and Other Pleasures*, London: Macmillan.

Mulvey, Laura (1981) 'Afterthoughts on *Visual Pleasure and Narrative Cinema* Inspired by King Vidor's *Duel in the Sun* (1946)', in Thornham, Sue (1999) (ed.) *Feminist Film Theory: A Reader*, Edinburgh: Edinburgh University Press.

Nunn, Heather, and Biressi, Anita (2009) 'The Undeserving Poor', *Soundings*, 41 (spring): 107–17.

Perkins, Tessa (2000) 'Who (and What) Is It For?', in Gledhill, Christine, and Williams, Linda (eds) *Reinventing Film Studies*, London and New York: Arnold.

Ross, Karen (2004) *Framed: Women, Politics and News Media*, Coventry: University Research Monograph.

Russo, Vito (1981) *The Celluloid Closet: Homosexuality in the Movies*, New York: Harper; paperback reprint 1987.

Shohat, Elaine, and Stam, Robert (1994) *Unthinking EuroCentrism: Multiculturalism and the Media*, London and New York: Routledge.

Wardle, Claire, and Boyce, Tammy (2009) *Media Coverage and Audience Reception of Disfigurement on TV*, Cardiff: The Healing Foundation and Cardiff University.

# CASE STUDY

# Images of migration

- DISCOURSES AND STEREOTYPES OF 'MIGRATION' AND OTHER KINDS OF TRAVEL
- NEWS MEDIA
- THE 'GRAIN OF TRUTH' IN STEREOTYPES?
- VARIETIES OF MEDIA REPRESENTATIONS
- CONCLUSION
- REFERENCES AND FURTHER READING

No representation can 'contain' more than a fraction of its real-world subject. In the case of migration and asylum seeking that 'referent' is enormous, elusive and hotly contested. Over the past five years many opinion polls indicate that UK, and some European, public attitudes towards asylum and immigration issues are generally, and increasingly, negative (Crawley 2009). These attitudes often lead to hostile behaviour and even attacks on immigrants. They also influence the content and direction of government policies and discourses – another kind of 'representation'.

Here we explore images of migration, asking:

- How are different migrating groups, or situations, represented, or under-represented in the media?
- Do some media *re*-present certain frames, images, words and 'scripts' over and over again, making certain discourses seem 'natural' and familiar?
- Does that help marginalise or even exclude other discourses?
- In what different media do such representations occur?

'Asylum seekers' are still, largely, at the first stage of struggles over representation, where there is a huge need simply to contest very limited and negative images, misinformation and prejudice. Let's first unpack the term a little.

**Who is an asylum seeker?** Anyone who has applied for asylum against persecution under the 1951 UN Convention on Refugees, and is waiting for a decision.

**Who is a refugee?** Anyone who has been granted asylum under the UN Convention (signed by the UK along with 144 other countries). The legal definition of 'refugee' is someone who, owing to a well-founded fear of being persecuted for reasons of race, religion, nationality, membership of a particular social group or political opinion, is outside the country of nationality, and is unable or, owing to such fear, is unwilling to obtain the protection of that country.

**Who is an illegal asylum seeker?** No one. It cannot be illegal to seek asylum: everyone has the fundamental human right to request asylum under international law. Even the term '*bogus asylum-seeker*' is misleading. It pre-judges the outcome of an asylum application – like describing a defendant as entering a 'bogus plea of innocence' during a trial. A more accurate term is '*failed asylum seeker*'.

**Who are 'illegals'?** Those who work without legal permits, for whatever reason. As a direct result they are often paid illegally low wages, and work in illegally poor conditions, sometimes organised by official 'gangmasters'. But such questions, also affecting other workers, are not the ones conjured by this word. Instead:

- it can be used to exploit fears of semi-criminal activities, such as prostitution and sex trafficking, drug dealing, theft – which do exist but are not confined to undocumented workers;
- the term '*illegals*' is often used as though it were the same as *asylum seekers*. In fact '*undocumented immigrants*' is probably a better term.

The Office of National Statistics, which records the net annual flows in and out of the UK, uses the terms '*in-migrants*' and '*out-migrants*'. And many prefer the term '*people flows*' for migratory moves.

## DISCOURSES AND STEREOTYPES OF 'MIGRATION' AND OTHER KINDS OF TRAVEL

Stereotypes, we argued, involve both a categorising and an evaluation of the group or activity being stereotyped. Like genres, they give the impression of absolute boundaries, though the idea of a spectrum or continuum of difference is more useful. In other words, they produce a narrow label for a large and unwieldy reality: 'southerners', 'northerners', 'football fans', 'students', 'immigrants'.

We've used the word 'migration' rather than 'immigration' to try to draw attention to different valuations given to the widespread movements of people to and fro, or 'people flow'. Migrations spark heated debates for different reasons: fears about unemployment, about globally mobile terrorist networks, as well as dislike of cultural practices like 'arranged marriages' and 'honour killings'. As reported in many media forms these can easily make exciting

and often misleading angles to all kinds of stories. They also ignore the ways in which other social groups may also have cultural practices which offend: fox hunting, large bonus cultures and so on.

### 'People flows'

Some journeys are represented positively, and are media-ted as 'natural', or even invisible. Tourists' journeys and students' 'gap year' travel are hardly ever seen as part of global 'people flows', though they are a key part of many economies, and may inspire later individual migrations. A historical example: the departure of the persecuted 'Pilgrim Fathers' from Britain to North America in the seventeenth century is rarely described as involving migrants.

Other large-scale journeys are not thus naturalised, let alone celebrated. Class is a key factor here, partly acknowledged in the use of the term 'economic migrants'. Broadly it has been said that if the journeys involve the poor they're called 'migration'; if they involve corporate executives, 'homes in the sun' or white, richer migrants, they are called 'relocation' and usually welcomed. Quite different discourses apply to high-paid executives leading semi-nomadic existences between different airports than do to women from poor countries who often have to abandon their families to work as nannies, sex workers or cleaners for wealthier families in rich countries. See Hochschild and Ehrenreich (2003: 4) for an account of this relatively undocumented global flow, a trade in what they call 'something that can look very much like love'.

The United Nations High Commission for Refugees (UNHCR) in 2009 was involved in work with 34 million people, including some 838,000 asylum seekers. Developing countries' predicaments produce most of the world's refugees. But they also provide asylum to most of them (see UNHCR website http://www.unhcr.org and also http://www.oxfamgb.org).

## EXPLORE 4.11

**Q:** How many kinds of 'people flow' have you and your family been part of?

Include holidays, or moving to go to university. Students are a huge part of global people flows.

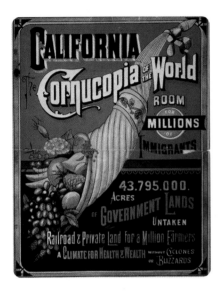

*Figure 4.10* Huge promises to 'immigrants' made in a nineteenth-century poster for the settlement (and sale) of parts of California. Climate guarantees included!

### Histories

'We are here because you were there' was the slogan of anti-racist campaigns in the UK in the 1980s.

The stereotypes of 'immigrants' resemble those of US slavery in some ways. By 'Other-ing' this group as utterly different, even inhuman, it becomes harder to ask obvious questions related to 'why?' People do not usually leave their homes on such long and dangerous journeys for trivial reasons. Even if they reach their destination, evidence suggests that many intend only a temporary stay in another country, and hope to return home once savings targets have been achieved. Complex issues arise: do modern states need to have

borders? What of the need for security against global terrorism, drug trafficking and so on?

Two more examples of absent histories:

a   The nation state of Pakistan ('a basket case', in the insulting language of some journalism) is partly a result of Britain, when it withdrew from imperial domination, dividing India into what it perceived as a largely Muslim state (Pakistan) and a largely Hindu state (India). How often is this mentioned in media treatment?

b   Global 'economic' migration patterns for the poor. Often these have been and are from within the same country – for example, Scots, Irish and Welsh migrations to wealthier England.

> The Welsh cultural theorist Raymond Williams used to tell of the class put-down his family used: 'Someone says his family came over with the Normans (i.e. are aristocratic) and we reply: "Are you liking it here?".' In *Politics and Letters* (1979) p. 36.

c   Somali 'pirates' make headlines, partly because of the exciting resonance of that word. But Somali fishermen (some of whom became 'pirates') had complained to the UN for years that illegal fishing by wealthier nations was driving them to the brink of economic collapse. Their coast had also become a nuclear waste dumping ground following a contract signed between local warlords and two European companies. Barrels of this toxic waste cracked open in the 2004 tsunami and waste washed ashore.

## EXPLORE 4.12

- Look at a week's news coverage of 'migration' issues.
- How much historical understanding is given as context for stories? Where? Which histories?

These huge 'back stories' are rarely adequately represented. One of the appeals of stereotypes is that they offer entertaining short-cuts through huge, complex and often painful sets of knowledge – for example, relations of inequality and dependency which it is disturbing to be reminded of. It becomes difficult to point out that migrants, working in low-paid jobs, often contribute *more* to hospitable countries in taxes, etc. than they take from them.

## NEWS MEDIA

News discourses and images of migration are key here, especially the choice of terms used in news headlines. A related part of news values (see Chapter 12) suggests that once a 'story', or theme, or set of 'scripts', is established as controversial or 'newsworthy' it tends to achieve further headline status more easily. Headlines often ignore the possibility that migrants might have anything to offer to the host country. As with celebrity coverage, alibi phrases like 'we hear that . . .' or 'there are fears that . . .' mean that almost anything can be alleged. Key words are repeated – 'swamping', 'stampeding', 'overrun', 'asylum capital of the world', 'flooding', 'tide', 'wave', 'sponging' and so on. These both dehumanise migrants and lock into (near-racist) rhetoric of Britain as a proud 'island race'.

### EXPLORE 4.14

- How much do your friends think an asylum seeker ('sponger') receives in state benefits? (According to a 2000 Mori poll most people believed this to be more than £110 per week.)

As of October 2009 the weekly rate for a single asylum seeker, aged over twenty-five, destitute and asking for support is £35.13 a week. It is justified because 'asylum seekers . . . typically live in UK Border Agency accommodation and so have no housing cost, or water, gas and electricity bills' (UK Border Agency). They are not allowed to work while waiting for decisions on their case.

### EXPLORE 4.13

Examine the next article you come across which raises migrant fears.
- List the key terms it uses and repeats, especially in the headline. What choices have been made?
- How is asylum seeking *framed?* What larger contexts are given, or withheld, such as the conditions being fled from? Which facts or statistics are used? Which organisations are quoted?
- How are photos used? Is it true that most images of asylum seekers are:
  - absent, replaced by images of UK government officials?
  - images of men, reinforcing the notion that the majority of asylum seekers are lone males? (UNHCR states that 49 per cent of 'persons of concern' to them are women, and 44 per cent of asylum seekers and refugees are children.)
  - not local to the area of Britain featured in the article?
- If the article is in a local paper, has there been any attempt to help local people imagine the plight, appearance, abilities, families of those written about?
- Are there any photos of families, in familiar, unthreatening work or home situations?
- Is there any sign that the reporters are 'on the spot' if the story concerns a British town?

The lure of a striking headline, and the brevity of responsible analysis in many stories, can mean that key information is ignored and thereby goes unrepresented – this borders on rendering a powerless group invisible. Misleading headlines in newsagents' shops, and online editions, are seen by many more people than buy or read the papers displaying them. So a retraction of downright misrepresentation (much later, and much less prominently positioned in the newspaper or website) is a very poor substitute for thoughtful and accurate journalism.

Bodies like the Refugee Council (http://www.refugeecouncil.org.uk, in their section 'Basics on asylum') attempt to correct the misrepresentations:

a   Applications for asylum are made in writing, so it is hard to justify the language of 'stampedes', conjuring a vision of panicking animals. Many more families than the Home Office expected await decisions for more than three years (2005) – again, hardly a 'stampede'.

b   In 2008, far from being the 'asylum capital of the world', the UK was ranked seventeenth in the table of industrialised countries for the number of asylum applications per head of population.

## THE 'GRAIN OF TRUTH' IN STEREOTYPES?

We argued that stereotypes take a recognisable feature of a group, put it at the centre of the image, and then go on to suggest it is always true of the entire group, and is even the cause of their situation.

Asylum seekers, like many powerless groups, are often ridiculed or even physically attacked because they cannot afford as much, or cannot access the same resources, as most of the rest of the host population. Negative images take the *results* of this deprivation, whether that be appearance, or difficulties with language, or desperation for money, or even a resort to crime. They put these at the centre of the description, as the *cause* of the group's situation. *All* asylum seekers are over and over again implied *by their nature* to be *always* on the look-out for scams or even criminal possibilities. This 'inherent' nature is then blamed for their predicament.

## EXPLORE 4.15

Imagine you are working on a popular soap such as *EastEnders*. You want to begin a storyline about either asylum seeking or economic migrants.

• How would you go about it? Which existing character would be the link to the new one? What would be the 'line': family relationship? illness? need to hide? employment?

• What problems might arise for casting, tone, gender and age issues, and possible religious and political controversy? How would you manage racist internet blogs? Jot down how these *refractions* might help account for the relative absence of such storylines in soaps.

**Example:** *Coronation Street* (spring 2007) began a politically sensitive storyline with an illegal immigration theme centring on Polish workers (who turned out to be 'legal') at the factory. It included a police raid after a disgruntled tip-off which turned out to be unreliable.

### Discussion points

I   If you plan for your asylum seeker character to become an integrated and popular character in the soap community, you might be accused of 'being PC ('politically correct'). However, if you plan to have them treated with suspicion, you might be accused of marginalising them. This conflict between soap opera role and the socially representative nature of key characters (as 'white British', 'female', 'asylum seeker', etc.) needs much better understanding.

2  Long-running hospital serials offer different possibilities, not least because new characters

    a  do not need to be introduced via an existing character.

    b  have an already existing degree of sympathy as patients in need of help.

**Example:** The BBC series *Holby City* in 2008 ran a long-running plot strand where a doctor became deeply involved with the plight of a pair of Korean asylum seekers, one of whom was pregnant with conjoined twins.

## EXPLORE 4.16

Repeat 4.14 above but locate your characters in a hospital serial.

## VARIETIES OF MEDIA REPRESENTATIONS

Different groups view migration differently: some may oppose migration for fear of worsened housing conditions, erosion of 'British national identity', criminal activity, 'swamping' via birth rates and so on. On the

### Example: 'The Irish'

Historically, groups who are hungry and hunted, with different cultures and traditions, have often been negatively imaged by the cultures they enter as (im)migrants. Terry Eagleton's exploration of stereotypes of nineteenth-century Irish immigrants argued against the perception that 'all Irish are lazy'. He suggested instead that many Irish immigrants fled from their small farms to the industrial cities of Victorian Britain in the wake of the Great Famine. (This 'famine' itself was partly the result of unfair trade arrangements, though the words 'Great Famine' make it sound biblical and therefore 'sent from God'.) Since the rural Irish poor were accustomed to a less crippling work discipline than their British counterparts, 'this could look like indolence, since their lives as small tenant farmers involved sporadic bursts of labour, but a fair bit of leisure too, with much enjoyment of fairs and feast-days' (Eagleton 2000).

British history later produced 'the Paddy' stereotype out of the men recruited for the backbreaking work of building nineteenth-century roads and railways, and also the abiding sense of the love of sociability and language which could be said to come from a largely rural society.

*Figure 4.11* A postcard satirising the anti-Irish racism of comedians (like Bernard Manning or Jim Davidson) by placing one against a wall of names of famous, even 'classic' Irish writers.

other hand, many employers may favour, or turn a blind eye to, the recruitment of illegally low-paid migrant workers. These conflicting pressures on governments make for mixed messages in immigration policies, let alone their refraction in media forms.

Not all news forms will take a hostile line. The liberal broadsheet press (*The Guardian, Independent*, etc.) will often follow up stories in sympathetic ways, as will some current affairs programmes on TV. Soaps like *EastEnders* have tried to broaden representations of British 'ethnic' groups. And some very popular comedians have arisen partly out of the experience of longer-established migrants to Britain.

British comedians (Omid Djalili, Shappi Khorsandi and Shazia Mirza) explore, in stand-up, radio, theatre and print, their experiences of Britain (see YouTube for sketches). In the case of British-Iranian Djalili this has gone along with a successful career in films such as *Gladiator* (US/UK 2000) and *The Mummy*, often, as he indicates, playing the OTT kinds of 'Orientalist' figures which his comedy undermines. As part of this self-representation, here's what Mirza, a British-Pakistani, wrote on some of her recent experiences:

> I may as well go back to where I came from. Which I'd say is Birmingham, but the BNP says is Rawalpindi . . . Nick Griffin was asked . . . how you could tell if someone was British. He said: 'You just look and you just know.' . . . In the past ten days I have been in Amsterdam, Cyprus and Paris [and] have been mistaken for French, Italian, Spanish, Malaysian and Egyptian. I was once even mistaken for an Indian (that really annoyed me!) . . .
>
> The irony is that there is no one more British than the Pakistanis I grew up with in Birmingham. I know women who wear Union Jack G-strings underneath their saris, young lads who can't eat chicken biryani without HP Sauce, and kids who have halal turkey on Christmas Day.

Such work resembles the confident, OTT play of comic TV series like *Goodness Gracious Me* (see the famous

'Going for an English' sketch, parodying the ways many British people treat Indian food when they 'go for an Indian'). It is a very different stage of representation to that of asylum seekers, who often dare not be filmed, photographed or quoted by name, for fear of reprisals in their homelands, or having their applications turned down, or of causing friction in their family or community, here or in their country of origin. This raises hard questions of 'representability' (see main Chapter 4).

## Film resources and close textual analysis

Many images of 'migrants' represent them as victims, which they often resent, especially given their often courageous initiative in travelling across continents from their desperate circumstances. Novels such as *The Road Home* or certain films can 'open out' such experiences. *Dirty Pretty Things* (UK 2002) and *Bread and Roses* (UK/US/Germany 2000) both focused on migrants employed as cleaners in corporate offices and hotels; *Maria Full of Grace* (US/Colombia 2004) centred on Colombian drug 'mules' and what drives people to such work. British TV series have included *Britz* (Channel 4 2006 – see website), a thriller about 'two Muslim siblings pulled in radically different ways', one of whom becomes a suicide bomber.

*Figure 4.12 Persepolis* (France/USA 2007), based on the director's graphic novel, is about a young Iranian girl growing up in regime-change Iran and fleeing to Paris.

Let's explore one sympathetic film in more detail: *In This World* (UK 2002), a drama-documentary following the perilous journey to Britain, from a huge refugee camp in Pakistan, of two Afghani asylum seekers, Jamal, aged about fourteen, and his older cousin, Enayat. The director, Michael Winterbottom, was partly moved to make it by a 2001 news story of fifty-eight Chinese immigrants found suffocated in a container at Dover. Here is a brief account of a key scene. Try to apply this approach to other texts if you find them striking in their representation of 'scripts' or situations you have not, and are probably not likely to, ever had to act out.

For part of their journey the two central characters, Jamal and Enayat, need to travel to Italy in a container lorry, illegally, having paid scarce money for transport. The journey becomes a nightmare; shortage of air, food and water leads to the death of Enayat and several others. When they arrive in Trieste, Jamal staggers out and then runs away from the container and the dead within it. The soundtrack holds a baby's shrieks, as the only 'illegal' left alive; the Italians' voices as they get to the bodies; the sound of traffic; Jamal's feet on the road; and a mourning musical score.

Jamal runs, the camera following him, first roughly, hand held, and then more smoothly, placed in front of him as he blindly runs away from the ghastly scenes in the container. This burst of energy is possibly a relief for the audience, taken out of a terrible claustrophobia. And Jamal changes from someone who has had to be watchful (of potential tricksters, of people who despise

him) to someone energetically expressing his desperation. For the first time he shows deep emotion, in tears, which the camera skilfully catches. The running goes on and on until we're invited to wonder: where is there for him to run to in this foreign land? And what has he learnt about the harshness of some lives?

Figure 4.14

Figure 4.15

Figure 4.13

Figure 4.16

There follows a fade to dark. Jamal appears again, the caption telling us two weeks have passed. He appears in the guise of a familiar figure to tourists and city dwellers: the begging, hassling migrant, involved in petty theft (he steals a woman's purse, after a waiter has offered her the luxury of choosing a kind of water – 'still or sparkling?'). The film, while not approving what he is doing, has given us a sense of how he has got there.

## CONCLUSION

This film, and especially these moments from it, challenges hostile discourses and stereotypes of such migrants. These will often blame the stereotyped group for their position, leaving their fuller histories out of the account. 'Host' media may also displace other 'domestic' issues on to them, blaming them for structures which have impacted drastically *on* migrants, rather than being caused *by* them – growing inequalities between rich and poor, both inside and across nations; the rise in unemployment; fears of terrorists; and for some, relatively sudden cultural changes in a few UK cities and towns.

The images and media representations offered of 'migrants' are often inadequate to their subjects. This can make it hard to voice justifiable questions, both inside and outside migrant groups. For example, criticisms of the oppressive gender practices of certain kinds of religious fundamentalism (see www.womenagainstfundamentalism.org.uk/ ) can often be too easily dismissed as 'Islamaphobia'.

But there are instances of self-representation, and of mainstream media making serious efforts to help 'host' audiences imagine migrants' situations. There are websites which work to welcome asylum seekers (see http://www.swansea-arrivals.net, for example) and among other campaigns, the 'Show Racism the Red Card' campaign against racism to football players (http://www.srtrc.org), the German site http://www.no-racism.net and http://www.exiledjournalists.net/page.php. We hope you will want to join the best, informed discussions on this growing global set of experiences.

## REFERENCES AND FURTHER READING

Crawley, Heaven (2009) *Understanding and Changing Public Attitudes: A Review of Existing Evidence from Public Information and Communication Campaigns*, London: The Diana, Princess of Wales Memorial fund.

Eagleton, Terry (2000) *The Truth about the Irish*, London and New York: St Martin's Press.

Hochschild, Arlie, and Ehrenreich, Barbara (eds) (2003) *Global Woman: Nannies, Maids and Sex Workers in the New Economy*, London: Granta.

Mirza, Shazia (2009) 'Shazia's Week', *New Statesman*, 11 June.

Tremain, Rose (2008) *The Road Home*, London: Vintage.

Williams, Raymond (1979) *Politics and Letters*, London: New Left Review and Verso.

# 5 Globalisation

The issues here, and around 'New Media', run through the book. But you should find the case studies on migrations and *The Age of Stupid*, and Chapters 10 and 12 especially useful.

This chapter explores a complex concept: 'globalisation'. We will consider:
- the extent of globalised media now
- what is involved in studying this field, including histories of global forms
- the changing and conflicting arguments which have been used to understand this area
- how we might approach it now.

## EXPLORE 5.1

- What would you call this large sphere? Earth? The world? The globe? The planet?
- What are the connotations of these different names? And of terms like 'international' now, as in 'the international community' which is said to be fighting in Afghanistan? 'Community' is another powerful 'hooray' word, which always rewards some scepticism. Within some 'development' discourses it can be a way of representing 'the other' in patronising ways: 'they' have community (in villages, etc.), 'we' (urban-based researchers, etc.) do not because 'we' are modern (another, different 'hooray' word).

Figure 5.1 A powerful image, visible for the first time by humans from space in 1966.

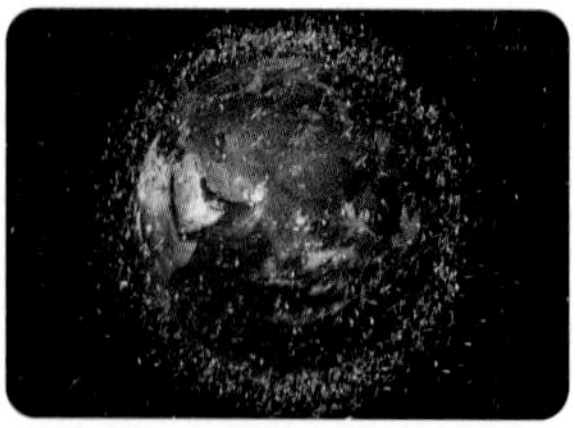

Figure 5.2 A more recent image, striking partly for its evocation of the earlier 'pure' photo, to which it disturbingly connects human technological debris around Earth. It perhaps makes it easier to feel that 'we' are not in quite such a cosy human 'community'.

## Your experiences of globalisation

You almost certainly have many, daily, experiences of globalised media. The internet alone offers resources which we all assume are global in reach, whether Google, Facebook, Twitter, blogs, email, links to mobile phone technology – and probably much else by the time this book is printed. Your favourite brand may draw on its global advertising power for part of its glamour. US TV series such as *Heroes* (2006–), *Lost* (2004–) and *Flashback* (2009–) display multiple, globally dispersed central characters and settings, as do many 'blockbuster' films with their global themes or glamorised tourist settings. All these add to the ease of 'transnational' imaginings – as do texts exploring the darker side of globalised migration, of which you or your family may have recent or past experience.

You may be one of the hundreds of thousands involved in massively multiplayer online role-playing game (MMORPG) groups such as *World of Warcraft* or *Second Life*. Or maybe you have felt involved with globally covered news stories, such as Hurricane Katrina in 2005, the 'swine flu' pandemic, the death of Michael Jackson in 2009 or the disappearance of Madeleine McCann in 2007. Perhaps you look forward to the next global mega-spectacle, whether a sports event, a pop concert or maybe a demonstration. Your image may even have been flashed across the world momentarily at such an event.

Among the pleasures of these experiences is that they are (amazingly, when you think of it) both globally dispersed and instantaneously shared, as a result of the scale of technological change from around 1970. One way of putting this is to argue that media (meaning any mediated set of meanings, beginning with written language) have gone from mostly one-to-one (print, telegraphy) to one-to-many (broadcast speeches, electronic media such as radio, TV) to 'many-to-many' or social media, as in online games and social networking sites. Another way of registering your own involvement is to think now about when you first became dimly aware of the 'distant others' who are now routinely made 'present' by media. Maybe the sound of a voice on a mobile phone? Or figures on TV or computer screens?

> Research the McCanns' website http://www.findmadeleine.com. Note the ways in which it operates globally, including its invitations to others to spread the story/search across the world.
> Q: Why do you think *this* missing child inspired such a global campaign?

> 'A typical car [of 1996 had] more computer processing power than the first lunar landing craft had in 1969.' *The Economist* (Balnaves *et al.* 2009: 5).

## Global histories

Power structures and activities on a larger than national scale have existed for many centuries, for example the Chinese, Persian, Roman and British empires, and the Roman Catholic church across medieval and modern Europe and beyond. All of these involved culture and 'media' (in the sense of documents, priestly speeches from pulpits, spectacular displays and so on) as well as displays of force.

But contemporary media globalisation is a rather different process. It occurs when activities:

- take place in a global (not simply a national or regional) arena
- are deliberately organised on a global scale
- involve some interdependency, so that activities in different parts of the world are shaped by each other
- often involve media and technologies which make possible *instantaneous*, as opposed to simply *fast*, communications.

Communications technologies began with the invention of papermaking and printing in China nearly two millennia ago. Paper use spread globally and allowed books and pamphlets to circulate well beyond the places where they were made – producing that sense of 'distant others' which is a resonant term in globalised media study.

## Early media technologies

Papermaking was one of the 'four great inventions' of ancient Chinese technology (the Egyptians invented papyrus, its predecessor, using fibres from the papyrus plant). First made of silk, it spread to the Muslim world, where the first paper mills were built. It was attacked by the official Christian world as a manifestation of Muslim culture – a 1221 papal decree declared all official documents written on paper to be invalid. This probably embodied the interests of wealthy European landowners in sheep and cattle, sources of parchment and vellum (other early kinds of paper). But the invention of the printing press in Europe, in the mid-1400s, changed attitudes. For more on this history see http://ipst.gatech.edu/amp/collection/museum_pm_euro.htm.

In 1924, at the British Empire Exhibition, King George V sent himself a telegram which circled the globe on all British lines in 80 seconds.

The expansion of trade between Europe and the rest of the world in the sixteenth century was accompanied and followed by the speed of Western imperialist and then post-imperialist conquest, languages and emerging media over much of the globe by the time of the twentieth. Crucial for later expansion was the development of underwater cable systems by the European imperial powers and companies such as Cable and Wireless, and the establishment of international news agencies (see Chapman 2002).

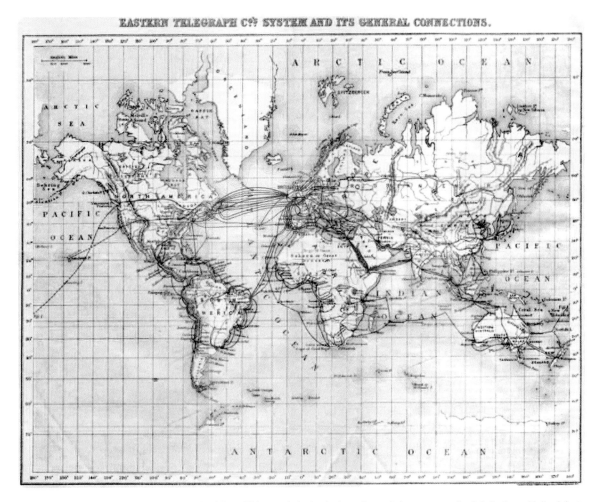

*Figure 5.3* A 1901 map of undersea telegraph cabling which reveals the beginnings of twentieth-century media globalisation, with its violent roots in European empires. Compare this to Figure 5.10 (p. 155) showing recent global internet connections.

It may come as a surprise to learn that underwater cables were so important, yet, until the 1850s, telegraph systems were land-based and thus quite restricted. By the 1870s submarine cables had been laid throughout South-East Asia and along the coast of Africa, and soon linked Europe to China, Australia and South America.

It was the first global system of communication to separate the sending of messages from the need to transport them physically. News agencies likewise gathered and disseminated news over huge areas, and eventually, in 1869, agreed to divide up the world into mutually exclusive spheres of operation. Such drives more or less corresponded, like the reach of the underwater cable systems, to the imperialist spheres of influence of the major European powers.

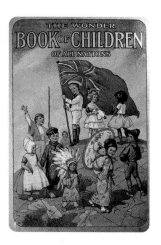

*Figure 5.4* The cover of a 1917 British book. It seems simply to assume 'global' hierarchies of 'race' and gender as being both part of empire ('like a family of children') and justifying it. See recent British 'race-ist' discourses such as those of the British National Party.

'Neoliberalism' (see Glossary definition) sounds very up to the moment and 'liberal'. But it defines policies of a globalised capitalism which attacks free or subsidised public provision of such social goods as education, health, the arts and housing. In Europe these had been won by social movements at the end of the Second World War (see Hall 2007).

Two recent watershed moments: the first, in 1973, was US President Nixon's cancellation of an agreement (called Bretton Woods) which had been signed in 1944 as the Second World War raged towards its end. This agreement had helped establish stable systems of monetary exchange and international trade regulation. President Nixon's cancellation of it, along with developments in electronic communication, advertising, attacks on trade unions, etc., opened up hugely speculative financial markets. It also accelerated the discourses and powers of 'free trade', 'deregulation' and a corporate capitalism newly able to chase markets and cheap labour across the world (see Grossberg in Bennett *et al.* 2005: 146–50). This process is also called 'neoliberalism', or globalisation, and, later, Thatcherism. Some economists argue that this founding moment of **neoliberalism** was one of the main roots of the 2008 – present global financial crises and recession.

The second 'moment' was the attack on the twin towers of New York's World Trade Center in 2001, now simply called '9/11'. This horrible, spectacular bombing, against, as it happened, a 'blue sky' background, took place in one of the most media-ted and imagined global cities in the world. Many saw it as like a scene from a blockbuster action-adventure film. It was a striking moment of silence in a world noisy with messages: the stunned silence of many of those witnessing it, on TV or in New York; the temporary cessation of the incessant advertising on US TV; and its anonymity, the absence of immediate claims by its perpetrators. Some of its long-term results included a huge increase in perceived threats, media amplification of 'terrorism' and actions for a 'global war' against it. It has been argued, speculatively, that an overall climate of fear – *of* others, and *for* children, especially – is partly a result of this atmosphere. In this the media play a key part.

## EXPLORE 5.2

If you can, see the film *11'09"01–September 11* (France 2002) in which eleven directors, from all around the world, were each asked to create an 11-minute-long film to comment on '9/11'. The ones by Chahine, Makhmalbaf and Loach are particularly striking, and the whole film a fine example of global film-making outside blockbuster structures.

- Sketch an outline of a film *you* would make on this theme, given 11 minutes.
- What are the difficulties raised?
- Argue for the strengths of your favourite film from those collected in *11'09"01*.

Another, linked result has been a heightened sensitivity to the experience of groups with recent or family history of migration, especially from countries labelled as sources of terrorism (e.g. some British Muslims, even though belonging to this religion is not itself a badge of national origin). A liberal response to this sensitivity has been to embrace 'difference' and to emphasise the ways in which differences extend across all groups.

> This approach sometimes risks ignoring inequalities, which are not the same as 'differences', though they may produce difference (see Therborn 2009, and Chapter 6 on Ideologies).

> A small history: Wheen (2004) cites a reputable historian: 'in the 1960s there was not a single religious or cult-based terrorist group anywhere, and as recently as 1980 only two of the world's sixty four known terrorist groups were religious' (pp. 182–3). He links this to US sponsorship of fundamentalist Muslim groups in the 1980s, with no care for the possible consequences.

> See the thoughtful discussions (and 'rant box') on the website www.womenagainstfundamentalism.org.uk for one feminist group's response to different kinds of religious fundamentalisms.

## EXPLORE 5.3

- List the last few media texts you enjoyed which relied on, or explored notions of, 'difference'. They might range from kinds of music, to games, to comedy, or TV programmes like *Heroes*, *EastEnders* or BBC2's *Who Do You Think You Are?* (emphasising how mixed, both in class and in geographical terms, are many people's family histories).
- What did you enjoy about their exploration of 'difference'?

Less liberal responses are exemplified by the British National Party, which claims to represent a 'downtrodden white majority' in the UK. 'British' is linked by them to the 'Anglo-Saxon-ness' of the 'folk' of 'this island race'. It is asserted to be continuous with the 'ancient world' which is said to have consisted of quite distinct and different races. This separation of races is then argued to be 'natural': these 'races' should be kept apart (as in apartheid). Hence the BNP's hostility to 'multiculturalism' which emphasises the virtues of a mix of different ethnic groups within modern globalised cultures.

## EXPLORE 5.4

- Make a diary of a week's encounters with different media which you can relate to a chosen definition of 'multicultural'.
- Do your notes suggest that certain kinds of multicultural effort are at work in the media? In which media? Which programmes, blogs or internet sites? What forms does this take?

**Marshall McLuhan** (1911–80) influential Canadian theorist of media communications. See fuller discussion of his work in Chapter 8.

The difference between 'universal' and 'global' is that 'What is universal is true everywhere and forever whereas what is global is merely a feature of the planet here and now' (During 2005: 87).

What are the meanings of 'cosmopolitan' for you? Expensive tourism, membership of a kind of elite global club, based on economic privilege? Or a kind of imagined community where people from different nations and cultures can meet with mutual respect despite different beliefs? (See Hall 2007)

'Shut up and shop': slogan from the 1980s as neoliberalism, the lure of 'free markets', the huge expansion of contemporary hyper-consumerism, shopping malls, global branding, etc. began to take effect.

## Approaches to globalised media

Despite the huge changes sketched above, one widely used image of our world is still as a 'global village'. The term was coined by the media theorist Marshall McLuhan in the 1960s. He was not using the term critically, to evoke the narrowness and boredom which some experience as 'village life' and which, along with the need for employment, helps drive many into cities in the hope of jobs and more freedom. His emphasis can be seen as the beginning of an optimistic (and nostalgic) theoretical take on 'globalisation'. Like Spielberg's talk of Hollywood's stories (simply resembling those ancient ones told by the fireside, effortlessly and 'naturally' travelling the world) this image attractively suggests that 'global' is the same as 'universal', that all of 'us' are cosily sharing the same imagery and products, warming our hands by the flicker of our shared screens. It goes along with recent reassessments of US empire-building as basically benign and civilising ('the global policeman') or even as happening 'by accident' (see Johnson 2007).

Other theorists have adapted this optimistic tradition in a less nostalgic way. Ingrid Volkmer (2003) argues that world satellite news channels are enabling a 'global **public sphere**' to emerge, in a phrase which draws on the work of Jürgen Habermas (see Chapter 12). She and other theorists deploy the terms 'cosmopolitan', 'citizen' and 'world citizenship', which celebrate, or try to further, the potential of globalised media to enlarge the capacities of nation-state media. The terms are further used in attempts to contest the global power of consumer-hood, or those identities as shoppers which we're often powerfully invited to see as our most important ones.

Less optimistic accounts are deeply sceptical about the supposed egalitarianism of globalised media and the 'freedoms' of the 'free market'. A key theorist here was Herbert Schiller (1919–2000) and others such as Robert McChesney, Noam Chomsky and Naomi Klein. Schiller argued not for global media's free-ing capacities, but its nature as 'cultural imperialism', acting on behalf of US capitalist interests. As Wheen argues: 'the problem is not globalisation per se, but the fact that the rules of the game have been set by the winning side – which, while enforcing them elsewhere, feels no obligation to apply them to its own conduct' (Wheen 2004: 245).

Schiller (1997) also suggested that traditional, local cultures are destroyed by the external pressure of more powerful countries, especially media and other cultural exports. Thus new forms of cultural dependency and status are shaped, mirroring older imperialist relations of power.

Two key points are parts of this broadly Marxist case. Firstly, the dominance of US advertising, and especially of branding-driven commercial media, forces a costly US model of production and trading on the rest of the world (even where commercial dominance may lie outside the US, as with South Korea/Samsung for electronic media). This very specific and, crucially, ad-funded form of culture becomes normalised, instead of other ways of organising media (such as via public service models, or perhaps via much more localised media, as may become necessary with global warming).

In addition, US media giants can often afford the rates charged to be held so low, for poorer markets, that they impact on local production. This is not lessened by the way that importers can modify the original to fit better with the preferences of their audience. African or Caribbean broadcasters, for example, cannot hope to produce programming of a similar technical quality at a lower price, and their station managers cannot afford not to buy in. Sometimes this now involves buying in to a global format or franchise, such as *Big Brother*, and translating for local tastes. Much of the time, however, a preference for local products holds up, and tax breaks and so on are experimented with to support this.

Secondly, the wide dispersal of the advertising/branding imagery which funds such media also, arguably, incites desires for US-style consumerism and upgrade fashions in societies which can ill afford them. Increasingly it is being argued that 'less advanced' cultures have, in some ways, better models of how to live, especially now, with the planet imperilled by the overconsumption in its 'developed' high capitalist areas.

Gender and sexual oppression within versions of various world religions cast a very different light on 'globalisation' and the 'traditions' it sometimes displaces. See the film *Moolaadé* (Senegal/France 2004) for a sophisticated, angry, but visually restrained treatment of female genital mutilation (FGM) in parts of Africa.

Where indigenous film industries have succeeded commercially they have often been labelled, from inside the country, by words deriving from 'Hollywood'. Thus 'Bollywood' names part of Indian cinema, and 'Nollywood' part of the Nigerian film industry.

Less often mentioned is the shadow of the 'hard powers' of the US: tough negotiations of trade treaties; enforcing copyright across the world; and the reminder of military might, embodied by about a thousand US bases worldwide. See Miller *et al.* 2007; Johnson 2007.

'Starbucks and stadiums' is one way in which urban planning experts now summarise the driving factors behind many would-be 'global cities'. Does it apply to a city near you?

The US Constitution cites 'life, liberty and the pursuit of happiness' as one of the 'rights of man'. But recent studies suggest that high-consumer capitalist cultures are not experienced as 'happy' by as many people as those in differently organised or even less 'advanced' ones. See http://www.happyplanetindex.org for an annual review which tries to measure a very different conception of 'the good life' than that in much global advertising and neoliberal discourses.

Several criticisms and refinements have been made to Schiller's position. In the first place, the case was researched and developed in the 1950s and 1960s when US world economic dominance seemed secure and unchallengeable. It does not adequately describe the shifts of the post-1945 period and it has arguably become more difficult, as Schiller recognised, to apply the theory to the 1990s and after.

Global restructuring has now to *some* extent eroded the economic pre-eminence of the US (though its military capacity to enforce trading and other relations in its favour remains hugely intimidating). There are debates, for example, as to who actually owns the US economy, with China cited as owning most of it through bonds.

Media examples of how major US media have been bought by foreign companies include:

- the Japanese company Sony bought Columbia and TriStar pictures in 1989, to add to CBS records;
- the German corporation Bertelsmann AG bought RCA and Random House publishers;
- the then-Australian Rupert Murdoch bought 20th Century Fox in 1986;
- in 2008 the Indian media corporation Reliance BIG Pictures took a large financial stake in Steven Spielberg's DreamWorks Studio.

But the brands remain US based, and it is in such shareholders' interest that they remain profitable.

A second objection was that the cultural imperialism thesis implies, in almost romantic fashion, that before the arrival of US and other media, 'Third World' countries were enjoying a cosy golden age of indigenous, authentic traditions and cultural heritage, untainted by values imposed from outside. Critics argue this attitude risks patronising what are seen as weaker nations, and romanticising their pre-colonial cultures. Sometimes cultures are called 'indigenous' whose sophisticated traditions and 'ancient heritages' have been shaped by long and brutal processes of cultural conflict and indeed exchange. These extend from well before the

Part of this condescension: bodily adornment and cover are called 'fashion' (and linked to modernity) in the West, but 'tradition' (and linked to the past, and to tourism) in the 'developing world'.

years of US intervention, often including hundreds of years of European (and other) colonial 'enterprise'.

Usually this case is applied to less 'developed' cultures. But in popular music huge importance attaches to specific cities, often ports, which register the impact of various migrations – from the Caribbean to New York and London, for example, themselves with origins in the slave trade with Africa. Think of Detroit and 'Motown' (standing for 'motor town', when it was the centre of US car production), or the big ports of Liverpool and Bristol, with their slaving histories, for, respectively, the early Beatles' music, and more recently Portishead and Massive Attack.

The West Midlands industrial area and specifically the city of Coventry developed 'Two Tone' music such as that of The Specials, The Selecter and The Beat, a hybrid of reggae, punk and ska which spread worldwide. See http://www.youtube.com/watch?v=ct8O3p0pgHI for its histories. These are examples of

a   the localness of some kinds of media, especially those which depend on networking and a degree of live performance, as much music does;
b   the (often painful) global histories and migrations that give rise to these;
c   the global corporations, usually US based, which can then spread this 'local–global' music globally.

## EXPLORE 5.5

- Can you trace such local–global connections for recent music?
- 'Emo' is said to have emerged from the hardcore Washington punk movement. Do other music waves have such origins? Or are communities of interest on the internet (Lily Allen's 'launch' on Facebook?) more important now?

For more on the global music industry see Webb (2007) and also http://www.ifpi.org/, http://www.mi2n.com/ and http://www.musicdish.com/ and for UK debates http://www.musictank.co.uk/.

Thirdly, globalisation has never been a simple process of homogenisation, or rendering the world all the same, though it is often characterised as just this, leading to 'McWorld' (see Herman and McChesney 1997). Rather than experiencing a 'homogenised' global

'McWorld' and 'McJob' (for low-wage, non-unionised repetitive work) are coined from the global spread of McDonald's food chain. Because of the standardisation of a narrow range of product in the 20,000+ McDonald's outlets, and its identification with US capitalism, the term often signifies a standardised, Americanised world.

147

*Figure 5.5* This Imax cinema in Hyderabad illustrates some of the rich visual contrasts involved in such media networks. In fact Hyderabad is one of the major hubs of the Indian information technology industry, and also home to the world's largest film studio.

Even the immensely powerful Australian media tycoon Rupert Murdoch had to take on US citizenship in order to acquire more US interests.

culture, we usually engage with hybridised texts. 'Indigenous' cultures and languages are enriched and complicated, as populations and imaginings flow this way and that across the globe. Globalisation is not simply the West expanding uniformly, in a 'blanket' way, into the rest of the world. For one thing, other countries' media forms have exchanges with, and even flow into and out of, 'the West'. Words like 'flows', 'networks', 'corridors' and 'transnationalisation' have tried to signify this more complex mapping. They try to suggest that when we talk of media 'covering' territories, there are always gaps and spaces in that only-apparent 'blanket' coverage. 'Web 2.0' and the possibility of instantaneous, globally interactive comments, campaigns, productions, form another complicating factor.

But we are also, always, talking about *corporate capitalist* strength, and flow, often hugely influenced, if not owned by US culture, which is also very powerful in 'new media' forms.

## EXPLORE 5.6

Consider this quote alongside the 'flows' discussed above:

'Really to work in its dominant form, capitalist globalisation must try to draw everybody into its web . . . everyone must come to look a little bit like an American, or to love a little bit like an American, or to walk a little bit like an American. That's why television and cultural industries are so critical, because you don't know quite how to walk and think in American until you look at enough television.' (Hall 2007: 150)

● Discuss the quote with friends. How far does it relate to your media experiences and enthusiasms, including brands?

● Which of such cultural forms are mediated, or delivered, through US-inflected routes or spellings or hybridities or accents – as, often, literally, in songs, in 'mid-Atlantic' DJ voices and so on?

Maybe you feel this account is inadequate, and that 'Eastern' cultural forms, for example, are important for you – 'The Dude' and Taoism in *The Big Lebowski*? Kung fu forms? Bollywood co-productions? Or perhaps 'Web 2.0' is your key media resource.

● How, if at all, are these mediated by 'American-ness'?

## Global–local flows

Let's look in a little more detail at the specific factors which both make for global US cultural power, yet can also complicate our sense of it and of the 'local' or 'transnational' reach which was always to some extent built into 'global' success. One name for this now is 'glocal', describing the capacity of contemporary consumer capitalism to proliferate difference along the lines of local preferences, cultures, etc.

*Figure 5.6* Banksy puts things into context, 2009. The child's T-shirt reads 'I hate Mondays!'. How do you think his image 'works' within this discussion?

### Example: US cinema

The US entertainment giants inherit and capitalise on huge accumulated experience in making commercially successful products, and from the start, in the 1890s, these had an international aspect. North America is a continent of immigrants, with ties to other continents, along with a history of brutal conquest of groups such as the Native Americans, and the use of slaves, originally from Africa, for much of its history.

Hollywood cinema is an example of the hybridising as well as the homogenising drives within the early dominance of US forms. The early 'American' makers and exhibitors in the 1890s were often first- or second-generation migrants to the US, and thus in very close contact with the European popular taste to which they were exporting. Canny textual strategies developed, which are still to some extent operative:

- adaptations of titles and publicity strategies for different markets;
- casting and even shaping different versions of films for global appeal to different audiences;
- plots chosen for cultural 'vagueness' or openness, so as to appeal to as broad a market as possible, avoid inflaming local cultural sensitivities and therefore threatening profits.

In addition, English being the main language of the US meant that early US products could ride on the back of the spread of that imperial language.

US exporters soon began to use differential pricing strategies for different parts of the globe. This has meant until very recently that once a US television series, for example, has been distributed in the North American market (large enough to allow it to recoup its production costs), it can be offered to every broadcaster in the world, but at different rates. The money made thus is often clear profit. In the 'developed' countries charges are based on audience size and disposable wealth (e.g. on the relatively affluent and concentrated audiences who can be contacted by media in big cities). But in, say, Africa the rates may be lowered dramatically, a process which both ensures *overall*

> It is worth remembering that the continent of America (north and south) is named after Amerigo Vespucci (1454–1512), a fifteenth-century Italian merchant and cartographer. By contrast, 'Canada' is said to derive from a French interpretation of a native word *kanata*, thus embodying the idea of a hybrid community.

> Arguably for British cinema it has been a double-edged factor: allowing easy passage to some English-language films into the US, but also meaning that they will compete for English-language markets with US 'product'.

profitability and also consolidates habits of enjoying US-style entertainment forms, and then the products and ways of life often modelled on screens. One local reaction, however, is to ignore rights and simply reuse US content without paying. Hence the effort of US media to control 'piracy' and copyright.

Co-productions are also involved, simply to afford the huge costs of media product which will 'travel' globally, partly via spectacular FX which connect to international experiences of 'magic' and conjurors, etc. All this means that big media corporations need to take some account of local sensibilities – though of course they try to shape them, or reinforce those parts of them which will fit broadly with global capitalist drives.

## EXPLORE 5.7

- Research the production details of a few days of TV programming.
- How many programmes are co-productions?
- In the case of primetime products, in what ways do you think the co-production funding may have shaped the resulting programme?

Areas to explore might include:

- Casting (even if non-fiction) – have stars been used? To what effect?
- Narrative shape and choice of characters: is there a 'vagueness' to the narrative which will 'travel well'?
- Locations and use of familiar kinds of (tourist?) spectacle.

## EXPLORE 5.8

- Get hold of cinema listings for your city or region, from a newspaper or the internet.
- Choose a major city with multiplexes, and, ideally, an independent cinema.
- Count the number of screens in the city which are running 'Hollywood' as opposed to non-US films. Calculate what proportion of the total these make up.

## Global futures?

We began with the different resonances of the words chosen to describe our part of the solar system. 'Planet' now invokes environmentalist discourses. 'Globalisation' often refers to the particular stage of 'neoliberalism' or global consumer capitalism we are living through. You'll find contradictory impulses in play – always a good source for debates – within different scenarios of what the next phase of our world will involve. One future envisaged is of imminent Chinese global dominance. Another involves a growing 'global village' of cool consumers, in touch with each other through the internet, global brands and networking possibilities. Another is of disastrous consumption-fuelled climate change, a consequence of the acceleration of consumer capitalisms, including the resource-hungry internet. A less examined one involves 'fortresses', whether that be 'Fortress Europe' barricaded against unwanted migrants (see Chapter 4 case study), or parts of the world barricaded against rising sea levels.

> In addition to home audiences, China (like India) has a huge non-resident set of audiences outside China, estimated by some at 40 million. Another term for such audiences is 'deterritorialised'.

### The 'Chinese domination' future?

In assessing media images of China's industrial and media power the following points are useful to bear in mind.

a   China has no major global brands (compared with the US's Coca-Cola, Google, Microsoft) and has only limited hopes for creating any. US companies and their hugely powerful imagery, placement and copyright power continue to dominate the lists of top global brands.

### Global media and China: *Avatar*

*Avatar* (US 2009) had the same massive commercial success in China as in most other countries, even though China only allows twenty foreign films a year to be imported. In January 2010 there were reports that Chinese authorities had prohibited screenings of the 2D version, perhaps because of the resonances of the film's story of the Na'vi's battle to protect their land and culture from outsiders. The forced removal of old neighbourhoods and destruction of some rural communities in China produced powerful echoes. Others have suggested that, in the US, the resistance of Native Americans, and elsewhere some anti-corporate struggles against the looting of the planet, are also embodied in the film.

A final twist was that tourism chiefs in central China renamed a peak 'The Hallelujah Mountain' – crags on which the film modelled one of its lovely floating rocks.

Chinese domination?

*Figure 5.7* Chart of top 2009 corporations from Interbrand, which calculates their worth annually.

| 2009 Rank | 2008 Rank | Brand | Country of Origin | Sector | 2009 Brand Value ($m) |
|---|---|---|---|---|---|
| 1 | 1 | Coca-Cola | United States | Beverages | 68,734 |
| 2 | 2 | IBM | United States | Computer Services | 60,211 |
| 3 | 3 | Microsoft | United States | Computer Software | 56,647 |
| 4 | 4 | GE | United States | Diversified | 47,777 |
| 5 | 5 | NOKIA | Finland | Consumer Electronics | 34,864 |
| 6 | 8 | M | United States | Restaurants | 32,275 |
| 7 | 10 | Google | United States | Internet Services | 31,980 |
| 8 | 6 | TOYOTA | Japan | Automotive | 31,330 |
| 9 | 7 | intel | United States | Computer Hardware | 30,636 |
| 10 | 9 | Disney | United States | Media | 28,447 |

Nevertheless China is enormously important in the huge and mineral-rich continent of Africa, in industries such as road building. See Edward Burtynsky's astonishing images in the documentary *Manufactured Landscapes* (Canada 2006).

b China lacks what is now often called 'soft power', which partly involves the spread of languages, or global cinema, sport and music hits. Language is key to the 'regional' flows and media 'footprints' of broadcasters like Al Jazeera or the BBC. They often embody the global spread of the earlier imperial languages: English, Spanish, French and Arabic. Yet, although an estimated fifth of the world's people now speak Chinese, it does not have the power inherited by the imperial 'footprints' of English or Spanish media.

The Chinese staging of the 2008 Olympics, costing an estimated US$ 70 billion can be seen as an attempt at 'soft power' or co-branding ('China' along with 'the Olympics'), trying to shift China's image from 'totalitarian communist' with oppressive foreign and internal policies into a more modern, spectacularised and broadly peaceful space (sport). Contradictorily, part of the display was quite militaristic, involving huge numbers of intensely drilled people (usually a part of Olympic ceremonies now), some in military uniform.

c Chinese global power does not result from histories of vast overseas empire. It largely lies in its capacity to manufacture cheaply, so far for 'Western' markets and trade, through exploitation of its labour force and 'economies of scale'. Its recent fortunes have been shaped by both decline and revival in these overseas markets.

d Overexcitement at Chinese power ignores the rise of the Indian economy and media influence, let alone the abiding power of the US, and European media.

e As with so much, climate change may sharpen the contradictions of China's image. It stands to lose much if catastrophic warming takes place. Equally, it is making huge investments in environmental technologies (though as yet seems unable to switch from a car-centred to a modern public transport economy). Part of its future global image may yet include 'saving the planet'.

> 'Soft power' is a political concept, developed from the 1990s. It signifies obtaining what you want through co-option, diplomacy, attraction (and, perhaps, successful 'nation-branding') rather than 'harder' power, such as force.

*Figure 5.8* A spectacular image, combining many of the elements which China wanted to project through this global event, including its military might. Research other Olympics ceremonies, including the plans for the London 2012 Games.

> As well as India's home audiences, NRIs or non-resident Indians, both Hindi- and Tamil-speaking, living outside India, make up hugely important audiences for Indian media – not least Bollywood, claimed as the world's largest film industry.

> Social change in China, especially the rise of car ownership, has led to a revival of radio. The notorious traffic jams of big Chinese cities are said to have created what is literally a captive audience for the medium.

## EXPLORE 5.9

- Jot down your impression of predictions that China will soon be the dominant global power.
- Where have you got these predictions from?
- What part have media images played? Which genres or media forms are they part of – TV? cinema? internet forms such as Google? games? comics? radio? sports coverage?
- Do you think traces of much earlier racist imagery ('the yellow peril', 'Dr Fu Manchu', 'the yellow hordes') are discernible in any of your chosen texts, e.g. via a fondness for images of masses of regimented Chinese? Or do you think there are differentiated and individualised images in wide circulation, perhaps in cinema and on the internet?

*Figure 5.9* Some global spectacles can help shift these inequalities. There was much excitement when South Africa was named as host for the 2010 FIFA World Cup™, though as we go to press there are rumours of low ticket sales. If you watched the event's ceremonies, what did you think were the emphases, and omissions, in the decisions on how to stage them?

> The Lone Ranger and his trusty sidekick, Tonto, face an overwhelmingly large group of hostile Apache. 'We're in real trouble, Tonto,' says the Ranger. Asks Tonto: 'Who's this "we", Paleface?'

> See *Burma VJ* (Denmark 2008) for a moving account of Video Journalists' (VJs') attempts to record the 2007 'Saffron Revolution' led by thousands of monks against the dictatorial power of the military regime ruling Burma. Part of the regime's power is its capacity to turn off internet connections to the rest of the world.

## The 'global village' future?

There are plenty of media invitations to think of the planet as an exciting global unity, a 'village' if you like, though that does seem a cosily nostalgic image of Web 2.0 and other kinds of global modernity. If it is a village, it is a huge, broadbanding, internet village, with shared fantasies and fandoms, conflicts and solidarities, diasporic and dispersed 'communities of interest'.

It is often flamboyant spectacles, for sporting and other events (the Olympics, various World Cups, exhibitions, conferences), which are cited as evidence of 'global unity'. Sport is particularly important. BSkyB, for example, agreed to pay a figure believed to be in excess of £1 billion to retain live television rights to most of the biggest UK matches, from 2010 to 2013 (*Observer*, 16 August 2009). Even if income from domestic live rights decreases, it is hoped that an increase in the value of overseas rights and new media platforms will make up the difference, plus possible auctions for 'near live' packages – on-demand highlights, mobile phone clips, overseas rights and radio rights.

Despite recession, there is still much celebration of the 'freedoms' of the internet and media 'free markets' where all are said to be equal, regardless of class, gender and other differences. Sadly these often work at the expense of understanding persistent inequalities in media power and other relations.

a First, who are the 'we' who have access to the literacy, electricity, computers and broadband flows needed to 'surf' the global internet (and let alone water, food and shelter in between surfings)? Though 'broadband penetration' is increasing, and mobile use even faster, we cannot assume that absolutely everyone has access to these technologies and the support systems they need.

b Second, in whose interests is Web 2.0 being shaped? It originated, like so many modern technologies, in the Pentagon's military research, as well as the 'alternative' enthusiasms of people like Bill Gates. But who now has overall control of which entries pop up first when you type a category into a search engine, or of Googlemail's capacity to retrieve every single piece of mail you have ever sent? A different kind of surveillance potential is that of some state regimes which occasionally exercise the power to turn off TV screens and the internet (e.g. in Burma, and in China during the violent conflict in Tibet in 2008).

How effective could global regulation be for the hugely damaging circulation of pornographic imagery, which experts cite as a growing source of HIV/AIDS deaths? See http://www.guardian.co.uk/commentisfree/2009/aug/30/pornography-corporate-responsibility-developing-world, and also Chapter 10.

## GLOBAL LIT SUBMARINE CABLE CAPACITY

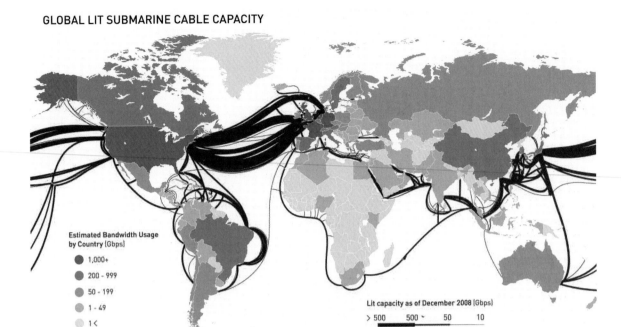

*Figure 5.10* This December 2008 map shows the amount of submarine cable capacity globally available for use (referred to in specialist terms as LIT, which distinguishes it from both maximum cable capacity, and from the bandwidth actually being used). Compare the map with Fig. 5.3. See also www.telegeography.com for more details, and the latest maps.

c    There are real pleasures in shared fandoms and other imaginings of distant others and possible identities. But there are risks in *uncritical* celebrations of active audiences, as though they were all *equally* equipped to construct resistant meanings and uses for media products, no matter what is on, or off, their screens. Many media users can resist or interpret news images for themselves (though that does ignore why other people choose to go along with them). But that is not to argue that 'the global market' in images will do everything for us. There is still a need for high-quality investigative journalisms or inexpensively available, well-researched and regulated national media which can work with the bloggers and 'sousveillance' images (see Chapters 8, 12 and 13 for more discussion) which are now enabled and circulated by global media.

Global news and information, a key part of dreams of 'global citizenship', are dominantly shaped by US profitabilities. This, as so much else in global media, is uneven and contradictory. The theory of 'the CNN effect' refers to this TV channel's pioneering of 24-hour global news. This resulted in a huge increase in saturation news coverage of wars, crises and disasters, and has had an impact on the

> The golfer Tiger Woods describes himself as 'Cablinasian' (a mix of Caucasian, black, Indian, Asian). This multiple ethnic identity was a crucial part of his global marketability for (former) sponsor Nike.

conduct of states' foreign policy from the 1990s. Such global coverage, funded like much else in US media by advertising, has indeed changed the world of news, even if it often seems aimed at a small group of predominantly male, well-educated and wealthy hotel users.

### The global–local future?

Whether we imagine a global village or a US-dominated world, it is too easy to downplay the importance of nation states and their media – and of even more specifically 'local' media and communities. Nation states are still needed, precisely to help manage global capitalism, even if corporations often override their laws, for example, by relocating production to lower-paid economies, or to somewhere closer to imagined markets, or where the currency rates seem more favourable. Far from being truly 'free' or 'deregulated', the 'free trade' treaties of the most powerful depend on thousands of pages of local regulations, and the co-operation of nation states to implement them (see Miller *et al.* 2005: 41). This is especially true as the US seeks to counter the threat to its huge copyright powers posed by internet forms.

And there remains a huge appetite for 'flows' of local imagery of our worlds, real and imagined, even in the most difficult conditions. In parts of Africa, for example, films tour in tiny mobile cinemas, where audiences often watch them several times. And the Pan African Film Festival in Burkina Faso has been operating successfully for forty years, though some films are cut or not shown in their home producer's nation, such as Morocco, and rely on success at other festivals to became known.

There are also substantial flows of 'local' material, such as the popular telenovelas, a form of melodramatic serialised fiction produced and aired in most Latin American countries and attracting a broad audience across age and gender lines. The Latin American *Telesur* news channel, attacked by the Bush administration when it began in 2005, is still operating successfully. And it seems that some recent preferences for 'homegrown' films are making dents in Hollywood's global profits. Such local produce has long been popular in France, but now the trend 'has spread to places such as Greece and Japan, which a few years ago earned just 5% of its box office from local language films but now earns 65%' (Pilkington 2009).

*Figure 5.11* A shot of the Burkina Faso Film Festival, 2009. No need to suggest how this differs from the Oscars setting, or those of other big global film festivals such as Cannes, London or Venice.

## EXPLORE 5.10

List the number of ways in which your own experiences of the media over the past week have been affected by:

- living in a *global* media economy
- living in a *national* media economy
- living with media which *mix global and national* characteristics
- living with media which connect you with 'distant others' instantaneously.

How many, and what kinds of local images of your world have you seen this week? Where?

### Fortress futures?

You may have come across the phrase 'Fortress Europe'. It originated in the Second World War, but is today associated with two 'fortress' discourses. One opposes the flows of unwanted migrants (business class travel is not threatened) into 'Europe', and is called the 'Fortress Europe' position. The other, emerging discourse argues that there is nothing to be done about disastrous climate change and that rich countries should, literally and metaphorically, build their flood defences (see below and case study for Chapter 6).

The term 'gated communities' is sometimes used to describe a similar phenomenon. They are residential 'communities' with strictly controlled entrance gates, and sometimes armed guards. In poorer countries they often provide security for the wealthy and can resemble fortresses.

*Figure 5.12* Spanish rescue services remove a dead body from the sea during a search operation for missing African migrants off the tourist island of Lanzarote.

'Feb 16th 'Two surfers on a Spanish beach yesterday tried to rescue drowning illegal migrants as their boat capsized off the Canary Islands in what looks set to be another major tragedy in the history of one of the world's harshest migration routes.'

A horrifying as well as a moving photo. There are several other examples of holidaymakers trying to help migrants washed ashore in the Canaries – a hopeful example of 'local' solidarities with now-not-distant others.

## EXPLORE 5.11

- What does 'Europe' mean to you? Through which media images and discourses has this image been constructed?
- Why is Israel allowed to compete in the Eurovision Song Contest? Do you otherwise think of it as a European nation? If not, why not? Again, relate to media images.

## EXPLORE 5.12

A related area: struggles to be defined as part of the 'modern world'?
- Explore recent media controversies over the image or brand of particular cities, nations or areas. Examples are the alleged damage to the national image of Khazakstan in the film *Borat* and to that of Austria by the reporting of the Fritzl case, 2008. Brazil also complained at its representation in an episode of *The Simpsons* in 2002.

### The climate changed future?

Like the other futures this one involves contradictory hopes and fears. The 'globe' in these discourses is conceived as a possibly ruined 'planet', which emphasises our shared place as 'humankind' in a material world. Yet the very capacity to imagine this, and to monitor minute changes to the planet's well-being, or to co-ordinate protests against ecologically disastrous kinds of consumption, and then flash them round the world – all this is partly down to globalised electronic media.

## EXPLORE 5.13

- Consider the following: 'weather forecasting is an area where global climate change issues a) might be treated but b) tend to be avoided'.
- Look at a week's forecasts and make notes on the tone of the bulletins. Is hot weather in usually colder countries almost always celebrated, without comment? What are the different connotations of 'weather' and 'climate'?
- Try to script a different forecast, taking global issues into account, and say what challenges that would represent for a short TV slot, within British attitudes to 'weather'. See Miller (2007) for US comparison.

There is a massive impact on the global environment in the amounts of waste from media industries such as film and TV, and in the lavish spectacles, building projects, etc. on which many cities now depend for entry to the elite club of 'global cities'. And the gorgeously lightweight, fashionable, shiny, super-efficient gadgets that enable swift global communications and enjoyments – these too depend on material resources.

## EXPLORE 5.14

- Research the substance known in Africa as 'coltan'.

*Figure 5.13* Children mining for coltan (an abbreviated term for '**col**umbite-**tan**talite'), a valuable mineral for corporations involved in electronics such as mobile phones, DVD players and computers. Its export is said to finance bloody conflicts in the Democratic Republic of Congo and elsewhere in mineral-rich Africa.

- Try to trace its usage by major media corporations such as Sony and Apple.
- What are alleged, on the internet, to be some of the consequences of this particular mineral hunt?

('Risk' is often used in global capitalist calculations, and in the writings of Ulrich Beck, a noted global theorist. But *predictable* risks, or rather known, already existing consequences, such as these to the health of the children driven to do such work, are rarely explored.)

## Conclusion

This chapter, and any writing on media globalisation, attempts to cover an insanely huge area. Nevertheless it is possible and useful to work with a few key approaches across a mass of theories and speculations, which we have tried to do here.

See http://www.timesonline.co.uk/tol/news/world/asia/article3646320.ece for an exploration of the power of Indian money taking over British corporations and companies in 2008.

Overall, the ways in which you understand and experience globalised media are likely to be contradictory. They make amazing, though uneven, transformations possible, almost instantaneously, whilst hard and stubborn conflicts and inequalities persist – even if they are rendered almost invisible in many media forms. It is useful to think of 'globalisation' through models of regions, networks, flows, a kind of 'liquidity' or mesh, rather than seeing it all, rather depressingly, as block domination by the US. But if we had to have one, most adequate description for globalised media, it would be as corporate capitalist – except for China, which operates as a state capitalist economy (i.e. the state operates as though it is one capitalist in competition with the rest).

This capitalist nature of globalised media has consequences which are usually taken for granted, or seen as unchangeable. For example:

- that the financing of most 'Western' media is by advertising, often overruling principles of a public right to quality media;
- that TV viewing or web browsing is interrupted by ads;
- that internet surveillance will routinely check your consuming preferences and many other personal details;
- that media are in competition for profits, like other capitalist firms;
- that 'free trade' drives apply to cultural goods, such as films and TV;
- that 'development' means developing towards this capitalist model, with its attendant overconsumption, cheapest possible employment patterns and massive rewards for those at the top (see Miller *et al.* 2005).

Nevertheless, capitalist 'globalisation' has produced, for example, the possibility of struggling globally, and nimbly, against threats to 'the planet'. The US space agency NASA offers both unparalleled opportunities for global surveillance, but also huge resources for environmental advances. Many cultures and individuals are adapting in intriguing ways to increased interconnections. And the possibilities for direct global participation in more democratic forms of media, and government, seem real, via the imaginative communities in which many of us take more and more part.

*Figure 5.14* A globalised welcome sign at a Cardiff school.

## References and further reading

Balnaves, Mark, Donald, Stephanie Hemelryk, and Shoesmith, Brian (2009) *Media Theories and Approaches: A Global Perspective*, London and New York: Palgrave MacMillan.

Bennett, Tony, Grossberg, Lawrence, and Morris, Meaghan (2005) *New Keywords: A Revised Vocabulary of Culture and Society*, Malden and Oxford: Blackwell.

Chapman, Jane (2002) *Comparative Media History: An Introduction, 1789 to the Present*, Cambridge: Polity Press.

During, Simon (2005) *Cultural Studies: A Critical Introduction*, London: Routledge.

Hall, Stuart (2007) 'Living with Difference', *Soundings*, winter: 148–58.

Herman, Ed, and McChesney, Robert (1997) *The Global Media: The New Visionaries of Corporate Capitalism*, London: Cassell.

Hochschild, Arlie, and Ehrenreich, Barbara (eds) (2003) *Global Woman: Nannies, Maids and Sex Workers in the New Economy*, London: Granta.

Johnson, Chalmers (2007) 'The Good Empire', *Soundings*, winter: 80–91.

Johnson, Phil (1996) *Massive Attack, Portishead, Tricky and the Roots of Trip-Hop: Straight outa Bristol*, London: Coronet Books.

Klein, Naomi (2001) *No Logo*, 2nd edn, London: Flamingo.

Klein Naomi (2007) *The Shock Doctrine: The Rise of Disaster Capitalism*, London and New York: Allen Lane.

McLuhan, Marshall (1964) *Understanding Media: The Extensions of Man*, London: Routledge and Kegan Paul.

Miller, Toby (2007) *Cultural Citizenship: Cosmopolitanism, Consumerism and Television in a NeoLiberal Age*, Philadelphia: Temple University Press.

Miller, Toby, Govil, Nitin, McMurria, John, and Maxwell, Richard (2005) *Global Hollywood 2*, revised edn, London: British Film Institute.

Pilkington, Ed (2009) 'Dark Future as Cash-Hit Hollywood Slashes New Films', *The Guardian* 19 October.

Schiller, Herbert I. (1997) 'Not Yet the Post-Imperialist Era', in O'Sullivan, Tim, and Jewkes, Yvonne (eds) *The Media Studies Reader*, London: Routledge.

Soderberg, Hans (2006) 'Is There Blood on your Mobile Phone?', http://danchurchaid.org.

Therborn, Goran (2009) 'The Killing Fields of Inequality', *Soundings*, 42 (summer): 20–32.

Volkmer, Ingrid (2003) 'The Global Network Society and the Global Public Sphere', *Development* 46, 1: 9–16.

THE MEDIA STUDENT'S BOOK

Webb, Peter (2007) *Exploring the Networked Worlds of Popular Music: Milieu Cultures*, New York: Routledge, especially Chapters 1 and 2.

Wheen, Francis (2004) *How Mumbo-Jumbo Conquered the World*, London: Fourth Estate.

# CASE STUDY

# *Slumdog Millionaire*: Global film?

- THE BACKGROUND TO A GLOBAL HIT
- THE PRODUCTION OF THE FILM
- DISTRIBUTION
- THE BOLLYWOOD CONNECTION

- CONTROVERSIES IN RECEPTION
- AFTER THE OSCAR CEREMONIES . . .
- CONCLUSION
- REFERENCES AND FURTHER READING

*Slumdog Millionaire* (UK 2008) is a cultural phenomenon. Worldwide, the most successful British film of all time (i.e. a British film made without American money), it was assumed to be American in some markets and Indian in some others. It could reasonably be claimed as a global text on the basis of both its textual content and how widely it has been seen, but also in terms of aspects of its production. But it has also created controversy and challenged audiences in different ways and in different cultural contexts.

## THE BACKGROUND TO A GLOBAL HIT

The story of *Slumdog Millionaire*'s production has been more widely circulated than that of most feature films – partly because the production story itself became part of the 'magic' of the movie as its creators embarked on a long promotional tour that continued even after its Oscar success. The story begins with Vikram Swarup, an Indian diplomat in London and author of the source novel, *Q & A*. He appears to have drawn on two specific news stories – one in the UK and one in India. A retired army officer in the UK was convicted of fraud after cheating on the quiz show *Who Wants to Be a Millionaire* (*WWTBAM*). Since the show was also massively popular in India, Swarup then thought, 'Who would be the least likely winner of the top prize in the Indian version – who might be accused of cheating?'

A scientist in Delhi experimented by putting a computer only accessible to children into a poor area of the city. The children quickly learned how to use the computer without any help from adults. From these two stories Swarup constructed the narrative of a young man from the slums who knows the answers to the quiz questions because they each refer to something he has experienced in his life, rather than knowledge he gained through education.

The novel was 'Indian' but it was written using the demotic language of English-speaking India. It draws on very traditional storytelling techniques such as that in the *Arabian Nights* (*The 1001 Nights*) in which Scheherazade has to tell a different story each night or the sultan will have her executed. In *Q & A*, the young man, Ram Thomas Mohammed, has to explain how he knows the answer to each quiz question by recalling specific aspects of his biography for his defence lawyer.

## EXPLORE 5.15 WHO WANTS TO BE A MILLIONAIRE IN INDIA?

Google the question above.

- Why was *WWTBAM* such a big hit in India?
- Which celebrities were associated with it?
- How do you think the programme might have been received by middle-class Indians? Would the poorest Indians even have seen the show?
- What themes do you think might be explored in an Indian film based around the show?

*Q & A* was well received in the UK and serialised on BBC Radio 4. It was also read before publication by Film 4 producer Tessa Ross who optioned the film and commissioned Simon Beaufoy to adapt it. Beaufoy decided to travel to India in an attempt to retain the 'Indianness' of the novel, but as an experienced screenwriter with a major worldwide hit to his credit (*The Full Monty*, UK 1997), he knew that the storyline would have to be modified considerably to sell to mainstream audiences in the UK.

Here are some of the ways Beaufoy changed the story:

1 The central character becomes Muslim and one of two brothers from a Mumbai slum. His name is changed to Jamal. In the novel, the character is an orphan brought up in an English clergyman's house in Delhi and there is an explanation of why he can speak English and why he has a name that spans India's three major religions.

2 Several of the sub-plots are removed to make the storyline clearer.

3 The romance element is made more important and runs across the whole storyline.

The story would be further tweaked when Danny Boyle came on board as director, but in the final script Boyle would claim that the narrative goal – essentially to bring the childhood sweethearts together – was not 'American' since it downplayed winning the money. Winning the girl seems to have worked with American audiences though.

*Figure 5.15* Jamal on the set of *Who Wants to be a Millionaire?*

While Beaufoy was doing this work, Ross was securing the property in partnership with producer Christian Colson. A well-known UK producer of smaller films, Colson was in 2005 still associated with Celador Films, part of the group that owned the rights to *WWTBAM*. Swarup had not used the show's title in the novel, but Ross thought that it was essential to be able to use it in the film. When Colson secured these rights, he was able to fund the production of the film and then sell the distribution rights of the finished film to Pathé in the UK and Ireland and France, Warner Bros in North America and other companies in territories around the world. With the revenue from this sale, Colson could cover the costs of production, but would retain control – meaning that the film would remain a UK production without interference from the Hollywood distributor.

## THE PRODUCTION OF THE FILM

When Danny Boyle finally agreed to direct, he chose to shoot the film entirely in India using an Indian crew but with most 'Department Heads' from the UK. Boyle has spoken about his Hollywood studio film shot in Thailand (*The Beach* 2000) and how he didn't want to repeat the experience of taking a Western crew to Asia. With his regular cinematographer, Anthony Dod Mantle (who often works in Denmark), he devised a complex shooting plan on location in Mumbai using film and digital equipment with second unit Indian crews shooting elsewhere in India.

One of the crucial decisions for the production team was the casting and communication with actors. Boyle's ex-partner and continuing professional colleague, the casting director Gail Stevens, worked on the film in London but in India the team turned to Loveleen Tandan to act first as casting director. Tandan worked so closely with the younger actors that she was eventually given the credit of 'co-director'.

### Indian cinema

India produces more films and has larger audiences than any other film territory in the world. But this is not one single industry. Film production is organised in a range of production centres according to language and the target audience of the films. Most people outside of India have heard of 'Bollywood' but although this is arguably the richest and most high-profile of the Indian film industries, it is not representative of all of Indian cinema.

**Bollywood** is a relatively recent term (perhaps in wide circulation only since the late 1980s). It refers to certain forms of popular cinema made in Hindi – the official language of India understood by about 40 per cent of the population, mainly in the north. The capital of Bollywood is Mumbai (Bombay) where around two hundred films with big budgets (by Indian standards) are made each year. But more films are actually made in the four south Indian languages of Tamil, Telugu, Malayalam and Kannada (around four hundred each year). These different language cinemas are rather disparagingly known as regional cinemas and this term also covers several smaller production centres using other Indian languages such as Bengali, Marathi, Assamese, etc.

A third type of film is sometimes referred to as parallel cinema. There is no hard definition of a parallel film but generally it refers to films that are more serious, possibly more realist and/or art-oriented. Such films appeal more to the middle-class audiences in Delhi, Mumbai, Bangalore and other major cities. The films could be made in any of India's languages, but are usually in Hindi or English in order to reach the biggest audiences. Diaspora film-makers such as Mira Nair and Deepa Mehta – Indian film-makers trained in North America – could be described as parallel film-makers when they work in India.

The large overseas population of first- and second-generation Indian migrants (termed NRIs or non-resident Indians) are an important market for Bollywood films and also, in some territories, for Tamil and Telugu-language films.

Danny Boyle watched a group of Indian films as part of his preparation for the shoot. These included mainstream Bollywood films starring Aamir Khan, the Bollywood star most associated with social issues, and all of the films made by Mira Nair in India. Nair's 1988 film *Salaam Bombay* deals with many of the same narrative incidents as *Slumdog Millionaire*. Boyle also studied the films of Ram Gopal Varma, known for gritty gangster films, and Anurag Kashyap, whose *Black Friday* (India 2004), with a story about the Bombay bombings of 1993, was quoted by Boyle as his inspiration for the chase through the Mumbai slums early in *Slumdog*.

The production team made a series of crucial decisions about casting which had a big impact on the subsequent reception of the film. The central protagonists in the story had to age from nine to thirteen to eighteen. Local casting sessions produced 'real' street children who were capable of performing for the cameras, but would struggle to do so using English. They therefore worked closely with Loveleen Tandan and used Hindi. The older local actors portraying the same characters were able to handle English but Boyle could not find an adult Jamal in

Mumbai. He explained that the young Bollywood actors were all 'pumped up' and gym-toned. This was why Dev Patel (then known mainly for appearances in the TV series *Skins*) was flown out from the UK.

In Indian terms, the star of the film is Anil Kapoor (the quizmaster), a prominent Bollywood figure, although Irrfan Khan (the police inspector) is also a well-known actor in both Bollywood and parallel films and is recognisable outside India for his roles in parallel and international films. Otherwise, *Slumdog* has a relatively unknown cast.

## DISTRIBUTION

The film was completed within budget (reported as £7–8 million) but its future was suddenly thrown into doubt when Warner Bros decided to close its 'specialist' film labels, one of which was handling *Slumdog*. There was every chance that *Slumdog* would be pushed straight to DVD in North America as a result. Boyle and Colson rushed to Hollywood to try to rescue the film and succeeded in persuading Warner Bros to sell the rights to another studio's specialist division, Fox Searchlight. Both Boyle and Beaufoy had experienced success with Fox Searchlight (*28 Days Later* and *The Full Monty*) and the company has a strong track record in taking low-budget 'independent' films into mainstream cinemas. Even so, the fact that much of the first part of *Slumdog* was subtitled was an issue (especially for television in North America).

Fox also agreed to release the film in India in two versions, the 'original' and one dubbed into Hindi throughout. The English version played in the urban multiplexes where Hollywood films usually play in India and the Hindi version was released as a Bollywood film would be released – in urban and suburban/smaller town cinemas.

The shift to Fox had no real effect in the UK (where Pathé released the film). But it was important that the American release and the swiftly growing profile of the film during the awards season leading up to the Oscars did help to open the film in territories all

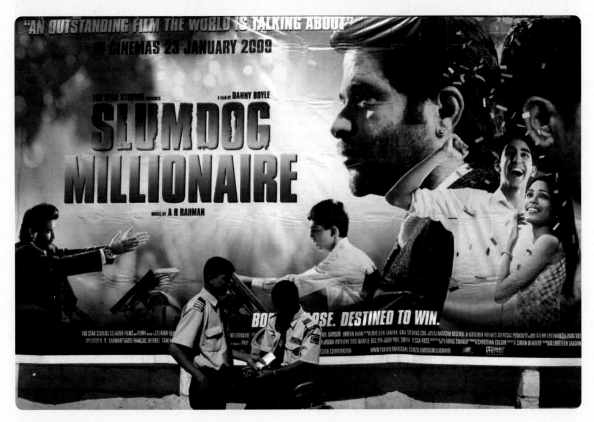

**Figure 5.16** The English-language version poster in Bangalore, southern India with two security guards.

over the world, culminating in $2.9 million in China in the first four days.

## An international hit

Worldwide, the box office gross of *Slumdog Millionaire* as of October 2009 was reported by Box Office Mojo as $377 million (http://www. boxofficemojo.com). It will probably be more than that as in some territories reliable figures are hard to come by. The UK figure was $52 million, US $141 million, with healthy numbers (i.e. by local standards) in all the major territories across Europe, East Asia and Latin America. The Indian total is given as $7.3 million, but it isn't clear whether this includes the Hindi-language total of $3.6 million (http://www.ibosnetwork.com).

Hollywood films are global in the sense that they are understood and enjoyed in film markets around the world. Ironically, in India Hollywood takes only around 5 per cent of the theatrical market, although its influence is arguably much greater since many Bollywood films openly 'borrow' story ideas from successful Hollywood films. (In 2008, one of the most successful Bollywood films, *Ghajini*, was a remake of a Tamil film which itself had copied the Hollywood thriller *Memento* (2000).)

*Slumdog* is not a Hollywood film, though it has been taken to be one. In fact, for several reasons, *Slumdog* has been caught between Hollywood and Bollywood. Few audiences around the world think of it as a British film. Partly this is because the film has been so successful that it has, by accident, fulfilled the strong desire on behalf of both Hollywood and Bollywood producers to create a film that could succeed in both markets and then around the world – the film that could replicate the success of *Crouching Tiger, Hidden Dragon* (China/HK/Taiwan/US) in 2000. As noted in Chapter 5, there have been several deliberate attempts to create this hybrid, none as yet as successful across the globe as *Slumdog*.

## THE BOLLYWOOD CONNECTION

Both the business analysis of *Slumdog*'s success and the cultural analysis of what the film means for audiences have struggled to deal with the film's relationship to the concept of Bollywood.

*Slumdog* benefited from the musical score composed by A.R. Rahman, the 'Mozart of Madras' and arguably the biggest name in film music worldwide. Although he began in south Indian film-making, Rahman has had a distinguished career in Bollywood and the UK/US as well. His music in *Slumdog* is important, but only one song, 'Jai Ho!', involves dance choreography and this appears in the closing credit sequence. Though seen in the West as a nod towards Bollywood, Indian audiences did not necessarily see the rather loose dance sequence as authentic Bollywood. On the other hand, the film no doubt attracted some audiences simply on the strength

of a score by Rahman. (Indian film soundtracks are important media products and not just elements of the films.)

## CONTROVERSIES IN RECEPTION

The best territory for the film (i.e. its box office take relative to the size of the market) was the UK, where audiences were not confused by the film's identity. Danny Boyle is a 'name director' and by the time of the film's release in early January 2009, the earlier success in North America (where the film had been released on a 'platform' of a small number of screens in November) had helped to build a major promotional campaign. Some audiences were taken aback when the promotional spin that this was a 'feel-good film' was contradicted by some of the violent scenes. Nevertheless, the film was highly praised and gradually built a large mainstream audience over several weeks (it didn't open as widely as most Hollywood films in the UK).

The controversies developed during the film's opening week in India, also in January 2009. The English version of the film appears to have outsold the Hindi

### What is Bollywood?

The two hundred or so Bollywood films each year span a range of genres and different approaches to film-making. There are horror films and gangster films as well as 'social' dramas and historical dramas and films such as those by Ram Gopal Varma and Anurag Kashyap and watched by Danny Boyle that might be described as in some ways 'New Wave'. Some of these films could be viewed as overlapping with parallel cinema.

Yet, despite this diversity, the biggest-selling Bollywood films still focus on comedy and romance. They tend to be long by Hollywood standards (though the two forms are now to some extent converging on 130–140 minutes) and to feature six or seven highly choreographed and expensively mounted dance sequences featuring big stars who must dance (and mime to playback singers). Most important, Bollywood is entertainment-led. The films create a fantasy universe, peopled largely by the wealthy middle class and focusing on moral values associated with the conventions of middle-class Indian family life – the realities of life for the majority of the population in India are not a primary concern. The attempt to appeal to an NRI audience means that stories often focus on characters who move between North America, Europe and India. Bollywood audiences expect glamour, excitement and stars – escapist entertainment.

*Figure 5.17* Posters for the Hindi version in Ahmedabad, Gujerat, in western India. Some posters carried the Hindi title represented in Roman script as 'Crorepati Slumdog'.

version in cinemas. However, Indian box office figures are notoriously difficult to check (each language cinema has its own chart) and because the Hindi version may have played in cinemas with lower ticket prices outside the major city centres, it is possible more people saw the film in Hindi. In the Hindi chart, the film was deemed an 'Average Hit'. Its Hindi box office was actually above the average (but a long way behind the 'Super-Hit' Bollywood films).

As soon as audiences began to engage with the film, opinion divided. It is worth remembering that the Oscar nominations (*Slumdog* received ten nominations) were announced just as the film opened in India. Critics and audience members were torn between praising the film and hoping for Oscar success for an 'Indian' film, and criticising it for being a film about India made by a Westerner. Here is a flavour of the comments:

> . . . This isn't the 'real' India. This is India as seen through the eyes of a Westerner who's selling *desi* squalor packaged as savvy slick entertainment
> . . . Yup, this is a film on a mission. It wants to exploit the Mumbai slums as a hotbed of tantalising images conveying the splendour of squalidity.
>
> (IBOS (Hindi Box Office Website) Review, Subhash K Jha, 23 January 2009)

> . . . allegiance to the West could have made this a bloodless, distanced copy of a fun book, but one look at *Slumdog Millionaire*, and you know that its spirit and soul is flagrantly, proudly Indian:

the Empire has been finally, overwhelmingly trounced.

It's not about poverty pornography. It's not about a White guy showing us touchy Brown-skins squatting by the rail-tracks. In the end, it's just about a film, which sweeps you up and takes you for an exhilarating ride on the wild side. Jai Ho.

(Shubhra Gupta, *Indian Express*, 22 January 2009)

An interesting view of the film came from a young Indian living in America who posted a favourable review on the 'Aint It Cool' website:

Most Indian movies are fairy tales, and fairy tales in popular culture are for two things: to highlight a moral value and escape the burdens of reality. Both of these have been the driving forces in the majority of our Hindi movies. They tried to induce morality but worked because of the escapism. We love our escapism. We would believe anything . . . *Slumdog Millionaire* is a fairy tale as well. But it's what a fairy tale would be if David Simon [creator of *The Wire*] wrote one.

(posted on: http://www.aintitcool.com, 26 November 2008)

What is interesting about the enormous outpouring of comments on the film is that many of the critics who denounce the film are only too aware that it is very knowing about Indian cinema and Bollywood in particular. They can't argue that this is an 'ignorant' Western view of India, since they have to acknowledge that it is an Indian story constructed for the screen by a Westerner who in turn openly admits his Indian influences. The argument for some critics then becomes: 'Would an Indian film-maker who had done the same job have won as many awards?'

The range of questions that the film raises within globalisation discourses is neatly summarised in the opening to a submission to the website 'Dark Matter':

Sound bites: poverty porn, slum tourism, imperialist guilt flick, post-colonial inequalities continued, Bombay's underbelly revealed-revelled, brilliant, feel good movie, accurate portrayal, gross misrepresentation, a visual Lonely Planet guide to Mumbai, an (anti-)Indian movie, Bollywood mania.

(Atticus Narain, 9 March 2009)

## EXPLORE 5.17 POVERTY PORN?

Read over the comments above and others you can find online.

- How did you respond to the images of poverty?
- What is at stake in using terms like 'real', 'feel-good' and 'escapism' in describing this film?
- What is the 'Indian' identity that these commentators disagree about?

## AFTER THE OSCAR CEREMONIES . . .

The stir created by *Slumdog* persisted in the months following the film's Oscar success. Danny Boyle became the focus of tabloid interest around the world when he was accused of not rewarding the youngest stars of the film sufficiently. Perhaps mindful of Angelina Jolie's and Madonna's adoption of poor children from Africa and Asia, Boyle had put money into a trust fund for two of the slum children to pay for their education and eventually for new accommodation. This didn't come quickly enough for the tabloid editors.

At the same time, some young Indian film-makers have seen Boyle as a film-maker who now has a global presence. Boyle has already announced that he was so excited by filming in Mumbai that he intends to make at least one more film in the city, based on a recent non-fiction bestseller *Maximum City: Bombay Lost and Found* by Suketu Mehta. He has also indicated that he wants to work with Indian film-makers Shekhar Kapur and Anurag Kashyap.

*Slumdog*'s impact on film studies and cultural studies has seen similar divisions between professional critics and scholars as between reviewers and commentators. For instance, in the American journal *Cineaste*, Robert Koehler lambasted the film (and Danny Boyle), suggesting that the success in awards ceremonies was evidence of the middle-brow taste of American audiences. In his view there is nothing original about the film and he suggests that Boyle copied well-known classical Hollywood directors such as Orson Welles. Boyle and Beaufoy simply offered a Western liberal's view of India. Most of this was refuted by Rahul Hamid in the next issue of the same journal. Hamid, while admitting the film's flaws, suggests that it is 'a film about globalisation' and that it offers sets of contrasts about rich and poor such as the scenes around the Taj Mahal – precisely not the usual tourist views but instead framed in terms of the boys' desperate urge to make money. It is not so important whether Koehler or Hamid is 'correct' in his reading, but that new kinds of global text raise new kinds of questions.

## CONCLUSION

There are balancing views pointing out the Indian sources for many of Boyle's stylistic ideas in the presentation of the story. Less common – and an indictment of film culture's general neglect of literary authors – is reference to Swarup's original ideas (including a similar Taj Mahal incident) in the debates. Whatever the commentary on the film in India and the West, it represents a new phenomenon – an essentially Indian story, created by an Anglo-Indian partnership of sorts, that has been widely seen around the world and earned thirty times its production budget at the box office. That kind of success demands to be repeated in some way.

## REFERENCES AND FURTHER READING

Blakely, Rhys (2009) 'What Do Real Slumdogs Think of *Slumdog Millionaire*?' *The Times*, 9 February 2009.

Hamid, Rahul (2009) 'A Hatchet Job on *Slumdog Millionaire*', *Cineaste*, 34, 3: 75–6.

Koehler, Robert (2009) '*Slumdog Millionaire* Review', *Cineaste*, 34, 2: 75–7.

Kumar, Amitava (2008) '*Slumdog Millionaire*'s Bollywood Ancestors', *Vanity Fair* 23 December 2008, accessed via http://www.vanityfair.com/online/oscars/2008/12/slumdog-millionaires-bollywood-ancestors.html

http://www.ibosnetwork.com/

http://www.darkmatter101.org/site/2009/03/09/rethinking-post-colonial-representation-after-slumdog-millionaire/

More links available on the **MSB5 website**.

# 6 Ideologies and discourses

> - 'Ideology' and its histories: Marxist approaches
> - Post-Marxism
> - Identity politics and critical pluralism
> - Discourses
> - Lived cultures
> - Conclusion
> - References and further reading

The concepts of **ideology** and of **discourse** have been key ones for media studies, especially in Europe. We argue that 'ideology' still has a key role to play in suggesting the often taken-for-granted and unseen connections between the media and different kinds of power, even as Web 2.0 gives more visibility to dissenting views of all kinds. 'Discourse' here can help us explore the 'in-between' area of how overarching and long-lasting ideologies become part of daily practices, especially language, its assumptions, its ways of positioning the reader, and user, on- and off-line.

## 'Ideology' and its histories: Marxist approaches

Some sets of ideas, though forming a system, even a rigid one, are not classified as 'ideological'. Someone may have obsessive ideas about personal cleanliness, and relate them systematically to the phases of the moon. But these are not called 'ideological' since they cannot be shown to relate to the distribution of social power.

Ideology refers to:

- sets of ideas which give some account of the social world;
- ideas which are usually partial (in both senses) and selective (as all positions are);
- the relationship of these ideas or values to the ways in which power is distributed socially.

'Ideology' is often taken to be:

- one of the means by which dominant economic classes extend their control over others (see Balnaves *et al.* 2009); and

- one of the ways in which dominant values and meanings come to seem 'natural' and 'obvious' rather than socially aligned, in other words, again, how they work with, or against, particular sets of power.

The place of religious beliefs in this spectrum is much debated. The first time it was argued that ideas are not free-floating but instead systematically linked to social power was in France, in the period leading up to the 1789 Revolution, which replaced feudal relations, justified by religious beliefs, with those of the 'Enlightenment' (a secular, not a religious view of the world; anti-monarchist politics, replacing a feudal monarchy with power centred on the newly rising bourgeoisie or middle classes).

Discussion of ideology in Western media and cultural studies usually comes out of the much later work of **Marx** (see Chapter 1). Writing in the nineteenth century, Marx questioned the supposedly 'natural' but unequal order of things. He analysed the then-new profit- and competition-dominated system – **capitalism** – and the power of two classes within it: the rising industrial manufacturers (or capitalists) and the working class (or proletariat).

*Figure 6.1* A 2009 film about Charles Darwin and his struggle with his religious upbringing when working on the theory of evolution. It received good reviews but struggled to find a US distributor and eventually was picked up by an independent company.

**Feudalism:** a system in which the poor had duties towards the landowners, those of 'noble birth'. Ideologically this was justified by a worldview in which the Earth was made by God, the sun revolved round it, and everything on Earth had a natural place in this divinely designed order.

**Capitalism:** a competitive social system, emerging in seventeenth-century Europe, involving private ownership of accumulated wealth and the exploitation of labour to produce profit, which creates such wealth.

### Some useful terms

The term 'capitalism' is suddenly in use again, following the 'financial crisis' and then traumatic recession(s) beginning in 2008. Michael Moore's new film in 2009 was even titled *Capitalism: A Love Story*. Desperate attempts to understand these events made visible this previously marginalised term. But it is rarely explained, and nor are related concepts. Here are some brief guidelines.

*Mercantilism* describes a class system emerging in the sixteenth and seventeenth centuries, led by merchants who accumulated wealth obtained through colonial exploitation, slavery and war. It's useful as drawing attention to the key role of money made from slave trading and the wealth of empire in the development of Western capitalism.

*Industrial capitalism* began in the late eighteenth and early nineteenth centuries when a new class of industrial entrepreneurs exploited technological innovation (such as the steam engine) using accumulated capital or money (from the slave trade, mercantile exploits, etc.). The factory system of production began and political power overall was wrested from aristocratic landowners, whose power dated from feudal times, by these 'capitalists'.

*Socialism* is an ideal arising partly from the experience of workers in this new factory system. It is broadly a belief in collective or public ownership, and

socialism

*Figure 6.2* In 2009, the Republican and private health firms' opposition to President Obama's socialised healthcare proposals used old-style fears of totalitarian socialism, as here. See Chapter 1 case study, and also Michael Moore's *Sicko* (2007) for contexts.

See Lawson (2009), who uses 'turbo-consumption' to describe our times; Klein (2007); and Wolff, offering a Marxist analysis of the crisis on http://video.google.com:80/videoplay?docid=7382297202053077236.

There's a key difference between European and US uses of the terms 'working class' and 'middle class'. In the more 'aspirational' US, 'middle class' is used to signify a much broader group than in European usage. It often covers groups which Europeans call 'working class'.

the rights of all working people to full representation in political systems. It was developed through trade union power, often supported by 'nonconformist' churches.

*Corporate capitalism* (sometimes called 'post-industrial') is the contemporary form into which capitalism has developed. Large corporations are mostly owned by 'institutional' shareholders (pension and insurance funds), making links between ordinary people (stakeholders, here) and big corporations. It is only 'post-industrial' in the sense that much manufacturing is moved around the globe – often to low-wage economies.

For the past few decades it has been combined with consumer capitalism, a term drawing attention to capitalism's inherent capacity to overproduce, leading to incitements to consume in every area of life, and arguably to environmental catastrophes.

Marx (see Chapter 1) argued that **class** difference, or people's relationship to the means by which goods and wealth are made and distributed (the 'means of production'), was key to the kinds of values and political ideas that they have. Do they *own* and *profit from* factories, banks, country estates, or do they have to earn their living by *working for* the owners of factories, banks and so on? The accounts of the world held by these two groups will be very different. Marx was especially interested in capitalists' relationship to those they employed, the working class, who, he argued, had the power to change history by their united action and their practical experience of having to learn how to work together rather than competitively. He saw class conflict, between these two groups, as the motor of history.

### Two contemporary applications

1   Though Marx was not very interested in fiction forms, and had no experience of our media, later broadly Marxist textual accounts of advertising, for example, can be related to his ideas. They emphasise how ads' focus on the product, the powers claimed for it and the joys of using it all render the work of producing it (labour) invisible, or even 'natural' – a deeply ideological move. The product can seem to appear from nowhere, without the exploitation of either human labour or the world's natural resources (see Williamson 1985 and 2008).

Car ads additionally raise issues of the toll on natural resources through manufacture (metals, glass, rubber, oil-based products such as plastic, etc.), whatever their fuel efficiency. Though understandably not treated by Marx's nineteenth-century work, such climate change related issues can be usefully explored in this context. (See Williamson at http://www.frieze foundation.org/talks/detail/the_culture_of_denial, Chapter 11 and the issues of 'greenwashing' it raises, and the case study for this chapter.)

> President G. W. Bush in 2000, at a dinner for New York's wealthiest socialites, remarked, 'This is an impressive crowd – the haves and the have-mores. Some people call you the elite, I call you my base' – an unusually frank statement by a member of the ruling order.

## EXPLORE 6.1

- Research a few car ads (TV/YouTube, and print or other online forms).
- Do they seem to have the kinds of relationship to dominant values outlined above? If not, say where and how.

2  Another interesting application of Marx's emphasis on labour, or work, and the ideological ways it is made invisible in capitalist cultures (except when strikes, etc. occur) might be the physical presence and ideological prominence of stars and celebrities. Unimaginable amounts of other people's labour go into not just the lifestyle of stars (nannies, chauffeurs, servants, agents) but also their appearance, which is often presented as 'natural' and as something we could, and should, all aim for (via cheap versions of their expensive clothes, beauty treatments, etc.; make-over programmes; 'easy' recoveries from pregnancies, etc.). In addition their presence in films is highly constructed (by the labour of lighting, costume, make up, scripting, etc.) but often celebrated as though it were 'just them',

*Figure 6.3* In 2009 Julia Roberts was in India filming *Eat Pray Love*. She had 350 guards, including forty gunmen, while being driven in bulletproof cars tailed by a helicopter (Hyde 2009). A sacred Hindu temple was closed for nine days for filming to take place – also involving labour.

## EXPLORE 6.2

Take your favourite star or celebrity and explore:
- their image, in relation to their idea that they are 'naturally' just themselves;
- any material you can find on how their physical presence has been constructed by the labour of others.

How gendered do these kinds of appeals seem to be?

Marx used the concept of ideology (as well as theories of force) to help account for how the capitalist class was able to protect and preserve its economic interests, even during years of unrest and attempted revolutions. Three of his emphases have been particularly important, (though of course he was writing well before the interactive media we now take for granted).

1   The dominant ideas, which become part of the 'common sense' of any society, are those which work in the interests of the ruling class, to secure its dominance. Marxism sees this as leading to fundamental misrepresentations of the real conditions of life, especially paid work. It is those who *own* the means of production who thereby, also, control the means of producing and circulating the key political ideas in any social order. This is said to be key to why the meaning-making bodies in any society (now dominated by the media) represent broadly political issues as they do. It implies that the working class needs to develop its own ideas and imaginings, and struggle for the means of circulating them, if it is successfully to oppose capitalist rule.

2   Related to this, Marx argued for a base–superstructure model of the social role of institutions, which would now include the media. He argued there is a clear relationship between the ways the basic needs of a social order are met (through factory production in industrial capitalist orders, or rural production within landlord–peasant relations, for example) and its superstructure, i.e. its 'secondary', less basic institutions, such as organised religions and cultural life. Such a model is also often called economic determinist, since the economic 'base', and who owns it, is argued to *determine*, not just to influence, cultural and political activities.

3   A final step is the argument that, through these sets of power relationships, the dominant class is able to make workers believe that existing relations of exploitation and oppression are *natural, inevitable and therefore unchangeable*. This ideological power 'mystifies' the real conditions of existence, and how they might be transformed. Crucially it conceals the vested interest that dominant groups have in preventing change, in whatever ways necessary, since they benefit from things as they are.

Later, for media and cultural studies, the Italian Marxist **Gramsci**'s term **'hegemony'** was taken up as a key way of thinking about how dominant value systems change. Gramsci emphasised their relationship to everyday *lived cultures* and to 'common sense' which he saw as having a core of 'good sense' which needs to be developed in trying to 'unmask' the reality of class-divided societies and to struggle successfully for change.

## Gramsci, Althusser and Klein

**Antonio Gramsci** (1891–1937) was a revolutionary Italian Marxist activist
and theorist who took part in political struggles in Italy, involving church and
state, north and south, peasants and modern industrial workers. As a result his
theories showed a keen awareness of the need for *complex* struggles and
negotiations and have been seized on and adapted by modern Marxist
writers. Instead of an emphasis on the imposed dominance of a unified ruling
class, and the determining power of the economic base, Gramsci argued that
particular social groups in modern democracies struggle for control of
consensus, or *hegemony*. In this they use persuasion and consent as well as
occasional brute force. He emphasised the importance of 'everyday cultures'
and the need to connect with the hotchpotch which he argued is often
'common sense' so as to make of it 'good sense'. Such ideas have been taken
up and applied to media which he could not even have imagined.

He was imprisoned by the Fascist leader Mussolini in 1927 and died in
prison, where he had written his *Prison Notebooks*, often using obscure
language to evade the attention of his guards and the prison censors.

Later, the French Marxist **Louis Althusser** (1918–1990) argued for the
concepts of ISAs (ideological state apparatuses), including the family, media,
religious organisations and education system, and RSAs (repressive state
apparatuses) resorted to at later stages by 'the state', such as the law, prisons,
armed forces.

Because of these struggles at different levels, power is seen as never
secured once and for all but as needing to be constantly negotiated in a to-and-
fro tussle. The key point from this for media studies is that people are not
forced or duped into a false consciousness of the world, but have their consent
actively fought for all the time – nowadays, crucially, through the media.

The emphasis on both force and consent in Marx, Gramsci and Althusser
is arguably developed in **Naomi Klein**'s theory of the 'shock doctrine' along
with her work on the importance of corporate branding. However, she does
not explicitly draw on classic Marxist models. See her website http://www.
naomiklein.org for the application of 'the shock doctrine' to disasters such as
the 2010 Haiti earthquake.

> The phrase 'making a difference' is often used now (where years ago the more ambitious 'change the world' might have been). In some ways it embodies a Gramscian rather than older Marxist view of what changes can be achieved, though without Gramsci's ambitions for revolutionary changes.

The financial crises and recession beginning in 2008 offer rich examples
of struggles for hegemony. The idea of 'the market dictating' recurred
over and over. Using the term 'the market' like this denies the extent to
which humans can shape their economic conditions, and, indeed, how a
few humans, mostly male, have made them as they are.

The delighted squeals of central characters in *Sex and the City* (US 1998–2004) as they open, or are given, high fashion accessories can be argued as both an OTT image of, but also as enacting the process of, a kind of fetishisation. Q: Do any products have the same kind of fascination for you? Does *Top Gear* act out a masculine equivalent for cars?

It is also part of what Marx called '**commodity fetishism**' or '**reification**' (from the Latin for 'res' meaning 'thing'). This describes a process whereby products and larger social processes, all made by people, are treated as though they had an almost magical reality and logic of their own, as though 'the market' was almost a real 'thing'. Wikipedia has a good discussion of Marx's ironic use of the term 'fetish' for his highly rationalist, nineteenth-century intellectual context. It was then normally used in study of certain 'magical' objects in 'primitive' societies. It is now useful in thinking about ideology as a 'masking' of actual social relations – as well as about some of advertising's strategies, and results, in 'fetishistic' appetites for certain goods.

## EXPLORE 6.3

- What is your idea of 'the free market'? Where do you come across it in media forms?
- See if you can find interviews, or news/current affairs items, where different views of the current economic crisis, how to name it, picture it (see news logos) and to get through it, are debated.
- Do any speakers use 'the free market' in the ways we've suggested above?
- What other views on 'the market' have you come across? Where?

Marxism's emphasis on the determining role of ownership and economic relations is active in **political-economy** writings (e.g. Graham Murdock, Nicholas Garnham, the Glasgow University Media Group in the UK, Robert McChesney, Ed Herman, Toby Miller and Janet Wasko in the US). This work is a corrective to some media theory's emphasis on textual elements, and to over-celebration of the power of 'active audiences', though at its best it tries to work alongside these approaches. As Janet Wasko puts it, political economy is

> an indispensable point of departure (for media analysis) . . . economic factors set limitations and exert pressures on the commodities that are produced (and influence what is not produced), as well as how, where, and to whom those products are (or are not) distributed.
>
> (Wasko 2001: 29; see also Wasko *et al.* 2006)

This develops Marxist nineteenth-century models of ownership and production as 'control'. It works better for the complex and now interactive conditions of twenty-first-century global media and ownership patterns, for which *distribution* is key. But it does this without sacrificing a sense of the key pressures exerted by *ownership*. Increasing concentration of power, and profits, into the hands of a very few enormous media corporations, and of a few executives within those, is argued to lead to:

- an overall decline in the *range* of material available (e.g. in satellite and cable television programming, or cinema) as global conglomerates exclude or swallow up all but the most commercially successful operators, or those remaining few which are state-funded;
- the dominance of corporate advertising and marketing within culture generally. This is especially true of 'lightly regulated' US television channels, where heavy advertising sometimes seems almost to equal programme time. It is also powerful in 'blockbuster' cinema, with films, full of product placements, tie-ins, marketing deals, etc., often seeming like adverts for the accompanying DVDs, theme park rides, clothes, computer games, fashions, food, drink;
- the prevalence of 'blockbuster' material as 'anchors' to the performance and branding of media corporations (whether certain Hollywood films or 'flagship' TV programmes, music performers, etc.). Some argue that blockbuster success 'travels' via material which is criticised for being 'formulaic, undisturbing, easily understood'. See Wasko *et al.*'s (2006) account of Disney and debates around the global reception of its products.

> Bruce Springsteen's 1992 line '57 channels (and nothin' on)' puts this position concisely.

### A final note on 'the dominant ideology' thesis

Some writers (see Abercrombie *et al.* 1980) agree that dominant ideologies do exist, and struggles for hegemony around them, but argue that these are not as important, in explaining how social orders hang together, as

- awareness of force, in the wings (huge state bodies for surveillance and armed control; see Klein 2007), and
- the 'dull compulsion of the economic' or need to earn a living

– and, we could add, the time- and energy-consuming work of child-rearing and domestic labour. All this leaves us little room, time or power to challenge systems of values which most people either disagree with or feel to be irrelevant.

In addition, positions drawing on psychoanalysis, such as the Frankfurt School, would argue for the pleasures involved in the fetishism and **disavowals** of many cultural forms, especially branding and celebrity, in securing an apparent 'consent' to deeply unjust and unequal social orders.

> **Disavowal**: in psychoanalysis, the process of refusing to recognise a troubling or traumatic perception. Applied by some media theorists to account for the apparent power of advertising, entertainment and fantasy forms, etc. to 'mask' unpleasant realities. The term suggests some awareness on the part of audiences, along with their desire to ignore that for the sake of the pleasures of these forms.

EXPLORE 6.4

- How far do you agree with this position?
- Do your friends' attitudes, or your media experiences, seem to support any parts of it?

## Post-Marxism

Several historical changes have affected the power of 'classic' Marxist theories:

- The collapse of Eastern bloc state socialism from 1989 was disturbing for those who thought those countries had put Marxist ideas into action.
- The renewed power of 'free market' or 'neoliberal' emphases and policies, from the 1970s, has permeated most areas of life. These arguably have their media theory equivalent: a tendency *simply* to celebrate audiences' powers in relation to media, as though corporate media were not in question, and the limits they set to the variety of media output, and to audiences' activities, on- or offline.
- Equally influential have been some so-called **postmodern** positions. Despite their emphasis on 'deconstructing' dominant ideologies, they often seem to have constructed their own: an abandonment of any political connections to help construct a better world.
- A growing scepticism about the claims of science or reason to possess absolute truth, or to involve necessarily benign consequences for the world. This has enriched some areas of media analysis, especially of fictional forms. But it mattered for Marxism, which had claimed scientific status for its theories.

Such changes resulted in key questions being asked, though arguably the strengths as well as the weaknesses of Marxism were lost when it was abandoned as an approach.

- To talk of just one dominant ideology, directly related to economic power, implies an improbably argument-free ruling class, which is able smoothly to 'make' the rest of us go along with its interests. We're talking of capitalism here, rooted in competition and certain kinds of contradiction. Such 'single ideology' approaches often make very patronising assumptions about anyone other than the person doing the analysing. If the wheels of ideology roll so smoothly to produce

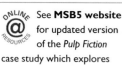

See **MSB5 website** for updated version of the *Pulp Fiction* case study which explores debates on postmodern theories.

conformity, how has the person analysing their workings come to have his or her 'outsider' perceptions?

- The challenge of newer politics has offered ways of analysing other kinds of oppression. These are based in the ways that gender or ethnicity, for example, crucially affects 'life chances'. They are not seen as absolute determinants, as class was in the Marxist model. And there are important debates now about the difference between 'diversity' and 'inequality' (see Orr 2009).

### The persistence of class and its shifting visibility

1  It used to be easy to signify, through physical appearance, that a figure was 'wealthy' or 'poor'. Nineteenth-century charity pioneers like Dr Barnardo used images of thin and raggedly dressed 'street urchins' to appeal to the conscience of the wealthier. 'Third World' charities often still do this, understandably. And until relatively recently, artists and cartoonists have used large body size, as well as clothing, top hat, accent and so on, as indicators of wealth: the 'fat capitalist' or greedy lord.

2  It is now likely that a well-toned, slim or even thin body is the result not of food shortage but of careful diet and some affluence. However, aspirations to this appearance often produce anorexia or bulimia, which further complicate matters – what are *those* slim bodies evidence of? 'Traditional' poverty can still, of course, produce rickets and thin bodies. It's also possible that expensive-looking clothes, jewellery, even cars, may conceal huge levels of personal debt.

    Such changes now make it difficult to 'read off' from physical appearance alone what might be the truth of someone's economic position. It is one of many factors making it hard to broach questions of social class, as compared with more visible identities, like gender, some disabilities, or certain ethnicities and religions.

3  Obesity, which in some cultures is prized as evidence of having plenty to eat, is, in the 'developed world', likely to be the result of both cultural and material deprivation and addictions (though genetics, and even a choice not to be a 'slave to fashion', may also come into play). As part of the complicated attitudes to such bodies, 'greed' (rather than addiction) is often said to be the cause of being overweight. Ideologically this view shifts blame away from the very addictions which often result from the marketing practices of major food brands.

4  Ideological contexts for such blamings include post-1980s celebrations of extreme wealth (as in much celebrity coverage) and justifications of

*Figure 6.4* A nineteenth-century photo of a British street child (c.1870–7) from the charity Barnardo's (www.barnardos. org.uk).

As you'll know, the area of 'approved' body shapes is now hugely gendered, despite general health concerns. The term 'body fascism' has been coined to draw attention to how ideological and coercive the images of airbrushed, surgery-enhanced bodies can be.

**Conspicuous consumption**: a term coined by the Norwegian-American economist and sociologist **Thorstein Veblen** (1857–1929) to describe the consumption of goods and commodities for the sake of displaying social status and wealth. (It is not used to describe eating disorders.)

Though 'everyone recognises' the 'underclass' figure of Vicky Pollard from BBC's *Little Britain*, it's very rare to hear the term 'the undeserving rich'.

corporate greed – which has usually been called 'growth'. Wealth, whether individual or corporate, is hardly ever represented, as in Marxist theory, as being directly related to the labour of those who produce it, 'by hand and by brain'.

Compare this to various make-over programmes, often dismissed as 'trash television' because of the people (women usually) on whom they focus in an effort to render them 'acceptable' (see Wood and Skeggs 2008). Or see the media hounding of some of the 'undeserving poor' or 'underclass', part of 'broken Britain'. These are often council estate dwellers, and especially women constructed as 'wicked mothers', whose family trees, supermarket bills if involving alcohol, and other intimacies may be ruthlessly paraded, especially but not exclusively in the 'red-tops', if the woman seems scandalous enough. See Nunn and Biressi (2009) for an excellent account, which they summarise thus: 'As the undeserving poor become ever more closely associated with negative characteristics, the well-adjusted majority can continue to enjoy the benefits of "meritocracy" with easy minds' (p. 107). 'The underclass' is a US-originated term which partly signifies not only the homeless, the addicted and even petty criminals, but also the most deprived part of the unemployed working class. The term inherits some of the derogatory values of the nineteenth-century term 'the undeserving poor', and also drains poverty of its place within unequal class divisions, which Marxism focused on.

Since the mid-1980s discussion of class, and especially working-class experience, has dwindled. The solidarities (unions, local communities, workplaces) which made for class identities were often destroyed, and replaced by neoliberal ideals such as 'social mobility' and 'consumer choice'.

## Identity politics and critical pluralism

As this shrivelling of an awareness of class identities happened, other, key identities (sexuality, ethnicity, gender and so on) claimed more expression and visibility. A good example of the difference of such **identity politics** is some feminists' argument that inequality derives from other oppressions than unequal pay in the realm of paid work, though that is key. Gendered inequality also stems from the realm of *reproduction*, meaning both the reproduction of future generations (the family) and the household work needed to reproduce social orders (caring for the workforce).

## EXPLORE 6.5

*Figure 6.5*
Taken-for-granted phrases and words form a key part of oppressive identities around gender. Cartoon by Posy Simmonds, published in the 1970s.

- See if you can devise a similar 'oppressive word mountain' for any 'identity group' which you are a member of – by age, ethnicity, sexual orientation, as well as class, perhaps.

*Figure 6.6* A postcard which highlights the different demands of different kinds of labour, domestic and industrial.

Men's social position and power can often be shown to exploit women's domestic and even emotional work for them and their children. And because of the assumed 'naturalness' of women's caring role in the home, they tend to be overwhelmingly employed in 'the four Cs': caring, cleaning, catering and cash registers (see http://www.fawcett.org.uk and Hochschild 2003). We might add call centres, though there are increasing numbers of men employed in those, as often happens in recessions with occupations previously gendered as 'feminine'. Call centres involve the kinds of 'emotional labour' skills which many women learn, both in caring for their families, and in growing up with the expectation they will have families, and will have 'natural' abilities to work/care in this way.

'Black' theorists have likewise explored not only the foundations of modern industrial development in the wealth accumulated through the slave trade, but also the ways in which inequalities between ethnic groups have been constructed and maintained, and how they have often cut across class and gender difference. Similar arguments have been made for different sexualities, for age groups (for both children and old people), disability and other key structuring experiences and struggles. All of these have become more visible, partly thanks to Web 2.0 communications in recent years, and there have been absolutely key changes to most people's experiences as a result.

Some would argue that too much of Marxism's key interest in class differences has been lost in 'identity' emphases. We still live in deeply unequal capitalist societies, driven by profit, high consumption and gross inequalities. But these now operate on a global scale, with relations of exploitation spread across and between continents, and with other kinds of oppression also producing deprivations.

Some would argue that neoliberal capitalist orders are quite happy with identity politics. Such politics are admirable and necessary, and related to class differences. But they are argued to emphasise diversity and not inequality, which is steeply rising and finding disturbing forms of expression, such as fascist movements focused on 'race' (see Orr 2009).

Pluralist models of media ownership have developed, seeing the media as floating free of power, and emphasising the apparent diversity and choice of media forms and products. They argue that, if certain values, or forms, are dominant, it is because they are 'genuinely popular' and have won out in this 'free market of ideas'. Time and again, for example, the 'popularity' of US cultural forms is attributed to 'universal' appeal rather than globally orchestrated power.

Of course there *is* diversity in media, especially in an internet/ interactive age. Both website owners and big corporations are driven to

*Figure 6.7* Banksy's image suggests not only global inequalities but the narrowed life it represents for both human sides of the rickshaw – even though they are so unequal in terms of monetary wealth.

See Wilkinson and Pickett (2009) for a massively researched study of the effects of inequality, and why remedying this needs to be prioritised above what is called 'growth'. It is estimated that 1 per cent of the world's population now own 40 per cent of its wealth, for example. Also research http://www.happyplanet index.org/.

Recall Spielberg's quote from Chapter 2: 'Once upon a time it was a small gathering of people around a fire listening to the storyteller with his tales of magic and fantasy. And now it's the whole world . . . It's not "domination" by American cinema. It's just the magic of storytelling, and it unites the world.'

circulate many different ideas and identities to remain profitable. But we still need an account of power to understand how some ideas and imaginings came to circulate more freely than others. Thus, developing the original Marxist and Gramscian emphases, others (e.g. Thompson 1997) suggest we now live in times of a complex play between several kinds of power:

- economic power
- political power
- coercive, especially military, power (see Klein 2007 on the 'shock doctrine')
- 'symbolic power', i.e. the means of information and communication, including religions, schools, universities and, crucially, the media.

Such approaches are sometimes called **critical pluralism**. They acknowledge that there may be a struggle between competing **discourses** or accounts of the world, but insist that this is not an amicable 'level playing field' free-for-all. Some discourses are parts of powerful institutions and have easy access to credibility, material resources, legal power, publicity: access which will be fought for if necessary. Others are routinely marginalised.

> There is an increasing tendency to talk of the 'narratives' instead of the positions or arguments of political players – for example, 'the Palestinians have their narrative, the Israelis have theirs'. This seems to replace 'ideologies' or 'values'. Q: What difference do you think the word makes in these contexts?

## EXPLORE 6.6

- How far do you think the internet has changed these sets of relations?
- Are there any ways in which you have experience of it:
  a   circulating marginalised discourses, or
  b   preventing such circulation?

## Discourses

We suddenly used the word 'discourses' rather than ideologies just now. It's useful to apply this complex concept to the multiple ideas and values running within bodies of power. Media studies tends now not to use the model of a single dominant versus a single oppositional set of ideas, both rooted in class struggle (the Marxist model). Indeed the Frankfurt School, a group of influential Marxist theorists who fled Nazi Germany for the US in the 1930s (see Chapter 14) began to choose to call itself 'critical' rather than Marxist, and abandoned the idea that class conflict was the driver of history.

Later theorists, responding to the struggles around identity, which focused partly on media representations of oppressed groups, have turned to a model of powerful and subordinated ideolog*ies* and identi*ties*, said to operate through *lived cultures* and powerful or marginalised *discourses*. These offer a more dispersed sense of how power structures maintain themselves, and they locate struggles for change at different levels of the social order – a more optimistic politics than that of overarching class struggle.

Let's look at the components of this approach.

'Discourse' has a long and complex history (see Bennett *et al.* 2005) and is often confusingly used in media studies, so we will spend a little time on it here. It firstly involves regulated systems of statements or language use. 'Regulated' here means that the 'appropriate' language for a given area operates, with rules, conventions – and therefore assumptions and exclusions. And 'language' can be expanded to include visual languages (as in semiotics). To put it another way, discourses are systems of language use (arguments, descriptions, theories, etc.) built up as part of particular areas of practice (e.g. the law, fashion, politics, medicine).

'Discourse' can also be traced partly to the work of the French theorist Foucault. He was interested in the organisation of knowledge in institutions, which partly involved language, but also the layout of buildings, the routine practices (accreditation, exclusion, 'the rules of the game') of the law, medicine, prisons, etc. They are an integral part of the power of some practices.

Foucault argues that discourses actually create 'regimes of truth' and therefore our perceptions. The term 'child', for example, has not always been used of 'young adults' and is notoriously hard to define, both in years and as between different cultures. But the power to define someone as a 'child' usually has enormous legal, financial and other implications.

Discourses have also, since, been argued to operate for oppositional and specialised practices and sub-cultures, such as punk fandom or the specialised language of some sport.

'Discourse', as a concept in media studies, now often explores the 'struggle for meaning' at the level of words chosen for news reports, the phrasings of interview questions, the 'rules of the game' such as the 'language-etiquette, speech-tact and other forms of associating an utterance to the hierarchical organisation of society' (Frow in Bennett *et al.* 2005: 92). Fairclough is an important writer for this linguistic aspect of 'discourse' study and its method 'critical discourse analysis', often abbreviated to CDA – see Chapter 15.

---

**Michel Foucault** (1926–84) post-structuralist philosopher, sociologist and historian of knowledge. Best known for his work on the relationship of the practices of power and knowledge, especially in the areas of madness and sexuality.

---

Often the choice of a single word – 'evil' – to describe an act or a person will serve as remnant of a fundamentally religious view of people, where acts are not to be understood or discussed as socially shaped but are seen as 'God-given' – and therefore unalterable.

The set-up of a studio, of a
lecture theatre, or of
buildings such as courts,
embassies, hospitals, big
stores – these usually
'address' and place their
users in different ways, which
some would relate to
dominant discourses and
power relations. Take notes
on any public (or virtual)
room or building you know
from this perspective.

## EXPLORE 6.7

This may sound obscure, but make notes on the next controversial interview
involving a very powerful person that you see on TV, or read an accurate account
of. Can you see the unspoken 'rules of the game', the signs of 'language-etiquette'
or 'speech-tact' in the interview? Does an atmosphere of 'some things are best not
said' prevail: certain questions clearly cannot be put; some challenging areas are
avoided or not pursued – for example, around large bonuses, or a politician's
possible prosecution at an International Criminal Court for war crimes?

If the interview or discussion involves a studio audience, how are their
questions, comments, shouts or even movements 'managed', by the interviewer or
chair, by systems of microphones, etc.? (Of course, some of the very powerful are
not even going to be available for interview. Or it may have to be on their terms,
having cleared certain issues beforehand. Equally important is the use of pre-
recording.)

Discourse analysis explores what values and identities are contained,
prevented or encouraged by the day-in, day-out practices and (often
unspoken) rules of a particular *discursive formation,* in Foucault's term.

We explore how you might use linguistic critical discursive approaches in
Chapter 15. Deacon *et al.* (2007) outline their value:

Discourse analysis can . . . point to attempts to close meaning down, to fix
it in relation to a given position, to make certain conventions self-evidently
correct, to do creative repair work when something becomes
problematic, and to make the subject positions of discourse transparently
obvious without any viable alternatives. (158)

'Subject positions' here refers to how we can be 'positioned' by the ways
certain discourses address us, in words gestures, etc. A related term is **mode
of address**. Coming out of critical linguistics, it refers to the ways a text
seems to 'speak to' its audience, or 'who it thinks we are'. In everyday
encounters, whether on- or offline, our way of addressing a teacher, a friend,
a bank manager usually incorporates a (different) 'position' for each of those
people in what we are saying: as someone being treated respectfully, with
intimacy or with caution. The further implication is that when we are

For a very funny dissection of many practices of UK news forms see Charlie Brooker's *Newswipe* (BBC4 2009–, extracts available on YouTube and a very popular one via the link http://www. broadcastnow.co.uk/news/ multi-platform/charlie-brooker-scores-global-youtube-hit/5010263.article).

The model Lily Cole recently, interviewed about her academic studies, spoke of 'banking' the experience and then seeing what she wanted to do. We routinely talk of 'investing' in decision, students are often called 'customers', we 'own' rather than are involved with projects and so on.

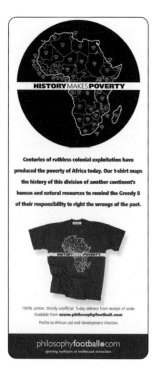

*Figure 6.8* 'Make poverty history' T-shirt

addressed in certain ways (as 'naughty children', as newly 'grown-up', etc.) we 'play along' and may even assume or perform the identity thus constructed for us, at least temporarily.

Or take 'professional' reporting of financial news. It often uses obscuring metaphors, such as 'the pound/stock exchange had a bad day/bounced back/took a hammering', or 'the NASDAQ dived' or 'getting the economy back on the rails', which later became 'the banks need to clean up their balance sheets; the government is cleaning-up the financial sector', etc. These both re-mystify the already mysterious workings of stock exchanges, and also 'naturalise' them, in the ways we outlined above via the Marxist idea of 'fetishism' or 'reification'.

Arguably related to this is the suggestion that everyday personal life, and not just 'business', is increasingly framed as a space of economic action and 'investment'. Payments of student loans, mortgages, credit cards, pensions and so on are obviously part of global financial networks. But we are also addressed by a range of 'private' cultural forms, like 'lifestyle' television and magazine features about home renovations, and many kinds of personal make-overs. These invite us to think of the future returns they may yield. We are thus repeatedly positioned in 'aspirational' ways, a classic ideological part of consumer capitalist discourses.

## EXPLORE 6.8

Consider this position for any recent 'lifestyle' programme or magazine feature you've recently enjoyed. Do you agree with the suggestion above? If not, why not?

### Examples

1  T-shirt for G8 protests in 2005. It reworks familiar discourses of African dependency by

   a  the words 'History Makes Poverty' (a variant on 'Make Poverty History' which was the slogan of many demonstrators, and already a striking phrase).

   b  the substitution of 'Greedy 8' for 'G8';

    c  (less visible) a map showing 'the history of this division of another
       continent's human and natural resources'.

2  Another example of turning a discourse around, drawing attention to the
    ways language and kinds of logic are used: 'When I give food to the poor
    they call me a saint. When I ask why the poor have no food, they call me a
    communist': Dom Helder Camara, Archbishop of Recife, Brazil (1909–99),
    a pioneer of Latin America's liberation theology movement, which argued
    the Gospels justified social change, not social acquiescence.

*Figure 6.9* 'Cool' is a powerfully fashionable attitude, one which does not easily combine with political activism, debate, etc. Kate Moss is considered by many to embody this, often performing a 'look' to camera which is haughty, unconcerned, remote, not 'needy', She is also renowned for hardly ever speaking in public, staying remote.

## EXPLORE 6.9

Look through your usual news sources, print, TV or online. Can you find any
metaphors which seem to be doing the kinds of ideological work suggested so far?
  Existing examples would include:

- the use of the metaphor of 'cancer' in political discourse, which is argued to
  encourage fatalism about a situation, and often to justify 'severe measures';
  it also suggests that cancer is always fatal, which is no longer true;

- 'downsizing' as a (pre-recession?) signifier for cutting down workforces. Other
  euphemisms include 'modernising', 'streamlining', 'restructuring', 'rationalising',
  'making leaner, fitter' and so on.

## Lived cultures

An interest in 'lived cultures' (loosely part of discourse approaches)
takes us back to some of the ideas of Gramsci, as well as out towards
the concerns of cultural studies. Gramsci argued that 'common sense',
an 'obvious' guide for many people, can be explored as a complex set
of traces, rather than simple 'wisdom'. These traces may come from
hundreds of years ago and may be contradictory ('God helps those who
help themselves'). But they are also constantly changing, and jostle with
much more recent beliefs and much 'good sense'. He emphasised that
hegemony is a lived process, never simply imposed, or existing in ideas
alone. The power of 'common sense' (rather than what he called 'good
sense') comes from its relationship to day-to-day material practices,
rituals and activities, as well as dominant ideas.

*Figure 6.10* A slogan in the form of a British Second World War **propaganda** poster which has had a huge revival recently, in mug, T-shirt and postcard forms – as well as being parodied ('NOW PANIC AND FREAK OUT'). See this chapter's case study for a companion image, and for discussion of 'propaganda'.

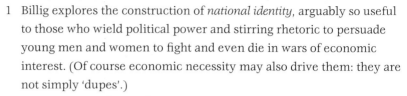

### Examples

1   Billig explores the construction of *national identity*, arguably so useful to those who wield political power and stirring rhetoric to persuade young men and women to fight and even die in wars of economic interest. (Of course economic necessity may also drive them: they are not simply 'dupes'.)

*Figure 6.11* Two girls in the ruins of Battersea, London, VE Day, 8 May 1945. Arguably their 'unknowing' use of the two flags makes the photo all the more resonant, or 'cute'. Anonymous US photographer, Imperial War Museum.

He suggests that such a 'strong' version of national identity is not something that is constantly 'there'. Instead 'one needs to look for the reasons why people in the contemporary world *do not forget* their nationality' (1995: 7; emphasis added), which is always 'there, and can then be called upon in moments of struggle'. He suggests this is achieved, in established nations, by 'banal nationalism', a set of banal, or everyday, lived practices. These form a continuous 'flagging' via everyday tiny reminders of nationhood: not a flag waved with fervent passion in the sports parade or war, but the 'flag hanging unnoticed on the public building', the daily salute to the Stars and Stripes in US schools, national symbols on coins and stamps, national history memorialised in street names, or the use of words such as 'we', 'us', 'them', 'home', 'foreign' in news reporting. Billig (2005) and Andy Medhurst (2007) have also explored the role of humour and its pleasures in sustaining dominant identities, as well as in subverting some of them.

---

## EXPLORE 6.10

- Research for a range of examples of signifiers of both 'banal' nationalist discourses and of more self-important kinds, such as commemorative or sports ceremonials, nationalist websites, etc. (The racist British National Party (BNP) was recently criticised for trying to adopt Second World War imagery as part of its image.)
- You might also watch for people who are declared 'national treasures' from time to time. What is the tone and role of this particular part of the nationalist discourse?

---

See Grindstaff and West (2006) for an interesting piece on cheerleading and the gendered politics of sport.

2   The lived cultures of sport, especially as constructed by corporate media, could also be examined for the ways they reproduce and 'refresh' our sense of categories such as gender and nationality. They also display/construct the desirability of physical and financial power (the 'big hitters', 'size matters'), part of the discourse of many big corporations.

Economic determinants clearly shape some of our sense of the relative importance of men's and women's sports. Overall media coverage of men's sports massively exceeds that of women's, which also usually has smaller prize money, except when the Olympics take place. But linguistic 'marking' and other 'natural-seeming' practices of the media reinforce the gender differences in sports.

- Women's sports are still likely to be subject to verbal and visual 'gender-marking', especially in internet imagery. Sportswomen are sometimes still infantilised in television commentary, as 'girls' (it's rare to hear male sports people called 'boys'); by the use of the first name; by repeated reference to their marital or family status (e.g. the tennis achievements of the Williams sisters were often related to their father's coaching in a way not seen with male sports stars). In women's basketball the images of the players are typically subject to sexualisation, and tennis players such as Maria Sharapova arguably attain celebrity status partly because of appearance.

- Women's achievements are less often held up as representative of 'the nation' (as happens for rugby teams, etc.). It is more usually seen as a personal affair, partly perhaps because they are less likely to be competing in the big team sports which depend on institutional funding and networking all the way from early schooling.

> 'The sports pages in newspapers are not optional extras . . . There are always sports pages, and these are never left empty. Every day, the world over, millions upon millions of men scan these pages, sharing in defeats and victories, feeling at home in this world of waved flags' (Billig 1995: 122).

## Conclusion

In summary, the Marxist emphasis on economics and class struggle as the basis of ideology has been replaced by an interest in other kinds of

- oppression
- power formations
- ways of circulating and challenging dominant assumptions.

For this there has been a shift from an emphasis on 'ideology' to one on 'discourses'. The media are no longer seen as 'concealing' or 'masking' the 'true' processes of a class struggle which exist in binary forms – capitalist/worker.

This approach has been replaced, in media studies, by

- a sense that, while concentrated levels of economic power do operate, they are complicated by other, often equally key sets of oppression;
- a sense that these are further complicated by the circulation of many confident new identities and related new ideas;
- an exploration of fiction, entertainment and fantasy forms, as well as 'factual' ones, as a way of exploring these identities;

- an interest in how audiences using many new media forms can be an active part of media processes and struggles.

Many would argue that much has been lost as well as gained in the move away from Marxism's emphasis on economic inequality, especially in present times of economic trauma and deeply unequal capitalist societies, linked globally. There seem now to be moves to re-explore some of that emphasis, for the very different times we are in – which this chapter tries to be part of.

Our case study focuses on one of the trickiest contemporary struggles, around climate change, which raises new issues for ideological analysis.

## References and further reading

Abercrombie, Nicholas, Hill, Stephen, and Turner, Bryan S. (1980) *The Dominant Ideology Thesis*, London: Allen & Unwin.

Balnaves, Mark, Donald, Stephanie Hemelryk, and Shoesmith, Brian (2009) *Media Theories and Approaches: A Global Perspective*, London: Palgrave Macmillan.

Bennett, Tony, Grossberg, Lawrence, and Morris, Meaghan (eds) (2005) *New Keywords: A Revised Vocabulary of Culture and Society*, London and New York: Blackwell.

Billig, Michael (1995) *Banal Nationalism*, London: Sage.

Billig, Michael (2005). *Laughter and Ridicule: Toward a Social Critique of Humour*, London: Sage.

Connell, Robert (2000) *The Men and the Boys*, Cambridge: Polity Press.

Deacon, David, Pickering, Michael and Murdock, Graham (2007) *Researching Communications: A Practical Guide to Methods in Media and Cultural Analysis*, London and New York: Hodder.

Fairclough, Norman (1995) *Media Discourse*, London: Arnold.

Foucault, Michel (1988) *Politics, Philosophy, Culture: Interviews and Other Writings, 1977–1984*, London: Routledge.

Golding, Peter, and Murdock, Graham (1991) 'Culture, Communications and Political Economy', in Curran, James, and Gurevitch, Michael (eds) *Mass Media and Society*, London: Edward Arnold.

Gramsci, Antonio (1971) *Selections from the Prison Notebooks*, London: Lawrence and Wishart.

Grindstaff, Laura, and West, Emily (2006) 'Cheerleading and the Gendered Politics of Sport', *Social Problems*, 53, 1.

Hochschild, Arlie (2003) *The Commercial Spirit of Intimate Life and Other Essays*, San Francisco and Los Angeles: University of California Press.

Holland, Patricia (2003) *Picturing Childhood: The Myth of the Child in Popular Imagery*, London: I. B. Tauris.

Hyde, Marina (2009) 'Julia Roberts Turns a Temple in India into a Closed Set', *The Guardian*, 25 September.

Klein, Naomi (2007) *The Shock Doctrine: The Rise of Disaster Capitalism*, London and New York: Allen Lane.

Klein, Naomi (2009) *No Logo*, revised anniversary edition, London and New York: Picador.

Lawson, Neal (2009) *All Consuming: How Shopping Get Us Into This Mess and How We Can Find Our Way Out*, London and New York: Penguin.

Lewis, Justin, Inthorn, Sanna, and Wahl-Jorgensen, Karin (2005) *Citizens or Consumers? What the Media Tell us about Political Participation*, London and New York: Open University Press.

Marmot, Michael (2005) *Status Syndrome: How Your Social Standing Directly Affects Your Health and Life Expectancy*, London: Bloomsbury.

Marx, Karl, and Engels, Frederick (1965; first published 1888) *The German Ideology*, London: Lawrence and Wishart.

Medhurst, Andy (2007) *A National Joke: Popular Comedy and English Cultural Identities*, London and New York: Routledge.

Munt, Sally (ed.) (2000) *Cultural Studies and the Working Class*, London and New York: Cassell.

Nunn, Heather, and Biressi, Anita (2009) 'The Undeserving Poor', *Soundings*, 41 (spring): 107–17.

Orr, Deborah (2009) 'Diversity and Equality Are *Not* the Same Thing', *The Guardian, G2*, 22 October, 10–11.

Therborn, Goran (2009) 'The Killing Fields of Inequality', *Soundings*, 42 (summer): 20–32.

Thompson, John B. (1997) *The Media and Modernity: A Social Theory of the Media*, Cambridge: Polity Press.

Wasko, Janet (2001) *Understanding Disney: The Manufacture of Fantasy*, Cambridge: Polity Press.

Wasko, Janet, Phillips, Mark R., and Meehan, Eileen R. (2006) *Dazzled by Disney?: The Global Audiences Disney Project (Continuum Collection)*, Leicester: Leicester University Press.

Wilkinson, Richard, and Pickett, Kate (2009) *The Spirit Level: Why More Equal Societies Almost Always Do Better*, London and New York: Allen Lane.

Williamson, Judith (1985) *Consuming Passions*, London: Marion Boyars.

Williamson, Judith (2008) 'The Culture of Denial', a talk on http://www.friezefoundation.org.

Wood, Helen, and Skeggs, Bev (2008) 'Spectacular Morality', in Hesmondhalgh, David, and Toynbee, Jason (eds) *The Media and Social Theory*, London and New York: Routledge.

# *The Age of Stupid* and climate change politics

- CONTEXT: IMAGES AND DISCOURSES
- THE TERM 'PROPAGANDA'
- TEXTUAL APPROACHES TO THE FILM
- 'CINEMA' AND ITS 'EVERYDAY PRACTICES'
- CONCLUSION
- REFERENCES AND FURTHER READING

'Climate change politics' is a complex, global and vigorously contested area. So it is no surprise that discussion of media imagery of this field can also be fierce and complicated. But at least, at last, it is now globally 'high profile'. The very idea that certain kinds of human activity were prime causes of disastrous climate change was denied for many years, often by polemicists funded by Big Oil (see www.exxonsecrets.org), who continue to be active in this area.

We are using a 2008 British film *The Age of Stupid*, funded, made, released and publicised globally in 2009, in highly unconventional ways. It forms a good case study for the ideological questions around media, including 'new media' or Web 2.0, raised by attempts to activate protest and change:

- how to 'represent' the issues at play in climate change debates;
- how to work these into a film designed for wide release, which has to make accessible and 'entertaining' cinema;
- how such re-mediation (from documentaries, political speeches, research, etc. to a hopefully engaging film) can relate to discourses and practices involved in making and distributing a 'global' film.

It was made for global release at a key 'moment': months before the Copenhagen summit of world leaders in December 2009. By then there was abundant evidence of the impact of warming.

1  The revolutionary theorist Gramsci wrote: 'The old is dying and the new cannot be born; in this interregnum a great variety of morbid symptoms appear' (1930; translated and published 1971).
2  'Other generations managed to abolish slavery, overturn apartheid or even land on the moon. We know what we have to do' (Director Franny Armstrong's email to supporters before the UK premiere, 2009).

## CONTEXT: IMAGES AND DISCOURSES

Advertising in general has claims to be the biggest propaganda system ever invented (see below). For cars in particular the ads often trade on 'planned obsolesence', as well as the fetishised glamour of the role of cars in films, games and *Top Gear* (BBC relaunch 2002–present). It's difficult to promote even the best public transport systems with quite the same sense of dangerous glamour, even though most people's actual experience of driving involves traffic jams.

Responding to evidence of accelerating climate change has for some time been hugely contradictory for car advertisers. Here a relatively 'eco-friendly' but nevertheless metals-and-minerals-hungry Prius car advertises itself. The eco-discourse is a familiar blend of

*Figure 6.13* Polar bear

*Figure 6.12* An ad for a relatively eco-conscious car, with 'good' mileage, use of recyclables, etc. By contrast you can easily find examples of car ads which flaunt their carelessness for the resources they use. See also the Prius 2010 ad on YouTube.

white colours, in car and backgrounds, a context devoid of other traffic, and signifiers of the prettier parts of 'nature'. Often car ads will 'offer to take you to places which are not likely to exist in the future, precisely because of the use of products like cars' (Williamson 2008).

Greenpeace has successfully drawn attention to the evidence of melting glaciers over the past decades. Antarctic polar bears have become figurehead images, looking forlorn but 'cute' on tiny ice floes, each seeming to be the last glacier. The slogan 'save the planet' tends to focus on such empty, spectacular landscapes. As a (dominant?) visual discourse it may carry a sense that something separate out there – 'the natural world' – can be studied, imaged and indeed 'helped'. This, though, ignores how it has long been shaped by human cultures, and especially high-consumer capitalist ones.

Even the BBC's global blockbusters *Planet Earth* (2006, first series) and *Life* (2009), wonderful in many ways, are mostly devoid of tourists, or other mention of human shaping, since that might impact on the purity of the spectacle.

The phrase, secondly, ignores the fact that 'the planet' arguably will survive any disaster affecting people. It has long mutated, and survived past huge changes. Perhaps insects, or other tenacious species, will be newly dominant?

## EXPLORE 6.11

- Are there equivalent images to this kind of warning, involving human beings?
- Would they need to come from 'hot spots', in both senses of the word?
- Then, how could such images be different from other, familiar, 'disaster' images?

*Figure 6.14* The 'dry' apocalypse of award-winning computer game *Fallout 3*.

*Figure 6.15* A poster for *The Day After Tomorrow* (US 2004), Hollywood's first eco-blockbuster film, with all the contradictions that involves.

In a wide range of images like those in figures 6.14–6.16, compelling visual discourses (especially in the US, with its long-established frontier myths) from survivalist narratives are often at play: how might you survive in a world without modern resources? These merge (certainly in parts of the US) into religious discourses of 'rapture' at what is seen as the coming, and oddly welcome, End of the World (see http://www.raptureready.com). 'The worst', here, is partly framed as yet another challenge to militaristic skills.

*Figure 6.16* *Wall-E*, big-budget animation with dystopic views of the future, but a fragile hope in its narrative.

## EXPLORE 6.12

- What are the limits and strengths to the ways that different media and media forms (fact/fiction, children's/adult forms, etc) are able to represent climate change politics? This is a challenging question for entertainment fiction forms, like cinema and some games. News, documentary, social networking sites can keep us up to date, minute by minute, with scientific debates, the latest floods and so on. Fictions perform other kinds of representational 'work', and take much longer to produce.
- Do film and TV representations have to be environmentally destructive, e.g. by showcasing expensive special FX, stars, stunts, etc. for the games and other spin-offs which are partly needed to fund the films?
- How do these relate to long-established post-apocalyptic discourses? Might they make 'the end of things' feel glamorous?
- Most important, might the repetition of such scenarios, without any sense of an alternative politics and different futures, deepen people's sense that there is nothing to be done – at least in non-'action adventure' politics and practices? (see Branston 2007).

The important British cultural theorist Stuart Hall used to refer to 'Thatcher's friend TINA' in trying to account for part of the ideological appeal of her neoliberal politics. 'TINA' stands for 'There Is No Alternative'. There are parallels with climate change politics.

## EXPLORE 6.13

List any such fictions you, or your friends, have seen, or played.

- Do you think they have they helped shape your sense of possible futures?
- How do they relate to the more practical, optimistic discourses in many children's books and news programmes, and some climate change protest movements? These offer immediate possibilities for small, everyday practices as challenges to 'inevitable' disaster. They can also build the political will for larger change, as in these solar power 'farms'.

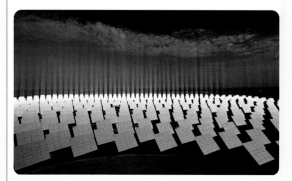

*Figure 6.17* Possible images of the future could include safe energy sources like these solar power generators in southern Spain, 2009.

- How differently did the film *Wall-E* construct these scenarios? Explore its vision of future human existence in the Buy'n'Large spaceship sequences. And at the X-Box game version, and the film's other tie-ins. Do these contradict parts of the main film's 'message'?

As a film trying to shift dominant discourses and political action on climate change, *The Age of Stupid* has to work firstly in a particular discursive context: key, familiar terms such as 'progress', 'development' and 'sustainability' need to be queried. Sustaining what social order exactly? Developing further what kinds of inequalities and unequal levels of consumption? Which impulses and sets of knowledge are effectively being *under*-developed and un-sustained?

Secondly, it inhabits several *formal* or *refracting* contexts.

- How well can films like this, needing wide circulation and to offer pleasures to big global audiences, represent complex arguments?
- How well can DVD extras, as here, usefully extend the main film?
- Key components of cinema are sensuous, audio-visual, entertaining. How to combine these with the message of the film? What genres seem to produce them?

## EXPLORE 6.14

- If you have not seen the film, jot down what you expect of it. This is often a powerful way of seeing how expectations have been shaped and circulated, even for non-blockbuster films, and also how precisely the film works.
  Areas to include:
  - how might it open?
  - what might the first scene consist of?
  - what exactly do you expect from Peter Postlethwaite's role?
  - is it to be 'propaganda'?
  - how will it end?

## THE TERM 'PROPAGANDA'

Some words can bring thoughtful conversations to a juddering halt. 'Propaganda' is one of these. To dismiss

197

a film as 'just propaganda' (a contemporary word seems to be 'preachy') is to locate or frame it as beyond the limits of acceptable discourse, as hopelessly biased and untrustworthy. On the other hand, *The Fast and the Furious* or *Top Gear*, which openly fetishise excessive carbon use, will not be seen as propaganda. They are classically 'naturalised' within consumer capitalist cultures.

*The Age of Stupid*, while loosely an SF film, is a documentary, making propaganda for action on climate change. Propaganda is a form of discourse which openly presents itself as wanting to persuade its audiences, often, but not always, by its argument and textual strategies. Advertising, public health and safety messages, as well as political ones, could all be classified as 'propaganda'. This film's title and the end credits involve the words 'AND YOU' – a very open mode of address, a way of positioning the audience which mainstream cinema usually avoids.

But 'propaganda' is commonly misunderstood as signifying only the manipulations of brutal governments, or lying political parties. The Frankfurt School theorists made use of these connotations. They had seen the unprecedented power of propaganda in the early years of German Nazism. Understandably they framed their critical approaches to early consumer culture in the US, where they fled to in the 1930s, in similar terms, provocatively likening it to 'propaganda'. Herman and Chomsky did likewise, later.

Yet if you accept our definition, it is not the *form* 'propaganda' which is to blame for its bad reputation, but some of the uses to which it is put. This means that if you disagree with a propagandising text (like this film) you need to argue *why*, in terms of the film's case, and not simply label it 'propaganda', and thereby stop discussion.

---

## EXPLORE 6.15

- Gather a few recent uses of the word propaganda, in print or in conversations. See if they correspond to the suggestions here.

'Ideology' is sometimes used in similar ways. Such marginalising usage can make it seem that it is always the other side – never one's own – that has an ideology, or is trying to propagandise for its position.

---

## TEXTUAL APPROACHES TO THE FILM

First, go to http://www.guardian.co.uk/environment/video/2009/mar/02/age-of-stupid-making-of, a 50-minute documentary on the six years spent making the film. Make notes on the makers' approach to the 'representability' of eco-politics.

Here's our discussion.

- As a documentary it is enjoyably *performative*. The two film-makers expose some of their weaknesses (e.g. Lizzie does not at first know about climate change politics and starts by booking a flight) and their anxieties during production (they wonder if

*Figure 6.18* The British 'Dig for Victory' campaign during the Second World War (1939–45) encouraged people to dig up gardens, flowerbeds and parklands to convert them to allotments for vegetable production (see Chapter 1). There has been a recent revival of interest it. This poster is '**propaganda**', as is 'Keep Calm and Carry On' in other parts of this book.

*Figure 6.19* Though not aiming for the expensive hi-FX work of *The Day After Tomorrow* (US 2004), the film has some short but impressive graphics sequences. They locate the beginning of the film in the 'disaster/post-apocalypse' field, and are also, shrewdly, part of the trailer. The music too is a key pleasure. How would you describe its tone and function?

they 'can sell the Alps footage' if it all fails, and so on).

- It also offers 'knowledge-related' or cognitive pleasures – about the stages of making such an innovative documentary. It could be called 'performative' in that sense too. It acknowledges glitches in production, the hard crafting of the Alpine shots to show the passing of time, the ethical questions of Alvin's involvement after the grief of Hurricane Katrina; the development of the computer graphics, and the music, as well as the networks of talent linked to Armstrong by this stage in her career. Now, watch the film itself.

There is no space to explore its complexity and 'crafted-ness' in detail. But it might be useful to organise your responses through the following questions.

How is it structured? How are the linked stories or characters woven into an argument?

Director Franny Armstrong says she took the idea of multiple heroes spread across continents from Stephen Soderbergh's big-budget Hollywood film *Traffic* (US 2000). This was itself based on UK Channel 4's *Sex Traffic* (2005) about sex trafficking: an example of the interconnections between media forms across continents now. See also the multiple hero/global narratives in 'blockbuster' TV entertainment series *Lost*, *Heroes* and *Flashforward*.

*Figure 6.20* Pete Postlethwaite as the archivist in this film.

1   Discuss the role of The Archivist/Peter Postlethwaite character. You might think about

   a   his location in a kind of SF narrative, set in 2055, and including one very melancholy speculation about the human race. What does this future setting and melancholy tone allow that a more conventional documentary form might inhibit?

   b   the small but important special effect of the 'screen' over which he pulls video clips. What does this enable and add to the film? How would these scenes be without it?

   > Compare the usage here to that of a similar screen in *Minority Report* (US 2002).

   c   his voice: how does this signify? Tone, accent, age, pace, etc.?

2   The film has been praised for including contradictions and conflicts, for retaining footage where characters express opinions which are not what you would expect of a simple piece of propaganda or 'ideology'.

Q:  Did you notice any examples of this? It seems to be an important part of ideological work like this to acknowledge the attractiveness or power of other positions and discourses (Alvin's pride in his work as an oil scientist; the seductiveness of images of US consumerism for Layefa in Nigeria). 'Fundamentalist' it is not.

3   As well as traditional documentary 'evidence', the film uses 'montage', where short sequences of film are juxtaposed so as to make a point via their combination. Again, these are not hammered home, but viewers, by implication, are credited with the intelligence. One example: the editing of the wind farm protesters' claims with filmed evidence of high winds which contradicts them. Can you think of others?

'Politics' is often seen as 'uncool'. This is for a whole raft of reasons, some to do with the place of irony and awareness of other discourses in interactive consumer capitalist cultures – often, for example, advertising acknowledges, with a 'wink', the absurdity of some products.

'Cool' is used of figures looking unconcerned, remote, not needy (see discussion by 'Lisa' in the blog http://sociologicalimages.blogspot.com and Chapter 6 on Moss). This is the very opposite of the feelings which political movements need to build and connect with. Some activists in recent campaigns, like 'Stupid' and 10:10, have adopted a very different style to that of older forms of protest, more humorous and inventive around stunts, for example.

## EXPLORE 6.16

- Do you agree with our suggestions on 'cool'?
- Look at the film's website, and at the documentary about its making. Is there a different kind of 'cool' at work here?
- What are the markers of this funny, smart discourse? In what ways does it seem to assume, or 'position', an intelligent 'media-savvy' audience?
- What are the pleasures of the film for you? Are there 'un-pleasures'? Did you enjoy the short 'films' (often animation) embedded in it which give entertaining potted histories of imperialism, advertising, 'Crap is Us' connected to China's growth, and so on?

We'd argue that the film does a fine job of intervening in climate change debates by seeking to engage with popular audiences (see responses on the website http://www.ageofstupid.net).

We could argue that, as well as the ideological work of making a coherent, smart and moving argument, the film has another achievement: it can produce hope, and a desire to join in change.

'To be truly radical is to make hope possible rather than despair convincing,' Raymond Williams, often quoted (but uncredited) in these contexts.

'Climate change deniers' often cite 'an apathetic public' as part of the problem. In an age of massively present interactive media, mostly funded by advertising, this is a very powerful 'denial' ideological position *all on its own*.

Some theorists, using psychoanalytic perspectives, argue that, as with personal traumas, it's often not apathy but caring too much that may be the problem. The threat of unchecked climate change may be too painful to engage with, especially if governments do not support or encourage actions that will make a difference (see Lertzmann 2009).

Hence our argument that part of the effort of the film is to produce hope on the part of ordinary people and everyday practices.

## 'CINEMA' AND ITS 'EVERYDAY PRACTICES'

The film also engages with the practices of cinema – taken for granted and therefore, arguably, deeply ideological. As we've said elsewhere, the media do not merely represent the environment; they help to *make* it the way it is. Part of this involves distribution and exhibition discourses – the power of big broadcast and cinema corporations simply to define/review/classify an oppositional text as 'uncommercial'. This helps guarantee it will *become* 'uncommercial' and be seen by only a few. 'Big Hollywood' is a key source of phrases like 'Size Matters', and the publicising of films and celebrity programmes in terms of how good it is to flaunt wealth and consume, consume, consume.

An interesting connection was made in 2008–9 between the L'Oreal cosmetics company's slogan 'Because you're worth it' and the hyper-consuming drives at the heart of the banks' crash.

How does this slogan compare with 'Because you deserve it'? Through a shift in the sense of how worth is measured? Might such tiny shifts, over time, help construct, or relate to, new dominant discourses?

In addition, at the level of funding and pre-production, blockbusters are massive marketing anchors for the corporations which own them. At pre-planning and then 'tie-in', 'product place' and franchise stages, other, often unnecessary, goods are sold on the back of them. Indeed for many big films these are a main source of income. All this just when the entire world needs new ways of living and sharing resources to be experienced as 'cool', and taken for granted.

This film makes what use it can of 'mainstream' strategies. Armstrong acknowledges developing Soderbergh's (*Traffic*) multiple internationally linked 'heroes'. It offers (modest) tie-in products: stickers, both 'Stupid' (found on some gas-guzzling cars) and 'Not

Stupid', T shirts, DVDs, a compost bin and so on. Its credits acknowledge help from funding bodies such as the UK Film Council and the National Lottery – important public sources. A version of 'authorship' will work for some in the audience. Franny Armstrong was known as the director of *McLibel: Two People Who Wouldn't Say Sorry* (UK 2005; available on video.google.com; see also trailer on YouTube). She is also a funny, skilled and engaging speaker, organiser and emailer – all important for the 'around' of such cinema. See this from a 2009 email about the US-based global premiere:

Glenn Beck [notorious Fox News anchor] is being very rude about our film, but we don't believe he even watched it as surely he would have noted that he is in it. (Funny Facebook response: *Beck didn't like this new film, therefore, it must be GREAT. I'm going.*)

Its production, distribution and exhibition practices, and its use of the internet, are innovative and 'sustainable'. 'Crowd funding' was used to raise the capital required. Large numbers of ordinary people were asked, often via the internet, for small donations. You can find on the website more about the global premiere (http://vimeo.com/6675157) as well as the pioneering 'Indie Screenings' model. This is a new form of film distribution allowing anyone, anywhere to buy a licence to hold a DVD screening of the film – with the price set according to the screener's means – and then to charge for tickets and keep any profits for themselves. There are no 'middlemen'.

And at the end of the film there is an account of how much carbon was emitted during its making. The 'Stupid' team also tried for the 'world's greenest premiere' with a projector powered by solar energy, a tent lit with gas from London landfill sites, celebrities arriving in electric vehicles, low $CO_2$ cars or bikes, to walk on a green carpet, of course, and so on. Altogether a premiere which produced 1 per cent of the $CO_2$ emissions of the typical blockbuster premiere: five tonnes compared with the usual five hundred.

## CONCLUSION

A Marxist analysis would emphasise the extent to which overconsumption is an inevitable outcome of capitalism, especially in its contemporary high-consumer form. As a system based on competition and profit, rather than co-operation and social sharing, it systematically leads to overproduction, 'planned obsolescence' (see Chapter 11) and an inevitable ravaging of 'natural resources'. The impact of the disposal of these products on the environment is now visible as a further problem.

Some big oil companies, despite their 'greenwashed' public image, are still busy funding the resistance to environmentally responsible politics. We, and the film, argue for understanding this economic and ideological 'driver' to the debate. But post-Marxist media and politics allow more than the prediction that this will be 'the end of the planet'. Climate change is produced unequally and will impact unequally – in fact is already doing so. Some parts of the world, and of specific cities, like New Orleans, are more impacted than others, for reasons of pre-existing inequalities – of race, class, gender, age and cultural capital. Some green activists have objected to the fact that the work of recycling, conserving, mending and so on will fall unequally on women and men.

The film's politics are 'red-green' in this sense, aware of the politics of identity as well as of political economy. Almost incidentally, it offers images, stories and histories which include some (but not all) the major key identities. It has *women* in significant positions, across the world, both in front of and behind the camera; an *old* mountaineer talking eloquently of the changes he has seen in the *European* Alps, and joining a *bicycle protest; Arab children* as important 'characters', and so on.

It has been argued that 'green' politics does not have quite the same sense of an 'enemy' or 'Other' which often drove earlier ideologies (the clearer 'capitalist versus workers' model of Marxism, the binaries which often drive fundamentalist religious ideologies and so on). To some extent, however small our power compared with that of the chairman of Goldman Sachs, or Shell, for example, it is *also* up to 'us' to make changes in everyday ways, especially to how we consume and conserve – as well as pressuring power to make big changes. This film valuably strengthens attempts to do just these things.

## REFERENCES AND FURTHER READING

Boyce, Tammy and Lewis, Justin (2009) *Climate Change and the Media*, Oxford and New York: Peter Lang.

Branston, Gill (2007) 'The Planet at the End of the World', *New Review of Film and Television Studies*, 5, 2.

Gramsci, Antonio (1971) *Selections from the Prison Notebooks*, London: Lawrence and Wishart.

Hansen, Anders (2010) *Environment, Media and Communication*, London and New York: Routledge.

Lertzmann, Renee (2009) 'The Myth of Apathy', *The Ecologist*, 38, 5 (June).

Williamson, Judith (2008) lecture, accessed via www.friezefoundation.org, October.

# 7 Media as business

> Creative rights are usually invested in a 'property' and referred to in legal terms as 'intellectual property'.

Media production is invariably an industrial process. It usually involves a creative producer and 'rights' to exploit creative labour, some form of technology and a system of distribution and then 'exchange' (the interaction with a user). Even if a producer is the legendary 'musician in a bedroom', each of the above applies. They have all been subjected to major changes over the past twenty years and media businesses themselves are in turmoil, some having found new ways to monetise their rights holdings – to make sure users pay something for their products – while others face the prospect of declining sales.

## EXPLORE 7.1  MEDIA BUYING HABITS

Reflect on your own media buying habits and compare them with what your family might have been prepared to pay for five years ago. Do you:

- buy a newspaper of any sort on a regular basis?
- ever buy CDs?
- go to the cinema at least once a month?
- buy or rent DVDs?
- play games online?
- have a television set?
- think about how much you spend on online services and phone contracts?

What conclusions do you draw from your comparison?

## Studying business organisations

Over the relatively short history of media studies, some scholars have argued that too much emphasis has been put on the media texts themselves and that more attention should be directed towards media use and media users. This is indeed what is happening to a certain extent, possibly as media studies cohabits more productively with cultural studies. Yet left out in this argument and seemingly always in the background is a focus on media producers – how they are organised and what kinds of practices they adopt and why. Our focus in this chapter is on the media industries. We've chosen to refer to this work in terms of media as a business activity. This signifies two things:

- we are mostly interested in organisations (public or private sector) rather than individual producers, although what 'bedroom producers' of music, or even individual bloggers and software developers do, can have an effect on media business as a whole;
- 'business' can act as a term to cover both industrial and institutional issues which in previous editions of the book we have kept separate; now we think that they might be better understood together.

The media industries are groupings of organisations producing both physical goods (such as magazines, DVDs and videogames) and 'live' experiences (a night's radio broadcasting, a screening of a 3D film in a cinema) as well as a range of services and facilities supporting media production and distribution. The totality of such media activity could be considered to be an ecosystem – a system which is sustainable over time with the different organisations interacting with each other in a productive way. They also interact with media users, with critics and commentators, and with regulators and governments.

The metaphorical use of **ecology** as part of media studies dates back to the work of Marshall McLuhan and others in the 1970s. McLuhan was discussing the interdependence of media forms at a time when the different media industries were clearly distinct, using different technologies and different forms of media language. Now we face a media environment in which **convergence** of technologies and applications means that we can access virtually all traditional media forms on a single hand-held device. By the time you read this, we'll know whether consumers will accept a touchscreen 'tablet' like the iPad as an attractive (and affordable) device that will allow users to play games, screen movies, TV programmes, newspapers and ebooks, play music and radio broadcasts, and provide full internet access.

> See Chapter 5 for Marshall McLuhan

But although all these media activities are likely to be available via a single device, does it mean that we will have a single media industry? It

*Figure 7.1* The iPad – on the way to becoming the all-in-one portable media player?

seems unlikely, but the ecological questions about which industries will survive, which will mutate and how the dynamics of the media environment can be managed, require us to consider a whole range of concepts taken from economics and business studies, sociology and politics, management studies and psychology.

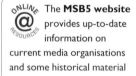 The **MSB5 website** provides up-to-date information on current media organisations and some historical material to provide context.

The ecology metaphor approach also has its critics who argue that a more adequate image would be one of capitalist markets. Words like 'landscape' and 'ecology' are argued to perform a 'softening' function compared with more commercially based ones.

## Ownership and control

**Political economy** was the original term from the early nineteenth century for what we now think of as 'economics'. Political economists were interested in who owned land, labour and capital and what the political consequences of their actions in using these resources might be.

Questions about public/private ownership and control have always been paramount for media theorists from a **political economy** background. They have been concerned about the possibility that concentrated ownership of media companies by small groups of 'major players' or control by government agencies could have a detrimental effect on the range of goods and services available to users.

This fear stems from the economics of monopoly supply (or more correctly, oligopoly supply – the control of a market by a few large organisations). By the early 2000s it seemed that the free-market capitalists who successfully lobbied to loosen regulatory controls and privatise some public sector organisations during the 1970s and 1980s were leading us inevitably towards a media landscape dominated by a relatively small number of 'media majors'. At the centre of this scenario was the contradictory notion of a 'free market'. The term suggested media users would be able to choose whatever goods and services they wanted. Yet deregulation actually fostered the growth of **conglomerates** that consolidated production resources into a few hands and potentially denied real choice to users.

See references to the work of theorists such as Janet Wasko in Chapter 6.

**Neoliberalism** is the term to describe a co-ordination of privatisation and deregulation. See Chapter 5.

## Media conglomerates

Conglomerates are companies made up of separate divisions, each with distinct identities operating in different sectors of the market – and possibly different industries altogether. They are most often formed through a process of 'mergers and acquisitions'. Where this happens in a specific market or sector it is termed **consolidation**.

In the 'narrative of free-market capitalism', consolidation is seen as inevitable in mature markets.

Discussion of free markets is included in Chapter 10. Let's look more closely at media conglomerates.

Such companies mostly:

- operate across national boundaries;
- operate across media sectors and also, perhaps, in associated industrial sectors such as telecommunications;
- are owned by shareholders (often institutional shareholders such as pension funds) and managed by a managerial business class who may have little direct experience of creative media;
- have headquarters in the US, Europe or Japan;
- are big enough, especially when working collectively through business or trade associations, to lobby effectively against restrictions on their activities proposed by national and international regulators.

There are still some individuals whose actions can be influential, but they have to work within a framework of corporate management systems and the ultimate power of shareholders. The corporate nature of modern media activity means that business decisions will be based on both short-term and long-term economic analyses – there is relatively little space for creative decisions aimed at purely artistic innovation (although good design will be an essential element in all media activities and product innovation will require research and development).

The most powerful trade association has been the MPAA – the Motion Picture Association of America, aka the six major studios – see http://www.mpaa.org/.

**Figure 7.2** Hokllywood has often turned to 'buying in' creativity by attracting film-makers from overseas or from other creative industries into film production. *Eternal Sunshine of the Spotless Mind* (US 2004) was directed by the French director Michel Gondry.

## EXPLORE 7.2  DO MEDIA MOGULS MATTER?

Here are three influential individuals in the media industries. Use a search engine to find out which corporations they have been involved in and why shareholders are often interested in what they are up to:

- Sumner Redstone
- Steve Jobs
- Jeffrey Katzenberg.

However, there are several other factors that suggest that the steady march of the media conglomerates towards complete domination of global markets might not be inevitable. They include:

- the failure to make large corporations work effectively for the benefit of shareholders and the decision to 'de-merge' in recent years (e.g. Viacom and AOL-Time Warner);
- the impact of the recession of 2008–9 and the sudden recognition that private industry sometimes needs public sector support;
- the development of new competitors in the growing markets of India and China;
- the emergence of new business models which threaten to undermine traditional ways of working.

## The experience of conglomerates

The idea of a 'media conglomerate' has its roots in the 1970s when the most famous media **'brands'**, the Hollywood studios, found themselves bought by larger corporations (e.g. Paramount by Gulf & Western) with no direct interest in media production as such. At this time, though, there was little interaction between the different companies within the same group.

## EXPLORE 7.3   HOLLYWOOD STUDIO BRANDS

- How many of these are familiar? Do you know which studios use: a shield, a mountain, a searchlight, a magic castle, a globe and a classical figure with a torch?
- These logos, most recognised all over the world for seventy years or more, are valuable marketing and sales assets – even if the studios themselves don't actually make many of the films branded in this way; http://www.neatorama.com/2008/12/03/the-story-behind-hollywood-studio-logos/ has stories about some of the logos.

> In 1969 Warner Bros was bought by a company operating a funeral business, a parking lot operation, a car rental agency and a building maintenance company.

## EXPLORE 7.4

- Go to IMDb (imdb.com) and look up a few of your favourite films. Use the 'combined details' presentation and check each film's distributor. The chances are that most of your film choices will be distributed by one of the Hollywood majors.
- Now take the first two Hollywood majors you come across and do an internet search to find out which other companies are part of the same conglomerate, noting which media sectors they are in. It's easiest to look for the 'investors' site for each conglomerate rather than the consumer site. It's more fun to do this yourself, but afterwards you can check out the 'Media Majors' page on the **MSB5 website**.

> **Synergy** – the concept that extra value could emerge from using the effort put into one product in the production and promotion of another. For example, a media conglomerate working with an author in a publishing division might also consider film, television and game adaptations in other divisions of the same company (or commercial partner company).

In the mid-1970s Hollywood cinema was in the doldrums and seemingly on the way out (even if some argue that the films were actually better). When it revived commercially in the 1980s, particularly with the rental and retail sales of films on VHS, and with various technological innovations such as cable television, videogames and music video, the possibilities of **synergies** between different divisions of a conglomerate became apparent. Gradually, each of the famous studio brands was bought by new owners who put together conglomerates solely concerned with media activities (see the 'The Media Majors' on the **MSB5 website**). By 2000, the media environment was dominated by a handful of major corporations, all with global interests and all bar one using a famous Hollywood studio as a significant brand.

The merger between the internet service provider AOL and the leading media major Time Warner early in 2000 was the biggest ever media merger and seemed to signal both the convergence of online and traditional media activities and further proof that the media ecosystem was experiencing a consolidation of interests which had only one logical outcome. But the merger never really worked and AOL was soon revealed to be far less valuable than had appeared the case when the so-called 'dot.com revolution' was being talked up.

In 2008 AOL was 'de-merged' from Time Warner. Earlier, in 2004, Warner Music had separated from Time Warner in a management buyout and in the same year, Universal Music was separated from Universal Studios after the breakup of the failed Vivendi Universal conglomerate. (The music business was the first of the core media industries to be threatened by online activity and piracy, and perhaps it is not surprising that it experienced the most turmoil at this time.)

One of the concepts that the move towards conglomerates involved was the process of integration, the term used to describe the purchase of other companies (or the founding of new subsidiaries) in order to extend control over a media market in one of two ways. **Vertical integration** has a long history in the film business. It refers to control over the whole process of making, distributing and exhibiting a film so that during the 1930s the major studios like Warner Bros or Paramount would produce their own films and distribute them 'domestically' and internationally – often to their own cinemas. The studios had their cinema chains in the US taken away in the late 1940s as part of 'anti-trust' laws designed to increase competition, but in the 1980s they were able to develop their own video labels and later to show their films on their own TV channels in many cases.

**Horizontal integration** refers to control over companies working across the same market sector. For instance, in the UK since 2000, the film exhibition sector has seen consolidation, with three large cinema chains (Odeon, Cineworld and Vue) taking over other exhibition companies so that now they each control significant shares of the overall market.

Another good example of horizontal integration saw all the major Hollywood studios in the 1990s taking over existing independent specialised cinema distributors, so that each studio acquired its own 'independent brand'. The whole idea of a different, independent approach to making and distributing films in the US (and elsewhere) was severely compromised. Recently these same studio brands have become vulnerable to further changes in the economic climate and in 2008, Warner Bros moved to close its three independent brands (New Line, Warner Independent and Picturehouse).

The dot.com revolution – the short period in which new online companies, sometimes little more than a website with a clever marketing idea, were founded and saw their share prices rise dramatically as they attracted new investors. But since these companies had no tangible assets as such, there was always the possibility that the new investment 'bubble' would burst, as it did during 2000 (soon after the AOL-Time Warner merger).

See the case study to Chapter 5 on *Slumdog Millionaire* and its 'escape' from Warner Independent to Fox Searchlight which made its US release possible.

*Figure 7.3* The London flagship of the Vue cinema chain (once the Warner West End) showing promotional material from 20th Century Fox and Paramount. Vue is one of three chains, all owned by investment groups, that dominate the UK market.

What is the motive for creating a conglomerate? Growth is only worthwhile if it secures and/or increases profits. But, often, there is no agreement on which strategy might be sustainable in the long term. Some managements look for **diversification** – operating in as many different media industries as possible. Others, driven by a belief in synergy, attempt to work in different media that share the same content. For instance, in the relatively short-lived Viacom conglomerate, all the divisions, including television brands MTV and Nickelodeon, were encouraged to initiate film productions for Paramount.

The identification of shared content also raised the question of whether it is more profitable in the long run to be a **content provider** or a **content carrier** – e.g. to own the rights to films or to own a TV channel. Some conglomerates have attempted to do both, but others argue that they are very different kinds of activities and that companies can be more successful (in producing profits for shareholders) by focusing on one.

Media content became more valuable as outlets/carriers began to multiply, since **back catalogues** could command a higher price as new

Film libraries do have a fixed cost of simply storing physical copies and maintaining them, but their value as assets is shown by the number of times whole libraries have been bought and sold – most British films are no longer held by their original owners and many are held by the French company Studio Canal.

carriers competed for material to fill their airtime. Content also has the advantage that during an economic recession a film library doesn't lose money, whereas advertising-funded television channels probably will. This also leads us towards another issue that we will meet later – the distinction between carriers that are subscription-based and those that are advertising-based.

What is heralded as a world-beating merger one day can be dismissed as folly only a few years later. Recognition of the importance of brands and the value of back catalogues is evidence that the 'old' media industries still have confidence in their ability to withstand the pace of change. However, as we see in Chapter 8, the concept of 'owning content' is beginning to look like a precarious investment if copying is inevitable in the world of Web 2.0. Kevin Kelly suggests that future income will come from the 'extras' that can be offered with the copy that will be effectively 'free' (see http://www.kk.org/thetechnium/archives/2008/01/better_than_fre.php). We aren't there yet, but it must be a frightening prospect for those whose income relies on royalties derived from repeat sales of their content. As well as these warnings, the 'traditional' media majors also face other new challenges.

## New players in India and China

The major media corporations emerged during specific periods of industrial development. For instance, the leading European media corporation (and the only major without a Hollywood brand), Bertelsmann of Germany, began as a printing company in the nineteenth century and as this statement on its website suggests, it is still aware of what this means for its corporate culture:

> Tradition-consciousness is a fixture in our corporate culture, which strives to integrate historically developed values with modern corporate policy.

(www.bertelsmann.com)

Bertelsmann is a rare conglomerate that is still mainly under the control of the Mohn family, descendants of Bertelsmann, who refounded the company in 1947. Reinhard Mohn, a hands-on figure known to his workforce in the company's base in Gütersloh, died in October 2009. Will his heirs manage to keep the company as a family business?

Other major European media companies such as Reed-Elsevier (Anglo-Dutch) and Pearson (UK) are also rooted in print publishing, but the famous names associated with cinema, the next media form to emerge in the late nineteenth century, are mostly American (even if many were built up by migrants from Europe). Since the 1980s new American 'players' in the global media business have emerged in the form of 'start-up' companies engaged in computing and online activity. Microsoft, Apple and Google have developed within a completely different business environment. Statements like this from Tim Cook at Apple are indicative of a different kind of approach to business:

> We're constantly focusing on innovating. We believe in the simple, not the complex. We believe that we need to own and control the primary technologies behind the products we make, and participate only in markets where we can make a significant contribution.
> (Tim Cook, 21 January 2009, Apple Earnings Conference)

We can see in this statement that Apple has a distinctive corporate culture, which includes the 'ownership and control' of both the hardware and software associated with its computers. Although Apple and Microsoft have different strategies (Microsoft focusing on its software for generic PCs), they share with Google a start-up company ethos (a 'West Coast' feel), driven primarily by ideas. But as they have become embroiled in both the consumer gadget and the media carrier markets (i.e. MP3 players and music and TV downloads) will they begin to behave more like the traditional media companies?

> Computer start-up companies appeared in the 1980s and featured new kinds of entrepreneurs, in one sense 'driven' by ambition, but in another, informal and opposed to hierarchical business traditions.

In Japan, publishing and motion picture companies emerged in much the same way as in Europe and Hollywood, although against a different cultural background and interrupted by the militarism of the 1930s and the subsequent defeat and occupation of Japan in 1945 – which in turn led to the post-war environment in which Sony developed. The Japanese experience suggests that hardware is easier to sell across cultural barriers, so that it is Sony, Panasonic (Matsushita) and the other hardware manufacturers that have a global presence rather than film and television studio majors such as Toho or Shochiku, which attempt to sell Japanese cultural content (and foreign content) to Japanese users.

> Sony's ownership of the Hollywood studio brand Columbia is a legacy of the period when Japanese electronics manufacturers decided that owning a studio would help them sell videocassettes – a form of vertical integration. Matsushita were briefly owners of MCA/Universal Studios from 1990 to 1995.

India and China had sophisticated entertainment forms well before Europe and North America (and Japan), but European colonialism and imperialism stifled the development of local media organisations in Asia up to the Second World War. In the decades following the war, China (apart from Hong Kong) was to a large extent cut off from the global business environment because of the trade policies of the Chinese Communist Party. In India government economic policy was also not encouraging for media corporations with global ambitions until the 'liberalisation' of economic activities introduced in 1991. Now, the two most populous countries in the world each have a rapidly growing middle class, providing a home market large enough to sustain large-scale media companies (always the advantage held by the US media companies over their European rivals with smaller single-language markets).

In the media ecosystem of 2010 and beyond there will be a range of global media corporations. It remains to be seen whether the emergent media corporations in India simply follow Hollywood models and whether Chinese corporations will be allowed by their government to develop further and to build a global identity (i.e. outside traditional Chinese markets in South-East Asia and the Chinese diaspora communities).

Shekhar Kapur, Indian director of *Elizabeth: The Golden Age* (2007), predicts that: 'In future sequels, when Spider-Man takes off his mask in Asia, he will probably be either Chinese or Indian. And he will no longer swing from the high-rise buildings of New York, but from Shanghai or Mumbai.' (Ramachandran 2008)

## EXPLORE 7.5 THE RISING INDIAN MEDIA CORPORATIONS

Each of these corporations has a Hollywood connection:
- UMP (UTV Motion Pictures)
- Reliance Big Entertainment (Adlabs).

Search to find out what the connections are. Are these corporations similar to US conglomerates?

The UK Film Council defines 'filmed entertainment' as including:
- theatrical (i.e. cinema)
- DVD/video rental
- DVD/retail
- pay TV
- terrestrial TV
- free multichannel
- nVOD (near Video on Demand) and VOD – includes TV and online.

|  | 2008 in US$ billion | % of global total | 2013 in US$ billion | % of global total | % change in global share |
|---|---|---|---|---|---|
| US | 34.8 | 41.5 | 40.9 | 40.0 | – 0.9 |
| Japan | 8.7 | 10.4 | 10.4 | 10.2 | – 0.2 |
| UK | 6.5 | 7.7 | 8.3 | 8.2 | + 0.5 |
| France | 3.8 | 4.5 | 4.3 | 4.3 | – 0.2 |
| Germany | 3.5 | 4.2 | 4.1 | 4.0 | – 0.1 |
| Canada | 3.4 | 4.1 | 4.1 | 4.1 | 0 |
| Australia | 2.4 | 2.9 | 3.0 | 3.0 | + 0.1 |
| Italy | 1.9 | 2.3 | 2.2 | 2.2 | – 0.1 |
| India | 1.76 | 2.1 | 3.4 | 3.4 | + 2.3 |
| China | 0.87 | 1.0 | 1.6 | 1.6 | + 0.6 |
| All other territories | 14.5 | 19.3 | 17.5 | 19.1 | – 0.2 |

*Figure 7.4* Filmed entertainment figures for 2008, and 2013 projection.

Source: *UK Film Council Statistical Yearbook 2009.*

What these figures show is the current underdeveloped state of the Indian and Chinese industries and their predicted substantial growth up to 2013.

China and India are important in other ways as well. Newspaper sales are going down in Europe and North America, but they are rising in India and China – and some Western publishers have taken the opportunity to buy into the newspaper business in India. The UK-based Daily Mail and General Trust (DMGT) took the maximum permitted 26 per cent stake in *Mail Today*, a joint venture with the India Today Group which also publishes Indian editions of many well-known American magazines (see http://www.indiatodaygroup.com/). India has been a major location for computer software companies for some time – it seems likely that some future web developments will be led by Indian companies.

*Figure 7.5* A Mexican multiplex built by Cinépolis, a major Latin American chain which in 2009 announced a major building programme in India – banking on growing Indian demand for new cinemas in different markets and drawing on its experience of similar conditions in Mexico (soon to become the third largest territory in the world in admissions).

*Figure 7.6*
The e-paper edition of *Mail Today*

## Public or private funding

The most startling news stories of 2008 concerned the intervention of governments, via the use of taxpayers' money, in the major financial markets to bail out failed banks and mortgage lenders in Europe and the US. Not so much of a surprise perhaps in Europe, but in the US government intervention has become much more controversial. We are conscious, in writing for students in a potentially global media studies community, that terms used to describe policies in the US may seem strange to readers in Europe and vice versa. The salvaging of international banking through intervention exposed attitudes to the public/private debate and points us towards thinking through what it means for media businesses.

In August 2009, two stories appeared in the UK media. In one, it was reported by the *Daily Mail* that the UK government had agreed to take 'tough action' against illegal downloaders of music and video files on the internet by requiring ISPs to cut off subscriber connections. This was much stronger action than recommended in the UK government's *Digital*

The hostile use of terms like 'socialised medicine' in the campaign against Barack Obama's health plans is one example of this confusion. Most people outside the US who have access to good levels of healthcare use some form of publicly funded service.

The 'silly season' refers to the holiday period in many countries, when there is little hard business or political news and the press and broadcast media tend to fill their space with frivolous or sensationalist news stories.

Public service broadcasting is discussed in Chapter 9 along with arguments about public funding via the licence fee.

Much of the credit for the BBC's successful venture into online media services is now being given to John Birt, the former director-general (1992–2000). Birt has been heavily criticised for his 'modernisation' and 'centralisation' policies, but in the case of digital media they seem to have paid off.

Cross-media ownership is a feature of many national regulation strategies designed to prevent strong market positions in different media sectors held by the same owner adding up to an overall monopoly position in the national media market.

*Britain* report. The action was prompted, the *Mail* suggested, by a visit to the UK by David Geffen, the wealthy 'media mogul' and founder of both Geffen Records and (with Steven Spielberg and Jeffrey Katzenberg) Dream Works Studio. Geffen is supposed to have had dinner with UK Industry Secretary Peter Mandelson. Perhaps this was just a 'silly season' story tied to celebrity gossip, but it is suggestive of the way in which media industries lobby for government 'protection' of their private interests at the same time as attacking public sector media and other forms of government intervention. The story did indeed later prove to have some substance in that Mandelson announced a policy along these lines in October 2009.

Barely a week after the initial story, Rupert Murdoch's son James launched an attack on the BBC investment of taxpayers' money in its extremely successful online news operation. James Murdoch was speaking at the Edinburgh Television Festival as the chair and CEO of News Corporation (Europe and Asia), the biggest shareholder in BSkyB, one of the main competitors for the BBC. The Murdoch family has a long track record of attacks upon the BBC and the whole concept of **public service broadcasting** (PSB), but this outburst was particularly well-timed (see below for Rupert Murdoch's comments on charging for online news).

With the advertising downturn and the gradual collapse of the newspaper market, the BBC's astute move into comprehensive online coverage – which provides video, audio and text services created by or for the corporation's radio and television channels – is a direct threat to the viability of the private sector media companies' attempts to exploit their own media output online. The BBC is able to use income from the licence fee to underpin its output, but the problem for the private sector companies is how to generate some income from their own online activities (to 'monetise' them in the current jargon).

Murdoch would like to cast the debate in terms of enterprising free market entrepreneurs such as BSkyB being constrained by a regulatory regime that supports public service broadcasting and views competition from the private sector with suspicion. This has been an ongoing debate since Rupert Murdoch's successful swoop into UK print media through the purchase and subsequent transformation of titles such as *The Times*, *Sun* and *News of the World*. It could be argued that the regulations governing cross-media ownership of terrestrial television carriers have been the major barrier to Murdoch's expansion in the UK. But as the television environment changes (to a completely digital system in the UK by 2012), BSkyB is emerging as a major player with only the BBC as a significant rival. The BBC has always been most vulnerable in its privileged position of receiving income from a compulsory licence fee.

### News Corporation in the UK

The global media conglomerate News Corporation is owner of News International, the company which publishes the *Sun*, *News of the World* and *The Times*. Another division is HarperCollins, a major book publisher in the UK. News Corporation describes BSkyB as its 'equity affiliate' (controlling 39 per cent of the company), Fox TV is available via BSkyB and 20th Century Fox has a UK distribution operation. See http://www.newscorp.com/.

The BBC responded vigorously to the Murdoch attack – as it needed to do. It was unusual to see Murdoch supported by several competitors who would usually side with the BBC. For instance, *The Guardian*, a centre-left newspaper with readers in many cases deeply opposed to Murdoch, actually faces the same problems as News Corporation. It has produced one of the most popular and well-used online newspaper services – all funded from within its own resources. But how can it compete with a BBC service backed by the licence fee (which represents 'protected' income at a time of economic recession)?

Some commentators have seen this and similar incidents as part of 'softening up' the BBC and paving the way for **top-slicing** of the licence fee – taking a share of the TV licence fee income and offering it to other media producers so that they can fulfil the public service remit currently covered by the commercial channels. ITV, Channel 4 and Five will lose significantly after the digital switchover as the subsidy implied through free access to the broadcasting spectrum is withdrawn. The subsidy currently supports the PSB remit for commercial channels. (See Chapter 9 for more on PSB.)

A joint campaign from the media unions, the NUJ (National Union of Journalists) and BECTU ('The Media and Entertainment Union') began in October 2009 to stop top-slicing on the grounds that the BBC needs the full income (and they need to protect their members' interests). The unions suggested that the 'funding gap' that would become apparent after switchover could be bridged by levies on BSkyB and Virgin Cable operations or ISPs and mobile phone companies. A report, *Mind the Funding Gap*, commissioned by NUJ and BECTU from IPPR, was published in March 2009. The report argues for the 'mixed ecology' of public and private and the plurality of different PSB providers.

*Mind the Funding Gap* is downloadable from the Institute for Public Policy Research at: http://www.ippr.org.uk/publicationsandreports/publication.asp?id=661

## EXPLORE 7.6  A TOP-SLICED LICENCE?

- What do you think are the benefits of having more than one PSB provider?
- Is it better to have one TV licence fee with the income divided up between different providers?
- Or should there be a commitment to PSB from 'new' players like the ISPs or BSkyB?

Some BBC material is not available online – rights issues for certain sports coverage, etc. prevent wider circulation.

*The Guardian* website example also refers to a second issue about the BBC spend on its online services. Both *The Guardian* and the BBC are now read/viewed widely outside the UK via an online presence. These overseas readers don't pay for access and are effectively subsidised by UK *Guardian* purchasers of the print edition and UK licence payers in relation to the BBC. *The Guardian* can decide its own policy, but all licence payers are entitled to ask about how the BBC spends its money.

The BBC remains in a difficult situation. Its high-profile TV programmes remain popular and BBC1 remains the most popular channel (21 per cent audience share). Its radio stations dominate the commercial opposition and its website is the most used media site in the UK. But maintaining this position involves contradiction. In the licence fee debate, making programmes that attract large audiences is essential to justify asking everyone to pay. But this commitment takes resources away from other kinds of programming that also need to be high quality to fulfil the range and diversity remits of public service broadcasting. The licence fee is set by Parliament and is due for renegotiation by early 2013. BBC Charter renewal will be necessary by 2016. Although it should be possible to plan expenditure with licence fee income guaranteed in the short term, the prospect of a change in government and the constant need to defend the licence fee in the face of concerted campaigns against it from other media producers can make BBC governance and production planning decisions time-consuming and problematic. (See further coverage of the BBC in Chapter 9.)

Working on 'bids' and accountable budgets, filling in evaluations and compliance statements is an important element of work in the publicly funded sector. How much is this also part of private sector work?

## Public and private in filmed entertainment

The public/private split runs through most forms of media activity. Film is perhaps the medium that seems most rooted in the free market world of 'global entertainment', especially in Hollywood and Bollywood. The international film industry refers to sources of investment funding as hard or soft money. Playing up the image of the movie mogul as a producer living by their wits in a dog-eats-dog world, Hollywood disdains **'soft money'** – funding support available via public sector schemes. Film industries without the large market that offers the possibility of financially viable releases, on the other hand, recognise that some form of public support is necessary to sustain a diverse range of film production over time. Soft money schemes include:

- tax breaks – allowances and concessions made available to companies producing in specific nations and regions;
- development funding – support for scriptwriters to work on ideas before production funds become available;
- direct investment from public funds in films made in specific nations and regions;
- distribution funds to enable more copies of films to be printed and exhibited and for associated promotion and advertising;
- venue and festival funding;
- training schemes and competitions for young film-makers, etc.

All countries offer something from this list. Even in North America there are various financial inducements to make films in different states in the US. Much of Hollywood's output (in film and television) is actually made in Canada (Vancouver and Toronto), partly because of indirect support available through Telefilm Canada.

The best source for researching what the various schemes offer is via the UK Film Council (http://www.ukfilmcouncil.org.uk/funding), or Centre national du cinéma et de l'image animée (CNC) (http://www.cnc.fr – English version available). Underpinning such schemes is recognition by governments that the 'creative industries' employ many people and create wealth on a large scale. See the 'Economic Impact Report' on the MPAA website (http://www.mpaa.org) for evidence of how Hollywood reminds the US government of its economic importance.

> 'Under French law, a film is not a product, but an artistic work. And the French movie industry enjoys the strong support of the State because of the cultural interest for the country of having a dynamic film industry.' From the Introduction to a guide to co-production for overseas film-makers in France – a rather different attitude to that found in Hollywood (http://www.filmfrance.net/ telechargement/France CoprodGuide09.pdf).

## The new digital environment

All the media industries have faced the same challenge in responding to new forms of competition from online services. Their responses have been variable. The music industry was one of the first to be hit and it was hit hard. After a period of dithering and believing that it could defeat both the pirates and the 'home copiers', it has now woken up to the possibilities of the new digital environment. We explore some of what happened in the music business in the case study that follows this chapter, but here is the bullish statement that opens the *2009 Digital Music Report* of the IFPI (International Federation of Phonographic Industries):

The recorded music industry is reinventing itself and its business models. Our world in 2009 looks fundamentally different from how it looked five years ago. Record companies have changed their whole approach to doing business, reshaped their operations and responded to the dramatic transformation in the way music is distributed and consumed.

The music business, like others, goes into 2009 under the uncertain cloud of the global economic downturn. However, we are no stranger to the need to reform, restructure and reinvent. Record companies began this process many years ago. They are, I believe, as a result, better placed than many other sectors to manage through more difficult times.

(John Kennedy, chair and CEO, IFPI)

This report has a sub-heading: 'New Business Models for a Changing Environment'. One of the proud boasts is that the music industry now generates 20 per cent of its income from online digital sales – whereas film and newspapers both languish with only 4 per cent of their turnover from digital platforms. We consider newspapers later in this chapter and film in the case study alongside music. Television also faces problems with new business models and these are covered in Chapter 9. But the most important media industry trading online is the games industry.

### The games industry

The games industry (aka the 'interactive entertainment software industry') is often now quoted as having overtaken the film industry as the biggest international consumer media industry. However, comparisons are difficult to make and far less has been written about the games industry in terms of media business. Here's an outline of the current industry.

The industry's roots are in the amusement arcade business of mechanical games in the 1930s with electronic arcade games appearing by the 1970s. It has developed in three major markets – Japan, Europe and the US. In the 1970s and 1980s the first home computers offered a new platform for games and by the late 1990s the dedicated games console (desktop and mobile) had become established. Online gaming also has a long history, developing to take advantage of new communications technologies since the 1980s.

One of the differences for the games industry is that several of the major players have at various times produced both dedicated hardware and software. A second associated point is that the software is much more expensive than films or music on discs and a thriving second-hand market for games might disguise an even bigger turnover.

One definition of the market from consultants Price Waterhouse Cooper tries to define the industry more tightly:

> The video game market consists of consumer spending on console games (including hand-held games), personal computer games, online games, and wireless games as well as video game advertising. The category excludes spending on the hardware and accessories used for playing the games. Retail purchases of a game are included in either the PC or console game categories. If those games are then played online for a subscription fee, the subscription fee is counted in the online game category.
>
> (http://www.pwc.com/gx/en/global-entertainment-media-outlook/index.jhtml)

### The players

The majors include Sony, one of the studio conglomerates, via its Playstation, and Activision Blizzard, the company formed from the games division of the French media conglomerate Vivendi and the software company Activision. Vivendi was briefly part of the studio major Vivendi-Universal. Harmonix, creator of the Rock Band series (see this chapter's case study Music and Movies), is part of Viacom, so some games companies are linked to the media conglomerates. Microsoft with the X-Box is also familiar as a computer company with media aspirations.

*Figure 7.7* Playing a console game

Sega and Nintendo are rather different as Japanese companies which started in *pachinko* (a traditional arcade game still popular in Japan) and playing cards respectively. Konami and Capcom come from the same background.

Finally, the independent games designers and publishers, many of them from the UK, have been gradually consolidated to produce major publishers like Square Enix (Japan), Ubisoft (France) and Electronic Arts and Take Two (US).

To make a comparison in which the hardware factor is stripped out, most of these publishers have a turnover from games roughly equivalent to a major Hollywood studio take from cinema box office (i.e. around $1.5 billion). According to Activision Blizzard, which has major strengths in online franchises, the combined European and North American market for gaming software in 2008 was $24 billion. There are undoubted parallels between films and games in terms of how the Japanese and American companies publish games that are then possibly distributed in certain territories by their rivals.

This business report gives an indication of the games industry thinking which embraces new distribution models (and takes up the ecology metaphor):

Renowned industry analyst Nick Parker claims that, according to his research, the tipping point ('the iTunes moment') will occur in 2014, when the games industry 'might have some parity between digital distribution and retail.'

. . . he was keen to speculate that it would not be too surprising to see Apple launch a dedicated gaming console based around Intel's Larabee chip.

The suggestion was that a company such as Apple could well take the gaming industry by storm, with Parker expecting 'one big new entrant to shake up the eco-system'.

(http://www.techradar.com/news/gaming/microsoft-dismisses-cloud-gaming-analyst-predicts-apple-console-645066)

## Business models

Wikipedia suggests that a business model might refer to:

> core aspects of a business, including purpose, offerings, strategies, infrastructure, organisational structures, trading practices, and operational processes and policies.

The problem for many media industries is that they face a situation in which what had once been a successful model is now no longer viable. Is there a new model that they can adopt – or, to pursue the ecological metaphor, is the organisation likely to adapt and evolve or become extinct like the dinosaur?

In 2009, Rupert Murdoch, a media entrepreneur widely acknowledged as a major figure in reworking the business model of the international newspaper industry in the 1980s, announced that his newspaper empire would begin to charge a fee for access to its previously free online content. Immediately a debate began about whether Murdoch had made the right decision in a competitive marketplace. If he charged for access, wouldn't internet users turn away to other free sites? Murdoch knows that it is very difficult to sustain an income stream from web operations – whether it is through selling online advertising space or charging a fee for access. But he also knows that when newspaper content is free to access online, it generally leads to a drop in sales of 'hard copy' newspapers. When circulation drops, so do advertising rates. How low must they fall before the paper has to close? Here is a good example of a 'failing' business model for newspapers. Will a web-charging model be more successful?

> See Chapter 12.

### EXPLORE 7.7

Do you ever buy a newspaper?

Read a free one?

Or do you expect to find all the news and features you want online?

Spend a short time at a newsstand checking out the newspapers and magazines on display.

- What strategies are they using to sell copies?
- How else could you gain access to a newspaper without paying the full cover price?
- Would you pay for newspaper content available online?
- What do you think of Murdoch's decision and its implications for the newspaper business model?

> The Y-pay? generation: '74% of 16-to-34-year-olds agree that paying to rent or see films in daily life is right and proper, just 39% think they should pay for the same content when they are viewing the content on the internet' (*The Guardian*, 7 September 2009).

Murdoch's change of stance over news made available online for free comes after what might be considered to be the relatively short life of the 'freesheet' model of newspaper publishing as a 'new model'. In MSB4 we discussed what in 2005 seemed like the quickly growing sector of free newspapers – especially for commuters in urban areas. But in 2009, the future for these media products began to look much less secure.

### The economics of newspaper operation

Like most businesses, newspapers have to consider fixed and variable costs. Fixed costs refer to costs that can't be easily changed as circulation goes up or down. To guarantee production of a paper every day, or even once a week, the publisher must have a printing plant which they own or have use of on a long lease. They must have orders for large shipments of paper and they must have at least some staff on long-term permanent contracts. These costs are there even if they decide to produce no newspapers for a short period. Other costs can be varied, so staff on short-term contracts might not be needed in a slack period.

Income (revenue) comes from the cover price of the paper and from the sale of advertising space. Revenue from the cover price will be reduced by distribution costs (payments to distribution companies, discounts to newsagents, transport costs, etc.) and the two forms of revenue are linked, so that as circulation goes down, advertising space will have to be priced at a lower rate to attract advertisers.

A free newspaper is attractive if the publisher has excess capacity – in other words they could print more newspapers on the same presses without incurring much extra cost (the plant is already there). At the same time, they may be able to use much more 'bought in' agency material and not use expensive reporters to create material. The marginal cost (the extra cost) of the free paper should be low and if advertisers can be attracted at reasonable rates, the proposition is viable. The big question is: how to distribute? When people want to buy a paper, they seek out a newsagent. Would you go out to a shop to pick up a free paper? Most of us wouldn't (probably because we don't expect something that is free to have much 'value'). The local free newspaper is usually distributed by a company that specialises in door-to-door delivery of 'direct mail advertising'. At railway stations and bus stations, newspapers will be given out or made available in special bins for easy access.

*Figure 7.8* Free newspapers

In London, for a brief period from 2006 there was a freesheet war every day, with Murdoch's *the londonpaper* competing with Associated News' paid-for *Evening Standard* and the same company's 'spoiler' freesheet, *London Lite*. The battle changed slightly when Associated News sold a majority stake in the *Standard* to Alexander Lebedev in January 2009. But in August 2009, after his father's announcement about charging for news online, James Murdoch announced the closure of *the londonpaper*. News International lost £12.9 million on the paper in the previous year, so perhaps we shouldn't have been surprised. Newspaper wars have often been bloody, with the last man standing 'winning' but frequently paying dearly. But if *London Lite* expected to benefit it clearly hadn't foreseen Lebedev's next move – to make the *Standard* a free paper.

The *Standard* has a history of more than 180 years of publishing and it's the only survivor of three London-wide evening papers in the 1960s and several other competitors since. The BBC News website was suitably taken aback and its report said:

> Many are reluctant to hand over the 50p cover charge when they have plenty of other things to entertain and inform – not least mobile phones and the huge range of news websites.

Alexander Lebedev is an intriguing figure and represents a very specific example of a new kind of global competitor for News Corporation. One of Lebedev's other interests is a 'liberal/oppositional' newspaper in Russia, *Novaya Gazeta*, with an English-language presence on http://en.novayagazeta.ru/.

That includes this one, where, within two hours of the story breaking, more people had read the news about the *Standard* going free than read the *Standard* itself.

But while the BBC is in a privileged position, with guaranteed income from the UK licence-fee payer, the *Standard* has to chase advertising income – despite being 75% owned by a Russian billionaire. And it is this potential revenue which lies at the heart of its plan.

(http://news.bbc.co.uk/1/hi/business/8287715.stm, 2 October 2009)

By the time you read this, the battle will have moved on. We can't predict the outcome. Will Murdoch be proved right and begin to make money from online news to compensate for falling sales of paid-for titles? Will Lebedev's gamble signal a way out for the traditional print newspaper? Gambling like this during an advertising slump looks foolhardy, but who knows? Perhaps the BBC News website will lose its licence fee backing – or perhaps some other form of PSB production outlet will replace it?

## Conclusion

We are suggesting that new business models and new players may be changing the way in which the media business environment evolves. To some extent, the traditional media conglomerates with their very rooted sense of how 'old' industries like newspapers, music and film work have yet to catch up fully. Web 2.0 and Media 2.0 (see Chapter 8) have attracted some optimistic supporters who argue that the traditional concerns of the political economy theorists over ownership and control have been side-stepped by the emergence of new models and new players. The focus has shifted to concepts like user-generated content (UGC) and more importance is being attached to how users actually engage with media products and services.

On the other hand, when we look at the new players in the media markets, whose entry has largely been via digital media and Web 2.0 applications, we note that fairly quickly they also work towards the consolidation of the new markets they have helped to open up. Microsoft, Google, Yahoo and Apple are still young corporations, but they dominate computer- and internet-based media activities just as much as the older media conglomerates have done in the traditional media industries.

It's also worth remembering that at the same time as consumer innovations such as the Kindle and Sony e-Reader started to challenge the book publishing industry in 2009, Hollywood was being forced to recognise the recession and its impact on what investment banks were prepared to put up for annual film production slates. *The Guardian* reported that a Hollywood financial consultant was predicting a 66 per cent cut in the investment funds available to the studios. In a triple whammy, Mark Gill from the Film Department pointed to a 25 per cent decline in DVD sales (and a rise in competition from video on demand (VOD)) and an increasingly competitive international film market with competition for Hollywood's English-language films from 'domestic' product in local languages in many countries.

The games industry is vying with filmed entertainment for leadership of entertainment media. Games companies have a strong base in Japan and in France and the UK as well as the US. So with Hollywood eyeing up the film-based competition from India and China, the US hegemony of entertainment is not perhaps as secure as it has been up to now. In Chapters 9 and 10, we consider broadcasting and regulation. The issue here is whether public service broadcasting in both traditional and Web 2.0 modes can maintain its presence, especially in Europe.

## References and further reading

Curran, James, and Seaton, Marie (2009) *Power and Responsibility: The Press and Broadcasting in the UK*, London: Routledge.

Hesmondhalgh, David (2007) *The Cultural Industries*, 2nd edn, London: Sage.

Institute for Public Policy Research (2009) *Mind the Funding Gap*, available via
http://www.ippr.org/publicationsandreports/publication.asp?id=661.

Miller, Toby, Govil, Nitin, McMurria, John, Maxwell, Richard, and Wang, Ting (2004) *Global Hollywood: No. 2*, London: BFI.

Ramachandran, Naman (2008) 'Bollywood v. Hollywood', *film & festivals*, summer.

http://www.ifpi.org/content/library/DMR2009.pdf

http://www.bectu.org.uk/news/230

# CASE STUDY

# Music and movies – digital and available

- THE CHALLENGE OF COPYING
- PIRACY

- CHANGING BUSINESS MODELS IN THE FILM INDUSTRY
- REFERENCES AND FURTHER READING

As the recorded music model becomes a less and less compelling one and the cost of bringing a new artist to market is so high, it becomes an easy fall-back for a music company which owns lots of old rights to exploit them. They are dealing with the tried and tested as opposed to the brand new and speculative.

(Jeremy Lascelles, chief executive of independent music company Chrysalis, quoted in the *Observer*, 20 September 2009)

For a generation used to viewing images on an almost continuous basis using a variety of screens that have just one thing in common – instant accessibility – the idea that there is an image-based narrative form that needs to be viewed in a special and not very attractive place must be beginning to appear almost quaint.

(Nick Roddick, *Sight and Sound*, March 2009, p. 14)

These quotes reflect the confusion over changing markets and changing business models in the media business environment. The music industries were the first to be fundamentally damaged by piracy and the relative collapse of traditional business models. The film industry has in some ways been the most reluctant to change to business models associated with digital media (and certainly to decide on how to pay for digital cinema projection). Yet in these two quotes, it is a film

critic calling for a change in attitudes and a music industry executive recognising the value of 'catalogue' – 'old music' distributed in new ways. The *Observer* article dealt with the worldwide release of remastered Beatles material. This included both 'retro' presentations of Beatles CD singles in 'hand-assembled' cardboard sleeves (in Japan) and a Beatles version of the popular *Rock Band* game for wii, Playstation and X-Box. Here, seemingly, is an industry which has found a way of exploiting rights in conjunction with new media business models.

The music industries and the film industry have a long history of almost symbiotic relationships, even though they have operated in different ways at different times. Recorded music has been an integral part of film's appeal since the 1920s and at various times the same companies have owned both film studios and record labels. (See the Classic Case Study on the **MSB5 website** – Music Industry, Technology and Synergy.)

They became more like each other in the 1980s with the increased reliance of the film business on ancillary rights, especially those associated with selling videotapes and later DVDs. Both industries were also influenced by the rise of a quite specific new media form, the music video. In the 1990s both could see that the new environment of the digital online world was going to challenge them. The main difference between them has been the means by which their products have traditionally been presented to audiences.

The music industries are really two separate industries dealing with live performance and recorded music. What we now call filmed entertainment is essentially the same or similar products, all prerecorded but available in different modes of distribution (e.g. in cinemas, on TV, on DVD, etc.)

## THE CHALLENGE OF COPYING

The music industry faced the challenge of copying first. From the 1960s onwards, anyone with an analogue tape-recorder could copy music from discs and radio broadcasts. Cassette recorders made this easier in the 1970s and the first official campaigns against copying began in the 1980s. In the UK this meant a logo on records proclaiming 'Home Taping is Killing Music'. This industry campaign (by the BPI – British Phonographic Industry) received some support from the Musicians' Union (who also ran their own campaign, arguing that taping was 'killing live music'). However, its main aim was to protect the income stream of the record labels (see McLeod 2005; Laing 1985). In reality, the home taping of the 1980s didn't damage the music industries significantly. Taping was, by the standards

of contemporary digital copying, a laborious process carried out in 'real time'. Most people still bought records but then made 'Mixtapes' to share with friends or to play in the car or on their Walkman.

Copying CDs produced better quality and also opened the way for piracy with mass copying. However, until the development of music compression and 'ripping' software, digital copying was not something that was easy to do at home. The changes that occurred from the late 1990s, as distribution – legal and illegal in terms of copyright infringements – of MP3 files increased, had various consequences:

- they changed the way people listened to music and the structure of the 'music industry' by promoting individual 'tracks' over the 'album' or 'single' in recorded music;
- they offered the potential for wider distribution of music by independent labels and performers; and
- the relationship between recording and live performance changed.

Services like iTunes operate on the **long tail** principle, stocking every kind of music. They also enable preview samples and along with other services enable access to podcasts, internet radio and playback of MP3s from artist and record label websites. Here is the democratising impetus of Web 2.0 making recommendations and a wide variety of user-endorsed music, rather than that simply promoted by the music majors. Alongside the 'internet jukebox' Spotify, YouTube and the My Space pages of musicians and fans, the recorded music environment explored by music lovers now is very different.

# HOME TAPING IS KILLING MUSIC

AND IT'S ILLEGAL

*Figure 7.9* An early industry campaign against copying.

## EXPLORE 7.8 HOW DO YOU LISTEN TO MUSIC?

Do you use an MP3 player or play music on your computer?

- If so, how do you organise the music you put on the player?
- How much do you recognise as user-generated content in how you classify your own music and how you use other people's advice?

Music industry practice used to be about exploitation of the rights gained in 'signing' artists to long-term contracts. Watch any of the biopics of 1950s and 1960s music stars (e.g. *Ray* (US 2004)) and note the trajectory from aspiring musician to a first signing for a small label, then a big label and then the development of a career. The label would hope to mould the career of the artist, persuading them to make music that could be easily marketed. Live performances were often designed to exploit different stages of the artist's career – initially gaining them exposure and then capitalising on chart success and consolidating sales through large arena shows. The label also exploited rights by selling them for ancillary uses (cinema, advertising, etc.) and later as catalogue (as in the Beatles example above).

Kembrew McLeod (2005) quotes an early instance of the cracks appearing in the music majors' model when the American band Wilco were dropped in 2001 by the major label Reprise because the album they had just recorded was 'not commercial'. Wilco managed to acquire the rights to their own material and streamed it over the internet to fans. In 2002 they released it on the independent label Nonesuch and sold half a million copies for their biggest success. The band discovered that, sometimes at least, the Web 2.0 gurus are right.

In Chapter 8 we quote Kevin Kelly as regards accepting that what you produce will be copied, but that people will still pay for the extras that can't be copied. These might include the chance to support the band knowing that the profits will go direct to them or that they will receive a bigger share when they are not with a major. Fans might appreciate getting the music first via the internet, but then also having the chance to own the physical copy. Wilco certainly didn't 'lose out' by embracing the possibility that fans would copy music.

The music majors (Sony, EMI, Warner Music and Universal) are corporate producers with large overheads. The arrangements they make to share profits with contracted artists are highly complex. Back to the biopics, and one of the most familiar narratives is that of the new pop sensation who sells tons of records and somehow receives very little income. With good management, he or she will eventually do well perhaps, but the business model is designed to generate profit first, and support for the artist is something that they have to fight for.

| | Albums (Physical) Millions of units | Albums (Digital) Millions of units | Albums (Total) | Change year on year (%) | Singles (Physical) Millions of units | Single (Digital) Millions of units | Singles (Total) | Change year on year (%) |
|---|---|---|---|---|---|---|---|---|
| **1999** | 121.6 | | 121.6 | +0.1 | 71.0 | | 71.0 | −3.8 |
| **2003** | 159.3 | | 159.3 | +6.8 | 30.9 | | 30.9 | −29.7 |
| **2005** | 159.0 | | 159.0 | −2.7 | 21.4 | 26.4 | 47.9 | +48.4 |
| **2007** | 131.8 | 6.3 | 138.1 | −10.8 | 8.6 | 78.0 | 86.6 | +29.3 |
| **2008** | 123.3 | 10.3 | 133.6 | −3.2 | 4.9 | 110.3 | 115.1 | +33.0 |

*Figure 7.10* Album and single sales in the UK in selected years, 1999–2008.

## PIRACY

The illegal copying and distribution of music and films and TV programmes is now generally referred to as 'piracy'. It's interesting that both the industry and some of the illegal copiers and distributors have adopted this reference.

> The term originated more than two thousand years ago to describe attacks at sea when ships were attacked by robbers seeking plunder. In the eighteenth century some pirates became celebrities. Wikipedia's description seems apt: 'pirates of the classical period were rebellious, clever teams who operated outside the restricting bureaucracy of modern life' (http://en.wikipedia.org/wiki/Pirates).

In more recent times, pirate radio stations have always had a certain amount of public support when they have attempted to play different kinds of music than that being offered by licensed radio broadcasters. In the UK in the 1960s pirate radio stations did indeed broadcast from ships offshore. They were eventually closed down by legislation but their popularity led to a major change in UK broadcasting. Radio pirates in inner cities still carry a romantic appeal of sorts, but they haven't had the same dramatic impact on broadcasting policy.

Internet radio knows no boundaries and neither do the various websites that have been set up to enable peer-to-peer copying and downloading. Using the BitTorrent protocol these sites allow anyone with a single computer and limited bandwidth to become part of a 'community' sharing large files. BitTorrent links computers together so that each computer 'feeds' others with a small part of a large file. The protocol is used by legitimate distributors to offer quicker and more reliable downloads, but large numbers of files are also shared without rights payments. One of the best known 'torrent tracker' sites is Pirate Bay, based in Sweden

and, as the name suggests, projecting the image of a community sharing material across national boundaries and challenging traditional forms of copyright law and regulation.

Alongside 'piracy', a second term, also with a romantic/heroic connotation, is 'bootleg' (derived from alcohol smuggling when bottles were perhaps hidden in boots?). The first widely circulated bootleg music recordings started to appear when portable recorders were smuggled into rock concerts in the 1960s or material was smuggled out of recording studios. Again, the popularity of such material eventually persuaded artists themselves and the record labels to issue legal versions of bootleg recordings, some of which, like *The Basement Tapes* by Bob Dylan and the Band, became classic albums (see en.wikipedia.org/wiki/Great_White_Wonder).

Much less romantic was the growth of counterfeiters – copiers of legal recordings creating facsimile tapes, CDs and DVDs. This practice is simply for monetary gain; there is no defence that the illegal copy is in some way aiding the artist or distributing material that wouldn't otherwise be heard. In the early days copies were poor and packaging unconvincing. Now it's better (apart from films recorded from cinema screens). There is little doubt that the practice has damaged the artists and the media industries as well as often delivering poor

*Figure 7.11* A 'demo' page on the Pirate Bay website. Sweden has three organisations using the Pirate name ('Pirat'). Go to Wikipedia to find out what they each do.

quality goods. As a criminal enterprise on an industrial scale it has many social disbenefits and in some countries it has virtually destroyed the local cinema industry (see Chapter 10).

It is difficult to avoid a moral judgement of some kind. Most of us would probably condone some forms of copying and distributing that avoids questions of copyright at the same time as condemning other forms simply designed to make a quick killing at a car boot sale. We are probably all fed up with the anti-piracy messages pumped out by the music and film industries, yet we don't want to be tricked into buying a poor copy. The single important issue for the digital media industries is that it isn't possible to stop the copiers (see the Kevin Kelly quote in Chapter 8) and therefore new business models are needed.

For an entertaining and thought-provoking perspective on copyright issues see the Larry Lessig video lecture on TED at http://www.ted.com/talks/larry_lessig_says_the_law_is_strangling_creativity.html.

The title of Lessig's lecture (see box) takes us back to the question of artists and creativity. As he points out, copyright laws (which differ from country to country) were instituted in a specific set of circumstances as popular music performance and then recording became institutionalised. But since then (early in the twentieth century) technology and media 'use' has changed. Perhaps we now need different interpretations of copyright law that recognise the globalised media environment within which media is produced? See Chapter 7 and the section on creative commons.

## EXPLORE 7.9 THE VALUE OF MUSIC

How do you value music?

- Do you make music yourself, use music in your media productions, collect recordings or just enjoy it for recreation?
- How do you think a price should be put on:
  - a new composition
  - a recording
  - a live performance?
- How do you find out about new music?
- How has digital distribution affected the value you place on music?

### Making music and making movies

What do you need to create a piece of music that people want to hear? Talent and imagination are essential, but not necessarily sophisticated equipment. High quality recording equipment costs only a few hundred pounds for basic 'live' recording. Local recording studios are available in many cities on an hourly basis. Recorded material costs nothing to distribute as MP3s with a laptop and broadband. Small runs of CDs are not expensive. If performers are willing to limit their ambitions to making the music that they enjoy performing for a fan audience that really appreciates it, they can make a comfortable living. Selling millions of 'units' and having a Christmas No. 1 is another story, but overall, recording artists and small record labels have proliferated as the majors have struggled to make the transition to a download world.

Making movies is rather different. The need for talent and imagination is the same, but the variety of skills required, the logistics of production and the higher costs of equipment mean that consistent production of movies people want to watch will cost more than the equivalent music production. Yes, you can make a movie for £5,000 (*Zombie Diaries* 2008) or even £45 as claimed for *Colin* (UK 2009), another zombie flick, but these are rare exceptions: £50,000 is now the bottom-end for a cinema production in the UK, e.g. *Le Donk and Scor-Zay-Zee* (UK 2009) from Shane Meadows and Paddy Considine, who have discussed setting up a scheme to help young film-makers make £50k films. Low-budget movies can survive with digital distribution only, but it is more difficult than posting a few MP3s on a website.

## CHANGING BUSINESS MODELS IN THE FILM INDUSTRY

The concept of feature films being instantly available whenever the viewer wants is not new. VOD or nVOD ('near' video on demand) has been around since the 1980s as an idea and since the 1990s as a feasible option on cable or satellite television. Now films are available for download on a home computer or a mobile device as well. But still the service provider faces the problem of deciding how much to charge for each download. This is made more difficult by the threat of piracy. If the charge is too low, the business may lose money; if it is too high, potential customers may turn to free but illegal downloads or less expensive pirate copies.

The service provider may also offer other filmed entertainment services. How will the new service impact on the others? After several years of spectacular growth, the DVD sale and rental business began to stutter around 2007–8. Hollywood saw a big fall in DVD revenue during 2009 and attention began to focus even more on release windows and in turn on questions about vertical integration, consolidation and diversification.

The feature film has often been regarded as one of the highest profile and most desirable of media products to access. Its value is to a large extent determined by an audience desire to see a film as soon as it becomes publicly available and to see it under the best conditions (best projection, sound, most comfortable seats; etc.). The distributor stimulates this desire through promotions and advertising, aiming to attract as many people as possible to the opening weekend (when cinemas will be prepared to pay distributors more to screen the film to an eager public).

DVDs available via self-service kiosks have launched in France and the US. But some Hollywood studios refused to distribute their films through the $1 per overnight rental service from Redbox as it 'undervalues our product'. Will the same scheme work in the UK where online rental has been a big success led by LOVEFiLM?

*Figure 7.12* 'pop' DVD kiosks at Piccadilly Station, Manchester, UK. 'pop' is a service from Universal and Sony. Most kiosks are in multiplex cinemas where they sell games and downloads as well as DVDs. The kiosks here target commuters who may not go to cinemas.

*Figure 7.13* Loveleen Tandan arriving at the premiere of *Slumdog Millionaire* in Mumbai in January 2009 (see the case study to Chapter 5). The film opened in India the next day.

Inevitably, over the ensuing weeks of the 'rental' of the film by the exhibitor, the 'newness' of the film in cinemas wears off and audience numbers fall to the point where there is no longer a commercial reason to screen the film. The business model suggests that the cinema window should now close so that a new window (DVD) can open. The DVD experience is different. Although the film is no longer 'new', the DVD may cost more to purchase than a cinema ticket, suggesting that the purchaser values the chance to view the film more than once – or more likely, to view it with others, making it cheaper on a per head basis. Rental is cheaper, but may involve waiting and then returning the disc soon after viewing. Each succeeding window (pay-per-view (PPV), subscription, free to air broadcast) will charge less for the viewing experience.

The problem with a rigid system of windows is that it is established by the major studios who enforce it for the most popular films. But it isn't appropriate for more specialised films and it can't be policed in a global market with online alternatives.

> . . . theatrical grosses are an increasingly inadequate indicator of how well a film is recouping – and yet they continue to be the sole measure of performance, considered a reliable barometer of a film's success when its revenue numbers on secondary windows are rarely if ever disclosed. It's no secret that distributors big and small are churlish about releasing DVD sales figures and even less for TV sales or per-picture pay-TV financials.
>
> So what happens to those theatrical grosses we all consume avidly every Sunday and Monday when theatrical distribution starts to share its first-window status with other platforms such as VOD, DVD or download-to-own?
>
> (Mike Goodridge, *Screen International*, 22 October 2009)

Goodridge in this quote accurately pins down the concerns of the studio majors when he points out that the current model is unsustainable. In the same paper (9 October 2009) he reported on two ideas being touted in Hollywood – a new blockbuster delivered to your living room on the day of its release for $250 or the same film on VOD for $30–50 only four weeks after release. This might be in the context of major studios closing or being **consolidated**.

### The cost of digital distribution

A 'home music producer' may be able to distribute music online for negligible cost, but it's not quite the same for professional producers. As well as paying staff, media businesses require professional websites and paid-for web services, including design, hosting charges and maintenance. This is where the hidden costs come in – not least the power consumption needed to operate fully professional systems delivering online films and music.

So far, most of the experiments in simultaneous theatrical, DVD and online releases have come from small distributors offering specialist titles. There have been interesting examples of using Web 2.0 services to promote and distribute specific independent films (see the Chapter 6 case study on *The Age of Stupid*). It is now almost the norm for art films to be released in the UK on only one or two prints just to gain a profile through reviews and commentaries, before all the effort goes into the DVD release a couple of weeks later (or, in the case of Fatih Akin's 2007 Cannes prizewinner, *The Edge of Heaven* (Germany/Turkey/Italy), a simultaneous PPV release on Sky Box Office). These figures from the UK independent distributor Metrodome illustrate the current financial performance of different distribution modes:

| | |
|---|---|
| Cinema sales | £293,000 (296 %) |
| Television sales | £228,000 (274 %) |
| Video on demand | £259,000 (46 %) |
| Other ancillary | £33,000 (6 %) |
| DVD rental | £273,000 (158 %) |
| DVD sell through | £3,459,000 (14 %) |
| Total | £4,545,000 (30 %) |

(From the Interim Report for January–June 2009, downloaded from http://www.metrodomegroup.com) The figures refer to only a limited number of around six theatrical films and six leading DVD/Blu-ray titles (out of thirty). The figure in brackets is the increase on the previous six months. This highlights a major issue – the huge impact of one successful title out of the six, and how it can mean financial security for a relatively small company. Overall, in this market DVD is currently the only game – but that could change. The majors are protected from the risk of the failure of a few titles in any year – the nightmare for a small distributor – but not if the whole business model collapses.

## EXPLORE 7.10 MAKING MONEY FROM FEATURE FILMS

What can you find out about the costs and revenue associated with a feature film?

Try to find out financial information on a major studio picture and an independent film (American or foreign) distributed in the US. You should be able to find a production budget, possibly a marketing budget (50 per cent on top of production budget on many Hollywood films), box office grosses and possibly DVD sales, at least in North America. Remember, only about 50 per cent of 'gross' box office goes back to the distributor as net rentals.

Try:
- imdb.com
- UK Film Council Statistical Year Book (free download from http://www.ukfilmcouncil.com/research)
- http://lumiere.obs.coe.int/web/search/ (admissions on films released in Europe – a rough calculation of ticket prices gives box office estimates)
- http://www.boxofficeguru.com/
- http://boxofficemojo.com/
- http://www.the-numbers.com/

In your university library, you should find *Screen International* or an equivalent industry trade paper with weekly charts and occasional market reports. If your library has a Screendaily subscription, the archives on http://www.screendaily are useful.
- How difficult is it to find useful information?
- What conclusions do you draw about how the current business models work?

The future is uncertain for everyone, especially during a prolonged recession. In 2009 it appeared that the market might still support big-budget blockbusters (but fewer of them) and low-budget independent films 'picked up' cheaply for distribution. The mid-range films from both Hollywood and other film industries might find life difficult with current distribution models if the distributors cannot see ways of making a profit given the cost of acquiring rights. The likelihood is that we will see more diversity in distribution models and less rigidity in the practice of the majors. But, of course, nobody knows for sure.

## REFERENCES AND FURTHER READING

Allen, Katie (2009) 'Back Catalogues Spin a New Generation of Profits for Record Labels', *Observer*, 20 September.

Laing, Dave (1985) 'Music Video: Industrial Product, Cultural Form', *Screen*, 26, 2: 78–83.

McLeod, Kembrew (2005) 'MP3s are Killing Home Taping: The Rise of Internet Distribution and its Challenge to the Major Label Music Monopoly', in *Popular Music and Society*, 28, 4 (October): 521–31. http://www.kembrew.com/documents/Publications-pdfs/McLeod-MP3sAreKilling.pdf

Mitchell, Wendy (2008) 'Sky, Curzon, Artificial Eye Work Together on *The Edge Of Heaven*', 3 January, http://www.screendaily.com.

http://www.musictank.co.uk/

http://www.musiciansunion.org.uk

http://www.theauteurs.com

http://microwave.filmlondon.org.uk/get_the_resources/

http://www.frequencycast.co.uk/ondemand.html

# Part II
# Debates

An internet application (Wordle) stylises our use of some key terms in these chapters.

Q: Which key term(s) do you think are missing, or wrongly sized here?

Q: How big would you make them?

# 8 'New media' in a 'new world'?

- 'Newness' and histories
- Academic approaches
- Openness, collaboration and 'users'
- 'The long tail'
- Digital copies and the 'enclosure' of information

- New media, old metaphors
- 'New media', vanishing resources
- Conclusion
- References and further reading

Most of you, reading this, will have grown up in a digital and online world – or at least, experienced the world that way since the time you began to access media products and services for yourself. You are called 'the internet generation' or 'digital natives' because you are presumed to be unprecedentedly familiar with such forms, and to expect an 'anytime anywhere' media, always 'on' (however far that may be from your experience). Some recent theories have suggested that Web 2.0, as this degree of interactivity is called, requires completely new theories of media. We're not exactly arguing for this, but equally we refuse some easy media panics suggesting that 'new media' are the end of civilisation as we know it.

We want to explore what is exciting and truly new about interactivity, as well as what existing theories can best be adapted to understand it, and to celebrate its enjoyments and potential, as well as its 'darker side'.

This has to include questions about the many different ways in which gadgets 'work' for us – as enablers of sociability; as training media (some games); as fashion accessories; as parts of domestic arrangements. The many uses of such media involve fears and hopes for broadly cultural developments, as 'Web 2.0' or 'new media' shape the relations of public/private, work/non-work, home/outside-home spaces and activities.

The term '**postmodernism**', emerging in the 1980s, can in retrospect be seen as an attempt to get to grips with changes we can now begin to grasp as materially rooted technological change within capitalist systems.

On 'digital natives' myths and issues, see the link to *Moby What?!* on PBS's Digital Nation section: http://www.pbs.org/wgbh/pages/frontline/digitalnation/learning/literacy/moby-what-1.html?play.

*Figure 8.1* Arguably mobile phones are often put to ancient purposes – weaving social connections, arrangements, gossip. But social networking sites can shape a quite new sense of privacy, as they report rows and intimacies. Q: What do you tell your mother (or son) if s/he wants to be your 'friend' on Facebook?

**Postmodernism** is a hugely confusing and often confusingly used term. It refers to several different approaches to contemporary media-tised experience, especially in 'developed' parts of the world. **See MSB5 website** for the updated case study *Pulp Fiction* which outlines and discusses its main features.

*Figure 8.2* The internet arguably began with the ARPANET a US military-related communications system, in 1969; in 1975 email was introduced, and in the 1990s the World Wide Web was publicised by Al Gore as the 'information superhighway'. During that decade it became an everyday technology – in parts of the developed world.

See Chapter 1 for a reminder of debates in this area, involving ideas of 'indexical' media. These are linked directly, if in fragile ways, with what they record – e.g. celluloid film stock and its 'trace' off the real, as opposed to digital forms.

Why the quotation marks around 'new media'? While celebrating the capacities of interactive media, we need to remember that study of media has always explored the 'new', and that some of the key theories for existing media are still relevant, alongside newly necessary concepts. Finally, nowhere is the interdisciplinary nature of media studies clearer than here, so you will find more than pure 'media' approaches in this chapter.

## 'Newness' and histories

When we wrote the first edition of this book, in the mid-1990s, users were still experiencing the arrival of what was then often named 'new media'. This referred to the move to **digital** and away from **analogue** media processes and products (see below). The internet was then still something that was the preserve of a few rather than a medium for everyone.

Analogue is the term for most media's pre-1980s reliance on recording sounds and images as physical forms – images captured in a chemical emulsion on celluloid film, sounds literally cut as grooves into a disc or as magnetic impulses on a tape. This physical transformation required skill and precision, and was prone to damage through repeated use. Digital data is easier, cheaper and less bulky to store. It's less likely to deteriorate and can be easily and accurately duplicated. It has also aided **convergence** because the same device (i.e. a computer) can be used to present all kinds of digital media.

But still some users prefer the old analogue forms – are they just old romantics or has the change in form created new problems? Is the sound or image still superior?

Digital data has several drawbacks:
- It can be easily 'corrupted' or accidentally wiped. Sometimes a small fault can render a whole file useless.
- Some digital files are not compatible with all kinds of equipment.
- Digital data is easily compressed – tempting commercial producers to release lower standard copies.

As a result, whole new industries have evolved to protect files from viruses, back-up data, convert between formats, etc. A reel of 35mm film is ancient technology, but it can still be projected after fifty years or more on equipment that hasn't changed over the same period. Other analogue media texts, such as vinyl records, have also returned to usage. And many would argue that Kindle technology is not a substitute for a printed book.

---

**EXPLORE 8.1**

- Find someone who buys or sells vinyl records. Ask why there is still interest in this 'obsolete' technology. Do you have any favourite 'old' forms, such as print, radio, books?
- How do these combine with newer media forms, such as games, in your daily activities?
- Look at http://www.youtube.com/watch?v=xFAWR6hzZek for a short satire involving the usefulness of books.

---

**EXPLORE 8.2**

Consider this quote on the practice of watching films on mobile phone and computer screens: 'few film- and TV-makers have yet thought much about how their films or programmes look on the tiny screens of hand-held devices . . . this situation begs for a "third aesthetic" after film and television' (James 2009).

- Explore these points with friends and fellow students. How true are they of your experiences?
- What might be valued in a 'new aesthetic' of smaller screens?
- If you use Kindle technology for reading books (on trains, perhaps?) does that seem to raise similar questions? Does the iPad?

---

Since the move from analogue to digital there have been two further stages in the development of online activity. The **dot.com boom** or 'bubble' (*c.*1998–2001) was a huge rise in the number of internet-based companies, with some of them subsequently 'crashing'. There then emerged what is called Web 2.0. This refers to several changes. Most important is the (often rather vague) idea of interactivity and user-generated content (UGC). The UK government's 2009 *Digital Britain* report rather optimistically calls this 'digital participation'. Web 1.0 had email, but in the early days this felt a bit like putting a message in a

---

**Convergence**: the combination of multiple services through lines of telecommunication from a single provider. See Henry Jenkins' blog at http://www.henryjenkins.org.

---

As one reviewer wrote of *Charlie Brooker's Gameswipe* (BBC4 2009): it's an indication of how ghettoised gaming is on television that it was a shock to see talented, popular contributors discussing the subject at length and in knowledgeable detail.

---

 See Chapter 14 and also **MSB5 website** for the case study on the BBC's uses of UGC.

Telex or teletype was a form of message sent by wire between two typewriters and was a common form of business, military and news communication in the twentieth century. Enjoy the comedy sketch on: http://www.youtube.com/watch?v=7pouCAOPfYg.

bottle and hoping it might arrive. Even electronic bulletin boards were a bit like corresponding by telex machine.

Web 2.0 makes direct communication easy and attractive, especially since wireless technologies and mobile (hand-held) devices mean that being online all day is now the norm for some. Ease of access also means that more of us are willing to 'post' material and help create 'content' online. Web 2.0 means that users expect to be able to do this and often expect any service to offer us this opportunity.

## EXPLORE 8.3

Your experiences? When you began your course, did you assume that you would be able to find everything you needed online, that your lectures would be recorded and podcast or slides or pdfs made available, and that you would be able to interact via them with your lecturers and fellow students? Printing or emailing your essays is probably now taken for granted.

Q: How else have interactive media shaped your learning?

Q: What is the place of 'face to face' learning (e.g. seminars) in your college?

Q: Go to http://www.youtube.com/watch?v=cL9Wu2kWwSY for a video which Sony played at their executive conference in 2010.

- How would you be able to check and further research the statistics used?
- How does this affect the usefulness or strikingness of this collection of statistics?

## Academic approaches

Henry Jenkins' blog (see p. 241), especially the Archive section, is a rich and well-theorised resource for this kind of exploration. See also Chapter 14.

Web 2.0 has led to utopian claims for Media 2.0 – as both a new form of media business and a new form of media studies. Critics have argued that the changes are so profound that the previous theoretical ideas developed in media studies have been rendered obsolete. What we need, they argue, is 'Media 2.0' a completely revised and updated version of the 'first form' of media studies, putting much more emphasis on 'prosumers' (consumers as 'producers' of content) and interactivity in general as challenging 'old' notions of 'representation', textual analysis, audiences and so on.

We agree that media studies needs to take on board the huge changes to media and the ways they connect users. It is no longer 'business as usual' for most media activity. But neither is it a complete break from the past.

'Newness' in media has been hailed before, and we can develop existing academic debates in engaging effectively with what is happening now. Two of these, from the 1960s, are sharply and interestingly at odds – the theories of Marshall McLuhan and those of Raymond Williams.

## Two different early approaches

**Marshall McLuhan** (1911–80), a Canadian literary academic and 1960s theorist and writer, was the most celebrated pre-internet theorist of media. His provocative phrasing and early TV-friendly presence helped make him one of the first academic 'celebrities' in the field (scan YouTube for clips of his many TV appearances). He argued that, irrespective of the content or audience use of particular media products, the technologies which 'carry' them change human perception of the world and practices within it. For him, media determine consciousness.

His most famous phrases are 'the medium is the message' and, differently, 'the medium is the massage', and 'the global village', evoking an optimistic, even redemptive view of electronic media, one which sees primitive 'community' virtues in the new world of broadband access. Wikipedia has a helpful account of his most famous book *Understanding Media: The Extensions of Man* (sic) (1964).

He also defined all media as extensions of the human body, forming new 'environments' for it in subtle ways and even making bodily changes, as media change from being 'ear centred' (acoustic) to being eye centred (visual). A famous statement of his: 'Media effects are new environments as imperceptible as water to a fish, subliminal for the most part' (McLuhan 1969: 22). His use of 'environment' does not directly relate to climate change politics, but refers to the balance between different media, such as TV and radio, as well as the 'sensorium' or combination of human senses.

Finally, in this very brief summary, he argued for re-mediation, that 'the content of any medium is always another medium'. By definition this is an older medium, and thus a reason to feel sceptical about completely 'new media'. (See Lister *et al.* 2009 for excellent fuller discussion of McLuhan.)

**Raymond Williams** (1921–88), a very different founding figure of cultural and media theory, agreed that media re-mediate. Examples would include early cinema basing itself on existing theatrical conventions and only gradually making its own forms, in the ways it mediated speed, spectacle and visceral potential. Later, some computer games could be said to re-mediate cinema, but with even more 'immersivity' or capacity to immerse players in certain

Arguably the term 'digital natives' for people who have grown up with interactive media (like you?) partly harks back to McLuhan's idea of a 'global village'. Both ignore issues such as class, gender and ethnicity in making internet access unequal.

Contrast McLuhan's 'sexy' pronouncements with Livingstone's point regarding media interviews: 'In terms of policy effectiveness the scholar's careful conclusions – "it depends on the context", "different children react in different ways", "the findings are indicative but not conclusive" – play out poorly in a fast paced and hotly contested policy process' (2009: 230).

*Figure 8.3* 'The Matrix is everywhere, all around us.' 'Follow the white rabbit,' says Morpheus in *The Matrix* (US 1999), a film which some see as a McLuhan-influenced view of all-pervasive media technology. *Videodrome* (US 1983), *Robocop* (US 1987) and *Strange Days* (US 1995) also speculated on futures where TV and electronic media are linked directly to bodily, perceptual changes.

kinds of game. In a recent turn around, the phenomenally successful film *Avatar* (US 2009) could be said to re-mediate the immersivity of computer games for cinema, especially in its 3D and IMAX versions. Livingstone (2009) develops this point: 'The contemporary conceptual toolkit centres on the prefix "re-".' She lists 'remixing, reconfiguring, remediating, reappropriating, recombining' as terms which 'recognise the activities by which innovations are rendered both continuous with and distinct from that which has gone before . . . adopting a frame of enabling and constraining rather than of determining or causing' (p. 25).

So Williams and others rejected McLuhan's view of technology as *in itself* determining human perception and social change – called **technological determinism**. Williams argued this was unhistorical and asocial, that it is impossible to study technology as though it were a sphere separate from social life. It is part of broader social processes, all the way from first ideas – that is, whatever seems, in different social contexts, to be feasible (i.e. fundable) projects – through to design, production, marketing, uses and consequences.

Williams wrote extensively on drama, literature, culture, Marxism and media. His book *Television: Technology and Cultural Form* (1974) is a milestone in thinking about TV as a specific medium, through emphasising the importance of the 'flow' of programmes rather than their existence as a set of discrete 'texts', like books or songs or plays. John Ellis (2000) took this further, suggesting TV can be understood through three periods and their specific cultural shapes:

- *Scarcity*, with mostly one or two national channels (BBC and ITV for the UK) where TV performed a socially integrating role, since most people could be assumed to be watching certain programmes. It was not, however, as easy to discover what they felt about these.
- *Availability*, with multiple channels, where he argues TV 'works through' traumatic happenings which viewers are made to witness but feel powerless to affect. Scheduling becomes key in ratings-driven systems.
- *Plenty*, which promises more of everything, and is the beginning of the 'being-together-while-apart' cultures which interactive media promise.

> You can probably see a reworking of older forms on your computer screen, e.g. 'cut' signified by scissors, or an egg timer signifying a task in progress, and so on.

92% use email to communicate with friends and family

Half of adults use webcams and social networking

7 in 10 access photos online

24% use a Twitter-like service

*Figure 8.4* For a well-resourced global snapshot of global digital usage take a look at the Norton Online Living Report 2009. Q: What do you find is the most surprising statistic there?

Later writers, working often with TV, have opened out the ways in which a 'technology' is more than just wires, plastic and circuits. New media are usually made commercially viable through also being design items, fashion items, something that fits into existing room layouts and usage, train journeys, etc. ways of keeping safely in touch with others (especially for parents and children) and so on (see Livingstone 2009).

Once we locate technology as socially *shaped*, and specific, in the ways Williams, Ellis, Livingstone and others have done, we have to allow that it can also be, to some extent, socially *shaping*. We can't simply generalise, in the way that often pressurised journalism likes to do, about new media, whether games or Facebook, as the latest threat to 'civilisation as we know it' (just like 'video nasties' or certain horror films did in the 1980s, and other media at other times).

Debates on **social media** can be shaped around two main attitudes, one pessimistic and the other optimistic or even utopian.

1  *Pessimistic positions* around the dominant technology of our time, the internet, include the following claims:

   - 'Social networking' via social media substitutes for actual physical relationships. It encourages banal and trivial communication, and leads to unhappiness because of lack of 'real' human contact – touch, ability to understand the range of face-to-face communication and so on.

   - It is shaping people in narcissistic, inarticulate and often autistic ways as a result of this lack of social contact with others. This accompanies internet addiction which is growing around the world, especially in China, where it is constructed as a threat to the nation's youth. Read and evaluate http://www.onasia.com/content/story.aspx?storyID = 669&page = 1.

   - A sense of public and private is being eroded, with Facebook and other sites allowing violent verbal abuse, bullying and ignorant comment in ways that would not be allowed in a properly 'public' space. There are also concerns about the global spread of pornographic discourses (see Chapter 5, p. 154) and of the global surveillance possibilities of interactive media.

   - Computer games are to blame for much violence and cruelty in their users.

2  *Optimistic, even utopian* positions are exemplified in this statement of 'where we are now' from the UK website of *Stuff*, the 'world's best-selling gadget magazine', September 2009:

   > We are living in a golden age. A time when the iPhone serves as a multimedia do-it-all app-fest, when all music is available DRM-free, when ebooks are on the verge of replacing paper books. You can wander down the streets of the world in Google Street View, get hi-def movies on Blu-ray for less than a tenner and buy a super-low emission hybrid car for Ford Focus money. This is it, people, we're living the dream.

   - A related utopian view is McLuhan's assertion that we are now

 **ONLINE RESOURCES** 'Social media' are usefully defined by Brian Solis as 'Any tool or service that uses the internet to facilitate conversations.' See **MSB5 website** for a link to further discussion on his website.

*Figure 8.5* Judging from some of its covers, *Stuff* constructs traditional gender roles as part of a kind of 'utopia'. 1) Analyse this magazine cover as a gendered representation of technology use. Contrast with Figure 8.4. 2) Make a survey: how gendered are your friends' uses of and confidence in internet forms? Is it true, as often implied, that the internet is free of gendered inequalities and preferences?

*Figure 8.6* This striking design publicised a *New Statesman* magazine piece on the internet's greatest success story, Google, and growing concerns about how it may be using the data it is amassing on its users.

living in an electronic 'global village' which can heal the sensory alienation of an era dominated by print forms and national boundaries.

- Many kinds of global and local protest, politics, arts, and charitable forms of action now use interactive media to shape a new world order. Obama's presidential campaign is a celebrated example, but see also indymedia resources for your country (e.g. uk.indymedia.org) and also www.zmag.org/znet the use of 'flashmobs', and Chapter 12.

Some developments produce explicitly *split* structures of feeling.

a Twitter social networking, for example, is often valued for its immediacy and for its short messages which can be followed up on elsewhere. It already has two amazing campaigns to its name.

---

**EXPLORE 8.4**

Research the 2009 Twitter campaigns around Trafigura, and Jan Moir's *Daily Mail* article on Stephen Gately's death (see Chapter 12).

---

Even its name sounds modestly self-parodying. But opponents point to the banality of some of the messages, and ask: how much can be communicated in 140 keystrokes?

b Here's John Lanchester (2009) on Google's power, a major cause of concern (as resembling Orwell's 'Big Brother' in the novel *1984*) for many:

> about a month ago my hard drive . . . crashed, and my backup . . . failed to restore my work archive. I was facing a gigantic bill for a by-no-means guaranteed hard drive recovery, when it occurred to me that every piece I'd ever sent by email might, just might . . . and sure enough there it was on Gmail. A copy of everything I'd ever written for publication, and everything else I'd ever emailed too. It's the kind of thing a big brother might do, help you in ways which make you feel simultaneously relieved and resentful.

## EXPLORE 8.5

Consider the assumptions of these three contrasting positions.

- Can you bring evidence from your experience of 'new media' to bear on them?
- How would you describe your position? On the basis of which media forms: games, texting, Gmail, internet-enabled political movements?
- Can you think of ways in which your position is shaped by your gender, ethnicity, social class?

## Openness, collaboration and 'users'

Web 2.0 has impacted on theories affecting both the study and the business of media, as you would expect for such a deeply embedded and socially 'shaping' technology.

As context, let's first reconsider the 'newness' of interactivity. The development of the internet and the opportunity to 'go online' to find something or simply to send email changed many aspects of communication and research. However, it was the possibility of *staying* online that really changed things. Pre-broadband working with computers used to involve a quick dash online, using a telephone 'dial-up' account to retrieve something, when connection time was expensive and often slow, and then working on it 'offline'. We can now use 'always-on' broadband connections – if they are available, and affordable.

*Figure 8.7* Workers haul part of a fibre optic cable on to the shore at the Kenyan port town of Mombasa, 2009.

1　The accessibility of broadband is not universal, nor easily come by. Figure 8.7, showing the arrival, in Mombasa, of the cable bringing access to those East Africans who can afford it, was taken in the summer of 2009. It's a reminder of the labour and materials involved in 'magic'-seeming goods, like computers and mobile phones.

2　A letter in *The Guardian* made this point about the unevenness of the pace of change in media usage:

> Alan Rusbridger asks when we last played a CD, owned a basic phone, went to a library for information or bought a map. The answer is that most ordinary people still do all these things. I can well believe media people live in the world he describes, but perhaps he needs to get out more?

(24 October 2009)

These connections have changed the media environment profoundly. They explain why we might consider the 1990s as a first internet age (the '**dot.com** revolution'), and why we need to think of 2005–6 as the beginning of a revised version of the experience. This is a shift not from 'Web 1.0' to 'Web 1.1', but to a completely revised 'Web 2.0'.

One of the striking aspects of the new media landscape, or ecology, is the creation of a kind of web-based 'academy', almost an alternative advanced education system, a new kind of 'media study'. This is primarily a North American phenomenon (though many of its members may have originated outside North America). It comprises a range of writers and lecturers who may be academics, media consultants, journalists, lawyers or other practitioners. But instead of publishing only for their main institutions, they write in journals such as *Wired* or write their own blogs or give video lectures sponsored by Google or less commercial organisations such as TED. Much of what they say is consequently free to access and a boon for impoverished students. We've used the writings of several of these Web 2.0 thinkers in different parts of this book. This doesn't mean we accept all of the claims for the extent of the changes that Web 2.0/Media 2.0 has brought. But they do allow new debates to open up.

> TED (http://www.ted.com) is 'a small nonprofit organisation devoted to Ideas Worth Spreading. It started out (in 1984) as a conference bringing together people from three worlds: Technology, Entertainment, Design.' In September 2009 there were more than 450 free TED Talks (i.e. video lectures) available to view.

Some useful new terms, used in accounts of media businesses, spreading into theories of audiences and interactivity are: *networking*; *user-generated content (UGC)*; *'the wisdom of crowds'*; *'crowd funding'*; *'the long tail'*; *'prosumers'*; *'tags'*; and *'clouds'*.

See also http://en.wikipedia.org/wiki/The_Cluetrain_Manifesto for a statement of belief in the new business model which is possibly offered by Web 2.0.

Let's begin with the concept of networking and **user-generated content (UGC)**. In June 2009 Clay Shirky gave a TED Talk observing that Web 2.0 was the fourth great advance in communication (following the printing press, telegraph and radio/TV broadcasting). This is not just because it introduced new possibilities of its own, but also because it includes easy access to all other media technologies. Whereas previous technologies enabled one-to-one instant communication (e.g. telephone) or one-to-many (e.g. broadcasting), Web 2.0 allows 'many-to-many' (sometimes called 'social media').

He outlined a recent example, from politics, of Web 2.0 possibilities. In 2008 individual US citizens, concerned at the potential for vote rigging in the presidential election, after serious allegations in the previous two, took video images and footage of voting activity at their local polling stations and posted it to a central website. They hoped this would deter possible illegal activity. It wasn't a new idea (Nigerians had done something similar in 2007, but used simple text messages rather than camera phones). Shirky commented that this was an example of 'global tech transfer' from Nigeria to the US – an unusual transfer in that the important resource that was utilised was 'social capital' rather than 'technical capital'. Nigerians had the pressing need to do this and so social usage developed because the technology was there to be adapted creatively.

This is an important observation about the introduction of new technologies – they don't usually spread until significant numbers of 'social users' (i.e. not technology *experts*) see a use for them. This can be hard to predict. Manufacturers of mobile phones did not expect the enormous take-up of SMS messages by teenage users. Shirky concludes that media have become 'social' because the technology has become almost boring rather than shiny and new. We can all access it, so it's argued that what then becomes important is what we can do with it.

Trivia: Clay Shirky teaches at New York University on a course entitled 'Social Weather'. See http://www.shirky.com/bio.html.

Interestingly Shirky is using an approach from the French sociologist Pierre Bourdieu (1930–2002) who pioneered the idea that inequalities persist through different kinds of 'capital' and their distribution. It is not simply a matter of 'money capital', though often closely related to it. See Chapter 3.

*Figure 8.8* Samsung's pebble design netbook, 2009. It seems designed as a 'cool' fashion accessory, like much computer advertising (see Apple) which also markets machines as 'pure', and certainly not as related to disastrous climate changes.

*Figure 8.9* Why do you think the founders chose the Hawaian word 'wiki' for their online encyclopaedia? (See Chapter 15.)

Firefox is a product from the Mozilla Foundation which used the coding released by Netscape, producer of the first widely used browser, Netscape Navigator, to develop a new internet suite. Mozilla also produces the Thunderbird email client.

---

## EXPLORE 8.6

Evaluate your own use of Web 2.0 services.

- Have you started blogging or participating in online groups because your peers and family seem to be doing it?
- Does your use mostly involve immediate friends and family? Or have you also joined a global 'community of users'?
- Have you identified activities that enable you to live your life differently or to work in different ways? How important are these 'new' uses of media technologies?
- How do you think the saleability of gadgets as fashion accessories, for male and female users, fits with Shirky's suggestions – or with your own usage?

---

Shirky's example (developed later for Twitter's role in the 2009 Iranian elections) evokes the wider phenomenon of collaborative media (such as Wikipedia, and also the 'crowd funding' of films like *The Age of Stupid*). Surowiecki (2004) argues that a large group of individuals, making independent decisions on the same issue, which can then be aggregated and averaged, are more likely to produce a 'correct' decision than a small group of experts. These are 'crowds' of individuals who voluntarily contribute to something – like Wikipedia – rather than simply respond to a sampling questionnaire. It is crucial for this argument that the 'crowd' is made up of diverse and self-selecting individuals, without attempts to 'second guess' what others are thinking. It is not the same as 'crowd psychology' (which suggests that individuals within a crowd are aware of, and react to, other crowd members), but it does mirror aspects of statistical sampling.

Tapscott and Williams (2006) argued for business activities undertaken by groups of individuals with no formal organisation. Wikipedia itself is developed through 'mass collaboration' (see http://en.wikimedia.org/wiki/Wikipedia#Editing_model for a statement of Wikipedia's aims and strategies). The basic idea goes back much further, to activities like software development, where free, open source software projects, like the Firefox browser, were produced by 'communities' of developers. Other software projects invite users to test products, file reports, help other users in support groups and then create extra applications or 'plug-ins'. The product of this labour may be distributed freely or as shareware. Those who contribute in this way might be described as **prosumers**, or a mix of consumers (they might still pay for the product) and producers.

A different possibility for collaboration comes via the use of tags, user-devised or user-selected terms for classifying media content. For instance, if you have a Flickr or Picasa account, you can post your digital photos to your website and tag each image to help you classify your collection. Similarly, if you blog about something you may wish to add several tags to link it to other similar posts you have made. But the tags don't just help you. They could allow others searching for something to find relevant images or posts on your sites. 'Categories' are also available on some Web 2.0 services as an alternative to tags. Both categories and tags can be related to clouds – a visual representation of word tags or categories such that the most used words are shown in a larger type size. You can see the effects of this by producing your own clouds using free Wordle software (http://www.wordle.net/). See the Part II title page image (p. 237).

> 'Prosumer' has several meanings, all related to collapsing the distinction between 'professional/ producer' and 'consumer'. Businesses might use it instead of 'customers', rather like 'semi-pro'. In some 'Media Studies 2.0', it might refer to users who are actually contributing to producing 'published' media texts – though nothing on the internet is fully private.

As an application, we might rethink informal classification of films (and other media texts, such as popular music) if we look at how 'users' describe specific films. Which tags and categories do they use? See the blog from the University of Amsterdam (http://mastersofmedia.hum.uva.nl/) on such uses of Web 2.0. In a section entitled Video Vortex (2008), visual artist Dan Oki suggests new ways of constructing cinema history by making use of databases of film 'meta-data' – full cast, crew, locations, etc. – on a large scale. This could map developments and innovation in cinema and overcome the elitist 'default' option of attributing change to the singular 'visions' of directors, or 'auteurs'.

## 'The long tail'

Combining the traditional attractions of economies of scale and the new possibilities offered by online databases, various retailers have prospered with Web 2.0. The most obvious example is Amazon, the online retailer that took over the Internet Movie Database and which also developed an online rental business (subsequently operated by Lovefilm in Europe). Amazon's simple business model is based on the idea of making any media text (books, DVDs, music, etc. – as well as non-media products) available, not only by storing the most complete range possible in a warehouse, but also by organising a host of other smaller retailers in a 'virtual marketplace' so that even second-hand and remaindered stock is included – and stock held overseas. In this way, Amazon has the

> The IMDb began as a project by a group of usenet film fans in 1989 and was based at the University of Cardiff when it was launched on the web in 1993. In 1998 it became an Amazon subsidiary.

*Figure 8.10* One of the warehouses storing the 'niche' goods of Amazon's 'long tail' ready for distribution.

The **long tail**, although known to statisticians for many years, was the focus of a 2006 book, *The Long Tail: Why the Future of Business Is Selling Less of More* by Chris Anderson. It is often used in debates on businesses more generally and is another example of the interdisciplinary interests of this stage of media study.

potential to 'prove' what has been termed the **long tail** effect. What's called the frequency distribution curve for popular media products would normally show that the most popular (i.e. the 'Top 20' or so) would at any time constitute around 80 per cent of the market, with sales of all other media products 'tailing off' to single figure or even zero sales. Thus the 'long tail' of DVDs/CDs, etc. traditionally destined for a 'niche' market. A traditional high street store would be unable to justify holding all the low-selling titles, but the marginal cost (the extra cost for a single item) of storage in a large warehouse is not significant.

The database that underpins Amazon's operation offers two benefits:

1  it helps to physically locate one item in the warehouse out of thousands (millions?); and

2  it helps the customer to be aware of alternatives. Instead of a single sales agent in a high street store, who may know relatively little about books, films or music, Amazon's database can immediately suggest that 'if you like this, you might also like this . . .' or that 'people who bought this, also bought this . . .' Because Amazon is a Web 2.0 retailer, it also invites users to provide 'wish lists' or suggestions. With links to IMDb and customer reviews available, the retailer prompts you to consider the 'wisdom of crowds' (of which your choice is presented as a part) in selecting your purchase.

The suggestion is that online retailing exploits the long tail, enabling consumers to have a much wider choice, and that creative artists outside the mainstream should, in theory, receive more royalties. Does this actually happen? How could we tell that the long tail is really there and that choice is really being extended? Many of such claims for Web 2.0 are very optimistic, even part of 'free market' emphases. They ignore possible disadvantages, let alone the impact of deep recession.

The long tail promise certainly helps a few larger Web 2.0 operators to drive out smaller 'niche' competitors, who face higher set-up costs in relation to their turnover. Consumers may be in danger of abandoning the services of 'experts' in favour of Amazon or Google (or all those 'compare prices' websites). We will pay less for advice, but we will need to be very sure about the 'wisdom of crowds': who is summarising it, and who has the power to act on it.

There are also social costs associated with the success of online retailing:

- not everyone has access to a broadband connection – or a credit card account, to pay online;
- it is difficult to work out the environmental costs and benefits associated with door-to-door deliveries of packaged goods (i.e. compared with buying them direct from a store); and
- the failure of high street businesses may trigger a collapse of high streets, with their associated public spaces in traditional trading areas in towns and cities.

## EXPLORE 8.7

What for you are the advantages and disadvantages of 'real' as opposed to 'virtual' or online shopping?

The growing success of online retailers suggests that the economics of the long tail makes sense – they can make profits by selling just one or two 'units' of a very wide range of products. But who are they selling to? Certainly a very well-informed consumer can now find more or less anything they want, be it rare music or obscure films. But what of the average consumer without the time or inclination to look far and wide? Amazon still pushes its 'bestsellers' or 'blockbusters' first, just as there is controversy over the order in which entries pop up on Google's search engine. It continues to make good business sense to maximise sales of a few titles, and there is little real evidence of a change in consumer choices. Perhaps we need to remain sceptical?

Some small internet sites have shown similar commercial potential. See http://www.youtube.com/watch?v=sxy-TxCXH6Y on Lauren Luke, a South Shields single parent who was bullied at school, started recording make-up tips on YouTube and is now manufacturing her own make-up range.

Watkins (2010) has argued that the 'community' of 'digital natives' is rather like those wealthy 'gated communities' only available to certain income groups, and often segregated by neighbourhood. See also Chapter 5 on 'fortress futures' and Watkins' interview on Henry Jenkins' blog archive.

The failure in the UK of the 'downmarket' F. W. Woolworth chain in 2008 saw empty shop spaces and deserted public space all over the UK. It also triggered the collapse of music and films retailer Zavvi, which relied on Woolworth's distribution service.

*Figure 8.11* A visualisation of part of Kelly's argument.

## Digital copies and the 'enclosure' of information

One of the most important advantages of the 'switch to digital' is the facility for making perfect 'copies' of media products, or rather 'duplicate originals'. The concept of a copy originally implied something that was 'fashioned to be like' the original, but was nevertheless inferior in some way – it was a 'reproduction'. Digital files can be duplicated so that they are identical (although often the copier chooses to make them lower quality if that is cheaper). Kevin Kelly, one-time founder and editor of *Wired* magazine, suggested (2008) that digital copies are usually 'free' to produce:

> Every bit of data ever produced on any computer is copied somewhere. The digital economy is thus run on a river of copies. Unlike the mass-produced reproductions of the machine age, these copies are not just cheap, they are free.
>
> (See http://www.kk.org/thetechnium/
> archives/2008/01/better_than_fre.php)

Kelly's argument raises fundamental problems for media producers. It is pointless to think that you can prevent anyone making digital copies – 'piracy' of different kinds is inevitable and media producers should think about other ways to make profits from their ownership of 'original' material. As Kelly succinctly puts it:

> When copies are super abundant, they become worthless.
> When copies are super abundant, stuff which can't be copied becomes scarce and valuable.
> When copies are free, you need to sell things which cannot be copied. Well, what can't be copied?
>
> (Ibid.)

Kelly answers his own question with a discussion of eight possibilities or 'generatives':

| | | | |
|---|---|---|---|
| Immediacy | Personalisation | Interpretation | Authenticity |
| Accessibility | Embodiment | Patronage | Findability |

## EXPLORE 8.8

Read his article to find out about each of these in detail.

- Jot down summaries, and try to apply them to the media you use most.
- Do you agree that most of us who can will pay, either to make our life easier (immediacy, accessibility, findability) or to improve the quality of what we have and our experience of using it (all his other 'generatives')? 'Patronage' may also cover wanting to give those who work on these media products some kind of income.

> One of online media's results has been a greater willingness for experts and academics to go to the blogs and websites of those who, like Kelly, might have been dismissed as 'geeks' or 'nerds' previously. Within a year of being published these ideas were picked up by industry film commentators as a possible solution to problems of piracy and falling revenues.

## New media, old metaphors

Information is often argued as something that is not 'used up' or 'consumed' when it is passed from one person to another – unless of course when you acquire information you refuse to divulge it to anyone else, a case where information becomes like any other commodity that is traded for monetary gain (see Balnaves *et al.* 2009).

The whole process of 'commoditising' information has been compared to the eighteenth-century British 'enclosure movement' and its global equivalents. The large landowners of the Middle Ages had allowed the peasantry – the 'common people' – to use what was seen as common or shared land as a basic resource on which they could graze some animals and grow a few subsistence crops. The developing capitalist system, however, offered the landowner the chance to make money through investing in new technologies, and in farming more scientifically and intensively. Landowners used their political power (at a time when they were amongst the few who could vote or sit in Parliament) to 'enclose' common land by law, forcing the peasantry to leave the countryside and find new work in the towns, where industry was developing – the 'progress' of the Industrial Revolution.

The commodification of information in the digital age has been called a second enclosure movement in which a number of large corporations such as Google, Corbis and Getty Images are exerting rights over the massive collection of digital files that they have acquired through commercial operations. One response to this has been the **Creative Commons** movement, offered as a solution to the problem of 'common knowledge' and authorial rights in the new media landscape. It proposes that authors should be able to decide what interest they want to retain in what they produce, and what they are willing to distribute freely.

> You can explore exactly how this is designed to work on the website at http://creativecommons.org/, and see also Wikimedia commons websites.

'Public domain' refers to the concept that a text is open for adaptation or republication without payment to a rights-holder.

*Figure 8.12* A screengrab 'fragging' moment from the computer game *Fallout3*, which reuses, but expands on momentary violent images of fragmenting bodies in cinema.

See Chapter 11 on the concept of 'built-in obsolescence', highly relevant here.

There are some contradictions in all this. Kelly seems to argue both that:

a  digital copies are essentially free – and therefore it is pointless to expect a return simply because you own the original rights, and that

b  it is a problem knowing how to support creative work in this new world of collaboration.

Some confusion comes from the concept of information itself. Balnaves *et al.* 2009 argue that traditional forms of copyright are granted to authors for their 'tangible expression' of ideas for a limited period. After that, the ideas pass into the public domain and are again free for anyone to use.

There are two problems with this.

1  Copyright laws are not universally applicable, so that they differ, for instance, between the US and Europe.

2  Most media texts are not 'information' as such (think of fictions, and the huge area known as 'entertainment'). These have always been seen as 'exploitable' in terms of payments for often costly processes of creation and/or 'performance'.

## 'New media', vanishing resources

One rarely discussed part of media study involves the materials needed for, and the later disposal of, fast-changing 'anytime anywhere' media, gadgets and equipment sold and enjoyed across the world. This evokes a different sense of 'environment' to McLuhan's.

Consider these points:

- Media corporations' global hunt for both minerals and water with which to make the complex equipment involved in global media, and for low-cost skilled labour, often female, needed to assemble it, and later to dispose of it. This is fuelled by changing fashions in status-driven media use, including international upgrades such as the analogue–digital switchover, or the 'race to HD', Blu-ray, etc.

- The amounts of electricity needed to power the internet, especially with Web 2.0's 'always on' norm, and power-hungry forms such as games and YouTube, as well as flat-screen TVs.

1 'We cannot continue to grow the internet in an energy constrained world' (Subodh Bapat, vice-president, Sun Microsystems (Johnson 2009)). Explore Johnson's other writings for *The Guardian*.

2 '... for every unit of energy a server uses to actually do some computing, it takes an equivalent amount of energy to cool it down again. US government statistics show that data centres now use as much energy as the whole of the car manufacturing industry' (Susan Watts, 'Two Go Mad in Silicon Valley').

See Watts' other reports for BBC2's *Newsnight*, especially on Google's secretiveness about its appetite for electricity, and the problems of cooling its servers.

Then switch off the link?

'Connectivity' usually refers to the internet bandwidth coming into and going out of a country, and the quality of the infrastructure linking computers to the internet (see Figure 8.14's caption about Samsung and South Korea, p. 258). This, of course, has implications for environmental politics.

- The tsunami of toxic waste resulting from analogue disposal alone will probably not feature much in the images on new 3D-HD large flatscreens or Blu-ray players. This disposal of hi-tech equipment has serious environmental consequences, especially for those children who will have to put their lives at risk in remote, poor areas of the world, dismantling sets for the tiny amounts of minerals, often toxic, which they can sell and live off. Sometimes, ironically, this happens in those very areas which are mined for the minerals in the first place.

*Figure 8.13* Children are among those picking a (toxic) living in the huge Steung Meanchy waste tip, Cambodia, 2009.

Research 'nanotechnology' here. See http://www.care2.com/causes/environment/blog/will-nanotechnology-help-or-hurt-our-environment/.

## EXPLORE 8.9

- Research this area, firstly through the sources given above.
- Script and storyboard a 30-minute film which would trace the routes and energy uses between switching on your computer, your fingers typing a link to, say, YouTube, and receiving video images on your screen seconds later. Perhaps use Susan Watts' reports.
- How would you script the film's comments on connections between
  a  the enjoyment of such internet resources, and
  b  their possible climate-change consequences?

*Figure 8.14* Research Samsung, the world's biggest conglomerate by revenue. Note the range of commercial activities (military, shipbuilding, etc.) which help fund, feed into and out of their cutting-edge technologies. A high degree of connectivity (South Korea's is the highest in the world) also fuels this.

## Conclusion

We've only been able to sketch the debates and contradictory impact of 'new media' technologies here, though they are part of most other chapters. Earlier approaches and concepts are still valuable in understanding and locating these changes. McLuhan's speculative generalisations, in the 1950s and 1960s, drew attention to the need to rethink media technologies. But Williams' insistence that we need to see them as always fully enmeshed in other social drives and power contexts remains key. It has been thoughtfully developed in recent work (Dovey and Kennedy 2006; Livingstone 2009; Lister *et al.* 2009). Re-mediation is a key term here, for understanding not only how 'content' is shaped anew by each set of media forms (parts of theatre flow into some cinema, then parts of cinema into some games), but also how 'new media' have older shapings within their radically new forms.

'Media Studies 2.0' is right to point out the need to learn and teach through and with the huge changes of the past few years, and to celebrate their potential. But:

- it is sometimes too cynical about 'theory', though itself draws on theorists such as Bourdieu and McLuhan;
- it celebrates the 'power of active users' in ways which sometimes ignore the commercial structures which still try to shape those powers, primarily for profit, rather than for more shared, public interests;
- it tends to ignore real material and cultural constraints, including unequal gender power relations, on truly open use of the amazing potential for 'digital citizenhood' and the real possibilities it offers for unprecedented collaborations.

**EXPLORE 8.10**

- On the basis of your own experience of and research into 'new media' (such as social networking sites, various games and so on) outline an educated guess at what three developments you expect in the next three years.
- Remember that part of the current attraction of 'new media' is the commercial effort put into designing and marketing gadgets and equipment as fashion accessories, their promotion as 'cool', their place in the layout of home spaces, etc. Try to include these.
- Try to factor in the increasing effects of climate change. How might these interact with marketing ever-more-upgraded media forms and the masts and cables and electricity supplies needed to sustain them?
- On the other hand, how might the possibilities for global environmental politics expand, using digital interactivity?
- Justify and debate your ideas in class if possible.

## References and further reading

Balnaves, Mark, Donald, Stephanie Hemelryk, and Shoesmith, Brian (2009) *Media Theories and Approaches: A Global Perspective*, London and New York: Palgrave MacMillan.

Dalby, Andrew (2009) *The World and Wikipedia: How We are Editing Reality*, Draycott: Siduri Books.

Dovey, Jon, and Kennedy, Helen W (2006) *Game Cultures*, London and New York: Open University Press.

Ellis, John (2000) *Seeing Things: Television in the Age of Uncertainty*, London: I. B. Tauris.

James, Nick (2009) 'Editorial', *Sight and Sound*, May: 5.

Johnson, Bobbie (2009) 'Power Failure: How Huge Appetite for Electricity Threatens Internet's Giants', *The Guardian*, 4 May.

Lanchester, John (2009) 'Short Cuts', *London Review of Books*, 9 April.

Lister, Martin, Dovey, Jon, Giddings, Seth, Grant, Iain, and Kelly, Kieran (2009) *New Media: A Critical Introduction*, 2nd edn, London and New York: Routledge.

Livingstone, Sonia (2009) *Children and the Internet*, Cambridge and New York: Polity Press.

Livingstone, Sonia, and Haddon, Leslie (eds) (2009) *Kids Online: Opportunities and Risks for Children*, Bristol: Policy Press.

McLuhan, Marshall (1964) *Understanding Media: The Extensions of Man*, London and New York, Sphere.

McLuhan, Marshall (1969) 'Playboy interview: Marshall McLuhan', *Play boy*, March.

Orwell, George (1949) *1984*, London: Penguin; new edn 1998.

Roddick, Nick (2009) *Sight and Sound*, March: 14.

Surowiecki, James (2004) *The Wisdom of Crowds: Why the Many are Smarter than the Few*, New York: Doubleday.

Tapscott, Don, and Williams, Tony (2006) *Wikinomics: How Mass Collaboration Changes Everything*, New York: Penguin.

Watkins, Craig S. (2010) *The Young and the Digital*, Boston: Beacon Press (and see his website http://www.theyoungandthedigital.com).

# 9 The future of television?

Addressing the Library of Congress in 2008, Michael Wesch described how television networks have failed to 'get' the internet. He calculated that over sixty years, the three main US TV channels produced 1.5 million hours of television. YouTube produced the same amount in six months and 88 per cent of it was original material (how does he know?) – a higher proportion than the networks manage today.

> Michael Wesch of Kansas State University is one of the most engaging evangelists for Web 2.0. See his work on YouTube or http://mediatedcultures.net/mediatedculture.htm.

## EXPLORE 9.1

- When did you last watch television?
- Was it live?
- Where were you and who with?
- What kind of material were you watching?

In most of the developed world television had become integral to daily life by the late 1970s, at the beginning of what John Ellis (2000) termed the television era of 'availability' (see Chapter 14). Television became the most important source of news and of entertainment, and the TV set became the focal point of most homes in the developed world.

Is broadband internet access now more important than owning a TV set? In the UK in 2009, 65 per cent of homes had a fixed broadband connection and 3 per cent used mobile access (Ofcom 2009). But many of

**Figure 9.1** Anna Paquin and Rutina Wesley in *True Blood*, one of the 'high quality dramas' from HBO, available internationally on many different platforms. A 'water cooler moment' for some?

In 2009 BARB gave twenty-five hours viewing per person per week as the average in the UK (www.barb.co.uk).

To make the best use of the material here, you'll need to work through it alongside Chapters 7, 8 and 10.

us still watch television broadcasts for several hours a day and the social impact of popular television programmes remains in the 'water cooler' moments when we discuss with friends or work colleagues what we have been watching and why.

Internet access and other changes in media activity have not so much reduced the importance of television, but changed how we watch it, where we watch it and what kinds of material we watch. The biggest single use of broadband capacity is for video material, either streamed live or collected via digital downloads. If we've reduced the amount of broadcast programmes we watch, we haven't stopped using the TV set to view boxed sets of TV series. Television is changing even as it remains at the centre of a range of media debates. Does it have a future as a discrete medium and a discrete culture, or will it just become another online 'application'?

We can't really understand where television is going without a sense of how it developed and why it is the way it is now. This chapter has three main sections:

- an exploration of the economic basis of television broadcasting systems,
- three examples of television business models, and
- a brief consideration of television and public culture.

## Ownership and control in the television industry

Radio services began as private enterprises in most countries, led by the US and UK in the 1920s, but in the UK and Germany the established model became one of public ownership by the 1930s. In the US, 'public broadcasting' has always been seen as an 'add-on' to a commercial system. One of the reasons for state involvement in broadcasting was the question of 'spectrum scarcity', with analogue broadcasting signals competing for space in a finite bandwith. This was far more important in more densely populated areas with more demand for services. It is noticeable that the effective ending of scarcity (i.e. when all broadcasting has switched to digital multiplex signals) has been much more complex in Europe, because of concerns about public sector broadcasting issues, than in the US where the whole country 'switched over' in June 2009. In the UK the **digital switchover** was scheduled to take three to four years.

A rather different concern about radio broadcasting focused on the capacity to develop propaganda. The Nazis demonstrated how effective this could be in the 1930s and all the main combatants used radio, cinema and posters extensively during the war that followed. After the Second World War in Europe, the Allied authorities made sure that complex regulatory controls were in place when new broadcasting licences were granted in Germany to regional public sector broadcasters within a federal structure. ARD, the broadcasting service based on this model, was formed in 1950. In Italy a monopoly state broadcaster (RAI) was established in 1954 and in France in 1945. TVE in Spain was established in 1956.

Television services began in the UK in 1936, but were shut down during the war. In Germany TV broadcasts began in 1935 and lasted until 1944. See http://smashingtelly.com/2008/07/14/television-under-the-swastika/ for a documentary based on material from East German archives. These broadcasts privileged Nazi members and the armed forces, as well as offering 'viewing parlours' in Berlin.

In most continental European countries, 'commercial' (i.e. profit-making) broadcasting by private sector companies had been introduced by the 1980s, but usually within a regulatory framework that sought to protect the 'public service' ideals vested in the state broadcasters. The balance between private and public sector broadcasting in television began to shift in the 1980s for two reasons:

- The new technologies of cable and satellite broadcasting offered opportunities to introduce new channels and new services.
- The general shift towards 'free market' economics and 'deregulation' of public services and utilities resulted in various forms of 'privatisation' and 'contracting out' to the private sector. In France, the privatisation of the main public broadcasting channel, France 1, in 1987 created the current French market leader, TF1 (with 26 per cent of audience share in 2009).

The new opportunities attracted media entrepreneurs from other sectors into the previously stable European television market, including News Corporation (US), Bertelsmann/RTL (Germany), Mediaset (Italy), Vivendi/Canal+ (France), etc., as well as the telecommunications companies Liberty Media (US) (a product of the US telecommunications anti-trust actions) and Telefónica (the privatised Spanish telephone company). These companies moved into terrestrial and satellite/cable television (including pay-TV) and they began to operate across national boundaries. They often have 'cross-holdings' of shares within each other's companies.

The impact of the privately owned broadcasters has put pressure on public broadcasters and the concept of public service broadcasting. It has also meant that many European terrestrial networks have succumbed to further penetration by US imports as their own budgets are not strong enough to make competitive programmes. Some broadcasters have failed in the marketplace. The UK's once powerful ITV companies failed in a bid to launch a digital operation led by live football and the German Kirch Group collapsed also as a result of its sports broadcasting policies. These two failures, both in 2002, signalled that competing with the likes of News Corporation, Bertelsmann, etc. as major media corporations is difficult for smaller European companies.

These changes were real and they were noticeable, but sometimes they can be given too much emphasis. Figure 9.2 shows that in the world's biggest TV markets, apart from the US, the public sector remains significant. The table also points to the decline in advertising and the rise of subscription as revenue sources, discussed later in the chapter.

| | UK<br>£ per head | US<br>£ per head | Japan<br>£ per head | Germany<br>£ per head |
|---|---|---|---|---|
| **Public** | 43 | 1 | 25 | 39 |
| **Subscription** | 71 | 111 | 48 | 37 |
| **Advertising** | 58 | 110 | 67 | 36 |
| **Total** | 172 | 222 | 140 | 112 |

*Figure 9.2* TV revenue expressed as per capita funding in four major TV markets (in pounds sterling).

Source: Ofcom 2008.

An associated development that involves some European producers has been the success of independent production companies operating internationally, mainly in gameshows and reality formats and serial dramas. Two of the most successful have been Endemol and Fremantle. Endemol began as a Dutch company, set up international operations in the US and UK, and in 2000 was bought by Telefónica. In 2007 it began a process which took it back into 'private' ownership by a consortium including the Dutch founder and the Italian Mediaset group. Its most famous programmes are probably *Big Brother* and *Deal or No Deal* (see http://www.endemol.com). Fremantle is 90 per cent owned by Bertelsmann through RTL, but it now includes companies like Grundy from Australia and Thames from the UK and creates programmes such as *X Factor* and *The Apprentice* (see www.fremantlemedia.com).

The future of television in all markets is going to be determined by a number of factors:

- the relationship with Web 2.0 and new media technologies (mobile devices, digital cinema projection, etc.);
- the development of new business models;
- the regulatory framework (including PSB and competition policies).

We'll focus mainly on the UK, but in the context of European media generally. Europe represents both a concentrated group of territories with the possibilities of cross-boundary flows and a 'single region' in which European-wide policies (sometimes covering not only the EU of twenty-seven nations, but the 'wider Europe' of thirty-six) attempt to sustain the audio-visual industries and a diverse media culture.

## Paying for television

In most European countries, there are at least six possible ways in which viewers pay for television:

- via some form of taxation (e.g. a licence fee or subsidy)
- higher prices for goods in order to support advertising

The television industry is awash with abbreviations: DTH is 'direct to home'; usually this is now digital. DTT is 'digital terrestrial television'.

- subscription to receive a cable, satellite or encrypted DTH broadcast system
- pay-per-view per programme (PPV)
- direct payment for 'interactive services'
- direct payment for merchandising and 'tie-in' products or TV programmes in other formats such as DVD.

## EXPLORE 9.2

- How many of these payment options do you use?
- Why would you choose one over another?

The BBC licence fee pays for a total of eight TV channels, thirteen national radio networks (including the home nations), local radio and online services.

The UK licence fee has several advantages:

- everyone pays but some groups have concessions (visually impaired, over-75s, etc.);
- efficient to collect so revenue is not wasted;
- in 2009 all BBC programmes were available for a charge of £142.50 annually or less than 40p per day (less than the cost of most daily newspapers).

But the main advantage is that universal payment means the possibility of broadcasting remaining as a public good – a service to provide something we could not buy ourselves (or perhaps would not consider buying, but may discover that we still need). Or perhaps something that is not completely 'consumed' by an individual, but remains available for everyone?

The weakness of the licence fee is that under 'deregulation' and 'liberalisation' it is increasingly open to attack by the free market lobby because it is compulsory (see Chapters 7 and 10). The main defence against this charge is the popularity of BBC programmes. As long as the BBC makes its fair share of the most popular types of programme it remains 'a channel for everyone'. If the BBC's share of the broadcast market were to fall below a certain figure, the licence fee could become difficult to defend on this basis. The actions of Ofcom as a regulator are crucial here. A policy that encouraged the BBC to concentrate on news, current affairs and arts programming at the expense of *EastEnders, Strictly Come Dancing* and *Match of the Day* could be very damaging.

The Dutch PSB system allows 'membership associations' of people with similar cultural background to access specific programming designed for them and broadcast on publicly owned channels.

In other European countries, **public service broadcasting** (PSB) is funded in a variety of ways, by licence fee in Scandinavia, by government grant or subsidy (i.e. from general taxation) in national or federal structures, or by combinations of government funding and advertising.

*Advertising* is losing ground as a source of television funding. In 2007 it fell to less than 50 per cent worldwide (Ofcom 2008):

- it is increasingly difficult for even well-established networks such as ITV to deliver large audiences because of fragmentation;
- technology now offers simple ways of avoiding advertisements on broadcast television (e.g. watching VOD or replay versions of programmes which strip out broadcast ads);
- at times of recession, advertising almost always produces less revenue;
- internet advertising is increasing its share of the overall advertising market and putting pressure on television advertising to reduce rates.

See Chapter 11.

Programmes broadcast by commercial TV channels have never been 'free', even if they have been 'free to air'. Advertisers have in effect paid for the programmes (i.e. provided the revenue for broadcasters) and these costs have to be covered by profits from increased sales from the goods advertised. Most of us have accepted or not really thought about this system, not making direct connections between the programmes we watch and the goods we buy. Note that the regulation of advertising on ITV (a limit on minutes per hour, a clear distinction between ads and programming, etc.) has arguably helped to maintain ITV as a watchable service.

## EXPLORE 9.3

- What is your experience of advertising on TV?
- Are you irritated by it or can you ignore it?
- How does it compare with advertising on the internet as an interruption to viewing?

A looser regulatory structure risks an advertising environment in which the narrative flow of a programme is constantly interrupted by commercial breaks, some of which may be difficult to distinguish from the programme itself. Rick Instrell (2005) examined a US broadcast of an episode of *Friends* and counted three advertising breaks, lasting over eight minutes in total, in a programme of less than twenty-two minutes. Regulation has helped to restrain the excesses of advertising-funded television and certainly up until the 1990s, the lack of any direct connection between advertisers and programmes allowed ITV, as well as the BBC, to be 'producer-led' – i.e. to make a range of interesting programmes that would attract significant audiences, large enough to satisfy advertisers – rather than make programmes designed to attract specific audiences for advertisers. This situation ended with the new offers from satellite and cable.

One of the ways in which ITV has tried to counteract the 'avoidance' of ads has been through programme sponsorship, which allows a closer connection between the programme and the ad, so that the brand appears as part of the programme title card.

*Subscription* television implies a willingness to pay for extra television services. In one sense this is similar to the purchase of consumer goods such as a DVD player, etc. It is a willingness to pay not for a specific programme, but for a new technology in the home – indeed, the purchase of cable or satellite services in many countries may have been accompanied by the purchase of a new TV set for digital reception.

Perhaps a majority of satellite and cable subscribers will purchase 'premium channel' subscriptions on top of a basic package. This has been the basis for the growth of BSkyB's business in the UK with the following outcomes:

- families with children were the first to create 'multi-channel TV homes';
- sport and movies have been the 'drivers' behind sales of premium services.

> **PVR**s or 'personal video recorders' are growing in popularity and allow viewers to record and create their own viewing schedules and to attempt to avoid advertising.

Families with young children are more focused on 'home entertainment' with a preference for a wider selection of entertainment channels – both for children and for adults who may be less able to leave the home for entertainment.

Older men or younger single men are arguably the 'early adopters' of other aspects of home entertainment such as 'home cinema systems' with Blu-ray and full sound systems.

Children (several different age-range segments) are important to advertisers and to the new television service providers. Advertisers want to reach parents as consumers (possibly via the 'pester power' of children wanting specific products seen on television) (see Livingstone 2009). They also want to engage older children – the future consumers.

BBC children's programming has not capitulated completely in the new environment and when new BBC digital channels became available, children's programming on CBBC and CBeebies was the most successful element of the new offer. In October 2009, CBeebies, the channel for younger children, was one of the most watched channels on multi-channel television with a 1.4 **share** and a reach of nearly 2 million daily, beaten only by the ITV entertainment channels (Source: Broadcasters' Audience Research Board – BARB). On the other hand, the availability of so many channels to young viewers introduces the idea of choice as 'natural' and as they grow up they will likely not think about the subscription payment. Will they resent the licence fee?

In 2009, BSkyB earned an average of £469 from each 'user' or 'subscriber'. With the licence fee, the average Sky subscriber is paying out around £600 per year on television services or around £12 per week. This isn't a particularly large sum compared with the average cost of a cinema ticket, a DVD purchase or a premiership football ticket – especially since the television set can be watched by anyone in the family. With 9.5 million customers for its various TV, telephony and broadband services and revenue running at £5.3 billion for 2008–9, BSkyB is now the biggest UK-based media player (figures from http://corporate.sky.com). The BBC had income of £4.6 billion for the same period (http://www.bbc.co.uk/annualreport/exec/financial/highlights/highlights.shtml).

*Pay-per-view television* (PPV) hasn't yet taken off in the UK or the rest of Europe to the same extent as in North America. Once again, it is primarily concerned with entertainment (movies or music events) or sport, with a focus on unusual high-profile events such as boxing matches (for which US viewers are willing to pay upwards of $40 dollars per event). The important point to note in the context of this chapter is that PPV offers the clearest sense of 'paying for television' just like any other product. Assuming you have already bought/rented the necessary equipment, a decision to 'pay to view' is no different from purchasing a ticket to go to the live event. This should give the clearest indication of what a 'free market' in television might look like – at least in terms of sports or music events.

A different form of PPV is offered via digital downloads such as the iTunes service from Apple. Here is an example of 'paid for' television competing with 'free' internet-available programmes on BBC iPlayer and similar services from broadcasters worldwide – as well as pirated shows via filesharing services (see discussion of piracy in the Chapter 7 case study Music and movies).

> Digital downloads or streaming video are usually grouped under the heading 'video on demand' (VOD) – see the Chapter 7 case study.

PPV also prompts consideration of one of the longstanding differences between cinema and television. When television first threatened the mass cinema audience in the early 1950s, some cinemas looked at the possibilities of showing television broadcasts in theatres. This didn't take off, partly because the technology wasn't yet suitable. With high-quality digital projectors in cinemas and satellite/broadband feeds, some of the 1950s ideas have now returned and UK cinemas have seen 'big screen' broadcasts of major football championships as well as arts events such as live theatre, opera and ballet performances. Here is an interesting example of technological convergence which raises questions about how different, but associated, media industries will develop.

In October 2009, England's World Cup game against Ukraine provided an experiment in PPV live streaming with the match only viewable online (or in cinemas) because of the collapse of the sports channel Setanta. Most commentators were not impressed with the quality of the computer coverage, which was hastily organised – but its time will come.

> 3D football? By the time you read this, you may have the choice between live football at home with a few mates, a larger crowd at the pub and the prospect of the ball (or a player) landing virtually at your feet in the cinema.

*Paying for interactivity* involves viewers choosing to spend money on extra services such as voting for gameshow contestants or entering

*Figure 9.3* Watching live football online.

competitions (gambling really, since many competitions require little skill) or telephone shopping. It could be argued that this moves television more towards the casino or general leisure activity.

Payment via voting on BBC channels is a move towards another US model which sees 'public broadcasting channels' supported by donations from audiences who want to see the channels continue to broadcast. We might call this a 'charity model' of funding – going back to the world before the welfare state and public services funded via taxation. Voting also raises a series of ethical questions which surfaced in 2007 when a whole range of television channels in the UK, commercial and BBC, became enmeshed in scandals about on-screen competitions with entries received by phone or text. What is at stake here (alongside the professional standards of broadcasters who have 'fixed' competitions, or perhaps allowed unfair decisions under pressure during live broadcasts) is the status of a publicly owned media organisation in an increasingly commercial environment. (See PSB in this chapter and in Chapter 10.)

*Direct purchase* mainly involves the sale of DVD series in box sets. It seems odd that these sales seem to be increasing just as DVD begins to falter as a format for cinema films. Perhaps the explanation is that the big sellers are long-running series (usually, but not always, American) that although available on different channels are difficult to find in the schedules and the times of broadcasting may not suit specific audiences. Being able to 'gorge' on several episodes consecutively could be an attraction.

> The relationship between broadcast serial drama (e.g. *The Sopranos* or *The Wire*) and its boxed set equivalent is not dissimilar to that between the stories written in serial format for magazines in the nineteenth century and their subsequent publication as novels or book collections (e.g. much of Dickens or the Sherlock Holmes stories).

## Business models for television broadcasting

In Chapter 7 we emphasise that the major issue in all media businesses has become the search for suitable business models – ways in which to monetise the value inherent in the media properties for which rights are held. In that chapter and its case study, we consider the crisis in music, cinema and newspaper publishing. Television is in a slightly different position, if only because it acts as a media carrier for music and filmed entertainment as well as creating its own unique media formats. But at the same time it is more vulnerable than any other form to the onward march of Web 2.0. Television's business models are in some cases very traditional and some broadcasters may find it difficult to survive. In this section we consider three models:

- public service broadcasting
- commercial network television
- subscription television

and we make reference to four specific broadcasters:

- BBC
- ITV
- Channel 4
- HBO.

### Public service broadcasting (PSB)

According to UK regulator Ofcom, PSB continues to be valued highly by UK viewers and has retained its importance despite the availability of many more television channels and viewing opportunities. Defining PSB is not straightforward and over the course of five editions of this book, we've seen definitions in the UK change. One issue is that since Ofcom became responsible for ensuring PSB remained at the heart of UK broadcasting policy, it has defined and redefined what we might understand by the term.

### BBC

Outside the UK, similar ideas about PSB can be found across Europe and in most other parts of the world. Wikipedia provides a useful thumbnail description of PSB in many countries (see http://en.wikipedia.org/wiki/Public_broadcasting). The BBC model has been influential not just in those countries linked to the UK by language and a colonial past, but also in Japan, Scandinavia and parts of Latin America. In the US, something similar is evident in the form of the **Public Broadcasting System** or PBS, but this is far less significant in terms of the general television offer in the US and it tends to be limited to educational or cultural programming. The US also has local television services which receive public funds. In many countries, public funding is also available for services in regional/national languages or in autonomous regions (e.g. Spain).

Public Broadcasting System (http://www.pbs.org/) and National Public Radio (http://www.npr.org/) are two of the many public broadcasting organisations in the US. See 'Public broadcasting in the United States' on Wikipedia for further links.

The BBC remains unique in the breadth of its offer, not only within a UK context, but also internationally via BBC World, programming sold to other networks via BBC Worldwide and also through its major online presence. For this reason, we will consider PSB issues in relation to the BBC as a central focus, while also considering other examples.

As well as providing a model for PSB, BBC training and work practices have also influenced service providers elsewhere, e.g. in setting up Al Jazeera, which recruited several ex-BBC personnel.

PSB does not necessarily require a publicly owned broadcaster, but it does require regulation that can bind private sector broadcasters to certain PSB objectives. In the UK, the BBC, Channel 4 and S4C (Welsh-language channel) are public sector organisations (although each funded in a different way) and the commercial terrestrial broadcasters ITV,

GMTV and Five have been charged with an increasingly lighter PSB commitment since the 1990s.

Before Ofcom, PSB was not defined separately in the UK but was embodied in aspects of the BBC charter, broadcasting legislation and franchising/licensing arrangements for private sector operators. In *Media Student's Book* 2nd and 3rd editions we referred to a checklist of features based on work by an independent agency, the Broadcasting Research Unit, during the 1980s (see O'Malley and Treharne 1993). Although the overall media environment had changed dramatically since the 1980s, we felt that the list remained useful as a guide. It suggested that PSB should:

- provide a full range of programming to meet audience needs for education, entertainment and information;
- be universally available (i.e. throughout the UK);
- cater for all interests and tastes;
- cater for minorities;
- have a concern for 'national identity' and community;
- be detached from vested interests and government;
- be one broadcasting body financed directly by the body of users;
- promote competition in good programming rather than in numbers of viewers;
- be run on guidelines which liberate and do not restrict programme-makers.

It's interesting to compare this list with Ofcom's presentation of PSB in its 2009 *Annual PSB Report*. The report begins with the 'public service purposes' outlined in the Communications Act 2003:

- to deal with a wide range of subjects;
- to cater for the widest possible range of audiences – across different times of day and through different types of programme; and
- to maintain high standards of programme-making.

It goes on to recast these as 'purposes and characteristics' of PSB.

PSB purposes:

- Informing our understanding of the world
- Stimulating knowledge and learning
- Reflecting UK cultural identity
- Representing diversity and alternative viewpoints.

PSB characteristics:

- High quality – well-funded and well-produced
- Original – new UK content rather than repeats or acquisitions
- Innovative – breaking new ideas or reinventing exciting approaches, rather than copying old ones
- Challenging – making viewers think

- Engaging – remaining accessible and attractive to viewers
- Widely available – if content is publicly funded, a large majority of citizens need to be given the chance to watch it.

To these, the report also adds:

- Trust – deemed necessary to monitor following concerns about the handling of phone-in voting and competitions on PSB channels (see above).

### Changes in PSB policies

If we compare the Ofcom presentation with the 1980s list, it's clear that there is little change in the perception of what constitutes worthwhile PSB programmes in terms of 'quality' criteria, range, diversity, accessibility, cultural identity, etc. – although 'widely available' is not the same as 'universally available'.

What *has* changed is the prescription about the nature of the organisation that is needed to provide PSB and questions about how programming should be produced. Ofcom makes no such stipulations and this reflects the political changes that accompanied the privatisation of many publicly owned utilities. This led to the subsequent application of 'internal markets' in the remaining public concerns as well as the ideological attachment to more open markets in production requiring, for instance, that UK broadcasters commission independents to make programmes and also use outside facilities rather than maintain servicing departments in-house.

Ofcom has responded to both current political and economic changes in its definition of PSB. In some ways its actions as a regulator for 'communications' mirror those of the UK Film Council. The latter is not a regulator, but is charged with ensuring the future of the UK film industry as an important revenue earner and employer in the UK as well as promoting a vibrant and diverse film culture. Ofcom has a similar 'cultural remit' in its regulatory role. It must also consider how regulation will affect the stability of UK television production (a consistent contributor to a balance of trade surplus in television programming and services). In this latter context it is likely to run up against those 1980s concerns about preserving the integrity of unique PSB providers. For example, any proposal to use part of the BBC licence fee to fund other organisations in order that they can fulfil PSB objectives is likely to be criticised.

The PSB remit undertaken by ITV and Five and the Teletext service offered by the Daily Mail and General Trust has been slowly diminishing since the 1990 Broadcasting Act. Once a major part of ITV's operation,

In 2009 the highly respected independent producer Tony Garnett wrote a passionate essay on the problems of BBC commissioning policy which he posted on *The Guardian*'s media blog. See www.guardian.co.uk/media/2009/jul/15/tony-garnett-email-bbc-drama.

Ofcom's remit is tied directly to the development of UK government policy in relation to the UK's 'digital future' expressed in the *Digital Britain* report, June 2009. By the time you read this there may be a new UK government with different plans.

the PSB function was built into the franchise agreements made by the independent companies that comprised the ITV network. The remit still covers news, regional production and the quality and diversity of programming as well as the requirement to carry party political broadcasts and listed national events. Subsequent amendments to the franchise licence have reduced the remit in a long process of 'lightening regulation'. However, all the UK's broadcasters are clearly still within a PSB system and there is still a distinction between UK commercial television and channels in some other countries.

> The PSB remit for ITV companies before the 1990s resulted in current affairs programmes such as *World in Action* (Granada) and *This Week* (Thames), which often surpassed BBC programming in both journalistic endeavour and popular appeal.

Before we leave Ofcom, it is important to note that its remit goes beyond broadcasting as such and applies to online media and telephony. In this sense it has extended the UK television role, just as the main UK television providers such as the BBC, BSkyb, Channel 4 and, perhaps to a lesser extent, ITV and Five have moved into different media. Ofcom is quite prepared to look for other ways in which the PSB remit can be fulfilled.

PSB in the UK also comes under scrutiny from the European Commission which has the authority to rule on PSB provision under EU regulations governing competition. In 2001:

> a Communication from the Commission on the application of State aid rules to public service broadcasting . . . first set out the framework governing State funding of public service broadcasting . . . Since 2001, more than twenty decisions were adopted concerning the financing of public service broadcasters.
>
> (see ec.europa.eu/competition/consultations/2009_
> broadcasting_review/broadcasting_review_en.pdf)

In 2009 the EC set out to review its policy on state funding, mindful of all the changes in broadcasting practices over the previous eight years. In the main, the EC is likely to concur with Ofcom, but sometimes its decisions can prove difficult for individual member states. On the other hand, the strength of EC rulings is their supra-national application which gives national PSB broadcasters some comfort in the face of actions by multinational media conglomerates.

### Network television

The oldest business model in television is the network concept. It's worth reflecting on the term 'network' which immediately prompts the connection to a computer network and suggests that it is a concept easily absorbed within a Web 2.0 world. But television networks go back to the beginnings of the television service in the US and in Europe and they are closely associated with spectrum scarcity. TV networks work by branding a television channel that could be broadcast locally by subsidiaries or affiliates/network members. The main programmes are made/acquired either by the single brand owner (in the US) or by the larger network members (e.g. the regional ITV companies in the UK before consolidation). Network programmes fill the peak-time hours with popular entertainment, drama, sports and national news/current affairs, and the affiliates produce their own local news programmes and other programmes in the off-peak. Commercial networks are funded via advertising which could mean airtime sold across the whole network or locally/regionally.

Networks in the current television environment have the odds stacked against them. With advertising revenue flat or falling they have little chance of fighting against the competition of multi-channel television, and once the digital switchover is completed, the advantage of being the 'known' button on a TV channel selector will start to fade. But this does raise the question of 'local television'.

In the UK two opposite scenarios developed as the digital switchover gathered pace in 2009. In England, ITV appeared prepared to give up its loss-making 'regional programming' with the prospect that this PSB

*Figure 9.4* Granada Reports is one of ITV's regional news programmes.

commitment will be transferred to another service of some kind. However, in Scotland and Northern Ireland, where the two ITV companies, STV and UTV, have remained independent and are not owned by ITV plc, they have begun to opt out of network programming on a more regular basis, including during peak-time. This is an expression of 'national identity' which also carries through to ITV Wales, but though some viewers are happy with this, others regret that they cannot receive their favourite network programmes. Once digital switchover is complete, the missing programmes may well be available via other channels or replay software – although they may be more difficult to find than simply pressing the ITV button on the remote.

> UTV Media owns UTV and several local radio stations in the UK and Ireland. UTV in 'Ulster' is not related to the Indian media company with the same initials.

> STV (Scottish Television) is owned by the Scottish Media Group which includes Ginger Productions and the cinema advertising company Pearl and Dean. STV doesn't broadcast to southern Scotland which is covered by ITV in the region once covered by Border TV. This was the first UK region to make the digital switch.

Different concepts of 'local' and 'regional' television have operated at different times and in different places. At one time the concept of very local television, a reality in a North American context, looked like appearing in the UK with 'community channels' via cable and in the original discussions about a fifth national channel that might include 'city-based' television. Neither of these was realised. City-based channels have appeared at different times in London and Manchester, but the overall concept has never taken hold in the UK. Channels associated with major Premier League football clubs are possibly more popular.

It could be argued that when ITV lost its regional distinctiveness, it also lost some of its appeal for audiences. That regional identity was part of the PSB remit of the ITV companies – an element that could be transferred to local/regional newspapers and delivered as an online service.

The major networks such as ITV and its European equivalents have tried various other ways of exploiting their brands. After the failure of ITV Digital, the network has recovered to some extent by setting up three digital channels via Freeview, the DTT platform, which offer mainly repeats and acquisitions but also some original programming. Although the terrestrial channel ITV1 has fallen behind BBC1, the addition of audience shares from ITV 2, 3 and 4 boosts the total ITV share in the UK to 24 per cent (including the breakfast service from GMTV).

> Ofcom refers to the BBC and ITV digital channels on Freeview as 'portfolio channels'.

ITV plc holds only eleven of the fifteen regional licences (the other four are those for the Channel Islands, Northern Ireland, and two in Scotland).

ABC belongs to Disney, NBC to General Electric, CBS to National Amusements and Fox to News Corporation. National Amusements is the private company that controls ownership of both CBS and Paramount.

Note here that BSkyB only attracts a 6.5 per cent share, yet its revenue massively outstrips that of ITV plc (2008: £2 billion). The once cash-rich commercial network that could lure talent away from the BBC now struggles with less than half the revenue of BSkyB or the BBC.

The four North American networks all face the same problems of declining advertising income, but their position is less precarious because of their ownership by large media conglomerates and the possibility of taking content from other divisions. They have the resources to put together high-quality programming, but even so, the network model looks out of date.

### Subscription

As a business model, subscription television could be argued to have the advantage of the security of funding of a PSB broadcaster without the requirement to fulfil a PSB remit. In practice, it doesn't work out quite so straightforwardly.

Subscription income does certainly offer some security, especially if packages are sold to viewers for set periods (e.g. a minimum one-year contract). Even so, a percentage of old subscribers will leave each year and there is a constant battle to keep existing subscribers happy and attract new ones. The indicator of success here is a low **churn** rate (i.e. holding on to subscribers).

Secondly, the launch period for subscription may need to be lengthy and the channel's owners will need deep pockets. In order to attract subscribers, the channel needs attractive programmes, preferably unavailable anywhere else. Producing or acquiring such programming is expensive, but until the subscriber base is established the channel is not generating revenue. This means that the owners must be prepared to invest heavily in programming and to sustain losses.

BSkyB saw off an initial competitor, BSB (which merged with Sky to form BSkyB in 1990). Its eventual success in the UK was based on sport – Premier League football and rugby league – and movies (sourced from major stakeholder News Corporation's 20th Century Fox and other Hollywood studios). BSkyB sustained losses for many years until it eventually forged ahead of the UK cable industry in signing up subscribers. Then it saw off ITV Digital and Setanta, both of which tried to compete, but with insufficient investment funds: the live football rights they acquired were not attractive enough to attract large subscriber numbers quickly.

As a satellite broadcaster, BSkyB has avoided the PSB remit in the UK. Its range of programming has been more entertainment-oriented and it

UK cable was launched through local franchises during the privatisation boom of the 1980s, but by 2005 95 per cent of the operation was controlled by Virgin Media.

has been severely criticised for the relatively low levels of UK-originated programming and poor support for British cinema. However, in a couple of respects it has taken on the mantle of a UK PSB provider with a strong news presence and recently with the development of the Sky Arts channels (acquired through a gradual takeover from 2002 onwards of Artsworld, the independent channel set up by Jeremy Isaacs, former head of Channel 4). In an environment where arts programming is being cut back as other channels' budgets fall, Sky Arts is a useful PR tool for James Murdoch as well as a means of attracting more AB (professional/managerial class) subscribers.

Although some of its channels carry advertising, BSkyB earns its revenue primarily via individual subscriptions either directly or via Virgin and other carriers. It also receives a 'wholesale service' income from these carriers when they take channels which are offered on a basic cable package (i.e. no premium subscription). Sky News is one such channel.

## CASE STUDY: HBO

**It's Not TV. It's HBO.**
  Time Warner slogan

HBO (Home Box Office) and its corporate sister Cinemax are subscription-based television channels that operate in North America and, in different ways, globally in Asia, Latin America and central Europe. The company first launched a cable operation in 1972 but soon became a subsidiary of what is now Time Warner. Its programming is available in both HD (high definition) and standard formats and is carried by cable, satellite and broadband services.

Figure 9.5 A plug for next month's highlights from the October 2009 schedule of HBO.

Because it is a subscription-only programmer, HBO is not dependent on advertising revenue. It is available in around one-third of American homes (approximately 40 million subscribers as of September 2008) and a further 20 million plus homes internationally. Those viewers who do not subscribe will be able to access HBO 'original' material on DVD and in some countries these shows will be available on free-to-air networks (e.g. in the UK). Many of the most highly acclaimed shows will not be networked in the US, however, because they are made without the self-censorship deemed necessary for general viewing by the Federal Communications Commission, the US regulator. In American terms, this refers to sex, violence and profanity.

### Financial viability

As a content provider with a guaranteed income, HBO can afford to make expensive programming for a limited (i.e. not broadcast to all) television audience and still make large profits. Time Warner does not issue separate financial statements for all its companies and HBO is included in the 'Networks' division with Turner Networks. The 2008 figures show a total annual income of more than $11 billion for this division, with $6.8 billion from subscription and $3.3 billion from advertising.

### True Blood

A contemporary vampire series based on the novels of Charlaine Harris and mostly co-written by Harris and Alan Ball, a well-known Hollywood screenwriter and creator of *Six Feet Under, True Blood* was first broadcast in 2008 in the US and quickly became a cult success. The website for the series carried this ironic statement: 'This website is intended for viewing solely in the United States. This website may contain adult content.'

As we note in Chapter 10, it is difficult to control access to internet material, so this is really an invitation to access 'adult content' for anyone, anywhere in the world. The sex scenes in the series are certainly 'stronger' than those in network series and the combination of action, sex and comedy draws in audiences. Although legal broadcasts/downloads of the series may be restricted in different parts of the world, illegal downloads over peer-to-peer sharing sites are almost guaranteed. It may well be that it is the intelligence on display in the writing that gains the channel so many awards and the attention of upscale audiences, but it would be wrong to place HBO alongside more 'worthy' offerings such as *Masterpiece Theatre* with its

*Masterpiece Theatre* airs on the Public Broadcasting System in the US (http://www.pbs.org/wgbh/masterpiece/).

screenings of BBC and ITV drama serials and mini-seasons – some with education support.

### Quality drama

The most common reference to HBO and its high-quality drama series found in television industry discourses in many countries is an envious observation about how difficult it is to emulate such production quality. In the UK system before the arrival of multi-channel television, such production was possible by all three broadcasters, BBC, ITV Network and Channel 4. This was because expenditure on drama could be justified in the context of large audiences for artistically challenging material. The fragmentation and segmentation of audiences has reduced the overall audience size for each channel and now only mainstream drama (often referred to as 'cops and docs') is able to attract funding. ITV will now spend £2 million or more on a two-hour crime mystery for Sunday evening, but not £15 million over several episodes of a literary adaptation such as *Brideshead Revisited* (UK 1981) or *The Jewel in the Crown* (UK 1984), highly praised serial drama series of the 1980s. Much the same is true for the BBC and Channel 4. 'Quality drama' is now often assumed to be bought in direct from HBO or to be the result of co-productions with HBO or public broadcasters in the US, Canada, Australia, etc.

At various times, the UK regulator Ofcom has suggested that public funding of television (i.e. via the licence fee) might be used to create an HBO-style production house in the UK.

### CASE STUDY: CHANNEL 4

Channel 4 (http://www.channel4.com) in the UK is an unusual broadcaster. It was founded by the Broadcasting Act of 1980 and launched in 1982 as a publicly owned PSB provider. It was charged with commissioning (rather than making) programmes that were in some way 'alternative' either in their formal structure or in their appeal to audiences who were not being properly served by BBC and ITV. (This new concept – as a 'publisher-broadcaster' – was considered as innovative and continued to be discussed as appropriate for various initiatives until fairly recently.)

Channel 4 was founded as a subsidiary of the then regulator, the Independent Broadcasting Authority, and its budgets were determined by the sale of advertising (initially by ITV with minimum guarantees). This initial approach did indeed produce a different programming schedule, with notable successes in developing African-Caribbean and South Asian programme content and other innovations in meeting its PSB remit.

However, from the early 1990s onwards the channel gradually lost much of its radical edge and began to look more like a conventional UK PSB provider. In 1993, following the 1990 Broadcasting Act, it became a public corporation (though the board was still appointed by the new regulator, the ITC), and it started to control its income through selling its own advertising space. In this period it gained its highest audience share (11 per cent) but also began the move towards more popular programming. Over the next fifteen years, while maintaining its PSB remit and commissioning a range of innovative and 'quality' programming (including drama series such as *Queer as Folk* (1999)), the channel also started to target specific audiences, primarily younger and more middle class. Young women in particular were targeted through imported series such as *Friends* and *Sex and the City* plus the format import *Big Brother*.

In some ways, Channel 4 has been a kind of experiment watched from within the UK industry. Its successes have included its film industry ventures, initially in the early 1980s into 'television films' but then into theatrical releases, and its prizewinning news programming. With the arrival of multi-channel television, the corporation started new channels, FilmFour, More4 and E4, initially as premium channels and then moving to the Freeview service.

> Channel 4 Films arguably 'saved' the British film industry in the 1980s, and in 2009 its production of *Slumdog Millionaire* won eight Oscars, but in 2002 an attempt to become a distributor and international sales company was abandoned as funding problems mounted.

## Red Riding

This trilogy of television films based on a quartet of novels by David Peace was broadcast on Channel 4 in 2009 and then sold for cinema screenings

*Figure 9.6* A scene from *Red Riding 1980*, the second film in the trilogy, showing the stylised presentation of the story.

internationally. Many commentators saw the production as an attempt to create 'event television' around a serious drama offer and consciously to seek to compete with the impact of HBO series in the UK (Channel 4 also began to broadcast *True Blood* later in 2009).

In some ways, the attempt worked: the films (shown in consecutive weeks) were eagerly discussed and the promotions worked well. However, the viewing figures were mixed, dropping considerably for the second film and only picking up slightly for the third. This may be a result of the subject matter and the cinematic style of the films. The story, about police corruption and brutal murders, is set in the period of the Yorkshire Ripper killings in the late 1970s/ early 1980s and was filmed on location in West Yorkshire. The films were made by the well-known British independent film company Revolution Films (Andrew Eaton and Michael Winterbottom) and directed by three experienced British film-makers (Julian Jarrold, James Marsh and Anand Tucker). The budgets for the three feature-length films were less than for comparable HBO productions, but two of them were shot in CinemaScope ratios (i.e. wider than widescreen televisions). The overall look of the films was often dark – the image on poorly adjusted TV screens may have been off-putting and overall they would work better in cinemas. However, in a UK context the average 2 million viewers for each film is certainly more than the cinema admissions achieved by most British films.

The stark truth is that, being advertising-funded, Channel 4 faces a difficult future. But its PSB status and history of innovation do offer possibilities: receiving part of the licence fee income, joining other organisations in extended PSB (and publicly funded) services, and merger/tie-up with a larger private sector organisation (e.g. Five owned by RTL/Bertelsmann).

## Conclusion

We've queried the future of television as access to video online increases. Whereas certain aspects of broadband usage seem inevitable, e.g. the migration of advertising from network television to the internet, others are contingent – will statutory regulators outside the US seek to protect forms of PSB by helping them to establish online? Equally contentious is the future of supra-national attempts to protect intellectual property rights. If media-user attitudes towards copying follow the Kevin Kelly hypothesis (see Chapter 8), even the currently successful subscription television channels are at risk. In Chapter 10 we explore the issue of regulation in more detail, but here we should emphasise that the future

UK politicians have taken several mistimed steps towards Web 2.0 (see http://www.youtube.com/watch?v=3ziDciRjxUo and http://www.youtube.com/watch?v=yELHemcQn10).

Figures quoted in *The Power of Print* (2009) showed that readers' faith in the credibility of Google News was not significantly different to that in US newspapers. It would be interesting to poll on the credibility of Fox News and CNN.

of television is very much about what is now being termed 'public culture'. If politicians of all kinds, business leaders and trade unions, religious and cultural agencies, etc. decide to operate primarily in a Web 2.0 world, how will the society at large follow the debate across different outlets? Perhaps Google News will be our first port of call?

## References and further reading

Crisell, Andrew (2006) *A Study of Modern Television: Thinking Inside the Box*, Basingstoke: Palgrave Macmillan

Ellis, John (2000) *Seeing Things: Television in the Age of Uncertainty*, London: I. B. Taurus.

Instrell, Rick (2005) 'The Economic Shaping of American Television Drama', *Media Education Journal*, 37 (spring).

Livingstone, Sonia (2009) *Children and the Internet*, Cambridge and New York: Polity Press.

Ofcom (2008) *The International Communications Market 2008, 4: Television*, http://www.ofcom.org.uk.

Ofcom (2009) *Public Service Broadcasting: Annual Report 2009*, http://www.ofcom.org.uk.

O'Malley, Tom, and Treharne, J. (1993) *Selling the Beeb*, London: Campaign for Press and Broadcasting Freedom.

*Digital Britain* (2009) Department for Culture, Media and Sport, http://www.culture.gov.uk/images/publications/digitalbritain-finalreport-jun09.pdf.

*The Power of Print* (2009) WAN-IFRA Strategy Report, Vol. 8 No. 5, www.futureofthenewspaper.com.

# 10 Regulation now

- Politics and media economics
- Regulation and 'freedom'
- Historical background
- Changes in the 'orthodoxy' of economic policy and new models
- Deregulation, liberalisation and media institutions
- The contemporary regulatory environment
- A 'free market' for classification, censorship and sex and violence?
- The public gets the media it deserves?
- 'Free choices' and 'free speech'?
- Conclusion
- References and further reading

Whenever 'the media' are discussed as an important feature of contemporary society, a whole range of assumptions come into play. As we might expect from Chapter 6, different ideologies suggest different ways in which media organisations might function socially/politically and how we might understand their activities and the ways in which we interact with them. In this chapter we want to investigate questions such as:

- Should society expect media organisations to perform certain actions and desist from others?
- Are there some forms of media use which are more desirable than others?
- Who should decide this and the kinds of controls there might be over media activity?

Before we begin, we perhaps need to consider the concept of the media institution which draws on ideas from sociology, psychology and politics as well as economics and business studies. Institutions have been described as:

> enduring regulatory and organising structures of any society, which constrain and control individuals and individuality – the underlying principles and values according to which many social and cultural

practices are organised and co-ordinated – the major social sources of codes, rules and relations.

(O'Sullivan *et al.* 1994: 152–4)

A number of key words such as 'control', 'values', 'organised', 'codes', etc. are important in any discussion of media institutions. Overall, the definition points towards an ordered and 'known' world. As new media technologies and then goods and services were developed from the middle of the nineteenth century onwards, what were at first the inventions of a few pioneering entrepreneurs or public servants were eventually both industrialised and institutionalised. On the one hand, media production was organised on an industrial scale, and on the other, the actions of media producers and users were gradually 'regulated'. How precisely this happened depended on the social, economic and political contexts in which specific media activities were introduced. Institutionalisation, although it usually followed a similar trajectory, tended to be specific to national contexts – so how films are classified for different audiences varies across the world.

But this seemingly 'ordered' institutionalisation has been disrupted by the same two factors which are discussed in many other sections of this book – globalisation (in the form of deterritorialisation) and the development of new media associated with internet use.

As Jonathan Bignell points out, television need not necessarily have developed as it did in the twentieth century:

*Let the Right One In* (see Chapter 3 case study) is rated '12' in France, '13' in Spain, '15' in the UK and 'M/18' in Portugal.

Deterritorialisation refers to the move away from media production and consumption being governed by national boundaries – and 'official' designations of limits to the rights held over a media text. 'Region 3 DVDs' may be intended to be watched in East Asia, but they can be purchased over the internet and watched via a multi-region player by anyone, anywhere in the world.

television could have been a popular medium, in the sense that it could have been made as well as received by the viewers themselves, and the making of television could have been embedded in their own lives. Instead, television became big business, where national governments co-operated to set up technical standards to control the mass production of television equipment. A professional community of highly trained technicians and production staff undertook the making of programmes.

(Bignell 2008: 45)

With inexpensive digital video equipment and any of the various Web 2.0 services (see Chapter 8) now available, it is possible to return to that vision of a 'personal' use of 'television' (i.e sound and image communicated across long distances). Digital technologies offer at least the possibility of unregulated media production by individuals and the internet has proved very difficult to institutionalise. But this doesn't mean that institutional questions have disappeared or that regulation has been abandoned. Consider some of these questions about media activity in recent years:

- Should a newspaper be allowed to print photographs or cartoons that it knows will be offensive to certain religious groups?
- Major retail chains (e.g. WalMart in the US) have sometimes refused to stock magazines or CDs/DVDs containing what they deem to be 'offensive material' – if they have a monopoly of supply in a specific area is this too much 'control'?
- In a democracy, should everyone, irrespective of where they live or their ability to pay, be able to receive certain media services (e.g. television or broadband) by right?
- Should advertising be withdrawn even if only a few people are offended by it?

Each of these examples refers to the power of media producers or distributors to do things that others would like to prevent or *not* do things

*Figure 10.1* Advertising in France is regulated by the ARPP (Autorité de régulation professionelle de la publicité, http://www.arpp-pub.org/1-ARPP.html), a self-regulating body for the advertising industry.

others want them to do. The examples also refer to our activities as users. Do we want to live in a society where anything and everything is available if we have the money to buy it – or do we prefer a society in which goods and services are provided for all, but not necessarily in the way we would choose for ourselves?

---

## EXPLORE 10.1

- If you were in a position to regulate forms of media activity, what would you try to constrain and what would you like to promote?
- Or perhaps you don't think the media should be subject to constraint or encouragement?

---

'Constraining' the power of organisations and how media users engage with them is one of the main functions of the process of institutionalising them. At the same time the ideologies of contemporary capitalism emphasise 'economic growth' and 'more choice for users'. Can we, or should we, attempt both to constrain or direct media institutions in certain ways *and* to encourage them to produce more, advertise vigorously and constantly strain to become more powerful? As we will see, this basic contradiction underpins many media debates.

## Politics and economics

Some media debates are concerned with political issues – the relationship between media institutions and government – or with public debates more generally. Others are primarily questions of economics – how to make the most efficient use of 'scarce' resources (i.e. labour and capital) to produce goods and services. For example:

- A government directive to internet service providers requiring them to disconnect broadband users or to report on their behaviour (i.e. which sites they visit) is a political issue involving debates about personal freedoms.
- Whether a film animation studio should carry out its time-intensive post-production work in the US or contract it out to a company in Europe or Asia is a business economics issue.

But the separation of what is 'politics' and what is 'economics' is not clear-cut – in fact it is a function of ideology. If we believe an action is 'purely a question of economics', we are less likely to think of its political consequences. So, in the example above, the animation studio's decision might mean less work in its own studio and more work elsewhere – with social costs and benefits to different groups of people.

After the Industrial Revolution in Western Europe began in the eighteenth century, the scholars who studied these momentous changes (**Adam Smith, Karl Marx**, etc.) were described as political economists. They made direct links between the growth in production and the development of new nation states in a capitalist system. It wasn't until the late nineteenth century that 'economics' emerged as a separate discipline, concentrating in a more 'scientific', 'mathematical' way on changes in prices for inputs and outputs without the impediment of political questions. This form of economics (usually termed 'neoclassical') has remained dominant, but some media studies theorists have returned to the original formulation and adopted a **political economy** approach to their work.

This isn't an economics textbook, but we do need to note how, in the twentieth century, economic theory developed and changed over time. Despite the supposed separation of politics and economics, governments changed their policies and worked with economic models created according to the prevailing ideologies within the economics communities of academics and advisers.

A **model** in social sciences is a theoretical construction which enables policy-makers to predict what might happen in the future – e.g. how the population might grow, whether the price of oil will go up, or, in media industries terms, what will happen to television in any country when the analogue service is 'switched off' or when broadband access is sufficient for everyone to watch high-quality streaming video. We will concentrate on two such models and the arguments that surround them. But first we need a clearer idea of what is at stake in terms of controlling or 'freeing' media activities. The arguments focus on ideas of **regulation** and personal freedom.

> **Adam Smith** (1723–90) is associated with ideas about 'free trade'. Like Marx, he has often been misrepresented by various political groups.

> '. . . the difference between political economy and economics is that, in economics, war is a temporary alteration in price variation, the old joke being that "World War III, should it come, will be noted in two sentences in the *Wall Street Journal*, with an article inside on its effect on soybean futures" ' (from the 'political economy' entry on Wikipedia).

## Regulation and 'freedom'?

Media activity has an impact on society in three ways.

1  As a *social* activity, it can bring benefits associated with better information, insights, understanding and, of course, pleasure in our enjoyment of interaction with media products and other media users. At the same time, media activity could be harmful if it led to increased ignorance, encouraged violent and anti-social behaviour, or interfered in some way with other forms of social activity.

Disbenefits refer to the social
costs of economic actions.
These may not be easily
measured in monetary terms
but can be damaging to the
social fabric. They form part
of a cost-benefit analysis and
are not always recognised in
free market calculations.

In October 2009, UK
Industry Minister Peter
Mandelson referred to the
£16 billion earned by the
UK's 'creative industries'.

Attacks on media studies
in the UK media rarely
mention the economic
contribution of the media
industries – and the need
to produce graduates
with media skills and
understanding.

One of the first modern
thinkers to address the idea
of personal freedom was
Jean-Jacques Rousseau
(1712–68) in *The Social
Contract* (1762). He argued
that individuals could only
gain freedom by submitting
to the 'General Will' of the
society embodied in the
democratic state – but the
state must also act in a moral
fashion and preserve the
freedom of its citizens.

2  As a *cultural* activity, it can be considered as art practice. It can
contribute to the cultural heritage of communities and enable us to
explore ideas in new ways and to enrich our experience. Viewing
media texts as art objects gives them a different status compared with
texts which have a more instrumental social use or for which
entertainment is a primary function.

3  As an *economic* activity, it can provide employment and a return
on capital, creating wealth for individuals, companies and
regions/nations. In a capitalist system based on the concept of risk, it
can also be associated with business failure and the social **disbenefits**
that can bring. The so-called 'cultural' or 'creative' industries are of
great importance in post-industrial societies that have managed to
shift most forms of heavy industry and manufacturing to economies
with lower labour costs. Governments are beginning to appreciate
the contribution of the media industries to this sector – but perhaps
it hasn't yet been appreciated by society at large?

One aspect of regulation that is clearly related to the 'economic'
is the aim of maintaining competition in the media marketplace. This
could mean competition between PSB providers as well as between
different commercial media producers and between public and
private producers. Certain monopolies may be allowable in a PSB
context, but pluralism is frequently the byword.

Competition is essential to the free market approach, but since
this only occurs 'naturally' in a perfect market, it is often necessary to
distort market conditions to produce competitiveness. (See comments
on the free market model below.) Regulators in some countries are
keen to restrict cross-media ownership. The European Commission
also hopes to limit too much competitive advantage across the
European Union as a whole (e.g. the long-running action against
Microsoft over its Media Player).

How do we as a society maximise the benefits – social and material –
and minimise the disbenefits of media activity? The solution is going to
depend on our approach to issues of regulation and institutionalisation.
What is problematic is that there are also broad issues about how far we
as individuals are prepared to allow other people to have a say in how we
conduct our media activities as 'producers' or 'users'. How do we resolve
the conflict between the public and private aspects of our media use? Is
the best form of regulation organised by:

• governments
• media institutions themselves
• the operations of the market
• some other way?

Before we try to explore these questions, we need to sketch in the historical background to the regulation of media industries and how it is aligned to economic models, since without it you will find it difficult to understand contemporary debates fully.

## Historical background

Knowledge is power and has been recognised as such throughout history. Rulers and powerful classes have always tried to keep the mass of the population away from 'dangerous knowledge'. In Europe in the Middle Ages this meant a Christian church which attempted to maintain a 'priestly language', Latin, as the basis for theological and academic texts. The church had control over education, which was restricted to those who could learn Latin. The invention of the printing press promised to introduce the first 'mass medium', circulating ideas to everyone who could learn to read in their own local or 'vernacular' language. It is no surprise that governments of every kind immediately saw the importance of exerting some form of control over what was printed. Sometimes they banned titles, sometimes they altered them and sometimes they taxed them – raising revenue as well as limiting their availability by artificially raising prices.

The 'mass media' developed as industrial activities from the end of the nineteenth century onwards. Until 1945, political events and associated economic policies produced a turbulent social and business world with revolutions, world war, economic prosperity (particularly in the US in the early 1920s) and then worldwide economic depression. In this context, a difference between US and European ideas about media institutions began to emerge. In Europe there was a tendency towards forms of government intervention in the new industry of radio and television broadcasting, largely for political reasons. **Public service broadcasting** (**PSB**) is also evident in other developed countries such as Canada, Australia and Japan, and is generally regulated by a set of requirements laid down in a founding charter or licence and then monitored for performance. But this was also linked to other forms of publicly funded activity in countries with ideologies developed to support collective, or co-operative, 'social' ownership. By contrast, US ideas about the new industries stressed 'unfettered' capitalist enterprise and only a very limited role for state intervention.

In the US, political events did give rise to some public sector media activities, such as the theatre programme devised as a means of employing writers, artists and performers to entertain and educate communities with limited arts access as part of Roosevelt's New Deal

Perhaps the first important 'media product' was the Bible printed in 1455 by Johann Gutenberg and celebrated by Marshall McLuhan in the title of his 1962 book *The Gutenberg Galaxy*. That Bible was in Latin, but the new printing technology was used for William Tyndale's 'Common English' translation in 1525 – he was burned at the stake in 1536 for heresy.

Stamp duty is still levied on certain legal documents in the UK, but in the early nineteenth century it was used as a means of suppressing radical newspapers. The Newspaper Stamp Duties Act of 1819 was an effective means of 'regulating' newspapers by making them too expensive for working people to purchase. After newspaper and advertising duties were removed in 1855, the popular press began to grow.

See the full discussion of PSB in Chapter 9.

*Cradle Will Rock* (US 1999), directed by Tim Robbins, depicts the true story of a leftist musical drama production in New York in the 1930s and the attempts to prevent its staging.

The House Committee on Un-American Activities (HUAC) began investigating Hollywood in 1947 and nine screenwriters and a director were eventually sent to prison for 'contempt' – refusing to 'name names' and to say whether they were members of the Communist Party. YouTube features footage on 'The Hollywood 10'.

'In US movies before the 1960s, [the] Production Code dictated that characters got shot without bleeding, argued without swearing, and had babies without copulating' (Linda Williams in Nowell-Smith 1996: 490).

Statutory regulation means that the powers of the regulator are provided by Act of Parliament and are therefore enforceable by law. In the case of the BBC, it has traditionally been allowed to self-regulate, with that status being conferred by Royal Charter.

during the 1930s Depression. This movement promoted the careers of many writers and directors, including Orson Welles, but was viciously attacked by some Hollywood executives. Many of those who took part in the programme were later attacked as dangerous radicals during the anti-communist 'witch hunts' of the late 1940s and early 1950s.

In the US, publicly funded media activities have remained marginal: media activity is essentially a business enterprise or the product of an endowment by philanthropists (who have often made large profits from business enterprise). From the development of radio stations in the 1920s onwards, US broadcasting has been dominated by networks selling advertising. Public service broadcasting on European lines has been limited. This means that regulation of broadcasting in the US has been conducted by a federal agency more concerned with maintaining competition than with laying down requirements about programming.

The non-broadcast media such as cinema, press and advertising developed systems of self-regulation as part of their institutionalisation in the twentieth century. Self-regulation means that institutions appoint committees or panels of individuals drawn from within the industry (and sometimes 'independents' from outside) who are charged with enforcing a code of behaviour.

The tradition of certificating films for cinema release dates back to 1912 in the UK. Hollywood introduced a restrictive Production Code in 1930, designed to head off criticism and potential boycotts from religious groups. The press and advertising industries have also developed 'codes' of behaviour as a defence against critics, and like cinema they have been subject to forms of censorship. However, they have not been subjected to the same regulatory environment that has faced broadcasters. (See the list of self-regulating institutions and their codes below.)

## The centrality of broadcasting

Broadcasting has usually required some form of statutory regulation. Jostein Gripsrud (2002: 260) suggests several reasons why broadcasting is often seen to be the most important medium and therefore as giving the most concern to governments (this would have applied to radio in the 1930s–1950s, but is now more a feature of television):

- enormous 'reach' – accessible to almost everybody;
- people spend more time with radio and television than with any other medium (but the internet may be replacing broadcasting now);

- television is located centrally in every country (despite local services, it is the medium which represents a national focus on events);
- television dominates the agenda of the public sphere;
- television is the most important medium for culture, both in the sense of a 'way of life' and in the sense of art – we gain our sense of who we are and how we live primarily from television.

For all these reasons, television (and, to a lesser extent, radio) is considered too important to 'leave to the market', and governments have decided it should be regulated. We should also note the public safety issue of the control over radio frequencies (i.e. interference with vital services).

However, in Chapters 7, 8 and 9 we explore how the traditional model of television is being challenged by online video services.

> **Public sphere** – a concept associated with the work of Jürgen Habermas, who used the term to refer to a social space in which everyone should be able to communicate their ideas about the state and the economy. In practice, the opportunities to do so are limited. In Chapter 12, we outline the concept of the public sphere and criticisms of it.

## Changes in the 'orthodoxy' of economic policy and new models

From the end of the Second World War (1945) until the early 1980s, the prevailing economic ideology in the developed world was 'Keynesianism' (named after the British economist **John Maynard Keynes**). This set of ideas saw government intervention in the economy as an essential tool for controlling inflation and unemployment across all the major capitalist economies. Keynesian policies saw governments 'regulating' their own spending so that, if a depression in the economy threatened, spending on public sector goods and services would be increased. The aim of government policy was to maintain economic prosperity and the general economic welfare of all aspects of society (i.e. 'full employment' and low inflation).

These policies provided relative economic stability and were accepted by all political parties in the UK and elsewhere. In Europe this allowed governments to fund public service broadcasters adequately so that programming could be 'producer-led'. Producers had budgets that allowed them to make a full range of programmes. The UK stood out in Europe as having a 'mixed economy' in television with a strong commercial sector in ITV, but one which was regulated alongside the BBC and had certain public service broadcasting obligations.

In the US, television broadcasting was a relatively stable market up to the 1970s, with two, and later three, big commercial networks competing with each other across the country and an array of local channels in each major city. The different approach to regulation in the US did not directly

> **John Maynard Keynes** (1883–1946) was a very influential figure, often credited with founding the discipline of macroeconomics, the study of the workings of the whole economy, rather than those of individual producers, consumers, etc. (microeconomics). The 2008 banking crisis prompted calls for a reconsideration of Keynes.

affect Europe at this time. In the era before full globalisation of media activity, the main issue for Europeans was the import of Hollywood films and filmed TV series (westerns, police series, etc.). At various times imports were restricted in an attempt to protect local markets.

In the late 1970s, the economic orthodoxy began to shift for a number of reasons:

- the 1973–4 oil crisis raised the price of oil dramatically and caused energy shortages in the West;
- social unrest at home and military disaster in Vietnam hit US confidence;
- worn-out industries in some countries were suffering from chronic under-investment and lower production costs by competitors in 'emerging economies';
- the whole post-war system of international trade and monetary exchange was collapsing.

Governments began to abandon Keynesianism, partly because what had previously seemed 'impossible' – unemployment and inflation rising together – was now happening. They began to turn towards 'monetarism' and later the promotion of so-called 'free market capitalism'. In its extreme form, as formulated by the US economist Milton Friedman, monetarism meant that governments intervened only in the flow of money in the economy: money was all that mattered, and investment decisions were made only by referring to the prevailing money market conditions (the 'interest rate') and the potential profit from investment (i.e. rather than by whether investment would produce a social benefit). It is important to note here that governments didn't all embrace the new orthodoxy with the same fervour and their actions generally followed the previous distinctions between Europe and the US. Generally, France and Germany were most reluctant to change, the US was most eager, and the UK was somewhere in the middle.

> Naomi Klein's book and the documentary film based on it, *The Shock Doctrine* (UK 2009), features Milton Friedman's ideas, in combination with unchecked political violence, let loose in Chile and other countries since the early 1970s.

## 'Free market' economics

Before we go much further, it is important to think through how an economic model works. In simple terms, economists study the actions of buyers and sellers in markets and the cost of factors of production such as labour, capital, raw materials, etc. in order to try to predict what will happen. To do this, they use hypothetical constructs. One of these is the 'perfect market' in which everyone has 'perfect knowledge' and buyers and sellers make rational decisions. These decisions act on the levers of the price mechanism and the market controls itself with an 'invisible hand'. When the supply of something goes down, the price goes up and more suppliers join the market until the price falls again, and so on.

But this is a theoretical market. In the 'real world', markets are 'imperfect' as knowledge is not equally accessible to all buyers and sellers. Because of social and political considerations, governments, businesses and other organisations and groups of individuals deliberately 'distort' markets, usually, but not always, for good reasons. In our discussion about regulation, we are concerned with different emphases on the importance of 'markets' and 'competition' on the one hand, and 'intervention' and price control on the other. At one end of the spectrum there are free marketeers who perhaps believe that a free market is possible and that it equates to personal liberty. At the other are societies that accept markets only within a general framework governed by other social priorities (universal access, 'quality' of products, etc.). If we accept that globalisation (see Chapter 5) has created a global market, we might expect a whole series of disputes between governments whose 'take' on markets is different. We'll look next at what happened in the 1980s and how it has affected the media environment (in particular the broadcasting environment) we now live in.

## EXPLORE 10.2  STUDY A MARKET

The street market is the closest we come in the real world to the idealised 'perfect market'. Think about online shopping (including digital downloads) as an extension of the street market.

- Check the prices of a film/DVD and a music album across several internet retailers and local high street/ supermarket suppliers – are they all the same?
- Are they actually the same goods – or different versions from different suppliers?
- If you can find the same titles on sale in the US or in Europe, are the prices similar? Is it helpful to use the street market as a model for the market in films and music?

*Figure 10.2* A typical street market in Italy – is this a good 'model' for the media industries?

## Deregulation, liberalisation and media institutions

Starting in the 1980s:

- the new economic orthodoxy saw a move away from government funding of public sector organisations towards support for more 'open', 'competitive' markets; this meant outlawing what were called 'restrictive practices', selling state-controlled enterprises to new shareholders ('privatisation'), contracting out public services to private companies and encouraging the formation of new markets;
- new technologies – cable, satellite and cheaper broadcasting technologies – offered a sudden increase in the possibilities for new broadcast channels, more choice, but fragmentation of the market;
- new global media players emerged, some the result of privatisation of publicly owned utilities, capable of moving across national boundaries; in some cases they were welcomed by national governments and in some accepted reluctantly.

These changes destabilised the existing broadcasting environment, with public service broadcasters having to react to the presence of US companies or new European private sector companies working to the US model.

In economic terms the introduction of new channels and new services meant that television was no longer something that governments saw as a public good, to be treated as a special form of media activity in which everyone shares. Instead, it became a 'private good' just like any other media product such as a newspaper or magazine (see Küng-Shankleman 2000: 29). The media market across the world moved into a phase of what some commentators called '**deregulation** and liberalisation'. Linked government policies in many countries saw:

- the privatisation of what had been public sector monopolies in broadcasting and telecommunications – what had been publicly owned utilities were now privatised; these new private sector companies were free to attract investment into new media products and services;
- the 'loosening' of regulatory controls, especially in broadcasting, which allowed previously tightly regulated broadcasters to lose some of their public service obligations;
- the 'opening up' of media markets with new licences for broadcasting services, particularly in radio, satellite and cable. Restrictions on 'cross-media ownership' were also gradually lifted. This was the liberalisation of the market.

---

New technologies were also important in other media industries such as newspapers and magazines. Newspaper owners, led by Rupert Murdoch, took advantage of new labour laws to break trade union power in order to exploit these new technologies. They were not constrained by public service requirements.

---

Utilities included gas, electricity, water and telecommunications – the last including some major media players such as Vivendi and Telefónica.

---

In 1984 in the new 'free market', the UK government decided that so-called 'video nasties' should be censored by law – some markets are obviously more 'free' than others. In 2009, the British Board of Film Classification reported that the 1984 Act did not comply with EC directives and any rulings were temporarily invalid (http://www.spiked-online.com/index.php/site/article/7320/).

## EXPLORE 10.3  THE LANGUAGE OF THE MARKET

Have you noticed how the language used to describe the market is always 'positive'? Markets are 'free', they have been 'liberalised'. Regulation is usually described in negative terms, such as 'restrictions'. Even a potentially positive term can be presented negatively, e.g. the 'nanny state' in the UK. Presumably the people who use nannies for their children think that they are helpful, but the term has become one of criticism.

● If you were asked to write promotional copy for a new form of regulation, what positive terms would you use?

### What does regulation really mean?

For most of us regulation is not something we think about unless it suddenly has an impact. If at the start of the banking crisis in 2008 you were lucky enough to have some money stashed in a bank or a building society, you were probably very glad that governments decided to step in and save the banking industry from collapse by guaranteeing your savings. But you might also have wondered why the regulatory system was so feeble in the first place as to allow the crisis to develop.

Nothing quite so dramatic has happened in media regulation, but we shouldn't be complacent. What follows is an example of a media world without regulation.

Guyana, situated on the Caribbean coast of South America, didn't develop a national TV service until 1988 – unlike the other main ex-British colonies in the Caribbean, most of which developed TV services soon after independence in the 1960s. In Guyana, a repressive regime in the 1960s decided that the simplest form of censorship of television was just to 'delay' its development – no TV, no problems with dissenting voices. Guyana's colonial history means that the country has two distinct ethnic groups: descendants of African slaves and Indian indentured labour shipped in to work in the sugar industry. The 1960s regime attempted to exclude the Asian community. When a new government lifted the ban on television in the late 1980s, Asian TV stations sprang up very quickly. With no regulatory controls in place, an 'anything goes' policy in some new television stations saw broadcasts of feature films and other programming for which no rights had been purchased.

In other countries these would be 'pirate stations' but in Guyana they flourished openly. Any criticism of this practice could be countered by a claim that at least some audiences were receiving services and 'cultural content' that they had been denied before. But there were consequences. Here is a 2001 report in one of Guyana's leading newspapers:

> Piracy on TV, through video clubs and via recorded cassettes in this country has assumed a certain legitimacy and is institutionalised, thus making it more difficult to oversee the interests of the cinema. There used to be a functioning Cinematographic Authority in Guyana, set up by the Ministry of Information, and it used to police the cinema industry. It seems as if it is now needed to protect it. This authority might well be resurrected since it can now assist in saving the cinema.
>
> (http://www.landofsixpeoples.com/gynewsjs.htm)

In 2009 only one cinema was still open on a part-time basis. There were fifty-two cinemas in Guyana in the 1960s.

See Halstead (1999) and Narain (2005) for more background.

## The contemporary regulatory environment

Since the 1990s many countries have seen changes in government and therefore some changes in the approach to the surviving public sector media activities. At the same time, media producers have found themselves faced with three other factors:

- the structure of the global economy has shifted with the emergence of China and India and significant other 'players' such as the wealthy Arab states funding Al Jazeera or the Iranian English language television service;
- national governments find themselves constrained in media policy by trade agreements – especially in the enlarged European Union but also in the wider context of GATT; regulatory regimes have also begun to meet and organise on a European-wide basis (see below);
- the growth of internet services, especially peer-to-peer sharing, makes it very difficult to monitor what is being distributed within national boundaries.

We can identify six different types of regulation that might be applied to contemporary media, distinguished by where the power to regulate is located.

## 1 Direct control by government

Some countries are controlled by authoritarian regimes which intervene directly in the activities of the media industries (Burma, North Korea, etc.). But such intervention isn't unknown in democracies. The UK has a long history of attempts by government to prevent certain news stories being reported. The appeal here is to the 'national interest' and includes the DA Notice system and the restraints placed on certain individuals by the Official Secrets Act. In this respect the UK has a relatively 'closed' form of government, which is often revealed as such in comparison with the 'open' US system. Aspects of telecommunications activity were regulated by a UK government department until the creation of Ofcom in 2003.

> 'The DA Notice system is a voluntary code that provides guidance to the British media on the publication or broadcasting of national security information' (from http://www.dnotice.org.uk). In April 2009 a DA notice was issued to prevent the publication of press photos taken with telephoto lenses that revealed secret counter-intelligence material carried by a senior police officer entering 10 Downing Street.

## 2 Delegation by government to an independent statutory regulator

Most European countries have some form of independent regulation of broadcasting/telecommunications with powers delegated by government to an appointed body. Such regulators are commonly charged with issuing licences, collecting data, monitoring output and conducting research leading towards policy proposals.

### European audio-visual regulators

The EPRA (European Platform of Regulatory Authorities) operates a website profiling all the European regulators (http://www.epra.org/content/english/index2.html). The site also lists selected regulators worldwide plus other networks of regulators, broadcasting legislation by country and links to associated websites.

*Figure 10.3* The websites of the broadcasting regulatory authorities in Nigeria (http://www.nbc.gov.ng/) and Jamaica (http://www.broadcastingcommission.org). Both sites signal the digital switchover.

The US regulator is the Federal Communications Commission (FCC), an independent agency funded by the US government 'working to make sure the nation's communications systems are working seamlessly and competitively in your best interest' (http://www.fcc.gov). Although by European standards the FCC appears a 'light touch regulator', there have been several cases of problems when FCC rulings have been contested in terms of the 'First Amendment' to the US constitution which upholds the right to 'free speech'. See http://blog.cdt.org/2008/07/25/another-free-speech-victory-against-the-fcc/. Attempts to regulate internet operations also face similar opposition.

### 3 Self-regulation by media producers

This has two meanings. In a formal sense the media institution itself appoints a panel to oversee regulation. But it also works 'informally' through individual producers constraining themselves to avoid any chance of later demands for changes or cuts. The older media industries such as newspapers and cinema tended to create their own regulation bodies. More recent industries are more likely to be regulated by statutory bodies.

## EXPLORE 10.4 PRESS COUNCILS

- Visit the website of the Alliance of Independent Press Councils of Europe (AIPCE) at http://www.aipce.net/.
- Check the 'About the AIPCE' page and the aims of the organisation. In what ways do the aims reflect/refract the discussions about regulation in this chapter?

### 4 The general legal framework as a restraint

Obscenity and blasphemy provide legal frameworks for actions against media producers in many countries. If legal charges are made against media producers, the results are often not satisfactory for either side. Laws on blasphemy are problematic in secular societies – as atheists ask 'Who protects us from offensive remarks?' Legal action based on laws of privacy may also provoke a defence of human rights argument and the intervention of supra-national legal bodies such as the European Court of

Human Rights (e.g. a case like Max Mosley v. News Group Newspapers Limited, 2008).

## 5 'Market forces' regulate

Audiences using their own judgement over purchases affect future industry activities through the price mechanism. This is the view of the free market model which assumes that it is possible and desirable to allow the market to 'look after itself'. In Chapter 9 we discuss what the price mechanism means in relation to television services. Two recent developments cast some doubt on the power of the market. First is the suggestion that internet retail via the **long tail** means that even an obscure product with very limited appeal may be able to find sufficient buyers over a long period to justify its production. Secondly, if media products are effectively free for many consumers, there is no price mechanism as such. This is relevant to the easy access to pornography at no cost – something which brings pressure on 'protection policies', especially for children.

> If you want to gain a sense of how the most vocal 'free marketeers' argue their case, go to the website of Tech Central Station (TCS) at http://www.techcentral station.com, 'Where free markets meet technology'.

## 6 Audience pressure regulates

There is a long history of action by groups of all kinds campaigning for changes in media activity. Sometimes this has been against the output of material thought to be offensive or 'morally dangerous' – cinema, rock music, television, videogames have all been attacked in this way. Other campaigns focus on the overall quality and diversity of output and lobbying has also come from specific groups concerned either about representation issues in media products or about participation by their members in media production. Such groups may be most effective by putting pressure on either producers to self-censor (or to be more inclusive) or governments to require statutory regulators to investigate grievances.

　　Protest groups are often not themselves consumers of the products that they attack and in this sense such protests are not part of 'market pressure'. However, media producers may respond as if to market pressure if they fear that being associated with controversial media products may damage their sales. But then, as the saying goes, there is no such thing as 'bad publicity' and notoriety may also lead to an increase in sales.

> In a celebrity-driven culture, charismatic campaigners sometimes have a significant impact. In 1985 four 'Washington wives', with partners involved in politics and business, created the PMRC (Parents Music Resource Center) which eventually persuaded the RIAA (Recording Industry Association of America) to put stickers on CDs warning of 'offensive lyrics'. The practice continues today, but its effectiveness is contested.

## A 'free market' for classification, censorship and sex and violence?

As we've argued, the price mechanism and the free market are associated with 'value-free' economics – in other words, an economics which deals only with the effects of a change in prices on supply and demand and not with questions about what economic policy should be or what would be a price that was 'good for society'. The importance of this distinction is clear when we consider issues of classification and censorship.

In a 'free market' we might expect to see a thriving trade in pornographic material, as in many European countries and in the US, if that is what people wish to buy. Indeed, developments in media technologies (video, DVD, the internet, etc.) have nearly always been adopted first within the porn industry – since it is the least regulated and most market-driven media industry. However, the very advocates of the free market are often among those who wish to control access to the marketplace for certain kinds of products. The result is that in terms of 'sex and violence' we expect to see the development of some form of self-censorship in all media, whereby the distribution companies in that medium agree to set standards for acceptable products. This has happened with film, magazines and, more recently, videogames.

The oddity of the debate about sex and violence in broadcasting (or in print or on film) is that the issue is rarely put to the market test. We don't know what would happen if 'hard' material were freely available – if it is unacceptable to a large number of media consumers, perhaps 'the market' would drop it from general release when it didn't sell? There are many pressure groups arguing for censorship but few actively campaigning against. One argument might be that the current attitude to self-censorship is patronising towards the audience. If someone is capable of making a decision about whether a media product represents 'value for money', why can't they also decide whether or not it is offensive and 'liable to corrupt'? And if they can't decide, what makes a programme-maker better qualified to decide? This is the argument as presented by the libertarian right and is a complete refutation of public service broadcasting, without the qualifications of the social market position.

In some respects this libertarian position looks acceptable (assuming that children are protected from 'offensive' material, though this raises more questions). However, 'freedom to choose' is also the freedom to be assailed by fierce marketing. With that comes the possible acceptability of more explicit sex or violence, leading to more of such programming and less overall variety of material.

## The public gets the media it deserves?

Much of the UK debate about television (and radio and, possibly, newspapers) is about the 'level' or 'seriousness' of programming and scheduling. Public service broadcasting in the period up to the 1980s was heavily geared to ensuring that certain kinds of programme were scheduled on all channels in peak time. Current affairs and news and arts programming were all prescribed, as well as education during the day and at other times. The loosening of such requirements allowed ITV and then Channel Five and the satellite and cable companies to target BBC programmes in the schedule with more 'ratings-friendly' shows. The BBC struggled within its remit to compete, and towards the end of the 1990s various 'test cases' were widely discussed in the press and by regulators:

- the disappearance of current affairs and arts programmes from peak time;
- reduction of news programmes on ITV and the move to 10 p.m. by the BBC for its main evening news.

In the 'free market', are these kinds of change inevitable? The market is reflected in ratings and these in turn are used in negotiations with advertisers. Scheduling is a strategy game in which the scheduler makes an 'educated guess' about how well a programme will fare in a particular time-slot. Because an instant response is important in ratings terms, the scheduler is likely to:

- risk only those programmes which are formulaic (have worked before);
- take off very quickly any programmes which don't achieve the target rating.

In the regulated market with strong support for the public broadcaster, the scheduler would often allow a programme to 'build' an audience – especially if it was a new kind of programme. This was 'production-led' rather than 'ratings-led' scheduling. In Chapter 9, we discuss the future of television in terms of the switch to television online or time-shifted via PVRs and VOD. Does this mean the end of scheduling arguments and the triumph of the free market? The proponents of the free market in broadcasting are likely to offer these observations:

- People want popular programmes: why shouldn't they have what they want? (This argument is often couched in class terms, with the public service supporters represented as being a middle-class elite, out of touch with the tastes of the majority.)
- The market is very conscious of 'niche audiences' who want very different kinds of programmes. These audiences are often ABC1 and

attractive to advertisers. As such they are targeted by schedulers (and online retailers).

- The market makes producers more focused and more efficient (an argument often made to explain the success of imported US programming).
- Were the majority of programmes any better under the old system? Yes, there were some great television plays and some classic sit-coms, but what about the rest?

## 'Free choices' and 'free speech'?

'Freedom of choice' is seen by the free marketeers as a winning slogan. But what does it mean? As a traveller walking down an alley in Baghdad a thousand years ago, you might well have been able to buy a carpet or a sack of dates from one of many sellers, making your choice based on knowledge of all the prices and a chance to see all the goods. Your purchase decision may even have led to another buyer lowering prices. Go to the 'media bazaar' anywhere in today's global media marketplace and your choice isn't quite so simple. The chances are that you will know most about the products with the biggest marketing budgets. Products from smaller independent products may not even be 'on sale' at all if the producers can't afford to hire a stall. What kind of choice is being offered?

Modern distribution methods have increased access to books, DVDs, CDs, etc. Although your chance of seeing a wide range of films at your local multiplex is not very good (i.e. the same nine or ten films play at most multiplexes), you have the opportunity via internet shopping (as long as you have a home connection and a credit card) to buy any one of thousands of DVDs to be delivered to your door or downloaded as digital files. That is the power of 'the market'. Of course, you may help to put your local video shop, bookshop and record shop out of business. That is the power of 'the market' as well. Are there any social benefits in having a record shop manager to talk to or to sell tickets for concerts or copies of your band's CD? If you think there are, keeping them might require some 'intervention' in 'the market'.

## Regulation in Europe

As we've indicated several times in this chapter, regulation of a directive and interventionist kind (i.e. as distinct from the US model) is strong in Europe and it has become one of the main policy areas for the European Commission. The latest EC directive came into force in 2010. Here is an extract from the EC promotion of its policies online:

### Audiovisual and Media Policies of the European Commission
(http://ec.europa.eu/avpolicy/index_en.htm)

The audiovisual sector directly employs over one million people in the EU. It also plays a key social and cultural role – TV remains the foremost source of information and entertainment in Europe, with most homes having a television and the average European watching up to 4 hours a day. Audiovisual content is also increasingly accessed through on demand services.

EU audiovisual and media policy is implemented in 4 ways:

- Regulatory framework – mainly the 2007 Audiovisual Media Services Directive, which aims to create an effective single European market for audiovisual media and amends the Television without Frontiers Directive, but also EU recommendations on protecting children/minors online and European film heritage.
- Funding programmes – e.g. MEDIA, to complement national systems.
- Other measures – e.g. to promote online distribution of content (content online and media literacy) and media pluralism.
- Action outside the EU – especially defending European cultural interests in the World Trade Organization.

The Commission also participates in the European Audiovisual Observatory.

And from the Press Release for the Directive 'Audiovisual without Frontiers':

The new Directive reaffirms the pillars of Europe's audiovisual model, which are cultural diversity, protection of minors, consumer protection, media pluralism, and the fight against racial and religious hatred. The Commission also proposes to ensure the independence of national media regulators.

This overall approach is well thought out, but regulatory decisions and the institutional frameworks that they help to create can lead to difficult situations.

## Dealing with race hatred and extremist politics

In the UK in 2009, the British National Party, a party espousing racial exclusion and therefore potentially open to prosecution, won two seats in the European Parliament. The BBC, a self-regulating PSB operating in a broadly regulated (i.e. by Ofcom) PSB environment, decided to invite the BNP leader Nick Griffin on to a *Question Time* panel. *Question Time* is a popular discussion programme on BBC1 with a studio audience pitching questions to a panel of politicians and others from different backgrounds. Questions were raised as to whether the BBC was obliged to invite Griffin as part of the 'impartiality' clause in the BBC Charter. Certainly the BNP would have to be given a 'party political broadcast' slot as this is an agreement amongst UK broadcasters. The justification that appeared on the BBC website suggested that:

> The BBC could not apply different standards to different parties because of their particular policies. That would be a breach of our charter, challengeable in the courts.
>
> (http://www.bbc.co.uk/blogs/theeditors/2009/09/
> question_time_and_the_bnp.html)

*Figure 10.4* BNP leader Nick Griffin on *Question Time*.

Stuart Hall (described on *The Guardian*'s website as a 'cultural theorist') was quoted thus:

> He should be interviewed when he's specifically involved in a news event – for example if someone throws a brick at a BNP meeting. He shouldn't

be banned from the media. But *Question Time* is something different – him being invited on suggests we're interested in his views on a whole range of issues, which we're not. His appearances should be related to news rather than general commentary.

(http://www.guardian.co.uk/politics/2009/
oct/16/does-question-time-accept-racists)

> *Question Time* is made for the BBC by an independent company, Mentorn.

During the programme, which usually covers a range of topical issues, most questions were directed at Griffin and his policies. Although many in the wider BBC audience thought that Griffin's poor performance in answering questions had damaged his position, many others suggested that by allowing it to become effectively a 'bash Griffin' programme, the BBC itself had been damaged as a credible PSB provider.

## EXPLORE 10.5

- Do you think the BBC was right to invite Nick Griffin on to the show and then allow the format to be modified?
- What does this example tell us about the impact of regulation?

## Conclusion

We've suggested that regulation is a function of all media markets. Even deregulated ones have some new form of regulation, rather than an abandoning of it. But different ideological positions favour both different levels of regulation and different forms of regulatory controls. In the US the tradition has been for limited intervention in media markets and certainly relatively low levels of publicly funded and regulated output. At the same time, certain aspects of easily accessible media are subject to elements of social control. By contrast, in largely social democratic or at least 'mixed economy' Europe, publicly funded output is still extensive in an environment that experiences much more intervention by national and Europe-wide regulatory bodies and conventions. Both these positions are challenged by aspects of Web 2.0 and difficulties in regulating online media. Finally, in all these different modes of regulation, we recognise that regulatory codes always need adjusting as the media environment itself changes – and the ways in which users wish to engage with it.

## References and further reading

Bignell, Jonathan (2008) *An Introduction to Television Studies*, 2nd edn, London: Routledge.

Gripsrud, Jostein (2002) *Understanding Media Culture*, London: Arnold.

Halstead, Narmala (1999) 'Television in Guyana: A Regulatory Nightmare', in (eds), Lees, Tim, Ralph, Sue, and Brown, Jo Langham, *Is Regulation Still an Option in a Digital Universe?*, Luton: Luton University Press.

Küng-Shankleman, Lucy (2000) *Inside the BBC and CNN*, London: Routledge.

Narain, Atticus (2005) 'Remote Control Nationalism: Media Politics in Guyana', *Journal of the Moving Image*, 4 (November), http://www.jmionline.org/jmi4.htm.

Nowell-Smith, Geoffrey (ed.) (1996) *The Oxford History of World Cinema*, Oxford: Oxford University Press.

O'Sullivan, Tim, Hartley, John, Saunders, Danny, Montgomery, Martin, and Fisk, John (1994) *Key Concepts in Cultural and Communications Studies*, 2nd edn, London: Routledge.

# 11 Debating advertising, branding and celebrity

- Advertising, marketing and branding
- Debates
- Histories
- Hollywood and branding
- Hollywood: the brand(s)
- Case study: 'Brangelina'
- Citizenship and consumption
- A note on 'spin'
- Conclusion
- References and further reading

'To advertise' originally meant 'to draw attention to something', often by word of mouth. It is now the media form we most often encounter, usually as part of **branding**. It funds most media, directly or indirectly. Product press releases are often used by news sources, since they are usually legally safe and ready written. And such contemporary activities now involve much more than 'drawing attention' to products. They extend into PR (public relations) and activities known as '**spin**'. And, finally, they sometimes seek to take products out of the public eye, or to 'spin' their meanings in processes such as '**greenwashing**'.

Ads now have usually been carefully researched via focus groups (see Chapter 15). More recently 'viral' or 'peer-to-peer' advertising is attempted. This is said to work like a virus (in the community or in a computer) – 'infecting' one consumer who spreads it to others. This uses the idea of a cumulative 'tipping point', here in the spread of good 'word of mouth' for a product. You probably notice the resemblance to ideas of 'the wisdom of crowds' (also explored in Chapter 8). It's all a long way from simple 1950s psychological or 'effects' models applied to single ads, or to myths of the power of subliminal advertising.

The 'tipping point' explores the ways that momentum for social change gradually builds up, until a 'tipping' point is reached, where the momentum is suddenly unstoppable. The term comes from Michael Gladwell's book *The Tipping Point: How Little Things Can Make a Big Difference* (2001). Other key terms there include 'connectors' (people with extensive social networks), 'mavens' (specialists who can connect 'us' to new information), and 'the stickiness factor', which you will hear in some discussions of how often visitors come back to a website, or a blog.

Lawson (2009: 243) quotes the famous saying of the architect Mies van der Rohe 'less is more', and the reply of Frank Lloyd Wright: 'Less is only more where more is no good.'

*Figure 11.1* Advertising has for some time featured in dystopic source fiction narratives. The mall in *Minority Report* (US 2002) is a striking visualisation of novelist Philip K. Dick's idea of brands which scan the consumer's eyes – an extension of the use of barcode information by some supermarkets?

Most chapters in this book have had to deal with one or other of advertising's social roles (see Chapters 7–10 for its involvement with media economics). Some would argue its costs are now not only monetary, but involve mental and physical health, and the future of much human life on this planet. The term turbo-consumerism has been coined (see Lawson 2009) to describe the pace of demand which advertising, especially branding, has stimulated in recent decades. It is arguably the most powerful and pervasive form of propaganda in world history. Try to avoid all advertising for a single day. You will find it very difficult.

## EXPLORE 11.1

- How many forms of advertising have you encountered so far this week (include branding – the visible sign of a brand on your trainers, jeans, shopping bag)?
- Where did you encounter them?
- Have you ever advertised? Where?
  In a 'free' student or other local paper? On e-Bay? As internet 'spam'?
  On a dating site, advertising yourself, or an image of yourself? (See Chapter 15)

Advertising has drawn the attention of generations of analysts and is an attractive way to begin study of media imagery. Often though, the implication can be that ads alone produce direct 'effects' on viewers – as claimed in the past by advertisers. There's often a fascination with **'subliminal ads'** as apparent evidence of the sheer power of this media form alone. Yet this is arguably another example of the strange attraction of a 'dupes' model of audience.

**Subliminal** means 'imperceptible but powerful' (from Latin for 'below the threshold'). It is used of secret messages said to be inserted into advertising and other media forms, and to have measurable effects on behaviour, 'bypassing' the 'conscious' brain.

The theory is now discredited, though still circulates. Stories of 'backward messages' in rock and roll songs, or frames included in ads and political broadcasts, have also persisted. See Wikipedia's useful account.

## Advertising, marketing and branding

Advertising works in the larger context of marketing, public relations (PR) and now branding, all of which try to identify, connect with or create the 'market' for a product. This involves not only the design of individual ads but also the sum of the ways (such as pricing, placing in distribution outlets, association with celebrities) in which a product is positioned in its particular market.

Advertising or marketing agencies co-ordinate different kinds of activities, sometimes in competition with each other. PR is one set of activities, involving publicising persons or companies. It uses some of the same techniques as advertising – competitions, free offers – but may also arrange incidents, 'spontaneous' happenings, the setting up of internet fan clubs, micro-blogging (crafting identities on Twitter, etc.), even staged relationships, reported by the media as news (see the career of publicist Max Clifford). All of these activities can overlap with those of the advertising agencies which make ads and manage campaigns, 'placing' or buying space for ads in particular media.

> The South African company De Beers sought in 1947 to redefine diamonds, saying they would 'make diamonds a cultural imperative in a woman's life'. How does their advertising now try to redefine these small, polished, sparkling rocks?

> A **market** is the total of all the potential sellers and buyers for a particular product (and the number of products likely to be at stake). The word has attractive connotations – local, bustling, sociable – for operations which are now often very different. See Chapter 10.

> Nielsen Media Research, the leading provider of US TV ratings and 'competitive advertising intelligence', tracks product placement on the top US networks, including whether the ad is placed in the foreground or background, its time on screen, integration into the storyline, etc. This is in a context where products such as TiVo DVR allow some viewers to skip commercials altogether. Go to http://www.nielsenmedia.com for details of this (very expensive to access) research.

Branding aims to give products and services resonant cultural meanings through various imaginative/imaginary connections (often to celebrities or powerful cultural myths). However, these meanings are grounded in

- distribution: commercial placings and pricings;
- often intense legal protection (ever tried to use a pair of Mickey Mouse™ ears in a commercial poster?);
- the ability to pressurise suppliers of raw materials and products as a result of the sheer size of the regular contacts the branding company promises (you could explore almost any major brand for evidence of these practices);
- the processes of globalisation (see Chapter 5).

Branding is said to be driven by the need for 'competitive distinction' within a crowded 'marketplace'. The physical form of the brand (shape of bottle, colour of packet, logo, etc.) can come to stand as the face of the parent corporation. It is a key means of shaping 'markets' and competitive relations between companies, as well as many consumers' sense of themselves.

Figure 11.2 Interbrand report cover 2009

**USP**: unique selling proposition: the supposedly unique quality of a product which advertisers seek to communicate to potential buyers. These attempts occur in a world with many possible substitute products for big brands (e.g. the huge numbers of more or less equally efficient detergents, toilet rolls, trainers).

## EXPLORE 11.2

Explore http://www.interbrand.com, the major 'brand consultancy', which publishes annual rankings of global brands' values based on the percentage of their revenues that can be credited to their brand. Only brands worth more than £1 billion and deriving a third of earnings outside their home countries are included.

Striking about their report cover, opposite, is the ease with which you can probably recognise the visible brands by mere slivers of the logos.

Branding often seeks to establish a **USP** or unique selling proposition. At the simplest level it involves trying to persuade customers, through this USP, of a product's quality prior to purchase or experience, by means of the reputation or image of the producing company. It is often argued that the versatility of modern capitalism means that individual products (e.g. a bar of chocolate) are not unique for very long: product specifications can easily be copied by rivals in a few days, and the difference between products anyway is often minimal. How many truly different kinds of shampoo can there be? Brands, however (e.g. Cadbury's, McDonald's), making a range of products, can be made to seem, and indeed often are, stable guarantees of 'quality'. Their legal teams will strongly defend the recipe or design of the brand, and if a problem arises with quality, there will be intense PR and other efforts to repair the damage to the brand – see the Cadbury's example below.

## EXPLORE 11.3

Take five shampoos or other everyday product. Act as a 'rational consumer' and assess the claims of their advertising (including labels).

- How long did that take?
- How many shampoo brands are there in your local supermarket?
- Estimate how long a full survey, as 'rational consumer', would take.

Monarchs, cities and nations, as well as products, are branded, and rebranded. Such 'image campaigns' arguably stretch to the work of the British Council or the German Goethe Institute. The British royal family has hired branding experts to work on their images, following fears that their unpopularity, surfacing after the death of Diana, Princess of Wales, would lead to republican changes.

Conversely, one of the results of '9/11' or, rather, of the massive military responses which the US Bush administration chose to make to it, was to provoke what is called COE or country of origin effect. This denotes consumers' awareness of the place of manufacture or ownership of some branded products, with purchases – or boycotts – becoming related to those. Slave-like conditions in the factories of suppliers in some countries, for example, have sparked huge protest campaigns, like the one against Nike.

Branding is now more than a key commercial activity, it is also a metaphor, within most cultures. Articles will ask 'Is it time to rebrand feminism/Glasgow/the games industry?' and so on. Individuals sometimes come to see themselves as like brands, advised to operate 'reputation management' or 'impression management', looking for their 'USP' for CVs, for dating agencies and so on.

## Debates

The major debates around advertising/branding have included the following points, each working with different assumptions.

- It brainwashes consumers with deceptive promises and appeals, designed to promote consumerist materialism, waste, hedonism (pleasure seeking) and envy.
- If we did rationally 'assess' all the claims of all the kinds of any one product, as defenders suggest in the 'ads help the rational consumer decide' case, it would take more time than most people ever have.

See Balnaves *et al.* 2009, Chapters 7 and 9 for a good account of these, and recent Chinese and Indian strategies for rebranding their nation states.

See http://www.royal.gov.uk for one face of a vast multimedia PR operation that projects the Queen 'as a surly but steady presence at the helm of the nation . . .' *New Statesman* editorial, 13 July 2009, p. 4.

See http://urbanlegends. about.com/library/weekly/aa0 22101a.htm for a famous email exchange on Nike trainers. It's an example of 'culture jamming' which Jordan (2002: 102) defines as 'an attempt to reverse and transgress the meaning of cultural codes whose primary aim is to persuade us to buy something or be someone'. See also http://www. adbusters.org.

Planned or 'built in' obsolescence: the process of making a product obsolete after a certain period, or amount of use. This is planned by the manufacturer rather than being the result of 'wearing out'. See Packard 1960.

- Advertising is part of the built-in drive to '**planned** or **built-in obsolescence**' and high consumption on which modern capitalism, with its capacity for overproduction, partly depends.
- It acts as an unnecessary business expense, adding significantly to the costs of goods for customers. Large monopolies such as Procter & Gamble spend millions advertising products (e.g. soap powders) that compete with those of their own subsidiaries.
- For all its 'free market' claims, branding produces barriers to competition. Young companies cannot afford the expenditure needed to break into markets via the costly work of creating 'brands'. Big corporations can 'shout louder' and ensure their goods are favourably distributed in crowded markets.

## EXPLORE 11.4

Re. 'built-in obsolescence': ask friends and family if they have ever NOT been advised, when mobile phones, DVD players, etc. break down: 'why don't you buy a new one? It will cost nearly as much to have it mended.'

'Why do beer ads never show guys with beer bellies?' Anon, Radio 1, an example of widespread scepticism about advertising's images, which partly leads to self-aware ads, apparently with no designs on our disposable income.

Let's look at one recent example as a way of exploring some changes. Advertisers often, now, happily go along with claims that readers of ads are free to interpret them as they choose, to ignore them, or to spot product placements in a spirit of sarcastic superiority. They are now well aware of some audiences' knowledge of their earlier strategies. Pricing, control of resource supply lines, their powers to 'place' or distribute both ads and products are less often discussed. Ads often now make self-reflexive play with their own discourses, with enjoyable and often stunning-looking results, which also flatter their viewers.

*Figure 11.3* A prizewinning 2007 cinema and TV ad for Cadbury's Dairy Milk.

In 2010, the 'gorilla drummer' was part of the Cadbury workers' campaign to try to ensure that the US corporation Kraft Foods kept its pledges to safeguard jobs when it bought Cadbury's.

Featuring a gorilla playing the drums to Phil Collins's *In the Air Tonight*, the Cadbury's ad pictured (Figure 11.3) tried to work as an 'entertainment piece' and provoke 'viral' marketing by word of mouth rather than, for example, by connection with *Coronation Street*, which the company stopped sponsoring in 2006.

See John Lanchester's fascinating piece on the art of chocolate manufacture and the questions raised by Kraft's bid for Cadbury's: http://www.Lrb.co.uk/v32/n01/john-lanchester/short-cuts.

The ad is severed from any direct claims for the product except for the colour purple, the final slogan ('A pint and a half of joy') which 'anchors' the short film, and perhaps the song's lyrics. Viewers seem to have been fascinated by the ambiguity of the images – was this a real gorilla? Why this choice of film? Of soundtrack? Many enjoyed adding their own music.

See Wikipedia for more on the production of, and reasons for, this campaign, including a previous salmonella scandal (2006) around Cadbury's products and other problems involving PR and the company brand at the time. And watch for work on the brand image now that Kraft Foods has taken over Cadbury's (2010).

Enjoyable though it is, looking at individual ads will not account for the power of ads in an age of branding. Let's explore some histories.

## Histories

Advertising can arguably be found as far back as Greek and Roman public criers, shouting the wares of local traders. But its recognisable modern form begins to appear with the nineteenth-century Industrial Revolution, the overproduction of goods for existing Western markets through new manufacturing techniques, and then the drive to expand markets as part of global imperialist conquest. In the 1850s in Britain, the then Chancellor of the Exchequer, William Gladstone, removed regulations and taxes on advertising. Manufacturers were soon able to appeal to consumers over the heads of retailers, through the young media industries. And, beginning in the US, potential customers began to be educated (informally, by advertising) into the possibilities and attractions of consumption.

For many years (as now) ads were described as though they operated in purely irrational ways, and as though that was why they had a 'brainwashing' effect – on women. 'Femininity' is still often constructed as irrational and bound up with consumption (shopping, fashion and the domestic sphere) rather than with production or 'serious', i.e. paid, work outside the home. But the apparent power of advertising for women in these years cannot be understood outside other powerful contexts, and it's worth reminding ourselves that these still operate for many parts of the world.

> 1916 saw the launch of the automatic washing machine and the opening of . . . the first grocery outlet [in Memphis] to allow shoppers to browse the shelves themselves rather than have a clerk make up their order. A new imaginative landscape was being assembled in which domestic drudgery would be abolished and personal choice extended. The home would cease to be the focus of continual worry about making ends meet and become an arena of self expression and social display. The labour of maintaining basic living standards would give way to the pleasures of constructing lifestyles.
>
> (Murdock 2004)

To understand the appeal of such advertising we need to appreciate the real gains and freedoms for women represented by many new products with which it was connected. These saved hard, repetitive labour in the home. They offered the sociable pleasures of the new shops where they were sold – safe and pleasant public spaces for women otherwise largely confined to the home. In cities, goods were displayed, usually at fixed prices, in large, attractively laid-out department stores, in safe shopping districts.

The attractions were like those of early picture palaces, which offered opulent visual display, comfort, rest rooms, restaurants and polite service – rare treats for many working-class people. Advertising and marketing still work in tandem with other consuming pleasures, such as the layout of stores and, now, malls – and often the absence of other safe, enjoyable public spaces and activities in many towns and cities.

## EXPLORE 11.5

Such stores are sometimes described as 'temples of consumption'.
- Make mental notes the next time you visit one, of how you are invited round the sections, as well as how the whole 'addresses' you through music, lighting, colours, etc.
- If irritated by it, what exactly do you find irritating?

Another store tactic: the constant filling of supermarket shelves is argued by Stuart (2009) to be an incitement to consumption and thus to the staggering amount of food waste in contemporary 'developed' cultures.

*Figure 11.4* The make-up section of a contemporary department store.

For stimulating discussion of recent US ads and images, explore http://contexts.org/socimages.

In discussing the power of 'advertising' or 'branding' it's always important to remember associated marketing and distribution activities, as well as the usefulness and pleasures of many products. Though the 'built-in obsolescence' of, e.g., various mobile phone fashions is unsustainable, the phones themselves have many, often vital uses, for many groups, across the world. As with other theories of 'effect', users are never dupes, and texts never work in a vacuum.

## EXPLORE 11.6

- Do shopping 'malls' work as 'safe' public spaces for you? What are their attractions?
- Many cinemas are now placed in malls, rather than being 'stand-alone'. How does this affect your experience of film-going?
- Do cinemas work (or seem designed to work) as kinds of 'utopian' spaces – the colours, lighting, comfort, the abundance of sweets, huge containers of popcorn, candyfloss and drinks, cleanliness, polite service?
- Grainge (2007) explores how Hollywood brands, such as Warner, developed 'Warner Village' cinemas which both extended the brand (here as 'quality multiplex') and grounded it locally (pp. 169, 171).

The positive connotations given, in advertising from the 1920s, to change, novelty and youthfulness undermined traditional attitudes. These had endorsed 'thrift, self-sufficiency, home cooking, family entertainment, hand-made and hand-me-down clothes' (Pumphrey

'Sometimes tradition is just another word for bad habit.' Anon.

Some of the most powerful and difficult dilemmas for environmental politics involve how to balance this kind of attitude with precisely the need for activities such as mending, conserving, recycling to become 'cool'.

See the case study *The Age of Stupid*, as well as the DVD boxed set for the film, for arguments and debates.

See Packard (1957). Adam Curtis's 2002 BBC TV series *The Century of the Self* (http://video.google.co.uk/videoplay?docid=-6784663632245206 14#docid=-472880436774272 9519) explores connections to the descendants and associates of Freud in US advertising's emphasis on self-gratification. (Such US contexts to some extent explain the critical stance of the Frankfurt School theorists.)

The US series *Mad Men* (2007–) fictionalises the corporate structures, casual sexism, racism and other working practices of a Madison Avenue ad agency in 1960. At the same time it explores the predicaments of 1950s housewives, objects of the very advertising which their husbands work on.

1984). Importantly, they were often oppressive for ordinary women, generally the only people expected to do the actual 'making' and the 'handing down', and thus usually confined to the home. The mass consumption of labour-saving products and ready-made food were often truly liberating – for those who could afford them. They remain so in many parts of the world – a real question for 'green' politics.

But early ads, even those encouraging the most paranoid levels of anxiety about 'germs' and 'dirt' in the home, in many ways did *not necessarily* treat their addressees patronisingly. 'The Housewife' was constructed as having a *serious* responsibility (keeping the home clean and safe) and as *democratically* joining 'hundreds of thousands of American women' said to have benefited from this or that product. She was encouraged to think of herself as both a private *and* a public figure, one being offered the opportunity to take advantage of modern devices – in other words, she was 'connected' with technological and social advances.

By the end of the 1920s, US advertisers began to try to accelerate the buying habits of shoppers or consumers (largely women). The success of the US government's propaganda during the First World War convinced advertisers that they too could use social psychology or **behaviourism**, the name given to research into human motivation and conduct. Lifestyle advertising developed, going beyond a simple outline of a product's uses towards encouraging potential buyers to associate it with a whole desirable style of life, and to feel that *not* owning the product might lead to 'personal failure', unpopularity and so on.

Feminist views of such advertising ask about gaps in these images:

- Why should 'labour-saving' devices actually mean *more* work for many women, via the much higher standards of cleanliness expected of them?
- If women's work in the home is so important, why was it not counted or paid as *work*?
- Why cannot men, or older children, share involvement with this work in the family?

Advertisers constructed, and continue to construct, a kind of *self-surveillance* for both the housewife and her 'opposite', the 'career woman'. Women were repeatedly invited to ask themselves how clean, how safe was their bathroom, kitchen, cutlery, and/or how appealing was their hair, figure or personal aroma. In recent years this self-surveillance has arguably deepened.

Research into anorexia suggests that young women's (understandable) absorption in fashion can very easily lead to dissatisfaction with, and an inability to imagine as desirable, any but a thin, or at least adolescent-looking body. It seems this is also becoming a problem for young men. Ros Gill (2007) argues that the body has become a new (identity) project, one fraught with difficulties, especially for young women and men. The men's 'double bind' is that they must simultaneously work on and discipline their bodies while disavowing any (inappropriately 'unmasculine') interest in their own appearance.

> See also both versions of *The Stepford Wives* (US 1975 and 2004) and the series *Desperate Housewives* (US 2004–) for contemporary 'ironic' approaches to the still powerful, now retro-1950s image of 'the perfect housewife'.

> Recall discussion of 'disavowal' in Chapter 6.

## EXPLORE 11.7

Look through TV ads during programmes which seem scheduled to attract female audience's attention (e.g. morning or afternoon television).

- Do you think self-surveillance is still invited? Evidence?
- Are there any ads addressing men in ways that encourage self-surveillance?
- In which areas – appearance, competence in particular skills?
- How are they similar to, or different from, those addressing women?
- Is the tone of the ads showing men doing domestic work different – playful, perhaps, as though this is not to be taken seriously?
- What kinds of questions are women shown putting to themselves in ads for cosmetics, clothes, household cleaners, fitness products?
- Look at related 'make-over' shows. How do they intensify self-surveillance by women?
- What kinds of 'make-over' to appearance, lifestyle, etc. are suggested?

One final historical stage of these industries was the advent of branding. Naomi Klein (1999/2009) argued that brands' current importance goes back to the mid-1980s. Management theorists began to argue that successful corporations (rather than the single companies of earlier advertising) should primarily produce brands, associated with a range of products, as opposed to advertising separately their actual, different products. The partial US recession in that decade went hand in hand with the startling success of new kinds of corporation, such as Microsoft and Nike, and later Tommy Hilfiger and Intel.

> These . . . made the bold claim that producing goods was only an incidental part of their operations, and that thanks to recent victories in trade 'liberalization' and labor-law reform, they were able to have their products made for them by contractors, many of them overseas. What these [parent] companies produced primarily were not things, they said, but *images* of their products.

> . . . Creating a brand calls for a completely different set of tools and materials [from creating products and simpler levels of advertising]. It requires an endless parade of brand extensions, continually renewed imagery for marketing, and most of all, fresh new spaces to disseminate the brand's idea of itself.
>
> (Klein 2009: 4–5)

In the UK the regulating body is the ASA (Advertising Standards Authority). Explore its website at http://www.asa.org.uk/asa/. See also the UK Foods Standards Agency website: http://www.food.gov.uk/, a mine of useful information.

Again, marketing and branding need to be seen in the full context of production, regulation, distribution and other commercial practices, and their histories. Often other contexts are important. In the 1950s, for example, advertising often took the credit for stimulating British consumer demand after the Second World War. Arguably, though, the welfare state was at least as crucial for this change, giving millions of ordinary people proper healthcare, pensions and secondary education for the first time.

Tempting though it is to stick with textual analysis, brands and ads do not work magic on us simply through alluring messages.

## Hollywood and branding

An area of branding you may have come across is the concept of **synergy**.

This refers to:

- the combined marketing
- of 'products' or commodities (including people, such as 'Cheryl Cole')
- across different media and other products (in music, toys, internet and television programmes, T-shirts, theme park rides and so on)
- which are often owned by the same corporation (e.g. Time Warner or Disney)
- such that the total effect is greater than the sum of the different parts.

Synergy has been around for some time and is almost inseparable from major entertainment industries, especially Hollywood. It's related to 'cross-promotion' and product placement, like Volvo's recent promotion of its XC60 through the Twilight franchise, following several Volvo product placements in the *Twilight* films (see http://www.brandchannel. com for more on such branding).

**Product placement**: a form of advertising where branded goods or services are placed, clearly visible, in a context usually devoid of ads, such as movies, and one where they are not critically treated. Product placements used not to be admitted to, and the extent of this commercial tie-in can still come as a surprise. But there is now some awareness, criticism and parody of them. See *Behind the Screens: Hollywood Goes Hypercommercial* (Media Education Foundation, Amherst Mass., 2000) for a dated but acute discussion of such practices in blockbuster Hollywood (extract on http://www.youtube.com/ watch?v=9eNs-CjxUu4).

---

**EXPLORE 11.8**

Explore the nature and limits of the celebrated 'anti-consumerism' of *Fight Club* (US 2000).

Do you agree that this cult film:

- is technically brilliant, often eloquent and funny about dissatisfactions with corporate working lives, branding and consumerist ways of living,
- but, ideologically, it seeks to solve these problems by 're-masculinisation', i.e. expressing nostalgia for pre-consumer, 'cave man' times and pranks, by implication without women, who are traditionally linked with shopping and consumption (even in the figure of Marla) (see Robinson 2000), and
- produces a huge distance between Brad Pitt's 'bankable' image and his role? This leads to moments like the one where, looking at a 'body beautiful' Gucci underpants ad, Tyler/Pitt asks, 'Is that what they think a real man looks like?' Much publicity for the movie centred on his transformed 'built' body, pecs, etc. – exactly what many real men *do* long to look like.

---

The 'escapism' of Hollywood entertainment forms is often into worlds which turn out to contain highly recognisable products. Hollywood pioneered the use of cross-promotional tools, though this has hugely intensified in recent decades (see Branston 2000; Grainge 2007). As early as 1912 there was alarm in England and Germany about the ways that American movies were functioning as an arm of US exports and marketing. Fashions, up-to-the-minute kitchen technology and furnishings were routinely showcased in 'women's films' and then TV, establishing global tie-ins with manufacturers and links to stores and advertisers. The cigarette industry regularly lobbied performers to

*Figure 11.5* A particularly patronising ad for cigarettes, used as late as 1969.

smoke on screen (and as a result many stars died of cancer). Fantasy forms, like the Bond films, have always glamorised conspicuous consumption via product placements and tie-ins for luxury cars, watches, clothes, champagne, tourist destinations, computers, gadgets and so on.

## EXPLORE 11.9

- Watch for product placements in the next movie or television programme you see. It is often argued, on the grounds of 'realism', that we live in a world of products and films 'simply reflect' this.
- Research the extent to which the products are not simply 'present' but insistently showcased – lit well, clearly visible, often with the logo facing the camera, and sometimes appreciatively used and commented on by a character.

In the big franchise films, like *Harry Potter* or *Star Wars*, the 'products' are the characters themselves, through toys, replicas and so on, often available in outlets like McDonalds for months before the film's release. Such characters are said to be 'toyetic'. Increasingly the sets and narratives are also 'product', for games allowing older children, and adults, to immerse themselves in the worlds of the films. Worth researching for the product links to recent films is http://www.brandchannel.com/brandcameo_films.asp.

## Hollywood: the brand(s)

Despite the image of the logo on the hills, 'Hollywood' has moved from being primarily an actual site of production to being primarily a collection of brands (also called studios) which structure a global flow of 'content' across 'platforms'. Grainge (2007: 71–105) explores how the static signature trademarks of Paramount, Warner Bros. etc. at the beginning of films are now replaced by logos which morph into the experience of such films as *The Matrix* (US 1999) and *Spiderman* (US 1999). These logos reference both the mythical past as trusted brand, and the new, immersive pleasures now on offer.

## EXPLORE 11.10

- Check the next, recent studio film you see and note whether the logos work in these ways.
- Watch too for the branding of the 'aural spectacle' of Dolby Digital Sound as part of 'the cinema experience'.

Grainge also documents how Warner Bros., after the franchise success of *Batman* (US 1989), a crucial moment in corporate studio branding, consolidated its global theming in the 1990s through studio stores, theme parks and the cross-franchise potential of the Looney Tunes animated characters, especially cross-branding (with Michael Jordan) in *Space Jam* (US 1996). Their later, staggeringly expensive franchise, *Harry Potter* (US 2001), and *The Lord of the Rings* (2001–3), produced 'independently' by New Line, a Warner subsidiary, are also branding landmarks in, among other things, the potential of the internet and games forms for reaching diverse audiences through the immersive worlds in and around the cinema. The marketing of these two films involved

- the impression that they were blockbuster rivals in every sense, including ownership (see Grainge 2007: Chapter 6);
- the different approaches which such fantasy blockbusters take to product placement, etc. (compared with blockbusters set in the contemporary world).

The histories of advertising above suggested how important were women, often acting as spenders of domestic budget, to many advertisers. We've argued that this has somewhat changed: some men are now encouraged to see themselves, too, as discriminating consumers. Celebrity, another global advertising-related form, has begun to work on notions of both female and, increasingly, male identities, especially appearance, and the sale of products associated with these.

Celebrities now blend into news and current affairs, as well as their own magazine forms. These include *OK!*, *Hello*, *Heat*, *Grazia*, *Closer*, though 'Bollywood' and other national film industries produce their own stars/celebrities, used in similar ways. In the UK and US huge amounts of apparently 'straight' news coverage are skewed towards them. Indeed it's been argued that some news forms and channels are so heavily reliant on celebrity forms as to be operating a kind of commercial bias against fuller news coverage.

Celebrity coverage is said to boost ratings via 'human interest' and glamour, helped by the ease with which PR firms, blockbuster films, fan

 For an updated case study on Stardom and celebrity see **MSB5 website**.

See Chapter 12. Some also argue that official politics is shaped no longer by mass parties but by the success or not of candidates' 'lifestyle' or celebrity images.

sites, etc. offer links to them. For branding they offer year-round possibilities of tie-in activities, from coverage of births, weddings, funerals, holidays, sporting events, diets, exercise and beauty products, cars, houses and so on. Their performances in their main media form (sport, music, film, TV) and associated tie-ins there, form, in theory, a perfect synergy.

## EXPLORE 11.11

- Attempt a simple piece of content analysis (see Chapters 1 and 15) across a week to determine how much news output is 'star'- or 'celebrity'-related. This can include high-profile cinema events, such as film premieres, festivals.
- Try to explore
  a   the prominence of their coverage, across different media, and
  b   what you think *should* have been the prominent stories that week.

Cinematic forms of stardom, and analyses of them, are useful for understanding 'celebrities'; indeed it is increasingly difficult to separate the two. Stars and celebrities, it is argued, fascinate us partly through the ways that *parallel narratives* of their lives are constructed, in addition to performances of one kind or another. Here's a brief case study.

## CASE STUDY: 'BRANGELINA'

The potential for easily accessible narrative involvements offered by coverage of the celebrity romantic triangle Jennifer Aniston/Angelina Jolie/Brad Pitt could go on for as long as the three of them live – and beyond. The 'triangle' is entering its sixth year, fuelled by the appetite of celebrity magazines and most recently (January 2010) strong rumours that Jolie and Pitt are planning to split up. Such magazines often sell lucrative advertising space on the basis of their front pages and the gossipy speculations those promise. They rely on weekly 'scoops' to distinguish them from their rivals.

Some components of this couple's/triangle's marketability:

1   Celebrities usually have a kind of talent based in one or two media forms (singing, film performances) which is profitably connected to their celebrity and 'off-screen' narrative, once established. So, the scale of later publicity around 'Brangelina' means, for many viewers, it is almost impossible to watch *Mr and Mrs Smith* (US 2005) without speculating on

how far the on-screen images did 'reveal' off-screen romance developing for Jolie and Pitt, who have both denied it.

In a parallel set of moves, Aniston's films and relationships are still connected to the 'loss' of Pitt, and Aniston's 'failure' to find another long-term partner/have a baby, etc. This will probably continue to be part of the market for films by these actors, though, note, it is the two women who are especially focused on.

2   The different constructions of femininity in 'Aniston' and 'Jolie' play across this open-ended narrative: 'Aniston' – East coast associations with New York via *Friends*, accomplished comic actor, 'nice girl' with 'ordinary' attractiveness – is endlessly pitted (sorry) against 'Jolie' – Hollywood parentage, does little comedy, extraordinary, almost freakishly exaggerated beauty and mildly 'scandalous' image, before her relationship with Pitt, who is himself a location for discourses of forms of masculinity and fathering.

3   In some ways the star/celebrity couple Jolie–Pitt is not typical, though they do illustrate the inescapable logics of people-branding. The two have performed some high-profile charitable work (which, in a world of branding, may be seen as part of a 'slightly different brand'). They have disappointed conventional expectations (e.g. of a wedding) – which immediately fuelled profitable speculation and interest. They also seemed to avoid the more obvious kinds of product-related activities.

> 'Yes, she won an Oscar for *Girl, Interrupted*, she was good and scary, even if somehow in that fancy asylum she got two hours in makeup every day.' David Thomson, whose writings on star presences are always worth a look, here at http://www.guardian.co.uk/film/filmblog/2008/jun/13/biographicaldictionaryoffil16.

## EXPLORE 11.12

Search the internet for references to 'Brangelina' and connections with branding.

● Do any of your findings either surprise you, or relate to points made above?

*Example 1*: PR firm 5W Public Relations promoted one of its clients' baby clothes through sending them to Africa to get the company's logo in the first million-dollar Jolie–Pitt baby pictures. When millions bought the magazine issue featuring the pictures of baby Shiloh they also saw an expensive four-page ad spread for the Dodge Caliber.

*Example 2*: How differently evaluated, by different media, are the humanitarian and political actions of celebrities like Bono, Geldof, Jolie, Madonna, Pitt?

● Are such valuations related to gender, ethnicity, or to whether film or music is the original source of celebrity?

> The George Clooney telethon for Haiti (January 2010) produced the news that Pitt and Aniston were spotted chatting backstage. 'Would Haiti bring them together?' asked the gossip papers. Others criticised the ways celebrity coverage had taken over 'the Haiti story'.

*Figure 11.6 and Figure 11.7* Two front pages, published close to each other (June and April 2009) and showing the endless stretch of celebrity speculation on the basis of little evidence. 'Cool' blank expressions (if visible behind enormous sunglasses) allow almost any caption to seem credible, however much it contradicts other coverage. The careful use of words inside the magazine ('it seems that', 'sources close to x suggest that . . .') not only avoid legal action but, again, can fuel readers' enjoyable speculations. The photographing of 'doubles' can also start some temporarily profitable rumours.

4   At the core of such star/celebrity material now is the use of paparazzi photos. These go far beyond catching stars in compromising or simply private moments. Magazines such as *Heat* and *Closer* patrol bodies and behaviour, using photos which, in earlier times, would have been rejected. This produces coverage of celebrities who are drunk or violent, or getting out of a car and revealing some cellulite (female celebs these, of course, and in shots often grotesquely magnified), or simply looking tired and ordinary, or perhaps not quite recovered from a pregnancy. The structures of feeling evoked for readers are often argued to be sadistic, and even to involve a kind of shame (see Rose 1998 for interesting discussion). This seems especially perverse since, at the same time, in other sets of photos, celebrities are visualised as models of bodily control and perfection, which we are invited to envy, and to emulate, via consumption of the appropriate products.

Paparazzi: photographers who take 'candid' photos of celebrities, usually by shadowing them in public and, especially, private activities. Technological developments (e.g. longer lenses and higher-speed film) enable paparazzi to shoot from afar, while digital cameras and Photoshop in their laptops allow immediate airbrushing, especially at the Oscars, and rapid distribution of the resulting photos.

*Figure 11.8* The 'scrum' of photographers, and demonstrators, around Britney Spears, a figure used to test cultural anxieties around class and gender, including appropriate dress, mothering skills and other forms of feminine behaviour.

## EXPLORE 11.13

Collect some photos at random, either your own, or from news sources.
● See if there are *any* captions which *cannot* be plausibly fitted to the facial expressions in them, of the kind used in celebrity coverage (e.g. 'Britney is a car crash', 'Cheryl's despair').
Burkeman suggests: 'Stories may start with nothing more than a set of photographs: Aniston looking happy, or sad – or happy one moment and sad the next, since if you take multiple shots of anyone with a fast shutter speed, you can capture a range of expressions' (2009).

'[A]lcohol companies have
. . . started putting "please
drink responsibly" on
billboards . . . a bit like
showing a Land Rover
coursing through a snowy
landscape chasing a spy and
saying "please cycle more"
at the end' (Zoe Williams,
'Morals Go to the Market',
*The Guardian*, 25 October
2005).

Go to http://www.alcohol
concern.org.uk for UK
campaign data.

See http://www.who.int/
tobacco/statistics/tobacco_
atlas/en/ for global WHO
(World Health Organization)
statistics, maps and histories
of the deadly drug tobacco.
*The Insider* (US 1999) is
a powerful fictionalised
account of this industry's
practices.

## Citizenship and consumption

We have tried to outline the varied activities involved in branding, advertising and consuming now. Here histories are important, suggesting advertising's relation to gender, class and the important attractions of modernity, in some consumer products. But earlier history is not simply overtaken on the road to universal progress. Older and discredited advertising practices persist alongside the flatteringly witty allusions of some ads. Despite ironic self-awareness, and some forms of regulation in parts of the world, many dangerous ads, pricing and marketing appeals are still used in the 'developing world' and Eastern Europe (as well as in poorer areas of the 'First World'). Tobacco and alcohol companies, for example, rushed to ensure that their brands were known there before more regulated health restrictions were imposed. Tobacco sales continue to produce ill health in the smokers and those near to them, as does unregulated alcohol consumption by targeted groups.

New mothers in 'developing' countries are often encouraged, in hospital, to begin the habit of buying expensive packeted baby milk, needing to be mixed in water, often in desperately short supply. They are not encouraged, like many women in the richer world, absorbing the message partly through celebrity images of mothering, to breastfeed as a cheaper and healthier practice – if the mother is well fed herself of course.

Wherever ads are circulated, they mostly address us as shoppers, as consumers, rather than as citizens, with other concerns, or rather parallel ones, than shopping and buying (see Lewis *et al.* 2005). In the process some rich contradictions are thrown up. Women's magazines often produce challenging articles and even campaigns around topics like women's guilt at their supposed inadequacy as mothers, wives, home-makers; the dangers of sexualising very young children in advertising imagery; of anorexia, etc. It's precisely on such civic or citizen-related topicality that they sell their magazines, and their space to advertisers. But ad messages often drive in the opposite directions – trading, however lightly and wittily, on anxiety about appearance, or housework standards, or relationships, or, images of highly consumerised and sometimes sexualised toddlers – all in the interests of selling products which promise to solve these problems.

Yet though ads help to construct some oppressive identities and environmentally destructive practices, shopping and the exchange of gifts can also be a major form of kindness and social connecting (see Miller 2008 and also the debate between Lawson and Nava). We'd like to close by opening out some other, more contradictory and perhaps hopeful issues.

*Figure 11.9* Suffragette board game.

Campaigning politics have also been conducted *within* 'consumption', and not only at the level of boycotts, such as against apartheid in the 1980s, or 'ethical shopping' which tries to avoid goods produced in sweatshops, or flown thousand of air miles, etc.

The suffrage movement (for votes for women) produced this 'tie-in product' board game (the object is to achieve universal suffrage). They also made their own plates, mugs, etc. with appropriate colours (green, purple and white) or slogans. Selfridges decorated its shop window in these colours for a time.

The anti-slavery movement also organised consumer boycotts. The image of the kneeling slave with the motto, 'Am I Not a Man and a Brother' introduced by Josiah Wedgwood in 1787, was used by many manufacturers of pottery and prints.

See Lawson (2009) on 'anti-consumerism' as well as 'post-consumerism', and a debate with Mica Nava on http://www.opendemocracy. net/ourkingdom/mica-nava-neal-lawson/is-shopping-all-bad. See also http://www. labourbehindthelabel.org, www.freecycle.org and www.tescopoly.org.

The DVD set for *The Age of Stupid* is another example of a 'product' which is both politically challenging and uses free tie-ins differently – such as the 'STUPID' stickers with the advice 'Sticking these illegally – like on cheap flight ads or 4×4s – would be very very naughty. Don't even think about it.'

## A note on 'spin'

'**Spin**' has several meanings, and usually negative connotations. They range from PR and communication skills through to consciously biased or dishonest versions of events or persons.

'Spin doctor', instead of 'press officer', certainly evokes 'witch doctor' and 'the dark arts'. It has been associated with Alistair Campbell and Peter Mandelson, though Tim (Lord) Bell arguably started the modern 'spin doctor' cycle, working for Prime Minister Margaret Thatcher, among other, global figures (see Wikipedia's history of his career and networks).

See the BBC's *The Thick of It* (2005–) for a dark (hopefully exaggerated) satire on the extremes of Parliamentary 'spin doctoring' – an interesting comparison with the US serial *The West Wing* (1999–2006), another way of fictionalising the inner PR and other workings of some modern governments.

Spin usually involves commercial forms of 'signification' (see Chapter 1) but can involve others. It is often used dismissively, like 'propaganda', which can exist in either 'black' or 'grey' forms (using lies) through to accurate but biased, or 'positioned' forms.

## EXPLORE 11.14

It's worth considering:

1   What is being 'spun', perhaps by a 'PR stunt'?
    - Do some dismiss an initiative simply because an imaginative stunt or a well-phrased press release is being used?
    - Or is the stunt, etc. arguably a piece of 'greenwashing'?

*Figure 11.10* This sculpture was launched

a   to warn MPs of the dangers of climate change and
b   to publicise Eden, a new natural history TV channel.
    Q: A 'sell-out', since it's arguably a commercial image?
    Or a sign of the interweaving of some commercial and campaigning initiatives now?

2   Is the 'spin' being used simply to mean 'lying'? Or is it objecting to *any* kind of attempt at getting meanings across imaginatively?
3   Do attacks on 'spin' assume that there is some eternal truth or 'fact' which 'we' could get at if only this work of signifying or making meaning weren't going on?
4   Does this fit with a cult of 'sincerity' and 'openness' which seems (understandably) nostalgic for a time of simpler, more authoritatively given meaning? John Tulloch (2005) makes interesting points on 'spin' and the ways it is used.

A related issue is that reputation and perceived quality are crucial to brands. Some have 'reputation management' sections and there are a growing number of 'corporate social responsibility' (CSR) employees, some of whom try to ensure that the environmental rhetoric of the company's annual report is made to mean more than '**greenwashing**', a term used to describe claims of being 'environmentally friendly' made by companies about activities which damage the environment. Notoriously, for example, BP in 2000 launched a campaign with the slogan 'Beyond Petroleum' and a green and yellow sun logo, even though oil production, their core activity, is one of the most environmentally destructive industries. Virgin, Exxon, Shell, Lexus and most other big corporations can be researched for examples of greenwash activities. Protesters have sometimes targeted the promises of brands like McDonald's, in the films *Food, Inc.* (US 2009), *McLibel* (UK 2005), *Supersize Me* (US 2004) and the book *Fast Food Nation* (2001).

Now-unavoidable concerns about catastrophic climate change, related to corporate and high-consumption activities, mean that activists, as well as protesting 'outside' the corporations, are often at the same time pushing in other ways for bodies of power related to them to 'mean it'. This opens out some of the genuinely difficult questions of what CSR in the fullest sense should really consist of, of how it could be scrutinised, motivated and regulated.

It's worth considering what can feasibly be done at these combined levels, especially if you, like so many others, feel torn between needing to get a job (perhaps in corporate PR, or CSR) and trying to save human environments. An earlier political anecdote is a striking one, often used by Naomi Klein, a prominent anti-corporate campaigner. US President Franklin D. Roosevelt (1882–1945), at town-hall style meetings, would hear calls for change from his supporters to which he would say 'Yes. Now go out and make me do it.'

So powerful are green discourses now that it could be a good slogan for some corporate social responsibility staff, and others involved in the consuming worlds most of us are part of.

## Conclusion

This chapter has morphed from discussions of individual ads, often attractive parts of teaching 'advertising', through to more economically embedded arguments about associated global branding practices. We've explored some of the histories of advertising forms. We've suggested, as a result, that to dismiss advertising all on its own as either irrational or all-powerful in its 'effects' is inadequate. The power of consumerism lies

The metaphor of a 'whitewash' has been used since *c.*1800 for a glossing over or cover up of scandals and crimes, and also for inadequate or casual investigations of allegations.

www.dontbuyexxonmobil.com

*Figure 11.11* A Greenpeace 'greenwash' image, on the Adbusters website, http://www.adbusters.org, itself worth exploring for campaigns (Buy Nothing Day, 28 November), 'culture jamming' posters and discussions.

not only in branding but also in the advantages and pleasures which some products offer, as well as in the global networks of supply, legal force, distribution and access to publicity and lobbying power of many kinds which brands now command.

We've tried to indicate how, far from being simply 'information' forms, branding and advertising are crucially tied in to global cinema and entertainment power, especially Hollywood, and its offering of brand-related spaces in its films, its publicity processes and in parts of 'celebrity' now.

Finally we have suggested that it's misguided to blame only 'PR', 'spin', 'branding' and communication practices for all the ills, inequalities and disastrous consequences of this stage of 'consumer' capitalism. Its powers are far from being purely irrational, or indeed peaceful. If you want to be part of a fairer world, you need to understand it as fully as you can in order to engage with it adequately.

## References and further reading

Acland, Charles (2003) *Screen Traffic: Movies, Multiplexes, and Global Culture*, Durham, NC, Duke University Press.

Balnaves, Mark, Donald, Stephanie Hemelryk, and Shoesmith, Brian (2009) *Media Theories and Approaches: A Global Perspective*, London and New York: Palgrave MacMillan.

Branston, Gill (2000) *Cinema and Cultural Modernity*, Buckingham: Open University Press, Chapters 1–3.

Burkeman, Oliver (2009) 'What's a Little Truth between Friends?' *The Guardian*, 24 June: 6–10.

Gill, Ros (2007) *Gender and the Media*, Cambridge: Polity Press.

Gladwell, Michael (2001) *The Tipping Point: How Little Things Can Make a Big Difference*, London: Bantam.

Goffman, Erving (1976) *Gender Advertisements*, London: Macmillan.

Grainge, Paul (2007) *Brand Hollywood: Selling Entertainment in a Global Media Age*, London and New York: Routledge.

Jenkins, Henry (2006) *Convergence Culture*, New York: New York University Press.

Jordan, Tim (2002) *Activism! Direct Action, Hacktivism and the Future of Society*, London: Reaktion Books.

Klein, N. (1999/2009) *No Logo*, revised anniversary edition, London and New York: Fourth Estate.

Lang, Tim, and Heasman, Michael (eds) (2001) *Food Wars: The Global Battle for Mouths, Minds and Markets*, London: Earthscan.

Lawson, Neal (2009) *All Consuming*, London: Penguin.

Lewis, Justin, Inthorn, Sanna, and Wahl-Jorgensen, Karin (2005) *Citizens or Consumers: What the Media Tell Us about Political Participation*, London and New York: Open University Press.

Littler, Jo (2008) *Radical Consumption: Shopping for Change in Contemporary Culture*, London and New York: Open University Press.

Meek, James (2001) 'We Do Ron Ron Ron, We Do Ron Ron', review of Schlosser (2001), *London Review of Books*, 24 May.

Miller, Daniel (2008) *A Theory of Shopping: The Comfort of Things*, Cambridge: Polity Press.

Murdock, Graham (2004) 'Building the Digital Commons; Public Broadcasting in the Age of the Internet', https://pantherfile.uwm.edu/type/www/116/Theory_OtherTexts/Theory/Murdock_Building DigitalCommons.pdf.

Orbach, Susie (2009) *Bodies*, London: Profile.

Packard, Vance (1957) *The Hidden Persuaders*, London: Penguin.

Packard, Vance (1960) *The Waste Makers*, New York: D. McKay.

Pumphrey, Martin (1984) 'The Flapper, the Housewife and the Making of Modernity', *Cultural Studies*, 1, 2: 179–94.

Robinson, Sally (2000) 'Putting the Stud Back into Gender Studies', *Times Higher Educational Supplement*, 15 December.

Rose, Jacqueline (1998) 'The Cult of Celebrity', *London Review of Books*, 20, 16, (20 August).

Schlosser, Eric (2001) *Fast-Food Nation*, London: Allen Lane.

Stuart, Tristram (2009) *Waste: Uncovering the Global Food Scandal*, London: Penguin.

Tulloch, John (2005) 'The Persistence of Spin', *Media Education Journal*, 34.

Wasko, Janet (2003) *How Hollywood Works*, London: Sage.

Williamson, Judith (1978) *Decoding Advertisements: Ideology and Meaning in Advertising*, London: Marion Boyars.

Wilson, Elizabeth (2003) *Adorned in Dreams: Fashion and Modernity*, London: I. B. Tauris.

# 12 News and its futures

- The importance of news, and views of 'the public'

- The construction of 'news'

- 'Impartiality' and accuracy

- 'News values'

- Debates on the influence of news

- Futures: 'new' news?

- Conclusion

- References and further reading

'News' seems easy to define, though hard and fast definitions are surprisingly difficult to find. It means interesting new happenings, surely? Most definitions cite this meaning, but then add: 'news is interesting new happenings as presented (or mediated) by news media'. This raises two questions: interesting, and indeed available, to whom, why, and for how long? And mediated how, and why?

See Chapters 7, 8 and 9 for more on the fast-changing ways is which news is now funded, produced and circulated.

By the time you read this book there will have been (even more) important changes to news than are being debated at present. It currently seems unlikely that TV and print news (and online versions) will disappear. But they may be part of a very different market for news, with new business models and employment patterns, endangered 'quality' and locally specific forms, and new relationships between Web 2.0 sources and traditional print and TV news.

These go along with new potentials for news raised by the internet: new ways of collecting and reporting information; a 'new journalism' open to novices which can come from almost anywhere, often using new writing techniques, and functioning in networks of fragmented audiences, delivered at great speed, and, again potentially, open and deliberative in dazzlingly new ways (see Goldsmiths Leverhulme Media Research Centre project 'Spaces of the News', 2010).

Here we offer you some sense of these changes, as well as key concepts and debates, such as:

- the importance of producing and circulating reliable news forms as part of the workings of informed democracies;

- how 'news' has been constructed as a category, and how it might be changed;
- the impact of 'new news forms' associated with Web 2.0 and the ease with which comment can now be made on traditional news content.

You will have to decide which approaches best help you understand, and perhaps take part in emerging news cultures, including the key questions of how news circulates.

## The importance of news, and views of 'the public'

News is a globally important and fast-changing media form. It now flows at incredible speed, 24/7, across internet, TV, print, radio – where they are available. It, and rumours around it, can leapfrog from local to international contexts, and from formal to informal ones, by means of satellites, broadband, blogs, 'tweets' and multimedia messaging services (MMS).

It matters that complex modern social orders, aiming for democratic forms of governance, have access to news forms which offer reliable and accurate information and analysis. You will come across the idea of 'the public sphere' here, a term coined by Jurgen Habermas (b. 1929; see also Chapter 14). It offers the ideal of a safe, guaranteed area in social life where individuals can freely identify, discuss and help shape public and social affairs. Habermas cited the coffee houses of eighteenth-century London as producing a kind of public rationality, through such discussions, which could act as a check on state (we could add, for this century, 'corporate') power. He argues that modern commercialised media have 're-feudalised' public discussion, with celebrity, PR image and spectacle-centred news cultures replacing such rational discussions.

His theory has been criticised for:

- its vagueness as to what exactly are the limits of the 'public sphere'. Does it include parliaments or assemblies? Could it include entertainment forms?
- suggesting there is a clear distinction between 'private' and 'public' rather than seeing them as determining each other. 'The family', for example, is not the heart of the private world. Families exist in many different forms, and are shaped by public legislation, kinds of exploitative labour and violence within and outside them, etc.
- not specifying women or other minorities as part of public sphere discussion, indeed for implying, in the examples he cites, that it is the conflict-free domain of gentlemen;
- like the Frankfurt School (see Chapters 14 and 6), often lacking specific accounts of institutions, different kinds of spectacle, their

> **Multimedia Messaging Service**, or **MMS**, is a telecommunications standard for sending messages that include multimedia 'objects' such as images, audio and video.

> See the excellent Global Media Monitoring Project, 'the longest and largest longitudinal advocacy project on gender in the world's news media'. Its website is http://www.whomakesthe news.org.

gendering and so on. Others now argue, for example, that imaginative use of 'spectacles of disaster' can be an asset to efforts at global solidarities.

Habermas has acknowledged some of these weaknesses (see Thompson 1995: 73) and aspects of his theories suggest that he had not appreciated the profound impact of modern media, let alone 'new media'. This is understandable given that his major work outlining the 'public sphere' was published in German in 1962, and only translated into English in 1989.

Despite these problems, many see the *ideal* of a 'public sphere', like those of 'objectivity' and 'accuracy' in reporting, as something to which news and reporting should aspire, especially if they are active within so-called democracies. One consequence of thinking about ourselves as members of 'the public' – a form of collective identity – is that the term 'citizen' becomes an appropriate word for thinking about that part of our lives. Discussions will emphasise 'the public realm' or 'public discourse' and some may use the term 'deliberative democracy' (see Cottle 2009) as a more useful way into this valuable idea of 'citizenship'. Our 'citizen identities', involving shared concerns and pleasures, will sometimes be contrasted with the highly individualised and self-centred identities we're made more familiar with as 'consumers' (see Lewis *et al.* 2005).

And finally: how are the 'public' represented in news programmes themselves, especially through the ways that 'public opinion' is constructed within them (see Lewis 2001; Lewis *et al.* 2005)? What is usually conjured up by news terms such as 'middle America' or 'middle England'? How do 'letters to the editor' work, locally and nationally, and alongside new forms of feedback such as blogging? How are '**vox pop**' interviews framed by news programmes?

## EXPLORE 12.1

- Which spaces are now, or might become, part of a modern 'public sphere' of rational debate?
- How might Web 2.0, and interactive forms of reporting, blogging and debate help make a modern 'deliberative democracy' possible?
- How might they change the news' representation of 'public opinion'? (See Chapter 14 for more on this.)
- How might this apply to local news forms and local governance? (See http://www.amarc.org/wccd/ a website focused on international community

media, especially radio, and its potential for democratic and sustainable development. See also some local, often investigative news websites, including the much praised www.voiceofsandiego.org and http://www.londoncitizens.org.uk/.)

## The construction of 'news'

This area has traditionally been explored through what are called 'news values' or 'news criteria', the structuring principles which, media analysts have argued, lie beneath the everydayness of news. Johann Galtung and Mari Ruge laid out a now famous pioneering list of 'news values' in 1965 (usually dated as 1981, when first published in English). You will come across their names, and their argument – that news is *structured* according to unspoken values rather than '*discovered*' – remains a key one. But it is now almost fifty years in the past, before 24-hour news coverage, as well as interactive media. We will therefore outline and update several, though by no means all, of their key terms and introduce others through which to approach this 'construction'.

News workers often hope to be part of truly democratic processes by offering impartial and accurate news, for use by citizens in democratic processes. Two key points have often been made, within media studies, about the category 'news':

- It is not transparent, not unbiased, not a 'window on the world' which simply 'presents' interesting happenings 'out there', as is often implied.
- It constructs versions of events (we'll leave fakes out of discussion for now) and these constructions have often served dominant interests, whether corporate, or those of government.

This relationship to power still applies but differently to Web 2.0 news sources and practices. Ownership pressures are somewhat different, as are some states' capacity to deny internet access. But it's hard to see how any kind of news could avoid being constructed. Even tiny news 'tweets' are phrased and circulated in particular ways (constructed) – see the Trafigura example below for a particularly effective one.

> Twitter, launched 2006, has become a globally popular, free 'micro-blogging' social networking site. It allows users to send 'tweets', of no more than 140 characters, from their page to their 'followers', though open access can also be allowed.

## 'Impartiality' and accuracy

In Britain, whatever the actual practices, broadcast media are legally required to be politically impartial and to make 'balanced reports'. In UK newspapers, however, there has traditionally been a slot for the paper's opinion – the 'editorial'.

See *Outfoxed* DVD and clips on YouTube, and its birthday greetings to Fox News.

But, partly in the scramble for audience figures and the swirl of internet comment available, the lines of 'news', 'comment', 'entertainment' and 'opinion' are becoming increasingly blurred. Fine, that could be a valuable development. But it matters in a different way that, for example, a major outlet, the US-based but globally circulated Fox News, sometimes reports its own opinion pieces as though they were news, and regularly strays into areas of hugely biased, anti-Democrat comment, or even campaigning.

## EXPLORE 12.2

- Research Jon Stewart's comments on Fox News on YouTube, including the charge (2009, 2010) that Fox completely blurs the lines betweens news, opinion and entertainment.
- Research his comments on Fox anchors, such as Bill O'Reilly with his bullying use of 'Shut up!', or Glenn Beck with his extreme, 'bear-baiting' views. See also http://www.huffingtonpost.com/2009/10/30/jon-stewart-takes-on-war_n_339788.html.
- If you have access to Fox News, say how accurate you think his charges are. If not, see if they help you distinguish between news, opinion and entertainment forms in your own favourite news sources.

*Figure 12.1* DVD cover of film

*Figure 12.2* Jon Stewart

*All the President's Men* (US 1976) was an inspiration for many journalists. It dramatised the true story of the discovery, by two *Washington Post* reporters, of the 'Watergate' scandal, involving the Republican 'high command' bugging opponents' offices. This led directly to the resignation of US Republican President Richard Nixon in 1974.

The film drew on and reconstructed powerful images of the male hero-investigator-reporter, literally going into the dark to find 'Deep Throat', a source of the leaks from the White House, whose identity remained secret until very recently.

Q: What might replace it as an inspiration now? For you?

Some students cite Oprah Winfrey, Hunter Thompson, John Pilger, Anderson Cooper, but for many it is Jon Stewart in *The Daily Show* (http://www.thedailyshow.com/) which is watched by huge audiences in the US and elsewhere.

Q: How would you compare Stewart and other 'anchor' type news heroes (apart from Pilger) with the earlier model of reporter hero in *All the President's Men*?

We'd argue that the *attempt* to make impartial or balanced news is worth renewed support, though terms like 'accuracy' may now be more useful. This is in the light of:

- increasingly partisan, biased and globally available TV news channels and other outlets, of which Fox News is the most striking;
- tabloid (or in the UK 'red-top') forms which are so heavily reliant on celebrity and PR-led forms as to be operating a kind of commercial bias against fuller news coverage;
- the overall drive towards cutting costs in journalism, which Nick Davies (below) and others cite as, now, much more important than interference with 'impartiality' by proprietors (though that does happen).

Rupert Murdoch has always wielded (occasionally direct) powers over his News Corporation editors and put pressure on the BBC via public statements. Such actions mean that even where he is not directly intervening, his news workers are aware of his overarching presence and political views.

Two examples:

- In 1998 he prevented publication of former Hong Kong Governor-General Chris Patten's memoirs, which were critical of the repressive

Chinese regime. He also took the often critical BBC World Service TV off his Star network, whereupon the Chinese government gave him permission to start a cable TV station.

- In 2007 he admitted influencing the anti-Europe stance of his British newspapers (*Sun*, *The Times* and *Sunday Times*) and Sky TV news channels. This seems connected to European resistance to his attempts to take over sectors of their media (see http://www.cpbf.org.uk and http://www.guardian. co.uk/media/2009/jul/27/newspaper-owners-editorial-control 2009). And see http://www.guardian.co.uk/media/2009/jul/13/news-of-the-world- phone-hacking for a sense of the networks of power in and around one of his UK papers, the *News of the World*.

The question of 'balance' or impartiality has always been a difficult one. In the UK (for TV) it can no longer be gauged by a stopwatch eye as to how much media 'time' each major political party is given. The political spectrum stretches further than a see-saw 'balance' metaphor can cover, as do news sources. Though 'spin' and PR sources for news are important, arguments which put all the blame there imply that a fully objective account exists somewhere. This kind of objectivity or impartiality is an impossible goal for any statement or story because:

See the highly relevant debates on these questions as they affect documentary forms, in Chapter 13.

- To decide to select an item for news coverage is to make a decision about other items that cannot be told, because of time or space restrictions. Any such story has already had some value set on it.
- There are always several positions from which to tell a story. It is impossible to produce an account from completely 'outside', since positions on it will inevitably have been chosen.
- To say that complete objectivity is possible is to imply that an unarguable interpretation of an event exists *prior* to the report or story. Few would now argue this.

See the website of the NUJ (National Union of Journalists) http://www.NUJ. org.uk for more on their code of conduct, and much else.

Nevertheless, we can reasonably argue that news can and should be as adequate, accurate and informative as possible.

So 'news' does not exist, free-floating, waiting to be 'discovered' in the world outside the newsroom. Even phrases like 'don't shoot the messenger', often trotted out by those defending media reports of bad news, suggest that message and messenger can be neatly separated. We'd argue that assumptions about what constitutes 'a good news story' systematically *construct* rather than simply *accompany* its 'gathering'.

'News' is the end product of complex processes of budgeting, allocating resources, evaluating events and PR handouts, and framing (or 'spinning') the events chosen (see Chapter 11 for more on 'spin'). The sense of what is 'newsworthy' develops according to professionalised news values, absorbed in forms of training, formal and informal, later kinds of journalistic socialising, gossip, the basing of a news channel in a particular city and so on. They include a particular (often very limited) sense of the audiences for that news programme or newspaper – how educated is it? how much context can be taken for granted? what are assumed to be its political interests? So the news will not be identical on all channels or front pages on any particular day.

## A global news provider

*Figure 12.3*  Recent home page of Al Jazeera English edition.

Al Jazeera (meaning 'The Island' or Peninsula – the Arabian peninsula – but also an idea of independence) is an Arabic news channel located in Qatar, an oil-rich monarchy. It was founded in 1996 and funded by the Emir of Qatar and other Arab moderates who believed in the need for uncensored news in the Middle East.

It was staffed partly by reporters, trained in BBC World principles of attempted impartiality, who had been made redundant by the closure of BBC Arabic services as a result of censorship demands by the Saudi-Arabian government. Its motto is 'We get both sides of the story', though critics would say stories of corruption in Qatar are notably missing.

It gave voice to previously marginalised Arab viewpoints, especially after US/UK-led attacks on Afghanistan (2001), during which it was the only live news channel broadcasting from that country. It was the source of messages from Osama Bin Laden, as well as some suicide bombers, and showed (and continues to show) footage of the devastating effects of the war on civilian communities which many Western news sources tend to avoid.

The image of such news sources (e.g. through attack by Fox News) needs careful consideration. For example, a widely repeated 2005 story that Al Jazeera had shown beheadings of Western hostages was not true, and had to be retracted.

However, see http://www. guardian.co.uk/media/2008/ jan/30/tvnews.television for a sense of the difficulties faced in the expensive launch of the English-language channel, and the cultural differences, as well as not-so-different cost-cutting regimes alleged.

The US Bush and British Blair administrations tried to stop such broadcasting. In 2001 the station's building in Kabul was 'accidentally' bombed and destroyed by a US missile. In 2003 the Baghdad office was similarly hit, with a reporter killed. In 2009, after intense controversy about the limited international news coverage of the bombing of Gaza by Israeli forces, Al Jazeera released some of its broadcast quality footage from Gaza under a Creative Commons licence (see Chapter 8, http://blip.tv and Al Jazeera website).

It is probably the most watched satellite channel in the Middle East, even though there was a huge growth in satellite channels there in the 1990s. Al Jazeera also provides a free news website, though the launch in 2008 of the BBC's free Arabic-language TV channel, with a 24-hour service from 2009, has presented stiff competition.

## EXPLORE 12.3

- Look at the Al Jazeera website(s) and listen to the BBC World Service for an hour or so.
- List any ways in which these differ from your usual news sources, especially
  - the items which constitute top, newsworthy, 'headline' stories;
  - the stories which they follow up;
  - how their stories and news practices are gendered;
  - their use of shocking images which are often censored from broadcast coverage in the UK and US, sometimes under 'watershed' scheduling policies.
- Go to http://english.aljazeera.net/focus/2009/10/2009101011512667509.html on the 2009 Bangalore floods, calling Bhola Island the ' "ground zero" of climate change' in a twist on the shock of 9/11.

'Scoop', 'newsflash', 'news extra' used to celebrate the speed of 'news'. There are now serious concerns about the effect this may be having on the accuracy and reliability of unchecked news stories. Social media stories are part of this, along with neoliberalism's 'freeing' of checks and regulation (see Chapter 10).

## 'News values'

1 *The overvaluing of speed in news.* News has become synonymous with 'the new'. With the coming of almost instantaneous satellite and internet communications there is now huge emphasis on 'fast' or even 'first' delivered news.

This time-scale of news now raises several questions:

a As the famous example shown in Figure 12.4 (a doll taken to be a soldier) suggests, fakes can be passed off as real stories, given cutbacks in staff to check reports and this relentless drive to be 'first' with stories, however inaccurate.

b  In such drives to immediacy, as well as with an eye to legal consequences, news workers are understandably driven to rely more and more on press releases and other PR information from both corporate and government sources.

c  Related, though not the same: an oil spillage will be perceived as a news story; but the slow work over time of legislation or protest which makes it less (or more) likely to occur will not. It could be argued that 'current affairs' (CA) is where such issues now surface, but CA is at least as pressurised as news, and usually follows its agendas.

Nick Davies (2008) argues that journalism (or **churnalism** as he dubs it), increasingly reliant on cutting costs, makes too-frequent use of unchecked PR and official news agency sources (mostly the Press Association in the UK), partly because there are fewer specialist staff employed to double check these sources. This arguably constitutes a kind of silence within journalism, leading to a silence, or gap of knowledge, within audiences, who are thereby deprived of the knowledge to take part in fully democratic debates on public issues.

## EXPLORE 12.4

- Watch a major news bulletin. What proportion of it can be related to the kinds of sources Davies cites? Discuss with others how you would try to research this.
- Follow a single such story through some of the following sources and related sites.
  Note the differences, if any, in their treatment of it:
  http://www.huffingtonpost.com; www.indymedia.org; www.medialens.org; www.opendemocracy.net; www.reportingtheworld.org.uk; www.zcommunications.org/znet; www.gfmd.info/.

2  *Threshold*. Galtung and Ruge (1965/1981) wrote of the 'size' of an event that's needed for it to be considered 'newsworthy' (their term was 'threshold'). Commonly occurring events happening to individuals will not usually count unless they involve either a celebrity or an unusually

*Figure 12.4* It is easy to fake things on the internet, even pictures, like this one using an action figure from Dragon Models USA. Big 'alterative' sites, like *The Huffington Post*, claim they have millions of checkers (they had 23 million 'hits' in August 2009), but smaller sites cannot even make such claims.

*Figure 12.5* Reuters is one of a set of global news agencies trading news, including Associated Press (AP), Agence France Presse (AFP), Cable News Network (CNN), Xinhua News Agency, China, Pravda, etc.

See Davies' book, and Lanchester's review (2008), for detailed figures of research findings.

The excellent US-based *Columbia Journalism Review* (slogan 'Strong Press Strong Democracy') recently ran a story (http://www.cjr.org/regret_the_error/speed_demons.php) about The Yes Men (see Chapter 13) faking a corporate announcement, as they do. Explore the issues raised, and the rest of the site: http://www.cjr.org.

violent or sensational happening. The authors have been criticised for neglecting local news in this.

## EXPLORE 12.5

- Discuss with others what annoys you about your local news coverage, whether TV, radio, print or internet. Is it partly the sense that 'local' is boring? How might this be changed? Research Nick Davies' work on the concept of 'Churnalism'.
- Try to account for the nature of local news via news ownership, advertising levels, self-censorship via the probable networks of local elites (sport, education, Masonic lodges, etc.). What differences could be made to it?
- Again, if you have ZNet (http://www.ZNet.org) or indymedia (http://www.indymedia.org.uk) covering your area, research its stories, this time for a sense of how differently 'local' news could be constructed.

### Another role for a 'local news' story?

In 1999 the Columbine school shootings took place, posing huge problems for news reporters. All advertising was suspended for twenty-one hours, with financial consequences for the stations, but marking this event as 'exceptional' for viewers. The story amplified cultural themes or myths such as 'violent America', 'the youth are out of control' or 'violent media are producing violent school kids', as well as publicising such events globally. A controversial psychiatrist, Dr Park Dietz, suggested news guidelines to avoid unintentional 'glamorising' of such events:

1  Don't start the story with sirens blaring
2  Don't use photos of the killer(s)
3  Don't make it 24/7 coverage
4  Do everything you can to avoid making body count the main story
5  Don't make the killer some kind of anti-hero ('dressed in black', etc.)
6  Give details to the affected, local community.

Make it as *boring* as possible to every other community.

---

## EXPLORE 12.6

See http://www.Journalism.org for more, including questions (adapted here) for trainee journalists:

- Under what circumstances should you withhold information or pictures once you have them? What issues should be weighed in that decision?
- How does a newsroom handle interviewing live eyewitnesses, especially 'juveniles' on TV or mobile phones, when they may spontaneously say something that's inaccurate, or that could put others, including themselves, in danger?

---

3 *Proximity* or the closeness of an item to the perceived values of the audiences for the headquarters of that news institution. This is now complicated by the international flows of news material. But even so major traders of news, such as CNN, PA, Reuter's, trading news as a commodity, 'slant' the choice and construction of items, etc. to perceptions of the various national markets or 'territories' which they sell it in. This, increasingly, includes entertainment items involving stardom and celebrity.

See the Global Forum for Media Development at http://www.gfmd. info/ for a counterpoint to the well-known tendency of 'Western' news to require a huge disaster 'abroad' in order for it to 'make the news', compared with much smaller events closer to 'home'.

4 *Negativity*. 'If it's news, it's bad news' – long-term, constructive events are said to be much less likely to feature as news than a catastrophe or images of violence. News does use 'positive' stories (e.g. medical breakthroughs), usually as the 'happy ending' of some bulletins. But generally it tends to take the assumed normal and everyday for granted. It is driven to make big stories out of the deviant: crime, dissidence, disaster. Again, Galtung and Ruge have been accused of ignoring local news in this formulation (though their article was focused on foreign news coverage).

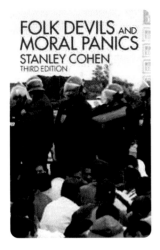

*Figure 12.6* The latest edition of Cohen's controversial and influential book.

'. . . it's interesting . . . not only have the public lost all faith in the media; not only do so many people assume, now, that they are being misled; but more than that, the media themselves have lost all confidence in their own ability to give us the facts.' Goldacre .

These comments are available on http://www. guardian.co.uk/commentis free/2009/apr/29/swine-flu-hype.

An earlier, and still powerful term, is 'moral panic', developed by Stan Cohen, Jock Young, and then Stuart Hall and his CCCS (Centre for Contemporary Cultural Studies, Birmingham, UK) colleagues in the 1970s, around 'mods and rockers', 'mugging' and other news constructions of (male) deviant groups. Moral panics could thereby be ignited to create public support for the need to 'police a crisis'. It includes the 'deviancy amplification spiral' in which news media overreact to an aspect of behaviour (which may indeed be seen as a challenge to existing social norms). The media response to and representation of that behaviour actually help to define it, communicate it and portray it as a model for outsiders to observe and adopt. Thus the media panic, arguably, fuels further socially unacceptable behaviour, which is in turn prominently represented in the media.

## EXPLORE 12.7

- Research coverage and construction of the panic around what was variously called Mexican pig flu, H1N1 flu, etc. before 'swine flu' was settled on (and see **MSB5 website** for a case study from a New Zealand perspective). Does it still fit Cohen's idea of a 'spiral'?
- Read *The Guardian*'s science correspondent Ben Goldacre (http://www.guardian.co.uk/commentisfree/2009/apr/29/swine-flu-hype) on how reporters invited him to dismiss it as 'hype', and outlining the complexity of the risk calculations involved. See also Simon Tisdall (http://www.guardian.co.uk/commentisfree/2009/apr/30/swine-flu-media1) on the opportunity it provided to various governments to 'bury bad news'.
- Assess their points. How did you and those close to you experience the first parts of the panic? What other attitudes to it did you come across in news or internet forms?

5  *Predictability*. News is assumed, by common sense, to consist of unusual, random events 'out there'. Yet much time is spent (at editorial conferences, etc.) trying to anticipate what is assumed to be 'newsworthy', and deciding where to employ expensive, and often highly endangered, overseas-based staff and equipment. Or, if a particular turn (say, 'violence') to events is expected, the drive will be to place reporters according to those expectations, and thereby amplify them.

Relatedly, events classified as 'news' are often known about weeks and months ahead – or years in advance for conferences, anniversaries, annual reports, sporting events, book or film launches and so on. 'The news should really be called the olds,' as someone once put it. Some newspapers even publish 'diaries' for the week ahead.

---

**EXPLORE 12.8**

- Research the anniversaries commemorated (or forgotten) in a day's news, sometimes by special invitations to bloggers and texters. Note how much space they take.
- Research what other anniversaries could have been covered. What values or ideologies are connected with/confirmed by the ones actually chosen?

---

Other kinds of events, and risks, such as famines, or the long-term effects of pesticides, are also predictable. But they are not usually part of the diary, since it's said they cannot be 'dated' or 'by the time the pictures are horrific enough to move people, it is almost too late', as one journalist put it. Where there are big but steadily present 'domestic' issues, such as unemployment, rape statistics or homelessness, there's a feeling that, though they go on happening, the journalist cannot keep on writing the same story. S/he looks for a 'twist', perhaps a way of personalising or even sensationalising it, or simply leaves it as 'not news'.

6 *Continuity*. If an event is defined by the powerful news companies as big enough, resources will be diverted to it for some time. Often even 'non-events' which seem part of that story will be covered: 'The bystander injured in climate change protests is recovering consciousness.'

7 *Composition*. Galtung and Ruge (1981) argued that 'stories' will be selected and arranged according to the editor's sense of the balance of the whole bulletin, or page. If many home stories have been used, then even a fairly unimportant 'foreign' one may be included. This 'news value' has been for some time challenged by 24-hour news, as well as Web 2.0 blogs and the existence of other news sources located in non-Western countries.

8 *Personalisation*. Wherever possible, events are seen as the actions of people as individuals, and more than that, news is usually *elite centred*. This runs all the way from endless shots of politicians getting in and out of cars (respectable 'personalisation'), through 'celebrity gossip and

Such terms (hard news, soft news) are arguably gendered, and can be seen as part of the ideological work of assuming, until fairly recently, that major news positions should be inaccessible to women. See Chambers *et al.* (2004) and also the Global Media Monitoring Project, cited above.

See Chapter 2 for more discussion and examples of these processes.

*Figure 12.7* A webcam was put into the BBC Radio 4's 'flagship' *Today* morning news programme, 2009. Why do you think this visualisation was made?

scandal', to child cruelty cases being put on the agenda by 'Baby P', used as a typical, dramatising, even if anonymous, case.

9 *Entertainment*. Despite the perception of news as 'hard' and 'factual', it usually contains an element of entertainment, from 'jokey' or gossipy tone, or freakish stories, through to the literal coverage of the entertainment industries, stars and celebrities. The proportion of this to 'serious news' will vary in different kinds of news media. In a further twist, 'serious' news, such as famines, are almost guaranteed coverage if stars are charitably involved, though on much debated terms (see Cottle 2009 and Chapter 11).

Three other areas of the construction of news deserve mention: *narrativisation* (which Galtung and Ruge list), *probable consequences* and *visual imperatives*.

- *Narrativisation*: items are from the start called 'stories' and, if long-running, they are shaped into narrative form, in which we expect a happy, or at least a 'neat', ending. War, and now often 'terrorism' coverage, draws on an existing repertoire from Second World War narratives, seen as about the last 'virtuous' modern war.

- *Probable consequences* refers to the selection of stories because they are likely to affect many people (tax increases, prices rises, wars, etc.). It's worth adding that the idea of 'probable' has been especially stretched in the case of recent stories about 'terrorism' and crimes; that, globally, coverage of famines and enforced diasporas are underreported; and that there's usually a capital-city-centred and 'official politics'-centred view of what will affect citizens.

- *Visual imperatives* are said to be especially important in TV news, and by implication for citizen journalism. They drive towards stories that have 'strong' pictures, whether of celebrities, 'biblical-looking' famines or scenes which resemble a blockbuster film, as in people fleeing from the explosions at the World Trade Center in 2001 or the 2004 tsunami. Increasingly, if wars are heavily censored, or inaccessible to picture technology, computer-aided graphics are used to give a sense of what might be happening. This is part of the re-mediation of a story, entering other media, but nevertheless the idea of visual imperatives deserves further consideration. For example:
  - Radio's agenda is very similar to TV's, although it cannot operate 'visual imperatives'. Why this similar agenda, if the visual is so important to news?
  - Television or press stories which lack pictures but are deemed important use computer-aided graphics to assist visualisation. Photographs do not always 'lead'.
  - 'Less newsworthy' stories, or ones involved with complex long-term

processes, are rarely helped in this way, though they could be, and sometimes are, within quality journalism. Again, so-called 'visual imperatives' tend to follow, not lead, existing news priorities.

1 'Soundbites' or vivid short phrases used over and over again in coverage of some stories ('the war on terror'; 'the credit crunch'; 'broken Britain'; 'social exclusion'; 'climate change'; 'the market dictates') could be argued to be at least as important as 'visuals' in shaping perceptions of news.
2 However powerful the photos taken by citizen journalists (CJs) or citizen photographers (CPs) on mobile phones, etc., they will always depend on words, and political struggle, to discover their context, why the events they record took place, and how to deploy the photos in political and legal contexts.
3 An important part of the study of news has been its language. Fairclough's (1995) critical discourse analysis approach, for example, allows us to explore wider issues of the drip-drip, day-by-day, tiny ways in which words, and the ways the news scripts position us, come to shape and solidify frames and interpretations of news (see Chapters 6 and 15). For example:

- The use of 'we', 'us' and 'them' in news language; the sense of where is 'here' and where 'somewhere foreign'.
- Why are military commanders called 'warlords' in the 'Third World' (including recent histories of Bosnia) but 'chiefs of staff' in the West?
- Why is the term 'defence budget' never queried? US arms expenditure ($651 billion in 2009), for example, is hugely bigger than those of its nearest 'competitors' and it's hard to imagine who might invade it, or threaten it with conventional weapons (see Lewis 2001).

> There is another meaning – the short passages selected from politicians' speeches for direct quotation. Academics researching this in the US argued that in the past forty years, the length has dropped by forty seconds. A president with complex messages to communicate may well find this difficult. See Sonia Livingstone on the challenges for academics trying to make thoughtful contributions to news discussions within 'soundbite' cultures of journalism, in Chapter 8, p. 243.

## EXPLORE 12.9

- Explore as many of these 'news values' as you can for today's news media, whether on- or offline. How would you rank them for importance, for different news sources?
- How have internet and citizen journalist (CJ) and video journalist (VJ) forms impacted?

## Debates on the influence of news

Herman and Chomsky (1988) also argue that (US) news is 'slanted', though they use a political economy approach, suggesting five filters which structure it towards the already dominant: ownership; funding; reliance on government or business as sources; 'flak'; and norms shared by news professionals.

British news studies were pioneered, from the 1970s onwards, by the Glasgow University Media Group (GUMG). They argued that news is constructed along ideological lines, usually ones friendly to the already powerful. GUMG investigated coverage of strikes (e.g. the so-called 'winter of discontent' of 1978–9, with images endlessly replayed in the years since, whenever public sector workers threatened strike action) and war stories (the Falklands). Much has changed in the news landscape since the 1970s, when the only two UK broadcasters, BBC and ITN, claimed enormous authority for themselves through their 'flagship' news programmes. GUMG interpreted stories through more polarised (split into only two sides) perspectives than would now be the case. There is now more awareness of how gender, ethnicity, religions, sexualities shape news – even wars and strikes. Meanwhile, class has arguably become a complex but often unspoken, or even hidden area (see Chapter 6).

More modest claims are now made for the influence of *particular news bulletins* (closely studied by GUMG) as opposed to broader kinds of influence, given that:

 **UGC** (user-generated content) refers to stories, views, pictures and other kinds of 'content' which are communicated to a news organisation from its users, usually via a website or mobile phone technology. See Claire Wardle's case study on **MSB5 website**.

- official or professional news forms are now joined by 'unofficial' or 'amateur' forms, such as citizen journalists (CJs), and user-generated content (UGC);
- '24/7 news' operates across a range of 'platforms', languages and cultures.

All of this makes it more difficult to suggest the huge influence of particular reports, though

a   the big news distributors and agencies (BBC, CNN, AP, Reuters) remain powerful;

b   they are most often the originating source for the opinions expressed in the blogs and 'user-generated content' (UGC) section of news organisations' websites;

 For more on such webs of ownership see Chapter 7 and 9 and **MSB5 website** as well as http://www.motherjones.com, www.cjr.org.resources and Nordicom's research.

c   'news' is often constructed and distributed by the same powerful conglomerates (such as News Corporation) which construct, own and distribute so many of the other meaning-making resources of global cultures, including fiction.

Though news programmes may not directly affect audience beliefs, many would argue that they can hugely *influence* audiences and politicians, if only by their selection of items for inclusion as 'news', or by the ways they set up issues and encourage them to be 'framed', discussed and understood. A mention of an issue in news forms may often give the 'green light' to current affairs and investigative documentary teams. And news seems still able to set the agenda of issues which we may find ourselves thinking about.

A conventional sense of 'news values' may also shape the ways professional reporters will filter and generally treat the blogs and twitters and other comment coming to them from users. They (rightly) experience huge pressures not to circulate racist, sexist or illegal kinds of abuse, etc. But they also have a sense of what will 'sell' or circulate, as 'acceptable' news stories and comment, and what 'should' be ignored.

'Isn't it amazing that the amount of news that happens in the world everyday always just exactly fits the newspaper?' (Guardian Unlimited ad, 2001).

Agenda: a list of items to be discussed at a meeting, usually drawn up by the person chairing it, who arranges them in what they perceive to be the order of importance. For news, terms such as 'agenda setting' and 'hidden agenda' draw attention to the importance of this power to frame and channel audiences' attention, discussions and often fears.

Gatekeeping: a related term, imagining news as flowing through a gate which is closed for rejected items and opened for chosen ones. The concept is criticised for not being sufficiently open to contemporary, more fluid news processes.

Framing: shaping and setting the limits to how audiences are invited to perceive certain groups, issues, stories. A good example, not limited to news, is the emphasis on a nation's 'budget deficit' as meaning that drastic cutbacks to government spending are necessary.

This could be framed very differently. Others, including Nobel Prize-winning economists, argue that a national economy is not like a household budget, needing to rush to pay bills. For most of the years of the British empire the deficit was higher than in 2009. Spending to try to get out of recession is much more urgent.

News is still hugely powerful, though sometimes in unexpected ways. Elizabeth Noelle-Neumann (1993), writing on the influence of opinion polls, suggested the capacity of some news coverage of some issues to encourage silence. Those already confident of sharing majority opinion voice their views, while those who do not conform fall silent. She called this a 'spiral of silence'. It could be related to the use of well-reported polls in news, often able to solidify the preferred meaning of events by suggesting a supposed overwhelming 'majority view' of them (see Lewis et al. 2005). The reporting of shock celebrity deaths, such as those of Diana, Princess of Wales (1997) or

This theory was severely criticised in the 1990s, partly because of Noelle-Neumann's political views, said to colour her research. Wikipedia outlines the debates.

Michael Jackson (2009), often excludes voices saying they were not particularly moved, or that they were even annoyed by the scale of news coverage. Blogs, etc. offer this opportunity – but how are they represented in the main news?

One area of developing debate is how far the control of news agendas is changed by internet news forms. The term 'news aggregator' is used of websites or search engines that select, retrieve and link news from the net.

## EXPLORE 12.10

- Make a note of a day's major news headlines. If you are interested in news, do they affect what you and your friends talk about, i.e. have they 'set the agenda' for your talk?
- Note the headlines two weeks later. Do you wonder what has happened to stories which, in the earlier agenda, seemed important?
- Are any panicking headlines now in conflict with the previous ones? (For example, a 2009 British media panic about 'Baby P' and negligent social services was followed, a few months later, by a ferocious tabloid campaign against record checks on unknown adults working with children.)
- How did these earlier stories recede into 'less important' status?
- Compare any mainstream TV news channel with Google News. What features do they share? What are the main differences? Do they share agendas?

## EXPLORE 12.11

- Can you think of a recent news phenomenon which you experienced as being greeted by a 'spiral of silence' around certain views?
- The death of Jade Goody? Of Michael Jackson? A decision to go to war? Or perhaps to mobilise a local regiment?

## Futures: 'new' news?

It has been argued that news values are 'professionalised', that you must acquire them in order
- to become a journalist
- to function effectively as a journalist (which may involve less-formal learning contexts, such as gendered socialising opportunities after work, or learning what is the 'house style' of your paper or radio station).

But 'amateur' news forms (blogs, photos, comments) now impinge on mainstream news suppliers, indeed are actively solicited by them. News is a porous form, and the dividing lines between 'amateur' and 'professional' have always been less clear cut than in some other professions.

This new 'content' can present problems for hard-pressed professional journalists.

a  How should the flood of messages be monitored for legal liability, racist or other offensive content, reliability or accuracy, let alone literacy? Journalism should be characterised by fact checking, but anonymity means that online debates tend to be polarised, and can be highly abusive.

b  Additionally, despite the flood of messages, content is often repetitive, leading to an 'echo chamber' effect.

c  How can this 'monitoring' work (often involving rewriting) be paid for, given the loss of jobs, cutbacks and further concentrations of ownership in the centres of the industry?

d  Journalists facing this blizzard of UGC (along with regular PR and other handouts) are still expected to produce more and more 'news'. Arguably this augments a reliance on 'tried and trusted' official sources which won't risk libel action, and are often already written.

e  Frenzied circulation and ratings wars, along with the possibilities of new technologies, have accelerated news forms' emphasis on speed, rather than reliability. The Iranian election protests of 2009 arguably made journalists realise again the role of the 'trusted guide' within a potential 'Wild West' of speeding rumours, untrustworthy or uninformed reports. But it takes real nerve to hold back when other news organisations are reporting apparently big stories ('First with the news!'), often with less checking and therefore reliability.

f  There are signs that journalists are developing professional values to cope with this, slightly dismissive of much user content as 'chaff', which has to be searched for the few grains of 'wheat' (eyewitness accounts and photos, tip-offs, and work for case studies which the newsroom may be making).

> Political pranksters such as The Yes Men have been as inventive as Michael Moore in the ways they have played with this reliance on trusted corporate briefings. See Chapter 13 for more.

> See http://reportr.net/2009/09/09/how-the-bbc-views-ugc-as-newsgathering/ for a summary of Cardiff University research on the BBC's use of and attitude to such content.

## EXPLORE 12.12

- Go to http://www.bbc.co.uk/guidelines/futuremedia/interactivity/communities.shtml to see how the BBC is trying to shape, frame and regulate this area. What problems does it face?
- How successful do you think these guidelines will be?

Arguably demonstrations deserve to be seen as part of public opinion. But Lewis *et al.* (2005: 25) cite recent evidence that they are the least commonly referenced form of expression of public opinion on TV news – less that 3 per cent of a British sample, and 2 per cent of a US sample. Research for your own news forms?

Slightly different to UGC (which despite its name actually often responds to rather than initiates 'content') are the contributions and organisations of 'citizen journalists'. These range from occasional images taken, say, on demonstrations (often not even by demonstrators), through to political campaigners and local coverage. Indymedia (http://www.indymedia.org), for example, is a global 'network of individuals, independent and alternative media activists and organisations, offering grassroots, non-corporate, non-commercial coverage of important social and political issues'. There are inspiring examples of alternative media forms which have been occasionally drawn on for news reports, such as http://www.riverbend-blogspot.com with its accounts of daily life in Baghdad under and after coalition occupation, or http://www.bringthemhomenow.org started by US troops and their families.

'**Sousveillance**' (a term coined by Canadian academic Steve Mann) dramatises the difference between 'top-down' and 'from-below' surveillance. It signifies

a   inverse surveillance, i.e. watching from below;

b   the recording of an event (e.g. a demo) by one of the participants instead of the expected 'outside' or official camera crew – sometimes literally placed 'above' the demo, or behind police or even army lines.

  See *Burma VJ: Reporting from a Closed Country* (Denmark 2008), mentioned in Chapter 5. This is a powerful undercover account of the monks' attempted revolution in 2007, made by amateur video journalists (VJs), a form of citizen journalism (CJ), and smuggled out of a repressive state, which strictly controls internet access.

Huge claims are made for these new kinds of journalism, and they, along with some UGC, could indeed be a vibrant source for different kinds of news, or of democratic forms.

*Figure 12.8* A child whose body is covered in lesions. According to the child's parents, the skin condition was caused by toxic waste. Trafigura disputes its role in this.

In October 2009 the editor of *The Guardian*, Alan Rusbridger, wrote about Trafigura, a London-based trading company accused of dumping toxic sludge in one of the poorest African countries, Ivory Coast. The company's lawyers, Carter-Ruck, sent many threatening letters to news agencies, launched an action against the BBC, and persuaded a judge to suppress a confidential but embarrassing document. The term 'super-injunction' signalled the making secret of court proceedings and court orders themselves. Rusbridger wrote:

an MP, Paul Farrelly, had tabled a question about the injunction and the awkward document in parliament . . . with . . . 300-odd years of precedent affirming the right of the press to report whatever MPs say or do . . .

And then there was Twitter . . . At five past nine I tapped: *'Now Guardian prevented from reporting parliament for unreportable reasons. Did John Wilkes live in vain?'* . . . 104 characters . . . By the time I got home . . . the Twittersphere had gone into meltdown. Twitterers had sleuthed down Farrelly's question, published the relevant links and were now seriously on the case. By midday on Tuesday 'Trafigura' was one of the most searched terms in Europe, helped along by re-tweets by Stephen Fry and his 830,000-odd followers.

Many tweeters were registering support or outrage, others were searching for suppressed information and obscure legislation. Common #hashtags were quickly developed, making the material easily discoverable. By lunchtime – an hour before *The Guardian* team were due in court – Trafigura threw in the towel.

> See http://www.guardian.co.uk/commentisfree/libertycentral/2009/oct/14/trafigura-fiasco-tears-up-textbook for the full article.

> These #hashtags are used to identify potential niche markets or users via groups of 'tweets' on Twitter or entries on Facebook. See www.techforluddites.com for one explanation.

### EXPLORE 12.13

- Research this story and see how many mixed sources and kinds of activist are involved.
- 'Crowd sourcing'? Maybe, though, these crowds have very knowledgeable 'guides', and a very specific sense of 'speed' and urgency. Part of the story goes all the way back to John Wilkes, of whom Rusbridger wrote: '(a) nod in passing to the memory of John Wilkes, the scabrous hack and MP who risked his life to win the right to report parliament. An 18th-century version of crowd-sourcing played its part in that, too.'

> When told by a voter that he would rather vote for the devil, Wilkes responded: 'Naturally' and added: 'And if your friend decides against standing, can I count on your vote?'

## Conclusion

We have summarised the ways in which perceptions of news (and of 'the public') are constructed, or even partly manufactured, by the assumptions built into news framing, 'gathering' and distribution.

The whole area now faces several crises:

- the decline in circulation of newspapers and cuts in employment of journalists and reporters;

*Figure 12.9* Journalists often encounter state violence. See responses to the murder of the Russian journalist Anna Politkovskaya in 2007. (Photo from a silent demonstration to protest against her murder and see also http://www.indexoncensorship. org/.)

Radio also plays a part, and it is suggested that local news has slightly growing audiences. See RAJAR (http://www.rajar.co.uk), the official radio audience measurement site, and, as before, http://www.amarc. org/wccd/index.php on global community media initiatives, especially radio.

- the decline in advertising revenue, much of it now available free online. Advertising has previously funded all except either part-privately financed news outlets (like Al Jazeera or The Huffington Post) or public service news (such as the BBC's).

These, and changes in the culture of audiences more widely (such as the demands on attention in a media-saturated environment, and on time, during people's attempts to survive a recession), pose a key question: who is going to pay for, and demand, serious reporting, on which many news sources, 'old' and 'new', draw, and comment, and on which democracies, and our activities within them as full citizens, depend?

There seems to be a crisis of authority or trust in news, and in forms of authority more broadly, which is not limited to 'tabloid' forms. News, especially at senior levels, is usually enmeshed with other forms of power. There have been shocking recent examples of the failure of many reporters to challenge official versions of events such as the decisions to invade Afghanistan and Iraq, or to question bankers' versions of how sustainable was the 'bubble' of the US housing market (see http://www.cjr.org). Equally there are examples of heroic journalism across the world. In the UK recently journalists were able, by a mixture of investigative and cheque book forms, to crack open a huge UK Parliamentary expenses scandal in 2009. And some internet news websites contributed in innovative ways to the election of Barack Obama.

We have tried to deconstruct, via an updated account of 'news values', the grander claims to 'objectivity', or 'being the first draft of history', sometimes made by journalism in the past. But we do not want to destroy them as ideals. The aspiration for accuracy, for reliable accounts of the social and political world, is fundamental both to good journalism and to new democratic forms where quality debates and investigations on behalf of all our futures can take place.

## References and further reading

Allan, Stuart (2010) *News Culture*, third edition, Buckingham: Open University Press.

Chambers, Deborah, Steiner, Linda, and Fleming, Carole (2004) *Women and Journalism*, London: Routledge.

Cottle, Simon (2009) *Global Crisis Reporting: Journalism in the Global Age*, London and New York: Open University Press.

Davies, Nick (2008) *Flat Earth News*, London: Chatto and Windus.

Fairclough, Norman (1995) *Media Discourse*, London: Arnold.

Fenton, Natalie (ed.) (2009) *New Media, Old News: Journalism and Democracy in the Digital Age*, London: Sage.

Galtung, J., and Ruge, M. (1981) 'The Structure of Foreign News: The Presentation of the Congo, Cuba and Cyprus Crises in Four Foreign Newspapers', in Cohen, Stan, and Young, Jock (eds) *The Manufacture of News*, London: Constable; first published in 1965.

Gitlin, Tod (2009), 'Journalism's Many Crises', http://www.opendemocracy.net.

Habermas, Jürgen (1989) *The Structural Transformation of the Public Sphere: An Inquiry into a Category of Bourgeois Society*, Cambridge, MA: The MIT Press. First published in German in 1962.

Hall, Stuart (2001) 'Out of a Clear Blue Sky', *Soundings*, no.19 (winter).

Herman, Edward S., and Chomsky, Noam (1988) *Manufacturing Consent: The Political Economy of the Mass Media*, New York: Pantheon.

Jack, Ian (2009) 'The Unstoppable Rise of the Citizen Cameraman', *The Guardian*, 11 April.

Lanchester, John (2008) 'Riots, Terrorism, etc.', *London Review of Books*, 6 March.

Lewis, Justin (2001) *Constructing Public Opinion: How Political Elites Do What They Like and Why We Seem to Go Along with It*, New York: Columbia University Press.

Lewis, Justin, Inthorn, Sanna, and Wahl-Jorgensen, Karin (2005) *Citizens or Consumers: What the Media Tell Us about Political Participation*, London and New York: Open University Press.

Noelle-Neumann, Elizabeth (1993) *The Spiral of Silence*, Chicago: University of Chicago Press.

Philo, Greg, and Berry, Mike (2004) *Bad News from Israel*, London: Pluto Press.

Rusbridger, Alan (2009) 'Trafigura fiasco Tears up Textbook', *The Guardian*, 14 October.

Schlesinger, Philip (1987) *Putting 'Reality' Together*, London: Methuen.

Scraton, Phil (1999) *Hillsborough: The Truth*, Edinburgh: Mainstream.

Sebba, Ann (1994) *Battling for News*, London: Sceptre.

Thompson, John B. (1995) *The Media and Modernity*, London: Polity Press.

# 13 Documentary and 'reality' debates

- Recent issues in documentary
- Documentary and assumptions about 'realism' and truth
- Verisimilitude and 'performance'
- 'Performance' in documentaries
- Ethics and documentary
- Recent hybrids 1: 'pranksters'
- Recent hybrids 2: 'reality TV'
- Recent hybrids 3: forms of 'drama documentary'
- Conclusion
- References and further reading

This chapter explores:

1   the constructedness of documentary, and how it relates to strong perceptions of its 'realism'
2   recent debates, including notions of 'performance', and of hybrid and 'prankster' forms
3   'reality TV' forms
4   different recent examples of drama-documentary.

## Recent issues in documentary

Many TV programmes can be considered 'documentaries' in a traditional sense (accounts of historical events and characters, of current controversies, of investigations, etc.). But there has also been celebration of 'theatrical documentaries' (i.e. those shown in cinemas) in recent years. Some of the most recent ones have been marketed as a blend of the documentary and fictional genres such as the thriller or the heist movie.

See the generic marketing of *Touching the Void* (UK 2003) and *Man on Wire* (UK 2008), especially their DVD covers and internet publicity.

Like everything else in this book, the idea of documentary, and its relation to the rest of the real, has changed in many ways recently, not least because of new, globalised technologies. Changes specific to documentary include:

- the massive cinema success of Michael Moore's recent political documentaries *Bowling for Columbine* (US 2002), *Fahrenheit 9/11* (US 2004) and, with an impact on Obama's presidential victory and the fierce US debates on healthcare, *Sicko* (US 2007). These, among the top six highest-grossing documentaries ever, were, for many, a revelation about the commercial and political potential of the documentary in cinemas as well as on TV;

- interest in 'reality TV' as being related to documentary, and sometimes blamed for documentary's commercial irrelevance; 'reality' shows are seen by many as a corruption of documentary, by others as its reinvention in the twenty-first century;

- what Gilbey (2009) calls 'prankster cinema', as an instance of recent developments at a meeting place of 'documentary, performance art, slapstick and satire';

- less often discussed, perhaps because assumed to involve older audiences and children, is the success of 'nature' or 'wildlife' documentary and spectacular 'planetary survey' blockbuster nature programmes, like BBC's *Blue Planet*;

- finally, hybrid forms, such as drama-documentary, have shown newly complex ways of working drama with documentary and performance.

> See Moore's website for details of his new film, *Capitalism: A Love Story* (2010). The way his work combines TV, film, book and internet presence has been a vital part of his impact.

> See the large audience figures for BBC TV's annual *Springwatch* programmes (BBC 2005–) – also working across media 'platforms' via TV and internet.

## Documentary and assumptions about 'realism' and truth

'Documentary' as a concept is often set up in opposition to 'fiction', and it tends to circulate, be labelled and reviewed, within the powerful binary:

| | |
|---|---|
| *the fictional = lies* | *the factual = truth* |
| entertainment films | documentary and 'realist' films |

This is partly why the form '**drama-documentary**' causes problems for some viewers: it confuses these apparently neat and powerful boundaries.

Actually such a sharp contrast does justice to neither side of the equation. Fiction is assumed to present utterly imaginary beings, places or events. But it is not necessarily unrelated to actuality, not even in its 'Hollywood' forms. Hollywood's representations of issues such as working conditions, contraception, etc. are often evasive, and can seem mainly there to provide a convincing milieu for their central focus: individualised stories of heightened drama. But it's worth reminding ourselves of the 'emotional truths' which some melodrama can embody. And fiction films located near the areas of fact or history, such as 'biopics' or *Hotel Rwanda* (UK/US/Italy/S. Africa 2004) and *Gomorrah* (Italy 2008), have similar obligations as documentary to try for kinds of truthfulness.

> Michael Moore drew on this binary when accepting his 2003 documentary Oscar, in the name of truth: 'we live in fictitious times . . . fictitious election results that elect a fictitious President . . . a man sending us to war for fictitious reasons. We are against this war, Mr Bush.'

See the discussion of 'verisimilitude' in Chapter 3. The concept signals the relation of even the most 'fantastic' film to the rest of (what's perceived as) 'the real'.

'Emotional realism': a term used by Ien Ang (1985), and others later, for a kind of truthfulness to certain emotions. She argued this could be found by some audiences even in glossy, wealth-centred fictions such as *Dallas*.

*Figure 13.1* A still from *The Bicycle Thieves* (Italy 1948), classic Neo-Realism in its very low budget, location shooting, non-professional actors, and 'realist' 'small' story of an unemployed father whose bicycle is stolen (adapted from a novel in this case).

*Snow* (UK 1963; find it on YouTube) could hardly be simpler, a mesmerising short film about a train's journey through the heavy snows of the winter of 1963. But even this is shaped, angled, given form. How?

On the other side, the constructedness of documentary is underestimated, assumed to be a simple matter, just pointing a camera at 'the truth'.

The term 'documentary' is absent from most accounts of genre classifications (e.g. Neale 2000, 2002). But it can be identified by genre-like aspects, which shift, like all classifications. Bordwell and Thompson (2004: 128) defined documentary as a form which 'purports to present factual information about the world outside the film'. It is labelled, classified, framed and, by implication, circulates as such. Like news, documentaries are commonly *seen as* particularly truthful, as being a kind of *trace* off reality, dealing with the 'factual' or 'unconstructed' as far as possible.

There are key differences from fiction films, which usually stage and pre-script their events, and generally use actors, even if they are untrained in the ways of professional acting, as in many post-war Italian Neo-Realist films. But documentaries are constructed, just as any form has to be. They don't simply point a camera at 'the truth' and, hey presto, there's a documentary. Documentarists have a choice of materials from which to shape their film – interviews, recording of events, sound materials (including music and sound FX), documents/evidence like charts, maps, cartoons, and archive footage. Less familiarly they may decide to stage or reconstruct some events, and may make some narrative *shaping* of the film, including necessary decisions about how to shorten, or perhaps emphasise, some parts of it. And throughout, there is the question of how events are framed, 'staged' and then edited – the 'angle' in both senses.

Even before a documentary starts shooting, there is the question of the initial selection of what to film, partly shaped by:

a the conditions under which consent is given or withheld by those that the documentary is to cover;

b and/or what kinds of access can be given by existing technology and resources. Is surveillance-like footage possible because of high-quality mobile cameras? Was the film made in a period when sound technology was not as developed as it is now? How many camera operators seem to have been used?

Below is a historical case study which explores the relationship of technology and access to documentary form. 'Direct Cinema' is one origin of the style of spontaneous-looking hand-held film-making which is most often called 'realist'. We hope to show that even the most 'realistic' documentaries, aspiring to give ordinary people their voices, very close to them in intimate uninterrupted filming, nevertheless have to be constructed.

### 'Direct Cinema'

In the early 1960s a new form of documentary developed in the US, known as **Direct Cinema**. This is sometimes seen as similar to *cinéma vérité* (French for 'cinema truth', and developing around the same time), though is arguably more observational. The modern term is 'fly on the wall' and describes now-fairly standard TV documentary techniques. It's now possible for those with digital and mobile phone technologies to eavesdrop or easily record 'real events' (i.e. ones not specially staged for the camera – such as lectures!). In this it now relates to surveillance forms, such as CCTV cameras around towns, cities and motorways – indeed some low-budget TV programmes are made up of such footage.

---

## EXPLORE 13.1

Where would you like to be a 'fly on the wall'? Select a subject you think would interest an audience, that you could cover with a small camera.

- Where would you place yourself to capture sound and image effectively?
- Could you capture all the material you would need to represent your subject satisfactorily?
- What strategies would you use to ensure that your subjects did not 'perform' for the camera?
- Do you think your subject would 'automatically' produce a story, or might you have to restructure the events in editing?

---

In the 1960s, however, the slogan of this approach to filming was that new techniques were needed in order to 'tell it like it is' about often inaccessible institutions. These techniques were:

- the camera and microphone should be as close to events as possible, with the film or tape running continuously;
- everything that happens was recorded, nothing was rehearsed or scripted; there was no use of voice-over narration or music – all this in order to try to give the subjects of the documentaries their own voice.

Certain technological advances were key for making this possible. The early 1960s saw the first:

- lightweight 16mm film cameras linked to audio recorders for synchronised sound, and

'Direct Cinema' film-makers included Robert Drew, Richard Leacock, the Maysles brothers, D. A. Pennebaker and Frederick Wiseman. Very few women either directed or were used as the central subject of these films. Today there are a number of distinguished female documentarists, such as Kim Longinotto.

See what clips you can find on the internet from Wiseman's films, including *Titicut Follies*. What difficulties did you encounter?

- film stocks sensitive enough to provide reasonable monochrome picture quality under most lighting conditions, including small hand-held lights. Unencumbered by large heavy equipment, the documentary crews were ready to go almost anywhere – and they did, covering rock concerts, high schools, presidential primaries and even a Massachusetts state asylum in Frederick Wiseman's film *Titicut Follies* (US 1967) which, however, was banned from being shown until 1992, partly because of the ethical issues of personal privacy which it raised, but also because of its portrayal of the appalling treatment of the inmates.

The pioneers of such work had three main problems:

- gaining access both to unobtrusive equipment and to permission to enter the institutions (schools, hospitals, etc.) they wanted to explore;
- avoiding causing their subjects to 'play to the cameras' or perform;
- deciding how to reduce the hours of footage to a reasonable length for audiences while avoiding a particular editorial position.

The problem of subjects who 'played to the camera' and therefore behaved 'unnaturally' was partly avoided by selecting subjects for whom 'playing to an audience' was simply part of their usual behaviour. Politicians (the Kennedys) were followed by performers of various kinds (Bob Dylan and the Rolling Stones). The issues of performance more broadly continued to be important for documentary – see below.

A major problem, especially for Wiseman's documentaries from inside institutions, was that the crew needed to spend long enough with the subjects, filming constantly, for them to begin to feel that the crew were 'part of the furniture' (an issue affecting 'performance'). When it came to the editing stage, though, there were miles of film to sift through. The question of how to edit those, and how that then shaped what had been filmed, became crucial. It is often said that these documentaries were not conventionally scripted, but were scripted in the editing suite.

The term '**shooting ratio**' is useful here, indicating the ratio of footage shot to footage actually included in the final edited product. So a shooting ratio of 30:1 (not uncommon for this type of film) would mean that thirty hours were shot for a one hour film, indicating a high degree of editorial shaping.

## Verisimilitude and 'performance'

All this relates to powerful assumptions about 'realism' or what we call 'verisimilitude'. It's always interesting to note *when* people describe media as 'realistic'. The term is often used about films like *Gomorrah* (Italy 2008) or *United 93* (US 2006) or Ken Loach's work. One, or both, of the following areas are usually involved:

- controversial subject matter, such as the southern Italian mafia for *Gomorrah* or, for Loach, trade union and other kinds of British working-class experience. Such attempts to represent that which is rarely represented are often identified *in themselves* as 'realist', however stylised the films themselves may be;
- a shooting style often simulating the jostled, hand-held shakiness which used to be a guarantee of the authenticity of news or documentary footage – the camera operator had to 'snatch' it, sometimes in the face of armed official hostility. Loach is known for not telling his actors what will happen in key scenes, so they look surprised. And the moment when someone speaks off camera, and the camera then has to turn apparently awkwardly towards them, as though caught off-guard, is another way of evoking a 'live' authenticity.

> Reread the discussion on verisimilitude in the Chapter 3 if needed.

> The same is true of other media forms. 'Punk' music was often praised for its 'realism', and this was said to consist of both subject matter and also use of basic chords and instruments, simple lyrics, shouts, groans, 'unpolished' voices, etc.

## EXPLORE 13.2

Think of the last time you called a TV programme or film 'very realistic'.

- Jot down what was it about that text which made you call it realistic – the subject matter? The way it was shot, lit, acted? A 'roughness'? Did the mascara run?
- Was the ending an unhappy one, in a genre where that is not expected?

Take notes on how and why friends or reviewers seem to use the term.

A striking example of this borrowing was the sitcom-drama-documentary-style series *The Office* (BBC 2001–3) – 95 per cent scripted but making unsettling use of awkward, reality TV-style camera work, pauses and silences, as well as 'the furtive, meaningful and unmet glances across the emotional gulf of the open-plan office' (see Amazon.co.uk).

The less polished a fiction film or a piece of TV looks to be, the more credible or 'realistic' it is often taken to be. Nowadays the codes of such 'realism' may mimic or involve mobile phone or surveillance camera footage. A much earlier classic example of the 'roughness' that's taken for

*Figure 13.2* Look at the Zapruder footage on YouTube for this work. See also the episode of the third series of the US TV series *Mad Men* (2010) which suggests how this event might have been experienced by different viewers.

'truth' is the footage accidentally recording US President J. F. Kennedy's assassination, taken by a bystander in 1963 and known by his name: the Zapruder footage. Stella Bruzzi (2005) uses this to emphasise how powerful is the sense that 'the truth' about the assassination can be found in these images. She contrasts this with the factual accuracy of the film – not the same thing, since a truth often seeks to go beyond 'the facts' to an interpretation. The Zapruder footage does indeed give us a genuine 'trace' of a historic event, facts if you like. But it's a step too far to assume that the film's roughness or accidentalness is a guarantee of 'truth' – i.e. that it will show you who killed Kennedy and why.

Sure, its rawness, date of making and preserved, 'amateur' status strongly suggest it has not been constructed – in the edit suite, digitally, by special lighting, expert camera operating, etc. It is striking historical evidence. But to show us more of the key truths about this assassination a camera would have had to be pointing the other way, towards the gunman or gunmen. As Bruzzi writes, using a contrast between fact and 'truth', 'the Zapruder film is factually accurate, it is not a fake, but it cannot reveal the motive or cause for the action it shows' (2005: 430).

See the trailer on YouTube for a flavour of the film.

The recent film *Burma VJ: Reporting from a Closed Country* (2009), made undercover by amateur video journalists or VJs, documents life inside totalitarian Burma, and in particular the 'Saffron Revolution' by monks in 2007. 'Film them all! So many! So many!' calls one marcher, and the camera pans up to balconies and rooftops crammed with cheering protesters – a moving scene, especially in view of the brutal crushing of the uprising. The whole film demonstrates the 'evidence-ness' of rough camera work and choppy editing which we're so used to seeing 'faked' or constructed. But the *reliability* of such a hard won 'look' as truthful includes which distribution networks were used, the reputation of the director, and of the VJs themselves, as well as comparison of the footage with news coverage and other analyses of the politics of Burma. It is possible to make faked images of such scenes; but their 'look' is not the only guarantee of their authenticity.

So, although rough and authentic footage retains a huge fascination, as seeming a kind of 'trace' off events, we should not mistake that for an unlocking of the door to 'the whole truth'. Indeed, there is now much more scepticism about whether a single truth or explanation of *any* complex event can be enough for adequate understanding. If the leap from 'this looks real' to 'this shows the truth' is impossible to make in the case of the Zapruder film, how much more careful should we be when presented with other footage, which may have been deliberately constructed to look rough and real?

## 'Performance' in documentaries

Bruzzi sums up questions of performance:

> [we need to] simply accept that a documentary can never be the real world, that the camera can never capture life as it would have unravelled had it [the camera] not interfered, and the results of this collision between apparatus and subject are what constitutes a documentary . . . documentaries are performative acts whose truth comes into being only at the moment of filming.
>
> (Bruzzi 2000: 6, 7)

Bruzzi's use of the term 'performative' and 'performance' is striking since these terms are present in many areas of media, and life more generally. Let's put them into context. Bill Nichols, in his influential writings on documentary during the 1980s and 1990s, developed a classification of what he called 'documentary modes' (Nichols 1991):

- *expository* – characterised by the soundtrack's 'voice of authority' and a general attempt to present a fixed meaning about the 'reality' that is represented (still present in some wildlife programmes such as *Blue Planet*, and current affairs documentaries, like *Panorama*);
- *observational* – the 'fly on the wall' approach, as in Direct Cinema;
- *interactive* – the presence of the documentarist is represented in the film, 'selection' of material is foregrounded;
- *reflexive* – the process of film-making is not only represented but 'interrogated' so that the reflexive documentary is as much about 'making a documentary' as about the ostensible subject material (see the work of Errol Morris, such as *S.O.P. (Standard Operating Procedure)* (US 2008) about torture in Abu Ghraib).

Bruzzi (2000: 2) argued that this suggested that documentary practice is a simple linear progression, from 'primitive' expository documentaries of the 1930s to a supposedly more modern 'reflexive' mode. She, by contrast, identified 'reflexive' practice as early as in the 1920s films of Dziga Vertov. On the other hand, she points to the continued use, even now, of 'voice-over' and other forms of controlled narration. Both of these suggest a far from simple 'progression' from one stage to another.

She also identifies a major problem with the polarisation of discussion about documentary. Some believe that technology will one day allow the 'perfect' representation of reality, and others argue that reality can

See Chapter 15 for ways in which this can be applied to interview situations. Interviewees are sometimes faced with questions that they may never have thought about, but in answering them they sometimes produce discoveries about themselves.

As well as denoting 'fiction' here, 'performance' often has slightly negative connotations. Children are told not to 'make such a performance' if they are 'acting up'.

**'Performance' in documentaries**

French film critic **André Bazin** ((1918–58) argued that film's 'automatic' origins in ...ography resembled ...of a death mask, a ...the real. But, at the ...essay on this, he ...other hand. ...is also a ...(7) What ...?

...esented in an objective way (and that, therefore, all ...'fail'). Bruzzi contends that 'the spectator is not in need ...inverted commas to understand that a documentary is a ...een reality on the one hand and image, interpretation ...her' (Bruzzi 2000: 4).

...ity' is a fifth 'mode' that Nichols introduced in the ...*erformative*'. Bruzzi sees Nichols as viewing ...ively, e.g. in Direct Cinema, because it reduces ...at performance more positively, in the work of ...emselves become performers in their films (e.g. ..., Michael Moore). In performing their role, she suggests, ...ocumentarist does not *disguise* the process of selecting from reality, but instead '*performs it*' for the camera. It is as though the film-maker says to the audience: 'Look, I'm trying to make an objective statement, but this is what happens when I do', rather than pretending the film could 'eavesdrop' on the real, which could be utterly unaffected by the process of 'documenting'. Even earlier documentaries, which might not seem to reveal the process of construction, were not necessarily taken as 'unconstructed' by their audiences, she suggests.

A related aspect of performance is the more specialised notion of 'performativity'. This emphasises how 'performance' has its own surprises, such that documentaries don't simply document a 'real' which stays still while it is documented. They are 'performative acts whose truth comes into being only at the moment of filming' (Bruzzi 2000: 6).

Theatre and film 'performance' involve the 'performed' rather than written text. But the props of performance (costume, make-up) can, in ordinary life, change experiences of identity.

### EXPLORE 13.3

- Have you ever had to perform a role – perhaps for work? Has this produced surprises, or meant you did things you did not imagine possible?
- Have you had the experience of performing a role which involved, for example, uniforms ('costume') or maybe even a different voice (telephone work)? Was this merely a role or did you partly 'become' that role via the props, and the ways in which you were treated?

An unpleasant recent kind of 'performativity' was the phenomenon of 'happy slapping' (making unprovoked attacks on people on the street in order to record the encounter, and especially the victim's shock or surprise, on a mobile phone). In March 2008 a 15-year-old girl, who filmed on her mobile a man being kicked and punched to death, was successfully prosecuted for aiding and abetting manslaughter. She was not simply 'recording' an event: her filming helped bring that event into being – a 'performative' act.

Finally, the work of Adam Curtis, loosely classified as somewhere between 'documentary' and 'art film', crafts together often rare film and news clips, music and occasional commentary to produce very striking hybrid films. Here the invisible director is 'performer' or 'author', raising intriguing challenges to 'reliability' and 'evidence'.

See *It Felt Like a Kiss* (2009) http://www.bbc.co.uk/blogs/ adamcurtis. His work began in the BBC, which currently shows this shortish film on its website.
Q: How would you classify it? Documentary? Art film? Rhetorical argument of an exotic kind?

## Ethics and documentary

Questions of ethics and documentary (mentioned in the reception of *Titicut Follies*) have existed throughout the history of documentary. Ethics is the study and practice of morality or behaviour which is 'good' or 'right'. You will come across it in the rules for any research you undertake, and in the way you are expected to conduct academic work such as interviews, acknowledging sources, etc.

For documentary it entails the responsibility of such forms, taken to be *factually* accurate, to be as *truthful* as possible, given that there may be disputing definitions of the truths of complex situations. Another way of seeing this is that they have a duty to contribute to the 'public sphere' which aspires to enable safe and robust debate, conducted in rational and morally responsible ways, as objectively as is possible (see Chapters 5, 10, 12 and 14 for more on theories of the 'public sphere').

There are two main ethical concerns for documentary practice:

1  Film's capacity, from its 1890s beginnings, to 'fake' material and therefore to be misleading. A famous early 'documentary' example: Robert Flaherty's *Nanook of the North* (1922) involved staging a walrus hunt, even though the Inuit had long since stopped walrus-hunting; constructing a special igloo with one wall removed so that an Inuit family could be filmed, in daylight, pretending to go to bed; and so on. The possibilities of faking material, both still and moving, with digital technologies are now even more easily available. They raise ethical issues around the attempt at truthfulness which has, until now, been one of documentary's prime ambitions.

Georges Méliès (1861–1938), a magician by training, and an early film-maker, said to have discovered by chance the 'special effects' created by stop trick, multiple exposures, etc. See YouTube extracts from his short films.

*Figure 13.3* Tom Hanks in *Forrest Gump* (US 1994) apparently meets President Kennedy (died 1963) in a film using digital special effects.

The 'right of final edit', or to say what is and is not to be included in the finished, edited version of a film, whether documentary or fiction, is highly prized. It is rarely given to anyone but the producing studio or company.

The full original article can be accessed at http://www.guardian.co.uk/film/2009/jul/17/prank-movies-bruno-sacha-baron-cohen.

The film proved to be the most successful cinema documentary in American history (though surpassed by Moore's later documentaries) and enjoyed wide critical acclaim, as well as controversy. In response, General Motors threatened to pull advertising on any TV show that interviewed Moore.

Pennis memorably enquired of Demi Moore: 'If it wasn't gratuitously done, would you consider keeping your clothes on in a movie?'

2  Broader ethical questions are also at stake, most importantly: how have the human subjects of documentaries been represented?

- Is the documentary as fair and accurate as it can reasonably be in relation to its subject or argument? What kind of right of reply do the subjects have, perhaps via an accompanying website?
- What are the implications of the degrees of closeness the film achieves? This might be an unacknowledged carefulness about offending one of the powerful – a celebrity perhaps. Or it might involve a greater degree of closeness (perhaps via zoom lenses, or secret surveillance mechanisms), or more pursuit of awkward questions than a less powerful subject was aware of when agreeing to take part.
- Was a right to anonymity given to the human subjects?
- Did they have a say in the final edit?

Considerable debate exists around what constitutes 'informed consent' and who is competent to give it (see *Titicut Follies* above, and also Chapter 15).

## Recent hybrids I: 'pranksters'

Ryan Gilbey suggests that a new documentary hybrid is 'prankster cinema', combining documentary, performance art, slapstick and satire. Gilbey dates it from Michael Moore's 1989 *Roger and Me* in which Moore tried repeatedly to stage a meeting with Roger Smith, the chief executive of General Motors, whom he accused of devastating his home town, Flint, with redundancies. Moore used false identities, pranks, wit, courageous confrontations – and interviews with some local people who may not have known how weird the context and Moore's editing made them seem. The roots of such 'prank'-based entertainment lie in US television, with *Candid Camera* (1948–), *Fear Factor* and MTV's *Jackass*, though these have none of Moore's political drive.

The controversial British television series *Brass Eye* (Channel 4 1997), written by and starring Chris Morris, staged straight-faced satire of moral panics, most notably in 'Drugs' and 'Paedogeddon'. Celebrities and politicians were fooled into pledging onscreen support for fictitious, and often plainly absurd, charities and causes. Another British TV prankster was celebrity interviewer Dennis Pennis (Paul Kaye), who made 'verbal hit-and-run attacks on the red carpet', unsurprisingly rarely longer than 10 seconds.

Gilbey argues that cinema was slow to see the potential of films featuring pre-planned pranks in public. But as documentary became more hybridised in the 1980s, the success of Moore's *Roger and Me* meant a style of filming associated with frivolous ('reality'?) TV acquired political direction. Sacha Baron Cohen ('Ali G', 'Borat', 'Brüno') has exploited this space, hybridising a number of 'prankster' conventions: the gleeful punk ethos of Dennis Pennis, some of the satirical impulses of Michael Moore, and some *Jackass*-style gross-out spectacle, often involving real danger to himself.

He controversially set up fake interviews (at first, but not always, with respected public figures), while playing excessively stereotyped characters such as Ali G (a pseudo-urban would-be 'rude boy'), Borat Sagdiyev (an anti-semitic, misogynistic, ignorant Kazakh journalist, obsessed with the idea of marrying Pamela Anderson) and Brüno (a flamboyantly gay Austrian fashion reporter).

*Figure 13.4* Michael Moore's latest film (2009), in the wake of the banking collapse and bonuses scandals.

John Corner (2001) adds to a discussion of the complex situation of TV documentary: 'Documentary within cinema . . . still has the strong contrast with its dominant Other – feature film – against which it can be simply defined as "nonfiction".'

Literal performance and its play with expectations is important here. According to *Rolling Stone* magazine, when playing Ali G, Baron Cohen would always enter the interview area in character, carrying equipment and appearing to be an insignificant crew member. He would arrive with a suited man, whom the interviewee thought was the interviewer. Baron Cohen, as Ali G, would sit down to begin conducting the interview by asking the interviewee some preliminary questions. The interviewee would usually remain under the impression that the smartly dressed director would be conducting the interview until just before the cameras rolled. This would grant the advantage of surprise, with the interviewee less likely to opt out of the Ali G interview prior to its commencement.

The ethical issues involved include whether, especially when 'ordinary' people are involved, they are duped or encouraged into expressing extreme attitudes and prejudices, and whether the format allows audiences to see 'a side of America you don't traditionally get to see through regular investigative journalism', as Mike Bonanno, half of *The Yes Men*, suggests.

Baron Cohen seems to have taken things a stage further in *Brüno* (2009). He was by then so well known that it was hard to find interviewees who did not recognise him. One interview raises issues for fakery, and the ethics of the abuse of less powerful interviewees. In it, Abu Aita, a non-violent Christian Fatah activist in Palestine, was described as a member of an armed terrorist group (Fatah also has an armed section). The interview with him lasted more than two hours and he was told it was meant to show young people life in the Palestinian territories. In a short clip in the film Brüno asks to be kidnapped, suggesting Palestinian terrorists are the 'best guys for the job' because 'al-Qaida are so 2001'. Abu Aita's actual reply was edited out of the

Full article by Neil Strauss, 14 November 2006, is at http://www.rollingstone.com/news/coverstory/sacha_baron_cohen_the_real_borat_finally_speaks.

*Figure 13.5* Baron Cohen in character as 'Brüno'.

short clip. This has had serious repercussions on his own life, and he is considering legal action against Baron Cohen (see Shabi 2009).

> ### EXPLORE 13.4
>
> ● Discuss how theories of documentary 'performance' can be applied to one of Baron Cohen's films.
> ● Has editing been key to the comedy? What kind of shooting ratio seems to apply? Some have suggested *Brüno* visibly ran out of ideas. How would you argue for or against this position, on the evidence of the film?

*The Yes Men*, more like Moore, establish fake credentials necessary to gain top-level access, including bogus websites. They embarrass irresponsible multinationals by delivering off-message speeches on their behalf, and frame their work as 'actions' rather than 'pranks'.

> To some extent Jamie Oliver's Channel 4 TV series *School Dinners* (2005) is pranksterish. There is no disguising identity but, for example, he presented school students with a bucket of the (revolting-looking) ingredients of their regular fried food, and more than a hundred swear words were bleeped out for the DVD version, intended for use in schools.

## Recent hybrids 2: 'reality TV'

'Reality TV' is used to describe *several* forms of factual television. It increased hugely in Britain from about 1989, often in prime-time pre- and post-watershed slots. The concerns about 'it' do not necessarily concern all of the formats, but often the ways that, in a ratings-hungry, cost-cutting TV ecology, these shows tend to drive out more expensive documentaries, news and dramas.

Though much 'reality TV' is cheap (owing to size of crews and preparation needed, use of audience members, absence of spending on sets, etc.), this does not mean that some of the ideas are worthless.

### Status and 'reality TV'

1　Wood and Skeggs (2008) explore the strong class discourses present in the distaste for such programmes, especially 'make-over' ones:
- derogatory descriptions ('trash TV');
- the perception that they invert public and private, and wrongly make 'the ordinary' (code for working class, especially female working class) central.

They also point to
- the overrepresentation of working-class people on 'reality TV' simply because of their economic situation, which makes the (smallish) performance fees alluring;
- the programmes' reinforcement of myths of 'self-management' and social mobility, when social inequalities remain grotesque, and social mobility rates remain stagnant;
- the 'spectacle of shame' around the human subjects, often using a 'judgement shot' of the moment of 'realisation'.

It is worth considering this complex assessment when you hear simpler accounts of such programming.

2　At the other end of the prestige spectrum, consider BBC's annual *Springwatch* series (2005–) as a kind of 'reality TV'.

It documents, via hidden, often remotely operated cameras, the fortunes of wildlife such as birds during British springtime. Most of each episode is broadcast live from locations around the country. A crew of a hundred and more than fifty cameras make it the BBC's largest British outside broadcast event, and one with considerable viewer input (see BBC website).

Q: Do you consider this to be 'reality TV'? Give reasons for your answer.

The first 'dramatic reality show', as we usually understand the term, was MTV's *Real World* (1992) based on 'fly on the wall' documentaries such as *American Family* (PBS 1973), a twelve-hour eavesdrop on the life of an unhappy American family. But it took the success of the European *Big Brother* and then *Survivor*, as well as cutbacks in some programme budgets, for the format to become a dominant one. In Britain the term was first applied to magazine-format programmes based on crime, accident and health stories or 'trauma television' (*Crimewatch UK, Lifesavers, America's Most Wanted* . . .), often blending 'apparently "raw" authentic material with the gravitas of a news magazine, combining the commercial success of tabloid content with a public service mode of

> In old thatched houses the 'eavesdrip' or 'eavesdrop' was the area of ground on which fell the rainwater thrown off by the eaves (or edge) of the roof. Someone who stood in this area, with their ear to the door or window, trying to listen to private conversations, became known as an eavesdropper.

address' (Dovey 2000: 135). Charities are often consulted about such shows, for the sake of accuracy and adequacy to the issues. A recent example: *Save the Children*'s role in the 2009 reality programme *How the Other Half Lives* (12 August, *The Guardian*). Can you find more?

---

## EXPLORE 13.5

Look at *Wife Swap*, or *Embarrassing Illnesses*, programmes which are often cited (sometimes without having been actually viewed) as the 'lowest of the low' or 'freakshows' or 'tabloid TV'.
- List elements which you see as worthwhile, or even related to public service broadcasting principles.
- List those you feel fit a classification as 'worthless' or 'freakshow' TV. Where and how did you draw these distinctions?

---

It's surprising how many different kinds of programmes, with very different budgets, are grouped under this heading. There are 'make-over' programmes (re-making homes, dating abilities, gardens, bodies, sex lives . . .); docu-soaps (*Wife Swap* or *Airport*); *Crimewatch* and less expensive 'cops' programmes, and so on.

---

## EXPLORE 13.6

Look at your favourite make-over programme or other kind of 'reality TV'.
- What codes, conventions and ways of addressing the audience does it employ?
- Have you ever felt ashamed to state your liking for it? Or only stated it ironically?

---

Type 'Burmese Big Brother' into a search engine. You will be reminded of the origin of the term in Orwell's novel *1984*, and of a contemporary totalitarian regime insulated from much of 'globalisation', including free use of the internet – and programmes such as *Big Brother*.

*Big Brother* is interesting to locate within work on documentary. In some ways it resembles 'Direct Cinema', not in using hand-held cameras (the many cameras are fixed and hidden), but in its 'eavesdropping' surveillance style. Yet it has always been much more 'scripted' than traditional documentary. It drives towards narrative (and therefore profitable voting) involvement on the part of the audience via:
- The casting process (45,000 people applied for the first UK series). Increasingly those who applied to appear expected, and possibly

welcomed, an unusual degree of exposure, and to experience some bizarre situations. Many of them said they hoped to become celebrities as a result. (Later versions cast celebrities, with their already existing 'back stories'.)

- Editing decisions. Nine thousand hours were recorded for the first series. The edits often helped construct 'characters' by selecting which clips to use, and the narratives thus constructed were often of a particular kind, and frequently centred on the sexual behaviour of the contestants.
- The choice of set. Half hi-tech prison, half trendy designer 'pad', it promises, and helped to ensure, different possibilities for each series.
- The capacity for extensions of the programmes into internet discussion of often unusual political areas (of 'identity politics'?). See Klein and Wardle (2008) on the discussions prompted by two contestants' use of the Welsh language in 2007. UK *Big Brother* was regularly attacked, and lowered viewing figures (see Lawson 2009) ensured the 2010 UK series was to be the last one.

The history of its UK success revealed much about TV institutions, their 'multi-platform' spread (which it helped pioneer) and corporate media connections or 'convergence'.

1  Scheduling it as a summer event (when surrounding programmes are usually made at much lower cost), available for showing in pubs, and then as an end of evening event for a 'youth' audience, were key elements.

2  'It achieved the rare trick of being visible even to those who don't watch it, through coverage elsewhere' (Lawson 2009). Once established it had flexible scheduling, along with huge press, internet and mobile phone coverage. But big news stories in summer 2009 ('swine flu', Parliamentary expenses scandals and recession) helped keep it off the key red-top front pages.

3  Viewers' ability to vote on who should leave the house (and, subsequently, on a number of other questions), via mobile phones, made it interactive, as well as hugely lucrative for its owners. Scandals around mobile phone charges, and some unrepresentative decisions on evictions, were part of its loss of popularity.

John Ellis speculated that the programme related to widely experienced work values and structures:

> Thrown together by circumstances, they are mutually dependent, but in order to survive they have to stab each other in the back by making their nominations for eviction. The experience is akin to a modern workplace with its project-based impermanence, appraisal processes and often ruthless corporate management.
>
> (Ellis 2001)

> Reread the section on 'format' in Chapter 3 to understand *Big Brother*'s commercial roots.

> As with any such big event, once it was 'on the agenda' it became the starting point for otherwise awkward conversations, allowed people to talk about other things through it, and even provided games.

## Recent hybrids 3: forms of 'drama-documentary'

As André Bazin, once wrote, 'Realism in art can only be achieved in one way – through artifice' (in 'An aesthetic of realism: neo-realism' (1948) (Bazin 1967/71)).
Q What do you think he means?

Many of the debates above concern the perceived distance between fact and fiction, or perhaps, drama and documentary. Hence the anxieties and controversy sometimes raised by forms which confuse these two. Let's explore two different, recent examples of 'drama documentary'.
1 *United 93* (US 2006) is often cited as a 'very realistic' film. It was a meticulously researched big-budget film about the real-life event of the hijacking of one of the aircraft used for the bombings of '9/11'. It's an example of the appeal of such reconstructions. The director, Paul Greengrass, like many directors and writers in this tradition, came out of British TV documentary and drama-documentary. He brings the 'reality effect' of this earlier TV work, such as *The Murder of Stephen Lawrence* (1999) and *Bloody Sunday* (2002), to 'Hollywood' action adventure, notably the Bourne franchise.

This 'realist' charge covers both form and subject matter, though some critics asked what could be learned about '9/11' from a meticulous, thriller-like reconstruction, especially since the political motives of the bombers on board are not explored.
2 *5 Minutes of Heaven* (BBC/Pathé 2009) is based on a shocking, true-life killing in Northern Ireland in 1975. It won the 2009 Sundance World Cinema Directing Award and World Cinema Screenwriting Award. The lengthy account of its processes here should give you a sense of the 'reach' and innovations involved in a quality TV 'drama-documentary'.

The funding route for this film ('greenlighted' by BBC4, partly because of the writer's reputation) is now unusual for the BBC, let alone other TV companies. See Tony Garnett and other correspondence at http://www.guardian.co.uk/media/organgrinder/2009/jul/15/tony-garnett-bbc-drama.

In 1975, 17-year-old Alistair Little, a member of the Protestant Ulster Volunteer Force, murdered his first and only Catholic, a 19-year-old, Jim Griffin, as he sat watching television. Griffin's younger brother, Joe, aged 11, witnessed the killing. Their eyes locked and Little admits that if he had known that Joe was Griffin's brother, he would have killed him too.

The film recreates this assassination carefully, but then deliberately goes into 'what if?' territory: what would happen if the two men were to meet up now, thirty-three years later? The real-life Little (played by Liam Neeson), having spent twelve years in prison for his crime, now works in 'conflict transformation', running workshops for traumatised people in Ireland, Israel, the Balkans and South Africa. Or, as the adult Joe Griffin/James Nesbitt bitterly puts it: 'He swans around the world telling people what it feels like to kill a man.' Griffin, irrationally blamed by his mother for doing nothing to prevent his brother's murder, is presented as a tortured adult. The meaning of the film's title emerges during the long scene in which Little and Griffin prepare to meet one another for a TV documentary, though in real life the two men have never encountered one another, and probably never will. Would there be 'truth and reconciliation' or something darker, more volatile? 'The film is about the complex psychological relationship that exists between the perpetrator of a crime and the victim,' said the producer. 'It is not about . . . finding easy answers.'

Clearly even the first, highly researched 'reconstruction' of the assassination is shaped in 'fictional' ways – casting professional actors/ stars, inventing dialogue, checking historical details. But after that the film uses a new form of drama-documentary. In real life Little and Griffin were asked to appear on a TV show where Archbishop Tutu brought together survivors from both sides of the conflict. Griffin declined, saying 'If ever I am in a room with that man I will kill him,', according to the screenwriter, Guy Hibbert, who began a long, slow and painstaking process of getting to know the two men in order to create a dramatic scenario in which they might meet – and explore what would happen if they did.

'My first question to each was "What if you had accepted that invitation . . .?" Alistair said, "I would go if Joe wants me to go" . . . Joe said, "I'd take a knife and have my five minutes of heaven." I'd say, "Look Joe if you [did that] what would be the next scene?" – and he said, "You're the writer, you tell me." I told him, "Your wife and two daughters would be watching TV and there'd be a knock at the door and . . . a policeman and woman [there] and . . . we'd cut to the two daughters crying." I said to Joe, "I don't want to write that scene . . ." '

The film dramatises events and scripts dialogue, but also has, as a main concern, the approving involvement of the two central 'characters' in what is still a potentially dangerous political situation in Belfast (compare Baron Cohen in Palestine, above). Guy Hibbert describes it as like drama therapy – 'working with them [for three years, on different days, travelling from London to Belfast] so they would never walk into each other in a corridor . . . serious . . . because we're dealing with the most dramatic and traumatic moments in their lives'. He made sure that everything was OK-ed by them, right down to ringing them when Neeson wanted to change one word of his dialogue.

'Probably the tensest part . . . was when I left them in peace for about six months while I wrote the script, and then presented them with it. That was the first time they'd come "face to face" with each other, if you like. Alistair then found out for the first time what Joe thought of him.'

Thanks to his participation, Joe Griffin is now receiving trauma counselling for the first time. See the material from which much of this case study is taken on http://www.independent.co.uk/arts-entertainment/tv/features/five-minutes-of-heaven–a-fair-share-of-troubles-1660787.html. The trailer is available on http://www.imdb.com/video/screenplay/vi30736921/.

*Figure 13.6* The poster for this film.

Distribution and circulation generally are important for all the films we've discussed. Hibbert, asked about preferred distribution for this film, screened in the UK and Ireland on BBC2 but internationally as a 'theatrical' (i.e. cinema) release, replied:

> You get 3.5 million people watching on TV. This is an art house movie, so in cinemas you might get 30,000, if you're lucky. In Ireland especially, a lot of people watched it. It had lots of press attention because it had their two biggest actors. You'd never have got that reaction in cinema, and it was key that Ireland saw it . . . The trouble with TV though is that two years work is over in one night. And if you were to clash with an England game, or an *Emmerdale* special, your two years would be finished for nothing. So in that respect we got the best of both worlds, because we have the general release around the world *and* festival showings . . .

## EXPLORE 13.7

Think of an incident, or news story, or piece of history that might make a good drama-documentary.

- Write a proposal for the BBC suggesting why, and how, you propose to make it *as a drama-documentary*.
- What do you need to take into account when making your proposal? Research Tony Garnett's correspondence, above, and see BBC's *WritersRoom* at http://www.bbc.co.uk/writersroom/.

## Conclusion

Documentaries have always been constructed, despite powerful discourses inviting us to see them as being simple kinds of transparent truth-telling. But film-makers have also always mixed forms, including kinds of 'performance' and even pranks. Hybridity is not new.

We've tried to explore these issues, as well as the ethical questions, both of faking footage and of 'representation' of real people and issues, which have rightly been at the heart of documentary debates. These relate to news aspirations and can contribute to a vibrant and responsible 'public sphere' which is more than simply commercially driven.

Despite some extreme 'postmodern' positions, we inhabit a real world, with social issues that can be represented, as long as audiences recognise that such representations are

- negotiated by film-makers, and
- will not be direct 'mirrors' of 'the truth' but more like refractions of (usually complex) situations.

This is especially true in a digital era, where the 'trace' element argued for photographic-based images is complicated by the possibilities of digital alteration.

Yet though reality, and the documentary, is always contested and constructed, an absolute pessimism about the possibility of 'knowing' or having convincing evidence of *anything* is misplaced. We hope you won't feel, at the end of this chapter, that there's an inevitable slide from the position 'documentary is *as* constructed as a fiction film' to 'there's no need to bother about untruthfulness'. It is right to expect some attempt at adequacy to the real in news and documentary, even though that will always be for particular purposes – an angry exposé perhaps, or a scientific investigation. This also relates to 'reality', 'entertainment' or 'prankster' forms of documentary, where the issues are at least as complex.

## References and further reading

Ang, Ien (1985) *Watching Dallas: Soap Operas and the Melodramatic Imagination*, New York. Methuen.

Bazin, André (1967/71) 'The Ontology of the Photographic Image', in *What is Cinema?*, 2 vols, London: University of California Press; revised edn 2004.

Bordwell, David, and Thompson, Kirsten (2004) *Film Art: An Introduction*, 7th edn, New York: McGraw Hill.

Bruzzi, Stella (2000) *New Documentary: A Critical Introduction*, London: Routledge.

Bruzzi, Stella (2005) 'The Event: Archive and Imagination', in Rosenthal, Alan, and Corner, John (eds) *New Challenges for Documentary*, Manchester: Manchester University Press, pp. 419–31.

Corner, John (2001) 'Form and Content in Documentary Study' and 'Documentary Realism (Documentary Fakes)', in Creeber, Glen (ed.) *The Television Genre Book*, London: British Film Institute.

Dovey, Jon (2000) *Freakshow: First Person Media and Factual Television*, London: Pluto Press.

Ellis, John (2001) 'Mirror, Mirror', *Sight and Sound*, August.

Gilbey, Ryan (2009) 'Jokers to the Left, Jokers to the Right', *The Guardian, G2*, 17 July: 3.

Klein, Bethany, and Wardle, Claire (2008) 'These Two Are Speaking Welsh on Channel 4!', *Television and New Media*, 20, 10.

Lawson, Mark (2009) 'Oh Brother', *The Guardian, G2*, 24 July: 5–8.

Neale, Steve (2000) *Genre and Hollywood*, London: Routledge.

Neale, Steve (ed.) (2002) *Genre and Contemporary Hollywood*, London: British Film Institute.

Nichols, Bill (1991) *Representing Reality: Issues and Concepts of Documentary*, Bloomington and Indianapolis: Indiana University Press.

Shabi, Rachel (2009) 'The Non-profit Worker from Bethlehem who was Branded a Terrorist by Brüno', *The Guardian*, 1 August: 3.

Wood, Helen, and Skeggs, Bev (2008) 'Spectacular Morality', in Hesmondhalgh, David, and Toynbee, Jason (eds) *The Media and Social Theory*, London and New York: Routledge.

# 14 From 'audience' to 'users'

- Academic representations of audiences
- The effects model
- The uses and gratifications model
- From 'effects' to 'influence': factual forms
- 'Cultural' approaches
- Re-mediating audiences
- Conclusion
- References and further reading

'Audience' has long been a key term for media studies approaches to people's responses and uses of modern media. It was a way of asserting that textual approaches alone were not enough. They were seen as still too close to earlier, scornful assumptions (from the nineteenth century and then, markedly, the 1920s) about the supposedly 'mass' audience for media, whose responses could be simply 'read off' the text.

'Audience', with its word origins in hearing, always implied a silent mass of people, 'attending' to some powerful 'text' – a sermon, a speech, a theatre performance. Ways of differentiating that 'mass', and thinking about their varied responses and groupings, have been part of media studies since then. A key development was to stop talking of 'audience' and use the term 'audiences' to suggest that many varied engagements might take place with the same mass-distributed text, such a blockbuster film.

Parts of the media, however, often slip back into much older dismissals of users as though they were still a doped, duped 'mass'.

A useful way of thinking of audience(s) is as 'the groups and individuals addressed, and often partly "constructed" by media industries'.

Q: How would you rewrite this, to include interactive 'users'?

'Audience' has several meanings, from the fourteenth century onwards. They range from a formal act of hearing (to be 'granted an audience' with a superior), to a group of people physically present in the same place and attentively listening (e.g. to a speech), through to contemporary *mediated audiences* (see Bennett *et al.* 2009).

**EXPLORE 14.1**

Keep a diary of a week's news, current affairs and/or 'reality TV' coverage of media audience issues.

- Are they framed so as to encourage a particular view of their audiences/users? This might involve 'children' and media, a regular source of often exaggerated or demonising concerns (paedophilia, internet addiction – though rarely the impact of advertising).
- If a piece of research into children's internet usage has been reported recently, look at 'red-top' and broadsheet news coverage of it. How carefully have issues such as 'internet addiction' or differences between 'children' been framed? How adequately does the report seem to have been quoted?
- Go to http://www.polismedia.org/news/newsdetail/internet-and-young-people-new-research.aspx for up-to-date research debates.

'Jump in' was the X-Box 360 slogan in 2009. See the banned X-Box 360 commercial on YouTube (http://www.youtube.com/watch?v=wBliYErXemo). Describe how it addresses and imagines its 'users'.

The term 'audience' is clearly also inadequate for covering the many ways in which people engage with interactive media. Do games, for example, have an 'audience' which is delivered to them? Players are attentive, but perhaps not in the ways presumed by 'audience', or even 'text' in earlier emphases. Yet we need some way to discuss the possible influence of the widespread distribution of 'texts' such as adverts, especially in combination with the marketing and other invitations to use, if not actually to 'believe' in, what they offer. This means that a single ad, part of a big marketing drive, is worth studying as a 'text', and is likely to be much more powerful than, for example, a single tweet against that ad. (See Ruddock 2008 on binge drinking, students, peer pressures and marketing campaigns.)

What concepts help us think through this area – which, after all, involves 'us'?

---

## EXPLORE 14.2

Many debates, and cultural valuations of some activities over others, are carried by the different terms you'll come across in this chapter:

*mass culture; 'the' audience; audiences; readers; two-step flow; users; UGC (user-generated content); consumers; prosumer; co-creators; lurkers.*

- When you reach the end of the chapter, check that you can briefly define these, and locate them within different approaches.

---

## Academic representations of audiences

Let's first update Kitzinger's (2004a: 168–9) helpful suggestions. She grouped audience research into four main areas:

- *'Market' driven*: originating in the US, and seeking to track audiences as consumers. It monitors such issues as attention flow, or the numbers of 'eyeballs' which your product is attracting. Corporations are now digitally highly proactive in researching what they perceive might be useful audience responses/information.

- *Concerns about morality and 'sex 'n' violence'*: focusing in an often simplistic way on the supposed corrupting power of media *all on their own*, isolated from social shaping and broader influences (see Huesmann and Taylor 2006, and debates around their position). This often deploys laboratory-based evidence. Social networking media and their supposedly often-malign influence on young users, in isolation, are now subject to this approach (see below).

> See the BBFC websites for interesting material on this debate now – http://www.bbfc.co.uk.

- *Responses to technological developments*: such as cinema in the 1920s, TV in the 1950s, when it was a new medium, through to children's, and other groups' use of interactive media today.

- *Questions about culture, politics and identity*: concerned with the media's role in framing public understandings, and also the ways that we use media texts and objects in relation to identities, pleasures and fantasies.

**EXPLORE 14.3**

'Your identity on the computer is the sum of your distributed presence.' (Turkle, 1995:13, quoted in Livingstone 2009: 100).

'It's quite fun having a jokey name but it's privacy as well. I don't like my mum and dad reading all the emails I send.' (Candy, aka 'Kissmequick', quoted in Livingstone: 2009 101).

- What is, or would be, your chosen email address as: a student? a contributor to your favourite social networking site? a fan? a job applicant.
- Have you ever 'performed' an identity on the internet?

We'll suggest that these approaches, shaped and funded by different bodies of interest, produce different images of 'audiences' and 'users', which have consequences in the world, and then for the users. Like many such images they often work in this kind of a 'circle'.

The key question is still: how to reposition our understandings between the two extremes – the idea of the all-powerful 'message', and that of the all-powerful user?

## The effects model

Across the spectrum of academic research, assumptions tend to cluster around one of these two extremes: the **effects model** and the **uses and gratifications model**.

The effects model (also called the **hypodermic model**) is the name given to approaches that emphasise what the media do *to* their audiences. Power is assumed to lie solely with the 'message(s)'. The media are often called 'the mass media' or 'mass communications'. This rightly emphasises the size and scale of their operations, but renders the rest of us somewhat passive – 'dupes' or 'dopes'. The language of this model often implies that meanings are 'injected' into the single mass audience by powerful, syringe-like media – hence 'hypodermic'. The next step is to describe the media as working like a drug, and then to suggest that the audience is drugged, addicted, duped.

But if something like addiction does form (as is said to happen with some groups and the internet: see Chapter 8, p. 245), it

a  fills as many *different* needs as do physical addictions (such as alcohol, tobacco);

b  does so as part of broader cultural shapings and commercial encouragements (perhaps lack of safe public spaces or opportunities to spend time in other ways, or the commercialised peer pleasures of using fashionable gadgets and knowledge).

To return to the 'mass culture' positions usually identified with the **Frankfurt School**. These also shaped the arguments of two nineteenth- and twentieth-century English literary figures, Matthew Arnold and F. R. Leavis. They conceived 'culture' (meaning 'high' culture such as 'the classics') as 'The best that has been thought and said'. This was contrasted with 'popular culture', generated by the mass media, though there was a somewhat nostalgic attachment to 'folk culture' of an earlier age, as well as 'literature'. Exploration of the responses of 'the masses' was not the concern of these literary critics.

The Frankfurt School, from the 1920s onwards, theorised the possible effects of then-modern media in response to German fascism's use of radio and film for propaganda purposes. Later, in exile from Nazi Germany, these 'Frankfurt' theorists explored the power of US media, including advertising and some entertainment forms. Its members developed a variant of Marxism known as *critical theory*, an interdisciplinary framework combining Marxism, Freudianism, philosophy and economic research. It emphasised the power of corporate capitalism, owning and controlling media, to restrict and control cultural life in unprecedented ways, creating what was called a 'mass culture' of stupefying conformity, with no space for innovation or originality.

Ironically, despite their grounding in Marxism, the group did not produce ideas of active and involved workers and audiences who might oppose such control, and in the 1950s they abandoned the model of class conflict as a motor of history. Nevertheless, as ultimate economic control of the media has become ever more corporate and concentrated, even alongside the potential of interactive media, their writings are worth revisiting. Habermas, a surviving figure, remains influential for his theory of the 'public sphere'.

While the Frankfurt School and others, coming from European experiences of fascism, theorised the 'effects' of popular media on a 'mass audience' in broadly cultural terms, different approaches developed the US in the 1950s. Researchers were alarmed by a perceived increase in violent acts (not including wars) which were argued to be a possible consequence of violence-as-represented-on-television (then a new medium). Unlike the Frankfurt School, they were not interested in linking these to a critical analysis of late capitalist society. They focused instead on the power of television to do things *to* people – or rather, to *other* people.

> 'There are . . . no "masses" but only ways of seeing people as masses' (Raymond Williams 1958). See Chapter 8 for more on this important cultural theorist.

> **Theodor Adorno** (1903–69), **Jürgen Habermas** (1929–), **Max Horkheimer** (1895–1973), **Herbert Marcuse** (1898–1979) and others were neo-Marxist cultural theorists who formed a group known as the Frankfurt School, though it was a grouping rather than an institution. They fled Nazi Germany for the US in the 1930s.

> See Chapters 5, 10 and 12 for more on the concept of the 'public sphere' and debates around its usefulness.

---

## EXPLORE 14.4

This position is alive and well, especially in Media Watch* and some parental and religious movements in the US and elsewhere, often working to have television and 'new media' more closely censored, or at least classified, based on this effects model.

- Look at the Media Watch website (http://www.mediawatchuk.org.uk/). Trace the assumptions about audiences you can find there, via choice of words, tone, evidence.
- Watch for
  - the use of 'them' rather than 'we';
  - any admission of researchers' or campaigners' own involvement in harmful viewing (they have to do a great deal of it to be credible censors, after all);
  - implications that 'things were all right' before, often thirty years or so ago;
  - visual and verbal stereotyping or 'other-ing' of the group or person being panicked over.

\* Media Watch was formerly the NVLA or National Viewers' and Listeners' Association, which had a striking history in UK censorship lobbies. NOT to be confused with the VLV, Voice of the Listener and Viewer, see http://www.vlv.org.uk.

---

**Burrhus Frederick Skinner** (1904–90) US behavioural scientist. Argued that all behaviour is explicable solely in terms of genetic dispositions and 'reinforcements', or rewards and punishments. Therefore, how behaviour is 'reinforced' is crucial, rather than its social shaping.

*Figure 14.1* See Adam Curtis's short film *It Felt Like a Kiss* (2009: BBC website) for a 'Frankfurt'-like account of the founding moment of advertising in the US in the 1950s, which mixed psycho-analytic inputs with the lessons of electric shock therapy. Compare its account to that fictionalised in *Mad Men* (US 2007–).

Often, now, intergenerational fears and insecurities from those unfamiliar with the new forms also enter the picture. The media in this model are argued to be *the most important* causes of 'violence', bullying, addiction and so on, and of the decay of standards of 'taste and decency'.

Another term you will come across is *behaviourism*, which influenced some researchers into the effects of media on 'children'. Behavioural scientists tried to understand human social behaviour by modifying the laboratory behaviour of animals. B. F. Skinner is one of the most famous. You may have also heard of Pavlov's dogs, laboratory animals whose feeding times were accompanied by a bell ringing, until eventually they would salivate whenever the bell rang, with or without the food. Clearly their laboratory behaviour had been violently modified. Scientists working on such experiments hoped that control by reinforcement could also be applied to human behaviour – though in different ways. American advertisers were interested, and some felt that there might be advantages in using 'repeated messages' or 'reinforcement' in television advertising.

A now notorious piece of research was the 'Bobo doll experiment' (Bandura and Walters 1963). It showed children some film of adults acting aggressively towards a 'Bobo doll', then recorded children acting in a similar way later when left alone with it. The implication (that children copy violent behaviour) was then extended to violent media content, which was asserted to have similar effects. This research method ignores several basic problems:

- Findings cannot necessarily be neatly transferred from experiments on laboratory animals to human beings in social situations, including encounters with media.
- If people are likened to laboratory animals, they will be assumed to be empty vessels, passively absorbing messages. **Cognitive psychologists** have argued instead that children actively construct meanings from the media, and that these interpretations are affected by prior knowledge and experience.
- People (including young children) are often very willing to please those conducting experiments, with a shrewd sense of what responses are the favoured ones. They also know quite well how to mess things up entertainingly.
- Outside the laboratory, the 'effect' of media may not be shown in our measurable *outward* behaviour, such as voting or shopping – or violent acts. Broadly cultural effects (on attitudes and violent subcultures, etc.) are harder to measure.

Within the effects model the power of the media, especially television, is usually assumed to be negative, never positive. If you look closely at the positions that urge censorship, they often fall into one of two contradictory positions, sometimes contributing to **moral panics**:

- 'The media produce inactivity, make us into students who won't pass their exams or "couch potatoes" who make "no effort to get a job".'
- 'The media *do* produce activity, but of a bad kind, such as violent "copycat" behaviour, or mindless shopping in response to advertisements.'

### A famous story

One story you may have come across involves the young Orson Welles' celebrated 1938 radio theatre broadcast of *War of the Worlds*, a science fiction story involving Martians landing on earth. The first two-thirds of the sixty-minute show were broadcast as news bulletins in a slot which, unusually, had no advertising. There were reports of mass panic by listeners. The whole incident is often used either

'As she entered a laboratory, one small four-year-old girl was heard to say "Look, Mummy, there's the doll we have to hit" ' (J Root 1986).

'Moral panic' is a term used most famously by Stan Cohen (1972) for a process where 'a condition, episode, person or group . . . emerges to become defined as a threat to societal values and interests'. Valuable for exploring, for example, media scapegoating of youth subcultures (e.g. 'muggers', 'hoodies', 'chavs') and media associated with them.

'In 1976, a group of friends from Los Angeles who often gathered together . . . to indulge in hours long sessions of television viewing, decided to call themselves "couch potatoes". With tongue in cheek publications such as *The Official Couch Potato Handbook* . . . they started a mock-serious grassroots viewers' movement' (I Ang 1991).

- as a way of lauding the power of 'realist' codes in radio, or
- as yet another example of how stupid audiences are.

In fact, as several researchers have suggested:

- some listeners heard only parts of the 'news bulletin-like' programme;
- nothing like such a 'spoof' had ever been heard on the new medium or radio;
- in the shadow of Nazism, on the eve of the Second World War (1939–45), an alarmed response to reports of invasion makes complete sense.

It's also the case that many newspapers were concerned that radio, then new, might make them extinct: they seem to have embellished and over-reported the story.

On 13 March 2010 there was panic in Georgia (in the Caucasus) where mobile phone networks were overwhelmed after a hoax TV report that Russian tanks had invaded the capital and the country's president was dead. Similar debates to the Welles' hoax apply, especially since Russia had invaded Georgia in 2008 as part of the oil politics of this region.

*Figure 14.2* Monument erected in New Jersey, November 1998, to commemorate where Welles' Martians 'landed' in 1938.

Media messages can indeed have 'effects' of a quite immediate kind: a weather forecast may encourage you to put on a coat; the flashings of strobe lighting can be dangerous for epileptics; too much sustained, close screen work can damage your eyesight and posture.

But usually a broader, more ideological *influence* is being claimed for the media, reasonable enough as an assumption, but often closely wrapped up with a derogatory view of 'audience'. 'The mass audience' in the effects model is usually assumed to consist of the 'weaker' members of society, especially the 'lower orders'. In the nineteenth century, novels were thought to be potentially harmful for working-class women. More recently there have been fears that romantic fiction, then soaps, then TV, and most recently the internet, render people (especially women) passive, helpless, drugged with trivia. 'Children', too, feature in such discourses: worried over in the 1950s because of the supposed harm done by American comics; then from the 1980s to the present in relation to horror films, computer games, gangsta rap, mobile phones, social media, text messaging.

> We enclose 'children' in quotation marks because it is such a wide term for so many different groups of young people. The differences are not only developmental but also involve very different levels of competence and familiarity with media forms.

Important concerns find (highly refracted) expression in such panics. But the debates are often isolated from other factors affecting children's use of media, such as:

- underfunded or unstimulating childcare, school and leisure activities;
- awareness that the computer skills acquired (e.g. through playing games) allow play with adult-status, exciting identities;
- awareness that computer skills, especially in games, are 'marketable' as well as enjoyable 'escapes' from often sheltered and possibly boring lives, as are the 'community' of social networking sites, games, mobile phone messages and so on (see Livingstone 2009: Ch. 2).

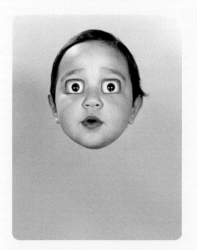

*Figure 14.3* The Guardian 'square eyes' mock up of child's face

A vivid visual image for an article (http://www.guardian.co.uk/society/2009/oct/14/tv-children-harmful-effects) on the possible influences of intensive TV viewing on young children, signified by the 'wide' absorbing eyes, almost seeming to signify fear, square-shaped like screens, and the red lipsticked slightly open mouth. It visualises widespread concerns – the uncomprehending but almost hypnotised attention ('slack-jawed'?), and the sexualisation of 'childhood' by media. Such fears, often fuelled by parental guilt at the convenience of TV as a 'babysitter', and by an outside world perceived as increasingly unsafe, are not always handled responsibly in media imagery. See Barkham (2009).

## The uses and gratifications model

*Figure 14.4* Using the media (here cinema) for particular kinds of gratification.

At the 'user-power' extreme of academic images of audiences, the 'uses and gratifications' model emphasises what consumers of media products do *with* them. Power is argued to lie with the individual **consumer** of media, who is argued to use TV, the internet, etc. consciously to gratify certain needs and interests (Blumler and Katz 1974). Far from being duped by the media, this 'audience' is represented as made up of individuals free to reject, use or play with them. The needs to be gratified include those for diversion and escapism, for information, for comparing relationships and lifestyle of characters with one's own, or for sexual stimulation. This approach was first formulated in the US in the 1940s and has been associated with television, and with socio-psychological approaches to media.

In the 1950s this approach seemed like a breath of fresh air, resisting the easy pessimism and crudely behaviourist emphases of effects work. Researchers (often well funded and sometimes working with advertisers) questioned people as to why they watched television. They concluded that 'personality types' in the audience gave rise 'to certain needs, some of which are directed to the mass media for satisfaction' (Morley 1992). These needs were grouped into such categories as cognitive (learning); affective (emotional satisfaction); tension release (relaxation); personal integrative (help with issues of personal identity); social integrative (help with issues of social identity).

The model is not interested in critiquing capitalist mass culture. Indeed some of its extreme adherents came close to denying *any* influence for the media, and never explored critically such concepts as 'social integration'. Just as metaphors of drugs, addiction and passivity characterise the 'effects' tradition, so the 'uses' approaches buzz with words like 'choice', 'consuming', 'freedom' and 'users'.

These words have one big attraction: we're much more likely to *want* to identify ourselves as active, empowered users of the TV or computer, than as the passive dupes of some media corporation. There are connections and comparisons here with 'free market' discourses in general. For example, celebration of 'the power of individual internet use' is now at the heart of cost-cutting policies towards public services (health provision, etc.) in many countries.

## From 'effects' to 'influence': factual forms

More sophisticated research into broader *influences* of the media or 'the new effects work' (Kitzinger 2004b) emphasise subtler, less direct media capacities to influence perceptions, frames and so on. These originate in approaches to news and 'factual' forms, especially a classic wartime US study by Lazarsfeld *et al.* (1944) which explored the influence exerted on voters by the media during an American presidential campaign. It concluded that voters were resistant to media influence, since individual predispositions or political preference influenced which media they consulted. The term *two-step flow* was coined to describe the important influence not of 'the media' but of local networks and opinion leaders, whose views often mediated those offered by the media. Media 'effect' began to be seen as one of reinforcement via such *intervening variables* – in fact, closer to 'influence' than to 'brainwashing'.

Gerbner and Gross (1976) suggested that the more television you watch, the more likely you are to have a fearful attitude to the world outside the home, a different kind of influence, more related to cultural approaches. Such questions have been revived recently around the suggestions of, among others, Michael Moore and Naomi Klein, and of Adam Curtis in *The Power of Nightmares* (BBC 2004), that we are living in a culture of fear, now deliberately stoked by politicians grossly exaggerating legitimate anxieties about 'terrorists'. Some parts of the media seem glad to have such 'sexy' headlines with which to boost sales and ratings.

Greg Philo's work over the years, with different members of the Glasgow University Media Group (GUMG), has suggested another form of broad influence or effect, on behalf of dominant groups. Two examples:

1 Long after the end of the British coalminers' strike of 1984–5, the group discovered that viewers had tended to forget important details of news reporting, but did remember key themes and phrases, such as 'picket line violence'. These, through repetition, became part of popular consciousness, and then memory about the strike, even if it could be shown at the time that they were mythical or greatly exaggerated.

2 Work in 2004 strongly suggested that perceptions of the Israel–Palestine conflict were skewed partly by the failure of news organisations to explain key terms, or to give historical background to

> When the 1984–5 coalminers' strike was over, the National Council for Civil Liberties reported that 'contrary to the impression created by the media, most of the picketing during the strike has been orderly and on a modest scale'.

> 'Every time it comes on [the Israeli–Palestinian conflict] it never actually explains it so I don't see the point of watching it .. . . It's like the Kosovo conflict. I don't want to watch it, I don't understand it – I switch it off' (comments from two members of GUMG focus groups, in Philo and Berry 2004: 240).

images of violent conflict and its perceived intractability. In one group, for example,

> it was apparent that a relatively straightforward piece of information, such as that the Israelis controlled water supplies and how this affected Palestinian agriculture, had a strong effect on how a [focus group] participant understood the . . . conflict.
>
> (Philo and Bery 2004: 241–2)

Further, 'a clear majority in the groups as a whole stated that their interest increased when they knew more . . . the relationship between understanding and interest in news was very marked'.

## EXPLORE 14.5

Look at the next time this conflict is featured on the news.

- Jot down terms (such as 'settler', 'Balfour declaration') which you are unsure of. What do you take them to signify?
- Research them. How might news have told the histories involved differently? Which media forms do tell such histories differently?

### Example: news audiences and 'compassion fatigue'

**'Compassion fatigue'** is a phrase often used of one set of possible audience responses to media images of terrible crisis, suffering and disaster. It's interesting here since it is located between media news 'messages' and audience responses to emotionally moving images, an area more usually theorised for fiction forms.

Like all images of audiences, it produces consequences. The term loosely evokes an 'audience' (presumed to be Western) which is supposedly weary of terrible images. This is at a time when TV, and especially news programmes, some blogs and associated interactive media, have raised the possibility of moral solidarity with, and action for, 'distant others'. But this powerful idea of 'compassion fatigue' can act as a prior constraint on news editors, who therefore may not assign reporters to global crisis reporting. They thereby shore up other kinds of sensationalist news coverage, which implicitly encourages the media to 'move on' in the fear that 'the audience' will get bored. It's becomes a kind of vicious circle.

> It has been argued that the warning 'this report contains images which some viewers may find disturbing' should be phrased 'which *all* viewers *ought* to find disturbing'. It's also argued that 'Western' viewers need to see *more* of the damage done to human bodies (and minds) by war if peace movements are to flourish.

Birgitta Hoijer (2004; see Cottle 2009 for summary and discussion) argues, in an audience-based study, that feelings of 'compassion' often depend on the use of visuals, and within them 'ideal victims' (notably women, children and the elderly), as well as on crises being located in generally Western-friendly nations. She thinks about 'compassion fatigue' through groups of different responses from her audience sample:

- *tender-hearted compassion*: focuses on the suffering of the victim and the spectator's own sense of being filled with pity;
- *blame-filled compassion*: registers a sense of indignation and may be directed at those thought to be responsible;
- *shame-filled compassion*: involves a sense of guilt at not having acted on such images; and
- *powerlessness-filled compassion*: involves the recognition that it may be impossible to affect the scenes of suffering.

---

## EXPLORE 14.6

Interview friends or classmates on their response to a recent piece of 'crisis' footage or other imagery (this could include radio).

- Do any phrases in their replies support Hoijer's differentiation of groups of response?
- Where, in her different groups, did your own responses lie?

---

This example, and many others, draws partly on work from the 1970s, at the Centre for Contemporary Cultural Studies (CCCS), Birmingham University, under Stuart Hall. Though not strictly speaking audience work, it enabled textual speculations about 'the audience' to take valuable new directions. It opposed approaches such as content analysis (which sometimes assumed an easily quantifiable relation between elements of the text ('violent acts') and audience 'response'). It also moved away from the idea of a single, dominant ideology expressed, or not, in texts. Instead it developed Gramsci's more complex model of hegemonic struggles (see Chapter 6).

But Hall's position did not simply fall into the then-current (and still fashionable) 'uses and gratifications' approaches. It insisted instead that, far from being autonomous and utterly individualised, audience members *share* certain frameworks of interpretation, and that they work

> **Stuart Hall** (1932–) British cultural theorist, especially of ethnicities, working with a mix of approaches (Marxism, discourse theory, history, sociology).

at **decoding** media texts within these frameworks, rather than being 'affected' in a passive way.

Subsequent research, including David Morley's (1980) small-scale work on *Nationwide* (an early evening UK TV magazine programme), took this further, focusing on:

- power structures *outside* the text which often shape audience members' responses: class, gender, ethnicity, age, etc;
- power structures *within* texts, part of media institutions – these would include legal constraints as well as ratings pressures. These mean that programmes often try to promote a 'preferred reading'. Though argued to be in line with dominant values, this struggles with other possible meanings in a text.

This broadly Gramscian model of hegemonic media power (i.e. power which is constantly having to work to win consent, rather than just being imposed from above) went along with Hall's three types of audience readings:

- **Dominant**, or *dominant hegemonic*, where the reader recognises what a programme's 'preferred' or offered meaning is and broadly agrees with it (updated example: the flag-waving patriot who responded enthusiastically to President George W. Bush's speeches).
- **Oppositional**, where the dominant meaning is recognised but rejected for cultural or ideological reasons (the pacifist who understood the speeches but rejected them).
- **Negotiated**, where the reader accepts, rejects or refines elements of the programme in the light of previously held views (the viewer who agreed with the need for some response to the attacks of 11 September 2001 but did not agree with Bush's military means).

## EXPLORE 14.7

- Can you think of a recent programme which produced similarly different responses from friends or family? Can you apply these suggested groupings to them? If not, what groups would you put their responses into?
- Do these ideological groupings work for fiction or fantasy forms?

One of the questions raised about this work takes us into our next section. It's fine to question a few people about videotaped programmes in a college setting. But to extend this to 'the audience' more generally, we need to know how likely they would be to watch those kinds of programmes outside that setting. This led to broader, cultural approaches, including domestic contexts for viewing and playing with media.

## 'Cultural' approaches

There has been a turn to audience **ethnographies**, or fieldwork research, largely derived from anthropology, in the past few decades. A researcher attempts to enter intensively into the culture of a particular group and provide an account of its meanings and activities 'from the inside'. S/he often employs participant observation methods, participating in the lives of the groups to be studied for an extended period of time, asking questions and observing what goes on. When the research is written up, it often tries to show a respect for the group studied by providing life histories, case studies and verbatim quotes from them. Problems remain, but such work tried to show real respect for audiences' own experiences. It seems likely that much can be learnt from careful, small ethnographic accounts along with equally careful treatment of theories, or textual readings, or from other empirical work such as questionnaires.

The key areas which media ethnographic work has investigated include:

- the domestic contexts of media reception
- genre and cultural competences
- media technologies and consumption (which spread into studies of interactive media uses).

Morley (1986) and others (Livingstone 2009) have explored ways in which the home – the 'domestic context' for most viewing – has structured TV viewing and internet use. Far from being simply 'the private sphere', our 'retreat from the world', the home is as cross-cut by kinds of social power as anywhere else. In particular, media use is often structured by gender and age power relations. The TV remote control, and who wields it, was/is often a key symbol of power within domestic viewing groups. So is the location and the hierarchy of uses of computers and games consoles, as well as parental anxieties and guilt about monitoring their children's use of them, sometimes via software.

All this has powerful implications for theories which imply a concentrated relationship between viewer and single text. But television/internet viewing has never felt like that a lot of the time. This is partly because of the flow which Raymond Williams (1974) and others have suggested is the characteristic experience of television, especially in commercially funded systems, keen to keep fingers off channel buttons, to keep 'eyeballs' on their channel. Indeed the main role of TV has been

**Ethnography**: direct observation of the activities of members of a particular social group and the description and analysis of such activity. Originally applied to other cultures (e.g. South Sea Islanders), and emphasising the need for immersion over time in the group. See Chapter 15.

Reminder from Chapter 1: 'empirical' means relying on observed experience as evidence for positions taken in debate.

*Figure 14.5* An image of the bored consumer, reduced to his or her zapping fingers?

The main audience assessment for BBC and ITV is conducted by BARB (Broadcasters' Audience Research Board, http://www.barb.co.uk), set up in 1981 to clarify the competing claims of BBC and ITV that each had the biggest audiences. BBC needed these to justify the licence fee, ITV to prove its attractiveness to advertisers.

described, by both academics and advertisers, as 'selling audiences to advertisers' – though 'selling audience attention' would be more accurate. Now, in a 'multi-platform', time-shifted, catch-up-TV, digital world, it is much harder to produce reliable figures for elusive audiences. Family members do not have to watch TV programmes in the order, or times, in which they are scheduled, or even on TV screens, let alone together. And TV is now joined by computer games, the internet and mobile phones. These have created a new world of 'living together separately' in the home – at least, in homes with broadband.

## Re-mediating audiences

Clearly a new phase of media use has been entered. UGC (user-generated content) is the term often used to describe supposedly new media input by audience members, often through the considerable interactive capacities of big media corporations like the BBC. But the concept of re-mediation can help us explore the extent to which 'audience material' (arguably a better term than UGC) has often been part of broadcasting, and other media, and has several meanings.

Audiences have rarely been simply those who had media 'delivered' to them. It is true that relatively few programmes emerge from outside TV's world, where professionals are sometimes said to make programmes partly for each other's approval, in the UK often with a very London-centred slant and view of 'the audience'. But audience members have previously been present *in* the media, especially TV, albeit in small spaces. They voiced concerns or pleasures with programmes, or with wider issues such as news coverage, in areas such as **access** programme-making (e.g. the 1980s and 1990s *Open Space* and *Open Door* slots on BBC2). Here power, including editorial control, was handed over to a group or individual outside the broadcasting institutions. BBC's *Feedback* slot is still a chance for listeners to comment on BBC programmes, though within broadcasting now the assumption often seems to be that audience members will interact directly with programme-makers on the website.

*Feedback* is produced by an independent company for BBC Radio 4.

It is described as the forum for 'comments, queries, criticisms and congratulations' on BBC programmes, by letter, fax, email (see BBC website).

### Opinion polls: audience 'voices'?

Public opinion polls are another form through which a supposed 'snapshot' of a sample of the audience is circulated (see Lewis 2001). These are highly constructed:

- the pollsters construct the questions;
- key phrases, likely to produce certain responses, are often used to

structure the direction and limits of discussion (such as 'illegal asylum seekers', actually a nonsense term since to apply for asylum is to go through legal channels);

- the work of questioning (on the street or door to door) is poorly paid and hard to check;
- it is suggested that opinion polls cannot pick up on the 'spiral of silence' (see Chapter 12) 'because people are responding to their perceptions of what the majority thinks' (Balnaves *et al.* 2009: 68);
- anonymity and even repeat voting is perhaps also a special problem for the reliability of some online polls;
- among some young people there is considerable peer pressure to perceive politics as 'uncool'.

## EXPLORE 14.8

- Have you experienced the pressure to perceive political actions as 'uncool'? (See Chapter 6 for discussion of this term, and its considerable power to marginalise political action.) For example, school strikes in protest at the invasion of Iraq were framed as 'simply about the desire to miss school'. Some students themselves began to see them in this way.

Whatever the results, polls can then be selected from, and parts of the results emphasised, amplified or ignored. There is repeated evidence, in both the UK and the US, that people polled want good health, education and public services and would consider higher taxes to pay for them. Yet this receives far less coverage in elections than the 'horse race' aspect: who's ahead? There is some pressure to ban such 'betting' polls during UK elections, given their potential influence on the perceived result.

## EXPLORE 14.9

Explore coverage of any recent or upcoming election.

- Take one opinion poll which has been heavily quoted. Find out as much as you can about its funding source, sample size, timing, media coverage and full results.
- Critically examine the questions it asked, and rephrase one or two of them, so as to encourage different results. How have the results been re-mediated in different media forms?

Many would say such audience presence has now been overtaken by the huge internet possibilities for blogging, texting, etc. Certainly big media institutions, especially news divisions, are keen to hear from their audiences, especially when they send what are perceived to be usable 'raw' material – photos, comments and video clips. Corporations are also very interested in free market research on their products: as Livingstone writes, 'the market watches closely and learns' (2009: 231).

---

## EXPLORE 14.10

- What do you think are the advantages and disadvantages of the 'anytime' interactive capacity for individual 'users' to send in comments, photos, etc. to broadcasting corporations (UGC)?
- How would you develop this, given the need for legal, anti-abusive, etc. filters which such material needs to go through for a big corporation to take responsibility for circulating it?
- Do you agree with the idea that being listened to is at least as important as having 'a voice'?

---

> **ONLINE RESOURCES** See Chapter 12 for more on UGC as well as a new case study on the **MSB5 website**.

> The 15-year-old female hero of *Fish Tank* (UK 2009), in a kind of rework of Ken Loach films, sees dancing to hip-hop music, TV make-up tips and a local 'talent show' as possible ways out of her grim and precarious life. The growing numbers of talent shows, such as *X-Factor*, in the US and UK, suggest the film makes a resonant link.

But audience 'material' does not only work via internet forms. TV entertainment formats, like talent shows, have not only put (highly selected) sections of 'the audience' literally on stage, in broadcast auditions as well as performances. They have also allowed viewers/fans to vote on contestants' performances, and to have their own discussion areas, at relatively little cost to the company involved. Illegal phone scams and voting frauds have also been part of this, a reminder of the power of the originating institution.

Such content is another example of longstanding re-mediation, into combinations of older and new media forms. Another is material co-produced by audience/users and institution, and shown on national TV, as in BBC's *Video Nation* shorts (though Channel 4 has a three-minute slot after its 7 p.m. weekday news programmes). BBC material now includes video diaries, developed into digital stories, lasting just two minutes.

Daniel Meadows, on http://www.bbc.co.uk/digitalstorytelling, describes an
intriguing new form, developed by BBC Wales, and viewable on the link
above. It's worth quoting at length.

> Digital Stories are short, personal, multimedia scraps of TV that people can
> make for themselves. They're 'mini-movies'. Desktop computers enabled
> with video editing software are used to synchronise recorded spoken
> narratives with scans of personal photographs.
>
> This project requires commitment for, as well as all the technical stuff
> that must be learnt, scriptwriting, picture editing and performance skills are
> also needed and these have to be worked on, which is why most Digital
> Stories are made by people attending workshops where participants can
> benefit from the help and advice of facilitators.

*Figure 14.6* BBC Wales' digital storytelling project.

> People of all ages and abilities make Digital Stories and many have
> testified how rewarding the experience is, for, when their story is shared
> with friends and family or posted on the web, they find they have
> discovered a new voice.
>
> There's a strictness to the construction of a Digital Story: 250 words, a
> dozen or so pictures, and two minutes is the right length. As with poetry
> these constraints define the form . . . and it's the observation of that form
> which gives the thing its elegance.

The dominant approach in media studies is one which celebrates the
powers of audiences, especially in their use of interactive media. This
goes along with powerful governmental, corporate and educational
discourses. This celebration comes partly from exploration of the activity
of fans and 'cult' viewers by academics such as Henry Jenkins, Matt
Hills, Lisa Lewis, Martin Barker and others, who emphasised that fans'
pleasures in certain texts (usually fictions) might be miles away from
either the meaning intended by their makers or the meaning produced
by most other viewers (see http://www.participations.org for current
research in this area). The entry of fans into higher education, as
students and then, some, as academics, has also led, via writings on
fandom, to greater visibility for audience creativity. This work somewhat

Jane Feuer, speaking in 1997,
suggested that for some
lesbian fans of the sitcom
*Ellen*, the 'coming out' of
the main character, while
politically admirable, deprived
them of the pleasures of
making their own secret
reading of phrases, etc.,
assumed to be 'not seen' by
the rest of the audience.

**'Prosumer'**: term coined by **Alvin Toffler** (1928–), described on Wikipedia as a 'futurologist'. It has several meanings, all of which collapse the distinction between 'professional'/ 'producer' and 'consumer'. In social media use, and some 'Media Studies 2.0', it refers to users (consumers) who 'produce' media texts.

resignified the image of fans as 'lonely obsessives', 'geeks', 'nerds' or potential stalkers. The fans were able, to an extent, to become 'producers' of their own episodes of favourite shows ('slash' forms), as well as consumer activists, lobbying television companies which sometimes, as a result, wrote episodes differently. Another step was then taken in academic study: terms like 'users' were replaced by 'co-creators' or even 'prosumers'.

**Example of a different kind of 'consumer' or 'fan' power: the boycott**

*Figure 14.7* Banner at the 2009 twentieth anniversary of the Hillsborough disaster of 1989, where ninety-six fans lost their lives.

- The *Sun* has been boycotted by many, on Merseyside, for libelling Liverpool soccer fans after the Hillsborough tragedy. The boycott has lasted for twenty years and is a powerful example of the actions of the relatively powerless (their 'audience' or consumers) against big media power. Boycotts are still potentially a site of 'user' power in this area, for print and (less easily) internet forms. This one was revived at the 2009 Labour Party conference when a union speaker tore up the *Sun* the day it headlined its switch of support to the Conservatives for 2010's General Election. (BBC Radio 4 produced a moving podcast, *The Reunion*, on the Hillsborough disaster, broadcast 12 April 2009.)
- Another example, in 2009, was Waitrose's decision to withdraw advertising from Fox News after their 'shock-jock' presenter Glenn Beck called President Obama an anti-white racist. Waitrose said it was responding to customer protests.

## Discussion: hybrid forms and *Mamma Mia!*

*Mamma Mia!* (US 2008) was the surprise cinema blockbuster success of 2008, is now the highest grossing musical film of all time, and became for a time the highest grossing film ever shown in the UK, surpassing even the phenomenal success of James Cameron's *Titanic* (US 1997). It is estimated that at least one in four UK households owns a DVD copy of *Mamma Mia!* The film is interesting to approach through ideas of the relatively low status of the audience (here largely women) and the form (a musical): hence the 'surprise' of its success. But further than this, the success and even the film itself might also be seen as the product of 'fans' or 'amateurs' (both ordinary and celebrity) in collaboration with a major US studio, Universal – a kind of hybridity.

Audience growth stretched right the way through repeat screenings and DVD sales, including a sing-along or karaoke version. Viewers were often fans of Abba, who first made their mark on the Eurovision Song Contest, and on whose songs the film was based. The film was directed by Phyllida Law, new to film, though an experienced theatre director.

*Figure 14.8* The cast and members of Abba at the premier of the movie version of the musical *Mamma Mia!* in Stockholm, 2008.

The film had an all-female producer/writer/director team (unusual, given women's lower status than men in Hollywood).

Its star, Meryl Streep, has talked of being a fan of the stage show, and of her glee at being offered the role, even though she was not known as a musical star. Not exactly an amateur, but her fandom was much publicised. Arguably the famously 'bad' singing of Pierce Brosnan was liked by fans both as 'having a go' (a classic amateur's pleasure) and as seeming, like much of the rest of the film, like karaoke for its stars.

## EXPLORE 14.11

- If you saw *Mamma Mia!*, how did you hear about it? What was your 'audience experience' – home or cinema? Karaoke user or 'straightforward' viewer? Enjoying the stars' (singing and dancing) performances partly as though they were amateur enthusiasts?
- Do you agree with these speculations about its connection to fan and other 'audience in the text' forms?

### Gated communities on the internet?

A darker connection to the rest of the real is suggested in Watkins' (2009) website and book (2010), arguing, in Jenkins' summary on his blog discussion, that racial and class inequalities are shaping internet access in the same ways that they do in some US neighbourhoods, involving

> a kind of 'white flight' as they escape the 'dangers' of their real world communities by seeking out other like-minded people in cyberspace . . . in what ways (do) our social networks online replicate – for better and for worse – our friendship networks offline, networks . . . shaped by continued segregation.
>
> Watkins [suggests] the language people use to describe and distinguish between Facebook and MySpace [has] long historical associations to our assumptions about race and class . . . MySpace is described as 'crowded, trashy, creepy, uneducated, immature, predators, crazy' while Facebook was praised as 'selective, clean, trustworthy, educated, authentic, college, private.' In other words, MySpace takes on values we associate with inner city slums, while Facebook is tied to the values one might associate with a gated community.

**EXPLORE 14.12**

- Discuss these comments. Do they correspond to your sense of these social networking sites? Or any others? Of 'trash' television and other kinds? (see Wood and Skeggs 2008).
- If you live outside the US, how far do the comments apply to your experiences?

## Conclusion

The image of 'the masses' and then of 'the (single) audience', mindlessly absorbing pernicious or corrupting 'messages', has mostly gone from academic research – though not always from certain kinds of media imagery and discussion. The concept of a single 'audience' shifted some years ago, to a sense of differentiated 'audiences' and 'readings'. This began the opening out to interactive media well before Web 2.0. This latest technological change co-exists with academic and business moves to using terms such as 'users', 'co-creators' and 'prosumers'. These signify the extent to which (some, broadband-ed) people seem to be increasingly active in their engagements with media, whether that be in political campaigns, in fans exerting pressure on companies to alter their favourite programmes, or even the business success of tiny initiatives such as Lauren Luke's make-up sessions on YouTube.

At the other extreme, 'active audience theory' has taken the stress on 'what people do with media' to its limit point, with an often hugely uncritical view of what 'empowered' audiences are able to do, or how they are differentiated (by gender, class, age, ethnicity and so on). It still makes sense to

a try to steer a way between these two extremes;

b reconsider some theories of audiences, and to try to combine, update or re-mediate them with newer approaches (see Livingstone 2009, Ruddock 2008).

In particular:

- textual approaches have not been rendered completely redundant: many blog comments are on texts which have been produced elsewhere, are massively circulated, and can be carefully or carelessly approached, as 'texts';
- the work of Bourdieu has been usefully rethought for the different kinds of 'capital' involved in competent media use, but approaches also involving gender, class, ethnicity and other familiar inequalities

> Think about how overworked and baggy this term 'interactive' is. Does it best describe what might be still called 'two-way' communication with distant others? See discussion of 'listening' below.

For a famous encounter between an articulate Falklands protester and Mrs Thatcher, on the sinking of the Argentinian battleship *Belgrano*, go to YouTube, 'Belgrano: A Reappraisal of Thatcher's Waffle'. An example of an earlier kind of TV 'interactivity', where 'power' was forced to listen.

remain useful ways of thinking of differentiated access to broadbanded activities;

- some theorists (see Crary 1999; Crawford 2009) are returning to, and reusing, the metaphor of 'listening' which is there in the word 'audience'. Corporations have long 'listened' to consumers' comments. 'Lurkers' on the internet (and in seminar and other discussions?), though named in perhaps a dismissive way, are partly 'listening' and learning from others' voices. So much media study celebrated 'having a voice', often in ways linked to neoliberal discourses, that it's refreshing to explore: who is listening? In how many different ways do we now 'listen' to different media? Could 'being properly listened to' (especially in 'flagship' media forms) be as powerful a demand as 'having a voice'?

When you read about 'audiences' or 'users', it's worth bearing all this in mind, as well as who is representing them/you in particular ways, and why that might be.

## References and further reading

Ang, Ien (1991) *Desperately Seeking the Audience*, London: Routledge.

Balnaves, Mark, Donald, Stephanie Hemelryk, and Shoesmith, Brian (2009) *Media Theories and Approaches: A Global Perspective*, London: Palgrave Macmillan.

Bandura, Albert, and Walters, R. (1963) *Social Learning and Personality Development*, New York: Holt, Rinehart & Winston.

Barker, Martin, and Petley, Julian (eds) (2001) *Ill Effects: The Media/Violence Debate*, 2nd edn, London and New York: Routledge.

Barkham, Patrick (2009) 'Not in Front of the Children?', *The Guardian*, G2, 14 October: 6–8.

Bennett, Tony, Savage, Mike, Silva, Elizabeth Bortolaia, Warde, Alan, Gayo-Cal, Modesto, and Wright, David (2009) *Class, Culture, Distinction*, London and New York: Routledge.

Blumler, Jay, and Katz, Elihu (1974) *The Uses of Mass Communication*, California: Sage.

Bourdieu, Pierre (1984) *Distinction: A Social Critique of the Judgement of Taste*, London: Routledge.

Bratich, Jack (2005) 'Amassing the Multitude: Revisiting Early Audience Studies', *Communication Theory*, 15: 242–65.

Brunsdon, Charlotte (1981) '*Crossroads*: Notes on Soap Opera', *Screen*, 22, 4: 52–7.

Cohen, Stan (1972) *Folk Devils and Moral Panics*, Oxford: Martin Robertson.

Cottle, Simon (2009) *Global Crisis Reporting: Journalism in the Global Age*, London and New York: Open University Press.

Crary, Jonathan (1999) *Suspensions of Perception: Attention, Spectacle, and Modern Culture* Cambridge, MA: MIT Press.

Crawford, Kate (2009) 'Following You: Disciplines of Listening in Social Media', *Continuum*, 23, 4 (August): 525–35.

Gerbner, G., and Gross, L. (1976) 'Living with Television: The Violence Profile', *Journal of Communication*, 28: 172–99.

Hall, Stuart (1974) 'The Television Discourse – Encoding and Decoding', *Education and Culture*, 25 (UNESCO); reprinted in Gray, Ann, and McGuigan, Jim (eds) (1997) *Studying Culture*, London: Arnold.

Hills, Matt (2002) *Fan Cultures*, London and New York: Routledge.

Hoijer, Brigitte (2004) 'The Discourse of Global Compassion: The Audience and Media Reporting of Human Suffering', *Media, Culture and Society*, 26, 4: 513–31.

Huesmann, Rowell, and Taylor, Laramie D. (2006) 'The Role of Media Violence in Violent Behaviour', *Annual Review of Public Health*, 27 (April): 393–415.

Kitzinger, Jenny (2004a) 'Audience and Readership Research', in Downing, John D., McQuail, Denis, Schlesinger, Philip, and Wartellia, Ella (eds) *The Sage Handbook of Media Studies*, London: Sage, pp. 167–81.

Kitzinger, Jenny (2004b) *Framing Abuse: Media Influence and Public Understandings of Sexual Violence against Children*, London: Pluto.

Lazarsfeld, P., Berelson, B., and Gaudet, H. (1944) *The People's Choice*, New York: Duell, Sloan and Pearce.

Lewis, Justin (2001) *Constructing Public Opinion: How Political Elites Do What They Like and Why We Seem to Go Along With It*, New York: Columbia University Press.

Lewis, Lisa (ed.) (1992) *The Adoring Audience: Fan Culture and Popular Media*, London: Routledge.

Livingstone, Sonia (2009) *Children and the Internet*, Cambridge and New York: Polity Press.

Morley, David (1980) *The Nationwide Audience*, London: BFI.

Morley, David (1986) *Family Television: Cultural Power and Domestic Leisure*, London: Comedia.

Morley, David (1992) *Television, Audience and Cultural Studies*, London: Routledge.

Philo, Greg (1990) *Seeing and Believing: The Influence of Television*, London and New York: Routledge.

Philo, Greg, and Berry, Mike, with Gilmour, Alison, Gilmour, Maureen, Rust, Suzanna, and West, Lucy (2004) *Bad News from Israel*, London: Pluto.

Root, Jane (1986) *Open the Box*, London: Comedia.

Ruddock, Andy (2008) 'Binge Drinking and Why Audiences Still Matter', *Sociology Compass*, 2, 1: 1–15.

Turkle, Sherry (1995) *Life on the Screen: Identity in the Age of the Internet*, New York: Simon & Schuster.

Watkins, S. Craig (2010) *The Young and the Digital: What the Migration to Social-Network Sites, Games, and Anytime, Anywhere Media Means for our future*, Boston: Beacon (and see his website http://www.theyoungandthedigital.com).

Williams, Raymond [1958] (1988) 'Culture is Ordinary', in *Resources of Hope: Culture, Democracy, Socialism*, London and New York: Verso, pp. 3–19.

Williams, Raymond (1974) *Television: Technology and Cultural Form*, London: Fontana; 2nd edn 1990.

Wood, Helen, and Skeggs, Bev (2008) 'Spectacular Morality', in Hesmondhalgh, David, and Toynbee, Jason (eds) *The Media and Social Theory*, London and New York: Routledge, pp. 177–89.

# Part III
# Research methods and references

Students doing internet library research, Cardiff University.

# 15 Research: skills and methods

- Basics
- Using the internet, and print forms
- Fear of 'theory'
- Methods
- Qualitative and quantitative
- Textual approaches
- Samples
- Focus groups
- 'Ethnographic' methods
- Footnote: Wikipedia
- References and further reading

This chapter will explore how you can best research the media, and theories of media. You already have skills for 'basic' academic work such as essays, which we will briefly recap and develop. Some of this chapter may also help your preparations for practical projects – a short film, a radio programme, or even 'practice-related' academic coursework.

See **MSB5 website** for updated material on production.

Most people feel qualified to comment on many aspects of media. But you have chosen to study and research them in more systematic ways. These involve:

- Learning how to find and use the resources available in your college (we'll use 'college' as shorthand for 'college or university' here). We can only give general guidance, and Web 2.0 has helped transform many of the resources available. Any worthwhile course will offer you specific help in using their libraries and their resources (books, journals, online databases, DVDs, etc.). We have also here recommended some excellent, more detailed guides to researching.
- Basics, such as how to reference correctly, and why this is important; how not to be afraid of the word 'theory'; why formulating your 'question(s)' and designing your research carefully is important, and so on.
- Key methods for media research, many involving distinctions such as qualitative and quantitative methods, already broached in Chapter 1.

Take a look at some of the recent articles listed in references, to gain a sense of what you could aspire to in your writing. We hope the rest of the book has already helped you with some of the skills and methods needed.

## Basics

The best academic work, such as a good dissertation, usually begins with a question. This is harder than it sounds: never worry about the amount of time you spend trying to get the right scale and angle of question or topic. You need to find it interesting, yet do-able, in order to produce well-designed, interesting work.

Some students first select very broad areas, like 'the representation of young men in British TV', maybe thinking it will be easy and interesting to find material and so they won't need to waste time formulating a research question. But the difficulty with such broad descriptions is that they don't help you search through an area, as a question does (after all, this is re*search*). A question should also produce worthwhile conclusions, which you will probably be asked to reflect on. How did it turn out, in terms of your expectations? What issues does it raise for future researchers in the same area? What would you warn them of?

You'll find that what's involved, for productive questions, is the right scale of topic area. Someone interested in 'representations of young men in British TV', for example, would do better to focus on one television genre, over a specific, manageable time period, and with a clearer question, perhaps involving the possible influence of some adverts, or popular programmes, perhaps on a specific aspect of being a young man (attitudes to cars on TV?). You will already know the basics of writing essays: take time to formulate the question or choose the best title for your interests; keep collecting ideas for as long as possible; read round the topic. As well as being interesting, this can actually *save* time: as your understanding increases you'll find it easier to structure and present your argument. Organise your preparation into a careful plan; use spell checks; fine tune your 'time management' skills so as to leave a space between completing the 'first draft' and handing in, when you can look over your writing almost like a stranger, reading it for clarity and other strengths, and weaknesses. Appreciate the slogan: *'writing is rewriting'*.

Add page numbers, and double check for accuracy (and sometimes for legality) and technical matters, such as adherence to what is called the 'house style' of referencing (usually the Harvard system, though your course may specify another one). Whichever system is used, it's important to be consistent and thorough in using it. We like giving the full first name of authors, for example, though others often use only initials. You should give the full URL of any web page you quote (see below) and it may also be useful to give the date on which you visited the site, since it may disappear or change in the meantime. You can pick up many slips at this stage of checking.

Finally: back it all up for the last time!

For practical work you're expected to think carefully about how to address your audience. For academic work too. Some find this difficult: how much knowledge are you supposed to assume the reader/marker has? Exactly how much 'proof' (references, etc.) do they need of statements you make? Discuss with your tutor if unsure. They want you to do well.

'Time management', a rather boring sounding term, is actually a tremendously useful skill, and for more than academic work. Also keep in mind the slogan 'Work smart not long', especially if doing a great deal of internet research (see below).

## Using the internet, and print forms

It is tempting now to do most of your research on the internet, partly because of its sheer speed. But to find useful internet material, you need to learn to search effectively. Check that the network in college is set up for your kind of research (i.e. don't just use the default search engine).

*Figure 15.1* A researcher wearing gloves to study primary documents in the National Media Museum, Bradford.

---

### EXPLORE 15.1

- Someone mentions in conversation that the following have useful websites: Ofcom; the British Library; the BBFC; the BBC; the Bradford Media Museum; the BUFVC ('especially the HERMES link and links to regional and local film archives'); the Colindale Library collection (at the British Library); *The Guardian* newspaper; the UKFC: the NFT Archive (via the BFI).
- We've deliberately not put web addresses in the above list, and not spelt out the acronyms, though you have a couple of other clues.
- Research and list their URLs. They are valuable resources. All of them are also called portals, offering extensive links to material on other sites. One non-academic US portal, www.findarticles.com, offers free articles from general interest magazines, academic journals and trade publications – all with some kind of reputation as credible sources.

---

**URL** stands for Unique Resource Locators, or internet addresses (e.g. http://www.nationalmedia museum.org.uk). URLs often have clues as to their nature in the last part of the address – see main text.

Make a list of the URLs you consult, stored as 'bookmarks' or 'favourites' on your computer, though if working on a college network it may be easier to keep a paper record. As a shortcut, keep the keyword in the address or URL, so you can use that word in your search engine to reach the site you want quickly.

Anyone can put up a website so check who is responsible for the ones you consult (on the home page). URLs have clues in the last part of the address: 'edu' or 'ac' marks an educational institution (though possibly a student page); 'org' is a 'not for profit' organisation; 'gov' is a government website; 'com' or 'co' is a commercial one; 'net' is a network provider, and 'mil' is related to military matters. Check how up to date is the page you're consulting. 'Dead' pages can linger for a long time and be fatally misleading.

Finding material on the web is often exciting: it can feel so fast, and it is enormously satisfying to find something after a long search. The hyperlink byways that sites invite you down are rather like browsing in a print-based library. Both activities can pleasantly while away the hours. But you might ask yourself, despite internet browsing feeling so fast, how

Recall our Introduction quoting Mayer-Schönberger's (2009) argument that the internet 'remembers' everything, and that this may give others, perhaps long in the future, informational power over you.

**Melvil Dewey** (1851–1931) created the library classifying system, updated many times. It puts library material into ten broad groupings. This book is likely to be included in the Social Sciences 300 group – '301 Mass Media'.

time-consuming is it if you have to verify what you find? Would it have been easier to look something up in a book? For this you need to navigate the Dewey decimal system of classification and know how to use the catalogue indexes.

However . . . books are rarely free from errors, and are always 'out of date' since it usually takes several months to process a manuscript through proofing and production processes. Textbooks, like this one, can take longer and are usually a mixed form, not referencing as much as other academic sources because of the need to explain clearly, unclogged by too many footnotes, etc. Textbooks also use a less formal mode of address than standard academic research.

Journal articles take slightly less time to produce, and are more readily put online. Some of them, whether online or print, will be 'peer reviewed', which means every article is assessed by a 'peer' or equal in the field. Depending on the word limit there will be specified roles for footnotes and other less 'official' spaces for tentative thought and talk. These avenues can be expanded on as part of blogs. We've cited a few previously. They can respond to media events immediately, though you need to check for adequate referencing. Indeed, a quality index is often worth looking for, whatever the source.

You need experience of using both the web and some print resources, preferably with expert help, and with practice at refining searches, in order to conduct the best possible research into your chosen topic.

## Fear of 'theory'

'Theory' has often been a 'boo word', especially in Britain. It is regularly opposed to 'hooray' terms like 'practice', 'experience', 'common sense', 'the real'. Or it's called 'airy-fairy', 'high', 'highbrow', 'grand', 'abstract' – all suggesting it disdains, feels above, the ordinary. See Branston (2000).

'I love it when you talk post-structuralist': a way of joking about the allure of 'theory', as well as a distrust of it? Or does it seem to be a kind of style accessory for some?

You will gather material in an attempt to demonstrate that a hypothesis (a question which will provoke useful argument) can be 'proved', usually in the context of major debates and theories. Theory is often a scary or even a derided term. But theory is ordinary: most people want to have an explanation of where and how their experiences fit into broader frames. These are often speculative or provisional, 'for now', and open to discussion. Some 'style' journalism and political discourses often imply that 'intellectualising' is unnecessary. Ironically they themselves operate a theory of culture, in the process of arguing against theorising! Yet as well as being 'ordinary' (about a desire to organise our experiences into broader explanations), theories are also 'special' and 'specialised' within academic discourse. They are explanatory frameworks for the area of your interest.

Sometimes students assume that theories are simply broad accounts of their field. But any theory, in order to be productive of debate, needs to carve out its own 'model' of its object, its key questions, its sense of what counts as evidence. This has to involve ignoring huge areas that it cannot or does not want/need to incorporate or see as relevant. Someone exploring 'the look' in the past ten years of mountaineering films does not need to produce a theory of audience responses to those films, though they may acknowledge them in passing.

---

**EXPLORE 15.2**

- Jot down a rough outline of any theory which you hold – it may be to do with a particular games maker, or to do with other parts of your life – the function of schooling, or Facebook.
- What is your evidence for your theory? How have you come to feel you 'know' about your chosen object?

---

This does not mean that you will be limited to just one theoretical approach in your research. Theorists are much more likely now to show an awareness of other theories of their object, even if only to acknowledge that those may not be the route they want to take. '**Thick**' description, in research, is a term you may come across. 'Thick' is used not in its everyday senses, but denotes research which combines different approaches, especially in social sciences, in order to explain not just human forms of behaviour, but also their contexts and histories.

> 'Thick' in this sense was coined by the philosopher **Gilbert Ryle** (1900–76), but most famously applied, to ethnography, by **Clifford Geertz** (1926–2006). See the long extract from Geertz (1973) at http://www.sociosite.net/topics/texts/Geertz_Thick_Description.php.

Very often in media studies the theories and approaches drawn on are interdisciplinary, emerging from social sciences, literature, economics, psychology and so on. They will also border on the area known as Cultural Studies. In this book, for example, we draw on Marxist theories of economics, theories of signification emerging from language study and so on. See **triangulation**, below, for an account of why you need to combine theories, methods and approaches.

## Methods

If a theory is put to research use, it draws on a **methodology**, or set of philosophical beliefs about its object, which will produce methods for research. You need to reflect on the skills you will need, or may already have, for this work. Your dissertation will probably have a Literature Review chapter.

The Literature Review is where you show what reading you have done for your research, but is not simply a listing of relevant print and internet sources. It is where you show an awareness of how the area has been theorised and explored, and how you have selected key reading for your particular piece of investigation.

So, you might cite some authors as very useful or interesting, with others as only relevant for different kinds of research in the area. Once you have done it you have achieved quite a lot of the hard groundwork for the dissertation. For one, you will have had to think carefully about what's special to *your* topic and chosen approach, and which methods flow from that.

When the Colindale Library newspaper collection was digitised in 2009 Catherine Hall, social historian, commented that when simply searching via keywords, you may miss questions of layout, as well as the coincidental discoveries you can make (as she did) when researching something else (Radio 4, Today programme, 18 June 2009).

'Ear witness' is a legal term for one who attests to something s/he has heard in person. We add it as a small flag to the new area of interest, in some media studies, to metaphors of 'listening' as well as of supposedly empowered 'voices' in media discourse. A possible research topic?

Though beware of 'taking on' highly speculative theories. A 'speculation' was defined by Raymond Williams as 'an idea that feels no need to prove its relation to practice' (1983: 316–18, quoted in Branston 2000). Make sure you are not trying to provide evidence for or against such a speculative theory where it would be inappropriate.

This is followed (or it sometimes includes) a statement of your Methodology, which again involves apparently scary words, referring to the basics of your selected approach. A couple of them: **epistemology** is the study of ways of knowing, of how sets of knowledge are created. It also involves an even more abstract term, **ontology**, a philosophical area involved in asking what we take to be real, and what is knowable. *The Matrix* (US 1999) was seen as being partly interested in this area, especially for digital cultures. So maybe it is not as remote as it seems. You will not usually be expected to spend a long time discussing ontological theories, but it is useful to have a sense of what such terms refer to.

Your methodology, then, should be coherently related to the techniques, or methods, which you use in collecting evidence for your research. This may involve primary or secondary sources. 'Primary research' implies that the researcher, or the source being used, is the first agent to collect and collate the material. For historical events this may involve those who are directly involved, 'eye witnesses', in an event, however large or small, via diary entries, reports, interviews very soon after. Often these are organised into archives. But autobiographies, reminiscences and interviews made quite some time later may also be used. For such events now, with digital and interactive resources, a photo or piece of footage taken by mobile phone is a likely source.

Secondary research labels accounts by those who were not present at the event. And, at a further distance, a highly theoretical piece of research may involve other people's theories, though the researcher will hope to shape their own, original position, or question, or piece of evidence. Though 'secondary' has connotations of being less authentic, because it's already mediated in some way, remember that every 'record' is a mediated account. It's always important to research the 'angle' of even witnesses to the event, large or small. Knowledgeable accounts,

*Figure 15.2* The French National Library (BNF) is one of many sumptuous, often ancient buildings, including universities, around the world. Like smaller, local libraries, they house books and journals, etc., as well as archive and other resources. In the age of Web 2.0 it is easy to ignore them, but they usually include facilities for digital research, as visible here.

sensitive to key details, are unlikely to be the same as 'unbiased' ones, which of course will themselves be from an angle – literally, in the case of many supposedly neutral filmed news reports.

One way of addressing the problems of possible omissions, unreliabilities or contradictions between reports is called triangulation. It's a metaphor from geometry, was developed in navigation, and is now used in Satnavs. It finds the location of a point by measuring *angles* to it from other known points, rather than measuring distance directly. For research it describes combinations of research methods, and often of witness accounts, whether 'primary' or 'secondary'. It is increasingly important given the convergence of different media forms, as well as a certain 'porousness' or blurring (e.g. between areas such as news, or even some fictions, and certain 'user' material present within it).

*Figure 15.3* Sea Island survey diagram, using triangulation, described by the Chinese mathematician Liu Hui in the eighteenth century.

## Qualitative and quantitative

In Chapter 1 we introduced two approaches to analysing media: **qualitative** and **quantitative**. We'll now go into a little more detail about these methods. As their names suggest, they are interested, respectively, in

- exploring the *qualities* of individual 'texts', interpreted broadly so as to include audience responses as explored in interviews, focus groups and so on, as well as in individual films, games set-ups, etc. and

- registering what can be discovered by counting repeated patterns of elements across groups (or '*quantities*') of texts. Quantifiable research is partly defined by being amenable to statistical analysis, which qualitative research is not, generally (though there are some computer programmes which do promise to perform this; see the helpful discussion in Deacon *et al.* 2007: 343–56).

An opposition between these approaches has often been declared, as though they were mutually exclusive. They are different, but they can be, and are often, used together, both in academic and in commercial or governmental research. Importantly, each of them is best used with an awareness of, or even alongside, the other one, as supplementing some of its own weaknesses. Celebrated analyses of individual texts like ads using semiotic approaches (essays by Barthes, or Williamson) implicitly suggested that such 'texts' do have some kind of typicality, or relation to representative *quantities* of other such ads, posters, etc. Otherwise, what would be the academic interest in analysing them, if they were simply random products? But exploring such 'typicality' is now much more possible.

> Remember that a 'text' can be anything that you are studying. Hence the sounds, gestures, speech of people in a focus discussion group can be studied as carefully as a photo or a computer game.

## Textual approaches

> Revise Chapter 1 and case study for specific examples from photographic, poster, TV, radio and other textual systems.

Whatever your 'text', in the broad sense – a news report, a transcription of a focus group discussion, a film, the design of a game setting – qualitative textual methods will help you pay attention to its specific qualities. These 'texts' exist as part of a specific form – words, moving images in combination with sounds, FX such as 3D and so on. This form will have its own traditions (especially genres) and these components in combination are *likely* to resonate for viewers and users. Clearly an accompanying study of audiences' involvement (triangulating your approaches) will help ensure you don't just fly away on speculations about the 'meaning' of this or that colour, word, etc. – enjoyable though that can be. It is possible to attempt **replicability** (see p. 420) here as with any other method. It is likely, for example, that within certain cultures the colour 'red' may signify in particular ways, or that a particular genre (say, horror) will be understood as playful in the ways it constructs certain kinds of violent deaths, or at least to be relying on viewers' familiarity with the FX used in gory scenes.

We don't have space to give full textual analysis examples here (though see other chapters and the **MSB5 website** for examples and connecting links). Good sources for *moving image analysis*, with methods which can be applied to TV, cinema and other 'moving sound-image forms', include Tim Corrigan's brief guide and David Bordwell's blog http://www.davidbordwell.net. Convergence and re-mediation (from cinema to some narrative shaped games, for example) of course mean you need to be sensitive to changed contexts, but to ignore any attempt at close textual analysis would be a real loss to many research projects.

For *verbal analysis*, media study has sometimes developed the close analysis of the spoken language art known as rhetoric, or that aspect of language which is designed to persuade. This has long been part of many elite educations.

> Rhetoric was seen as an art in both 'ancient' Greece and Rome, where issues of public policy and so on were decided by 'public' spoken debate (quotation marks around 'public' because it usually excluded women and slaves). Its devices (points made in groups of 1–2–3, some repetition of key phrases, an argument leading to a 'grand' conclusion, etc.) can still be observed in political speeches and debate.

Media studies sometimes built on and developed such analysis, sometimes for visual forms, via semiotics. Later the work of language theorists such as Norman Fairclough was also incorporated. Fairclough developed approaches often called critical discourse analysis (abbreviated to CDA) or sometimes critical media linguistics. This seeks to centre analysis of media language forms in social power structures, and to explore their relation to ideology, especially where its workings are least visible (see Chapters 6 and 12). Words are explored, especially in news forms, with an eye to what are called lexical choices – what other words could have been deployed? (See Chapter 12.) With what effects on flows of sympathy, feelings that some news characters are familiar and comforting while others are not, and so on? Are some terms melting into others, as seems to be the case with 'activist' and 'terrorist' in some discourses? How do some news forms invite us to imagine that 'the

Explore the BBFC website http://www.bbfc.co.uk/ for discussion of the slightly different classification approaches they have used for horror films in recent years, precisely because of the assumed specialist audience who will tolerate extreme FX.

A related example: in November 2009 US politician Al Gore argued, in relation to climate change, that 'civil disobedience has an honourable history, and when the urgency . . . crosses a certain line I think [it] is quite understandable' (in Burkeman 2009). This revived a key term, from Civil Rights and Gandhian politics.

"We leave 'will not be swayed by polls' in the speech. The focus group loved it."

*Figure 15.4* From http://www.CartoonStock.com

The quality of the statistical methods or the software used is also important, though a slightly different area. See Deacon *et al.* (2007), Chapter 14, 'Using computers', for detailed discussion of such aspects of statistical methods.

public' somehow does not include 'strikers' or 'protesters', that such groupings are neatly separate? A related term from linguistics, nominalisation, refers to the way that processes are transferred into objects (often by verbs becoming nouns) so as to weaken a sense of responsibility, or who is doing what. Deacon *et al.* (2007), in their helpful account of this field, give the example of 'Roof bolt fury after second pit collapse' where the noun 'fury' hides who are furious, and why.

Similarly 'passivisation' deflects questions of who is doing what into a passive form, as in 'airline staff are expected to return to work tomorrow', where we are not told who exactly has this 'expectation', though it arguably helps make a non-return to work seem 'disappointing'.

Such strategies can result in what is called the **mode of address** of a text. What assumptions are embedded in the way that 'you' and 'we' are positioned in relation to the speaker ('most viewers will feel anger that . . .', etc.). Is it assumed you are with the lynch mob, or group of adoring fans, or at a distance from an event or person? Though Fairclough and others focus on linguistic positioning, a familiar query in some news media research asks about visual and gestural placings: where is the camera positioned? Which sources are asked for opinions, and of these, which opinions are followed up, or given credibility whether in language or respectful gesture, etc. Many 'we' terms can be hard to opt out of, such as the national 'we', or the 'we' that is 'of-course-outraged'. For example, many news bulletin presenters now make quite clear, via gesture, tone of voice, frowns, smiles, etc., as well as by certain words, how they are feeling about a story, and perhaps by implication, how they assume we too feel, or should feel.

To return to the ways that quantitative and qualitative overlap: for quantitative methods, such as content analysis of texts or audience surveys, the *quality* of the questions asked, and the conclusions drawn, is a key factor. Indeed, your research will only be as good as the questions you ask. Very often research combines short, 'closed' questions, for which Yes or No, or a selected number is the only answer, along with more open ('qualitative') questions. The closed questions will produce numerical data that can be easily input into a spreadsheet to produce analyses. The 'open' ones invite more qualified/qualitative responses, but they are much less easily counted or given statistical form.

## Samples

Sampling is also 'ordinary' – flicking through cable channels or a magazine is an everyday sampling activity. Researching an area means that, whichever approach(es) you use, you will usually be arguing from more than one example. Even if you focus on, say, a single film, you will need to locate it in the context of generic frames, perhaps films it is contrasted with, its industrial or production history, and so on. The size and selection of your sample is a key part of the quality of evidence you present.

One term used in a specialist way here is 'population'. As Deacon *et al.* (2007) put it: 'Samples are taken from "populations" [which, here] are not necessarily made up of people; they can be aggregates of texts, institutions, or anything else being investigated . . . [they] are defined by specific research objectives, and alter in relation to them' (2007: 43). They then give an everyday example: the difference between sampling a bottle of milk to see if it is sour and testing for infective agents in a whole nation's milk supply – different questions, different sample sizes and methods.

Many research stages and methods are involved with each other. Defining the 'population' for your project, for example, will not only help you decide whether your sample is appropriate, that is, representative of the area you want to research. It may also help you refine your initial question. Your sample can be random or non-random. As the terms suggest, random sampling (also sometimes called probability sampling) signifies selection by chance – maybe people in the street or students on a module. But it also means that each unit selected has an equal chance of being selected. Small samples often need to use random sampling, but equally need to acknowledge that.

Non-random sampling involves deliberate selection processes – perhaps to try for age balance or other kinds of representativeness (though representativeness need not always be a research aspiration). The larger the sample the more convincing it may be, especially for quantitative research. Qualitative approaches, to texts or audiences, tend to use smaller samples, and to put the research effort into arguing in other ways for

a   their specific qualities

b   their connections to broader social and cultural processes (the Frankfurt School and other highly theoretical writings are sometimes cited as operating 'qualitative' methods).

The composition of your sample is important, as is the 'counting' method you use. This includes debates around different computing programs which may be available to you, for both methods.

Ethical issues should also play into your sampling and other methods. For one, you need to ask any participants, even on the internet, for consent, and to make sure you have given them the information they need to give you informed consent, often in written form. They must

'Karl Marx was the first to conduct a modern survey . . . [sending] over 20,000 questionnaires to workers in factories asking about their relationship with their bosses . . . Apparently Marx received no replies' (Balnaves *et al.* 2009: 281).

Possible methodological problems here?

Sometimes the metaphor of a 'snapshot' is used for samples that acknowledge their smallness within a huge area – perhaps because they are student explorations, for example. Nevertheless they usually seek some kind of representativeness.

There's a strong connection here to material in Chapter 13 pp. 367–8 on ethical issues for documentary. On some courses it may be possible for you to submit an academically researched dissertation as a documentary.

know what they are taking part in, that they can withdraw from the research at any time, that they need not answer all questions, and can be assured that your use of the data will be confidential, know they are not being misled, or will suffer distress, and so on. Your institution should have a policy on research ethics, which may apply to your work, and even be laid out as a form for you to complete and sign.

Not even the official British subject association, MeCCSA (Media, Communication and Cultural Studies Association), has yet thought it appropriate to write a special code of ethics for this broad, and interdisciplinary subject area.

If you want to go further than the guidelines of your institution, you might try these links, for whichever is the nearest subject area to that of your project.

- British Sociological Association: http://www.britsoc.co.uk/equality/ Statement+Ethical+Practice.htm
- British Psychological Society: http://www.bps.org.uk/downloadfile.cfm?file_ uuid=5084A882-1143-DFD0-7E6C-F1938A65C242&ext=pdf
- the Social Research Association – for both a code and relevant discussion documents: http://www.the-sra.org.uk/ethical.htm
- another valuable overview, developing a code for 'all socio-economic research' in the 'respect project', is at http://www.respectproject.org/ ethics/412ethics.pdf
- for the Market Research view of this: http://www.mrs.org.uk/standards/ codeconduct.htm
- see also by Haigh and Jones (2007).

Another ethical area, whether in the actual discussions, etc., or in the ways you write them up, involves avoiding the use of language which ignores the sensitivities of groups who may elsewhere be subject to racist, sexist, ageist and disablist labels. See the BSA guidelines above.

Plagiarism also deserves to be seen as an ethical issue and is rightly a term you will repeatedly come across. It describes a form of cheating and is sometimes classified under the heading 'academic honesty'. Remember you are not only cheating other students in your class by trying to gain this unfair advantage. Properly referenced writing embodies valuable aims: it is not just a way of making an argument look weighty. It is special – and does not usually exist outside 'the academy' (only rarely will journalists put references to their work, and some will not even name their sources in their stories). Academic writing usually makes more effort than most to be scrupulous: in the use of clear referencing, in avoiding plagiarism, in trying to make explicit its own conceptual basis, in guaranteeing anonymity for research interviewees and so on.

By accurately referencing whatever quotes or reading (internet or print) have been used in your research, you acknowledge other people's work. That work is thereby made accessible to others, who can then go on to check the full source, if that is their interest. In addition many examiners now use services such as TurnItIn.com which instantly references your work against the entire internet. Or they can Google a phrase from your essay and find all other instances of its occurrence online.

> Some kinds of plagiarism are more serious than others. In 2003 then-UK Home Secretary David Blunkett and Prime Minister Tony Blair apologised for the so-called 'dodgy dossier' used to help justify the invasion of Iraq, with all its bloody consequences. This had been largely lifted, often word for word, from a student's PhD thesis, published on the internet.

## Focus groups

A popular method in both academic and commercial research (e.g. by advertisers and PR organisations) is bringing together small numbers of people into what is called a **focus group**. This is part of a qualitative emphasis, from the 1980s onwards, on how audiences 'read' media output (see Kitzinger and Barbour 1998). It can provide rich qualitative material, via careful discussion of the transcripts of the discussion, often including notes on body language, hesitations, group dynamics and so on. Selection is still important, and you need to explain how you have made it, as well as other parts of the construction of the group.

- How have you contacted them?
- Where did you decide to hold the discussion, and why? In your home? In a room at college? Somewhere else?
- Did you decide to use markers of informality, such as offering tea, biscuits, comfortable seating?
- How did you interpret silences, or patterns of listening or not on the part of some participants?
- How did you try to cope with someone who seemed to be unduly dominating discussion?
- How did you decide to record the discussion and why? This is a major part of your evidence, and important for the replicability of your findings.

*Figure 15.5* As with unwanted statistics (see Chapter 1, p. 28), this cartoon suggests how tempting is the impulse to 'tidy up' the often messy or ambiguous phrasings and hesitations of an interview, or a focus group.

Replicability is an important methodological ideal. It refers to the attempt to make the quality of a research method unambiguous, so that 'different researchers at different times using the same categories would [interpret] the [material] in exactly the same way' (Rose 2001: 62). It cannot be absolutely guaranteed, but it is a valuable ideal, whatever methods you use. (We know we also mentioned this in Chapter 1: it's important!)

This relates interestingly to theories of 'performativity' in documentary debates (see Chapter13), as well as to notions of epistemology and ontology, see above.

Though focus groups are useful, you may be asked to operate triangulation (see p. 413) or a careful combination of methods which can enrich research findings. A focus group might usefully be combined with a questionnaire, which itself perhaps mixes multiple-choice type questions (with possibly a ranking of responses) as well as allowing some 'open' questions. As with all research you need to keep trying to understand the extent to which your questions, or presence even, have affected the group 'under observation'.

- Have your questions, and what you think you hear in the answers to them, been over-selected to fit a pre-existing agenda or theory?
- How are you addressing the inevitable imbalance in power between researcher and researched. How might this affect the findings?

There are no perfect answers to these questions, and they make research intriguing. But your tutors will expect you to show evidence that you have considered and tried to work with them, and, at the end of your research, have reflected on their strengths and shortcomings.

## 'Ethnographic' methods

There are a range of other methods you may feel fit your topic better. You might ask your participants to fill in diaries, perhaps of media use or of a developing story in the media, comparing interactive and other coverage. These can then be analysed, using whatever methods you carefully research. The usual questions of performativity (see Chapter 13) arise – e.g. how far have the diaries been shaped by the knowledge that you will be using them? Or you might try to avoid such problems and simply observe people, inconspicuously – in a multiplex as they queue and choose films for example.

Reminder from Chapters 1 and 13: 'empirical' means relying on observed experience as evidence for positions taken in debate. Though often attacked as 'untheorised' it will usually have a theoretical base (involving the value of such observations). Sometimes also called 'positivist'.

More ambitiously you may attempt a small **ethnographic** study, a key empirical method. We broached this in Chapter 13, and explained there how it uses a tool from anthropology fieldwork, or the study of other peoples/cultures. Ethnography tries to capture a way of life as it actually happens, not simply as related in later accounts. Researchers try to immerse themselves in the lives of a particular group, over significant periods of time, and to provide an account of its meanings and activities 'from the inside'. Media studies adaptations of this have usually taken less time, and used much smaller samples and activities from cultures with which the 'observer' is familiar, such as TV viewing. Rather than actually living with people, the media researchers mentioned in Chapter 14, for example, simply observed closely people's uses of the internet, TV or videos.

*Figure 15.6* Margaret Mead

Margaret Mead's pioneering work *Coming of Age in Samoa* was first published in 1928. It was a groundbreaking piece of cultural anthropology and a case study in such research methods itself. It tried to 'give voice' to parts of a very different culture, and to respect very different ways of shaping assumptions about adolescence from those current in Mead's native US.

Like many celebrated pieces of research, it fitted contemporary agendas – here, heated debates on 'the state of American youth' and changing attitudes to sexuality, as well as, later, to the more relaxed attitudes to childcare associated with Dr Spock (not 'Mr Spock' of *Star Trek* fame).

The cover (2001 edition) here suggests perhaps some of the issues raised for such anthropology. What would you speculate (and this is highly speculative) that the expressions, dress, deportment, look to camera, etc. here suggest about the attitudes of these three women to being photographed? Or indeed the limits of photography in suggesting the differences between the three?

Though speculative, interpreting such body language, etc. can be a valid part of this type of research, on large and smaller scales (as for media studies of audiences). See Wikipedia for accounts of controversies around Mead's research. Later interviews (themselves contested) with Samoan women said they were joking or exaggerating in what they told Mead. Even using later methods, such as Web 2.0 research, such questions are key ones for this kind of ethnographic work.

More recent adaptations of fieldwork have employed participant observation methods, i.e. participating in the lives of groups to be studied for an extended period of time, asking questions and observing what goes on. The immersion is nowhere near as extended, either in time or space, as in the ethnography described above but it can still produce valuable findings.

You might study either 'real people' in live, real-time contact, or increasingly, you may take part in Web 2.0 chat rooms, blogs and so on. This internet work raises issues around anonymity, identities, ethics (there are especial problems researching areas such as paedophilia) and the nature of the evidence you collect. Other decisions need to be made: do you 'lurk'? What information do you give the chat room about your presence, purpose and so on. Web 2.0 usage may also mean the research unavoidably spreads from local to global contexts, which you may or may not wish to happen.

Finally, in this list of updates to a method developed before the advent of the internet, the boundary between observer and observed can be blurred by researchers who are themselves pre-existing members of the group to be explored – most often in 'fan' research – fanthropology if you like. Some of the same rules and problems apply – how far can any observation avoid affecting what is 'observed'? What are the power relations between the two cultures of 'observed' and 'observer'? Many would argue this represents a welcome shift in the balance of power between 'fans' and 'academics', or the researchers and the researched.

> One interesting area to research might be the phenomenon known as 'lurking', all the way from why is it named in this way, through to: what are people doing when they lurk? Are different kinds of listening going on? Is there a drive to lurk in 'hot spots', 'watching' heated debate or even abuse of various kinds?

See Balnaves *et al.* (2009) for a detailed account of participant observer research into online dating agencies and the experiences and motivations of those using them (pp. 286–9). This is followed by a thoughtful section on global cyber-bullying and how it might be researched – and avoided (pp. 289–91).

Ethnographic approaches have been used in media and cultural studies, usually in smaller scale work. There have since the 1950s been studies of how newsrooms produce their output, often focusing on the role of editorial 'gatekeepers'. The late 1990s saw a renewal of interest in such studies as a way of understanding the impact of technological change in newsrooms (see Cottle 2007). Such production studies are much rarer for other media forms. There have also been studies of TV audiences, and also internet usage (see Chapter 13).

## EXPLORE 15.3

You, like many others, may be a cash-strapped student doing paid work to support your studies. In addition to this you will probably be addressed by the alcohol industry as a key consumer. You may feel (or have felt) under enormous pressure to seem to be 'having fun' (often identified as alcohol related), especially during Freshers' week.

*Figure 15.7* Enid/Thora Birch in *Ghost World* (US/UK/Germany 2001) is put through a training scheme in how to sell 'large size' and avoid mentioning 'chemical goo' or otherwise comment on the 'concessions' in her local multiplex.

*Figure 15.8* See **MSB5 website** for the case study on 'Researching mobile phone technologies' which explores internet research in more detail. It raises the issue of different terms being used across the world, making searches complex – the US usage is 'cell phone' rather than 'mobile phone'.

- With this dual identity you could observe, as well as participate in, experiences related to your studies (we're not joking). Bar work, its 'training' procedures and assumptions, its pricing and surrounding advertising could be used, in your research, as a perspective on cultures of drinking and the marketing of alcohol. Ruddock (2008) has some useful suggestions for context (in a piece we've also cited in Chapter 14) though working mostly with students as 'audience' for alcohol ads.
- Cinemas and other entertainment 'hubs' are additional spaces where you might observe, as well as participate in paid work, with a view to exploring distribution and exhibition practices, the role of 'concessions' as part of branding, pressures to high 'container size' consumption and so on.

## EXPLORE 15.4 SO FAR . . .

Supposing you wanted to research the adequacy of journalists' suggestions that the huge increase in the numbers of students enrolling on degree courses in forensic science (from 2 in 1990 to 285 in the UK in 2009) is due to the popularity of *CSI* and series like it.

- You think they may be making patronising assumptions about such students. What skills and methods might you expect to need? The hypothesis might be pursued via interviews with a relevant sample of students, located in media theories of audience. It might further include ('triangulation') textual analysis of the relevant articles, their location in particular newspapers and research summaries, if they are being drawn on (or not). Your 'population' would be all students enrolling on these courses (and all articles on the phenomenon, but we'll leave this for now).
- What would your sample be? If your university has a forensic science department, you might interview students there. Some alluring questions arise about it:

    Qs: First years? All? How to manage gender, class or ethnic, etc. mixes?

    Qs: How does the time scale of the reported increase in student numbers (1990 to 2009) correlate with the run of *CSI* in its different versions, and of other series?

    Qs: What methods would you use, and why? Focus group discussion? Survey? Questionnaire, with open and closed questions? Personal interviews? Textual analysis, e.g. of parts of the programmes, or of students' verbal responses?

> With undergraduate research it is understood that your time and resources
> are not those of professional researchers: 'convenience sampling' ('snapshots'), or
> using interviewees who are close to hand, is often used to describe one of the
> necessities of such work. But even so you can do some intriguing research into
> questions which interest, or even baffle, you.

You need experience of using both the web and book resources,
preferably with expert help, so as to conduct meaningful research, and
practise refining searches.

## Footnote: Wikipedia

Let's turn finally to a controversial source. In the past decade a new, free,
web-based resource, Wikipedia, has emerged. It was first launched in
2001 by Jimmy Wales. 'Wiki' is from the Hawaiian 'wiki wiki', meaning
'quick' or 'informal', and 'pedia' from the Greek for 'education', echoing
'encyclopaedia'. It claimed 65 million visitors monthly in 2009, and
3 million articles in English – twenty-five times the size of the
*Encyclopaedia Britannica*.

It is designed, and constantly updated, by mostly anonymous
volunteer users. It has editors overseeing what happens (like
'moderators' in chat rooms) and anyone who uses the site can start a
new page or edit an existing page. It has page links from each major
article to smaller 'stubs', which print encyclopaedias could not include.

The 'About Wikipedia' section of the website suggests that older
articles tend to be more comprehensive and balanced, while newer
articles more frequently contain significant misinformation, or even
vandalism. There's also a useful guide to researching with the site, and
a section ('Why Wikipedia is not so great') explaining that

> any given article may be, at any given moment, in a bad state: . . .
> in the middle of a large edit or . . . recently vandalized . . . [The site]
> is also subject to remarkable oversights and omissions. There is no
> systematic process to make sure that 'obviously important' topics are
> written about, so at any given time Wikipedia may be wildly out of
> balance in the relative attention paid to two different topics. For
> example, it is far more likely that the English-language Wikipedia
> will have at least some material about any given small US village than
> about a moderately-sized city in sub-Saharan Africa.

Wikipedia founder Jimmy Wales on the BBC Radio 4 *Today* programme cited the Wikipedia disclaimer 'the neutrality of this article is in dispute' and said he wished BBC News would use such disclaimers about its stories (31 January 2009).

In this sense it is more like a library than an encyclopaedia, where articles would be shorter, and would 'end' or produce a final summary of an area, at least until the next edition. In theory Wikipedia's pieces never will end.

Wikipedia has turned into

a relatively reliable source of information on the widest possible range of subjects because, on the whole, the good drives out the bad. When someone sabotages or messes with an otherwise sound entry, there are plenty of people out there who see it as their job to undo the damage, often within seconds of its happening.

(Runciman 2009)

Academics will often rightly caution use of it as a primary research tool, as with any reference work (though the links on it will often take you to primary web-based sources). And Reuters News, for example, say (2009) they do not use it.

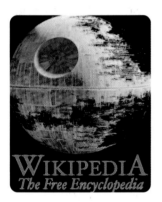

*Figure 15.9* An internet image of 'the dark side of Wikipedia'.

Siobhan Butterworth (2009), readers' editor of *The Guardian*, explored a recent Wikipedia hoax (see http://www.guardian.co.uk/commentisfree/2009/may/04/journalism-obituaries-shane-fitzgerald). Her piece is far from a condemnation of Wikipedia, but does raise issues around its journalistic usage, the regulation of such usage, as well as 'research methods' in the age of Web 2.0.

A March 2009 obituary of French composer Maurice Jarre began and ended with quotes, apparently by him. The words, however, were those of Shane Fitzgerald – a 22-year-old student at University College Dublin who had put them on Jarre's Wikipedia page a day earlier, shortly after the composer died, and just as writers were working on his obituaries. *The Guardian's* obituary writer had only a few hours to produce a substantial piece on Jarre's life for the following day's paper and used the quotes, as did several other print and web obituaries. The timing was deliberate for what Fitzgerald called his research. In a later email he apologised for deliberately misleading people, saying his purpose was to show that journalists use Wikipedia as a primary source, and to demonstrate the power the internet has over newspaper reporting. The absence of a footnote containing a reference for the quote ought to have made obituary writers suspicious.

Wikipedia editors were more sceptical about the unsourced quote. They deleted it twice on 30 March and, when Fitzgerald added it the second time, it lasted only six minutes on the page. His third attempt was relatively successful – the quote stayed on the site for around 25 hours before it was removed again.

*The Guardian*'s editorial code advises that quotes taken from another publication should be acknowledged. But it is less strictly adhered to in obituaries, features and blogs than in news stories, and it wasn't followed here.

In some institutions, and modules, use of Wikipedia will even result in a low or fail mark. As the editors write: 'The threshold for inclusion in Wikipedia is verifiability, not truth – that is, whether readers are able to check that material added to Wikipedia has already been published by a reliable source, not whether we think it is true.' If you decide to cite Wikipedia, remember that its articles are constantly changing: cite exact time, date and version that you are using. But don't expect it to offer you analysis. That's up to you. Many of the issues it raises could make very good research areas, connecting many of the topics in this book, as well exemplifying the rich opportunities as well as the risks that such new media forms present to those using them.

> You should be cautious about any web resource, not just Wikipedia. You will get most out of them by 'registering' as a user. This gives slightly more access and control over how you view things, though it may not be possible from your college network.

## References and further reading

Balnaves, Mark, Donald, Stephanie Hemelryk, and Shoesmith, Brian (2009) *Media Theories and Approaches: A Global Perspective*, London and New York: Palgrave MacMillan, especially Chapter 14: Research.

Branston, Gill (2000) 'Why Theory?', in Gledhill, Christine, and Williams, Linda (eds) *Reinventing Film Studies*, London and New York: Arnold.

Burkeman, Oliver (2009) 'Millions have Suffered Infinitely Greater Losses than I Have', *The Guardian*, 7 November.

Corrigan, Timothy (2003) *A Short Guide to Writing about Film*, 5th edn, London: Longman.

Cottle, Simon (2007) 'Ethnography and News Production: New(s) Developments in the Field', *Sociology Compass*, 1, 1: 1–16.

Deacon, David, Pickering, Michael, and Murdock, Graham (2007) *Researching Communications: A Practical Guide to Methods in Media and Cultural Analysis*, London and New York: Hodder.

Fairclough, Norman (2003) *Analysing Discourse: Textual Analysis for Social Research*, London: Routledge.

Geertz, Clifford (1973) *The Interpretation of Cultures: Selected Essays*, New York: Basic Books.

Haigh, Carol, and Jones, Neil (2007) 'Techno-research and Cyber-ethics: Challenges for Ethics Committees', *Research Ethics Review*, 3, 3: 69–108.

Kitzinger, Jenny, and Barbour, Rosaline (1998) *Developing Focus Group Research: Politics, Theory and Practice*, London and New York: Sage.

Mead, Margaret (2001) *Coming of Age in Samoa*, New York: Harper Perennial; first published 1928.

Morgan, David (1997) *Focus Groups as Qualitative Research*, Londno: Sage.

Rose, Gillian (2001) *Visual Methodologies*, London: Sage.

Ruddock, Andy (2008) 'Binge Drinking and Why Audiences Still Matter', *Sociology Compass*, 2, 1: 1–15.

Runciman, David (2009) 'Like Boiling a Frog', *London Review of Books*, 28 May.

Silverman, David (2000) *Doing Qualitative Research: A Practical Handbook*, London: Sage.

Skeggs, Beverley, Thumim, Nancy, and Wood, Helen (2008) ' "Oh Goodness, I am Watching Reality TV": How Methods Make Class in Multi-method Audience Research', *European Journal of Cultural Studies*, 11, 1.

Thompson, Paul (2000) *The Voice of the Past: Oral History*, Oxford: Oxford University Press.

Williams, Raymond (1983) *Keywords*, London: Fontana.

# Glossary of key terms

Listed below are some of the key terms we have used, with short 'thumbnail' definitions. Some common words are referenced only when they have special meanings in media studies. Use this glossary in conjunction with the index, contents list, chapter menus and, of course, the online resources on the **MSB5 website**, to find the material you want.

**analogue**   a form of representation which works by registering a physical change in a measuring agent (e.g. the silver nitrate on photographic film which changes colour in response to light). See **digital**.

**anchoring**   (1) written or spoken text (e.g. caption, voice-over) used to control or select a reading of a visual image; (2) also a person ('anchor') who introduces news items and often conducts interviews – both roles which can try to secure interpretation of news, one way or another.

**arbitrary signifiers**   term used in semiotics; signifiers with no resemblance to the referent or the signified; see **iconic**, **indexical** and **symbolic**.

**authorship**   approach originating in film studies which places emphasis on an individual author (usually the director) rather than the collective and collaborative nature of production.

**avatar**   a computer user's computerised representation of her/himself, as in *Second Life* or other online environment.

**back catalogue**   library or archive material, mostly in the music industry, but also films, where artists will expect to sell previous recordings for many years through re-releases and simply keeping copies 'in print' (now as digital copies).

**behaviourism/behaviourist**   movement in psychology which sees human behaviour as something which can be moulded by punishment and reward.

**blog**   shortened form of 'web log': a web-based publication consisting primarily of periodic articles (normally in reverse chronological order). Can often exist as coverage of news.

**Bollywood**   contentious term, sometimes wrongly used in the UK to refer to any form of Indian cinema (which has many 'regional cinemas' making films in regional languages). A corruption of 'Bombay Hollywood' – Hindi films made in Mumbai (Bombay).

**branding**   attaching powerful meanings or associations to products, especially in markets where one or more other products may be very similar. Involves work on the reputation or image of the producing company. Often extended now to images of people, nations, cities, etc.

**broadsheet**   type of 'serious' newspaper (UK) with larger, less square pages than tabloids, though recently 'broadsheets' have adopted tabloid sizing, referred to as 'compact'.

**burden of representation**   the problem arising when a previously under- or misrepresented group begins to be imaged in the media, and too few characters and producers have to bear the burden of being seen to represent the whole group – as 'positive role model', etc.

**capitalism**   a competitive social system which emerged in seventeenth-century Europe, involving private ownership of accumulated wealth and the exploitation of labour to produce the profit which helps create such wealth.

**celebrity**   someone seen as having the same access to fame as stars, and with a constructed 'parallel media narrative' of their life, but without the same level of achievement in the cultural sphere which initially made them famous.

**censorship**   decisive acts of forbidding or preventing publication or distribution of media products, or parts of those products, by those with the power, either economic or legislative, to do so. See **classification**.

**churn**   measure of the rate at which media service providers lose customers compared with the number of new customers signed up.

**churnalism**   term discussed by Nick Davies for journalism driven by cutbacks, competition and reliance on PR handouts – hence 'churning' out news.

**class**   (1) one of the groups into which people are divided as a result of socio-economic and other inequalities; (2) a specific group of consumers as recognised by advertisers, six classes now usually grouped into ABC1 ('upmarket') and C2DE ('downmarket'). See http://www.statistics.gov.uk.

**classification**   placing into categories, such as genres, or the BBFC's ratings, though there are a range of other ways in which understandings of texts are prepared by different ways of classifying them.

**closed**   term used of a narrative which is 'resolved' or comes to a conclusion, as opposed to an 'open' or more ambiguous narrative ending.

**CNN effect**   term for supposed effects on foreign policy, especially of US governments, of 24-hour 'rolling' news, including less easily controllable images, from about 1980 when CNN (Cable News Network) was launched.

**codes**   systems of meaning production, both within texts and at production levels (e.g. professional codes of conduct, standards of filming, etc.).

**coding**   that part of content analysis (also known as quantitative analysis) which applies a set of categories (and sometimes sub-categories) to the chosen sample, e.g. 'images of disability' might be broken into 'mental and physical disabilities'.

**cognitive psychology**   movement in psychology (opposed to **behaviourism**) which argues that human behaviour is changed by appeals to thought processes.

**commodification**   a commodity is anything which can be bought and sold; commodification and the idea of **commodity fetishism** are terms used, in Marxist theory, to argue against the undue spread and unnecessarily high valuation of certain services, items, values. See also **reification**.

**commodity fetishism**   in Marxism and Frankfurt School thinking, the belief that value lies in commodities instead of being added to raw materials by labour. More recently, for advertising and its argued consequences, a process whereby products (such as cars and handbags) are given an almost magical appeal and status. See **reification** and **commodification**.

**common sense**   in discussions of ideology, especially from Gramsci, a set of widely held assumptions that the world's meanings are obvious and can be understood without recourse to analysis or theory. Opposed to Gramsci's concept of 'good sense' which combines theory and experience.

**compassion fatigue**   loosely used term which suggests viewers are fatigued and numbed by the number of terrible events reported in the news. Aid organisations prefer 'media fatigue'.

**conglomerate** large industrial corporation comprising several distinct companies in more than one industry or in different sectors of the same industry.

**connote/connotation** in semiotics, the meanings interpreted from a sign which link it to other concepts, values, memories.

**consolidation** in media markets, the trend for large corporations to acquire smaller companies, producing an **oligopoly** of large **media conglomerates**.

**conspicuous consumption** term used to describe the consumption of goods and commodities for the sake of displaying social status and wealth. Not used of eating disorders.

**consumers** term for media audiences which emphasises their commercially shaped choices (in a supposedly 'free market') as opposed to older models of 'an audience' or 'the mass audience'. See also **prosumers**.

**content analysis** form of analysis focusing on manifest features of texts via a coding frame of carefully chosen questions and ways of valuing what is found through them.

**content provider** media companies which produce programme material for specific delivery or distribution systems, especially cable, satellite and internet, i.e. content carriers.

**convergence** the 'coming together' of previously separate industries (computing, printing, film, audio, etc.) which increasingly use the same or related technology and skilled workers. A feature of the contemporary media environment, convergence is a product of mergers between companies in different sectors as well as an outcome of technological development.

**creative commons** an international non-profit organisation devoted to expanding the range of creative works available for others to build upon legally and to share, using creative commons licences. These allow creators to communicate which rights they reserve, and which rights they waive for the benefit of recipients or other creators. Wikipedia is a notable web-based project using one of these licences.

**critical pluralism** a theoretical approach which acknowledges the co-existence of different sets of ideas (as in pluralism) but recognises that some are more powerful than others, and that they are in a struggle for ascendancy.

**cross-generic** blending different genre elements, e.g. horror and comedy. Arguably only a very few texts do *not* combine in this way.

**cult** term used of media texts around which 'cults' or groups of enthusiastic users have developed.

**cultural codes** meanings derived from cultural differences; see **codes**.

**cultural competence** from Bourdieu, the idea that ease of access to media texts depends on cultural difference and experience.

**cultural imperialism** position that the globalisation of communication has been driven, particularly since the Second World War, by the 'military industrial complex' of the large US-based corporations and state. Sometimes used interchangeably with **media imperialism**.

**cycle** related to genre, a series of films with very similar content or themes, often quite clearly referring to each other, produced over a short period.

**decoding** semiotic term for 'reading' the codes in a media text. Now seen as problematic since it implies a single, clear-cut meaning, waiting to be 'decoded'.

**denote/denotation** in semiotics, the work of that part of the sign (the signifier) which is immediately recognisable to the reader and which has a direct relationship to a real-world entity (the referent).

**deregulation** removal or 'lightening' of government restrictions on media industries, sometimes called 're-regulation' to draw attention to the ways in which it is not simply a liberation from rules.

**diegesis** the 'fictional world' of the audio-visual narrative. Most useful in distinguishing between 'diegetic' and 'non-diegetic' sound.

**differential pricing** means of accumulating maximum profit on a product by differentiating its price depending on what different markets (i.e. the wealth of potential consumers) will allow.

**digital** a form of representation based on discrete units of numerical information.

**Direct Cinema** documentary movement in 1960s US using new lightweight cameras and microphones, which kept as close to events as possible, with nothing rehearsed or scripted, no voice-over or music track, and a high **shooting ratio**.

**disavowal**  in psychoanalysis, the process of refusing to recognise a troubling or traumatic perception. Applied by some theorists to account for the apparent power of advertising, entertainment and fantasy forms, etc. to 'mask' unpleasant realities. The term suggests some awareness on the part of audiences, along with their desire to ignore that for the sake of the pleasures of these forms.

**discourse**  any regulated system of statements or language use (e.g. in the law or medicine) which has evolved rules, and therefore exclusions and assumptions involved with the social practices of which it is part. For media the term extends to include visual as well as verbal languages, and also work on discourses' different connections to power.

**diversity**  (1) the range of different types of programmes available on broadcast networks; (2) policy target for equality of employment or access to media for people of different ages, genders, ethnicities, etc.; (3) **diversification** (operating in as many media industries as possible) is an aim of some managements.

**dot.com**  businesses which use the internet as their primary marketplace, sometimes with little more than a clever marketing idea. Also **dot.com bubble** which refers to the sudden expansion of such firms' cash value, and the ensuing crash of 2000.

**drama-documentary, 'drama-doc'**  a re-enactment of 'real' events presented using techniques from fictional drama narratives.

**dystopia**  term used in science fiction; a dreadful future society, the opposite of utopia.

**ecology**  term used by McLuhan to suggest a kind of balance between different kinds of media, and their relation to human perception and understanding. Very loosely connected to the use of 'ecology' in what are now called environmentalist discourses. Some have suggested 'media ecology' avoids the different connotations of 'the capitalist media market'.

**editing**  (1) sequencing of text, images and sounds, the 'shaping' of a narrative; (2) the overall control and direction of fact-based publications in print and broadcasting.

**effects model**  model concerned with how the media 'does things to' audiences.

**empirical**  relying on observed experience as evidence for positions. A controversial term, often caricatured by opponents to imply an approach opposed to any kind of theory and relying on sense experience or simplistic facts alone.

**epistemology**   the study of ways of knowing, of how sets of knowledge are created.

**ethnic (n. ethnicity)**   usually signifies non-biological, broadly cultural distinctiveness and identities, produced through such activities as language and religion, as well as geographical location. As such it does not, like 'race'-based divisions, collapse historical human differences into supposedly fundamental 'racial' divisions – white/black or Aryan, Caucasian, Arab, Semitic and so on.

**ethnography**   a method of research, involving spending considerable periods of time with a particular community or group of people. Audience ethnography was an important development in media studies and now includes internet forms.

**feminist**   belonging to movements and sets of ideas and arguments which advocate women having equal rights and opportunities to those possessed by men.

**focus groups**   method of audience research which assembles small, representative groups whose fairly informal discussions are facilitated, recorded and analysed.

**format**   (1) different size or shape of common media products (newspapers as formatted as tabloid or broadsheet, film as 35mm or 16mm, etc.); (2) a TV category allowing for the international trading of TV show concepts and set-ups: e.g. both *The Weakest Link* and *Who Wants to Be a Millionaire?* belong to the genre 'quiz show' though their formats differ; (3) 'format radio': station using only one kind of music or speech.

**framing**   (1) referring to an image selected to show a person or object; various framings from 'long shot' to 'extreme close-up' are defined by the size of the human body in the frame; (2) referring to the power of media to 'frame' or shape and set the limits to how audiences are invited to perceive certain groups, issues, stories, especially in news forms.

**franchise**   (1) generally a licence to use a brand name in retailing or the service sector. Now used in Hollywood to describe a successful film title that can be developed into new films and associated products, e.g. *Harry Potter*; (2) in the UK, a term for the licence to broadcast specific services.

**Frankfurt School**   German critical theorists of mass culture working from the 1920s and 1930s. Later worked in the US, in exile from German fascism.

**genre**   theoretical term for classification of media texts into type groupings.

**globalisation**   a process in which activities are organised on a global scale, in ways which involve some interdependence, and which are now often instantaneous.

**greenwashing**   term used to describe claims of being 'environmentally friendly' made by companies about activities which in fact damage the environment.

**hegemony, hegemonic**   concept from Gramsci suggesting that power is achieved by dominant groups through successful struggles to persuade the subordinate that arrangements are in their interest.

**horizontal integration**   when an organisation acquires or merges with competitors in the same industry sector.

**hybrid (n. hybridity)**   combining differences, of style or technologies or cultural form (e.g. *Men in Black*'s combination of horror and comedy).

**hypertext**   text which includes links that take readers directly to other texts; hypertext mark-up language (*html*) is used to write pages on the **World Wide Web**.

**hypodermic model**   critical term for a model of media effects on audiences which it characterises as over-simple, seeing meaning as resembling the injection of a drug, with guaranteed effects.

**iconic**   (from semiotics) resembling real-world objects (of signs); see also **arbitrary signifiers, indexical** and **symbolic**.

**iconography**   art history term, used to describe the study of familiar iconic signs in a genre.

**identity politics**   the values and movements which have developed since the 1960s around issues of identity, in particular gender, age, race, sexuality and disability. Class has tended to be displaced by such politics.

**ideology (adj. ideological)**   complex term involving ideas, values and understanding of the social world, and how these are related to the distribution of power in society. Also involves how such values come to seem 'natural'.

**immersion**   the experience of being inside the world of a media product, which appears to surround the user. Term usually involves games, though recent films such as *Avatar* (US 2009) seek the same effects via 3D, IMAX, etc.

**independent**   any company in a media industry which is not seen as a major.

**indexical**   (in semiotics) referring to concepts via causal relationships (e.g. heat signified by the reading on a thermometer).

**internet**   the global 'network of networks' which links together computers and servers.

**intertextuality**   the variety of ways in which media and other texts interact with each other, rather than being unique or distinct. Especially relevant for the proliferation of media forms now, and audience familiarity with them.

**long tail**   theory of the ways that media businesses and economics have changed due to the impact of the internet and networking, so that smaller niche markets can be tapped, rather than the 'top-down' mass producers simply profiting from standardised markets.

**ludology**   the study and theory of games, both pre- and post-internet.

**market**   the total of all the potential sellers and buyers for a particular product (and the number of products likely to be exchanged).

**marketing**   the process of presenting a product to its target audience; the ways in which it is positioned in its particular market.

**masochism**   broadly, a medical/psychoanalytic term for the pleasure or gratification of having pain inflicted, or of being controlled. In film theory it has been used to explain some of the pleasures of cinema.

**Media 2.0**   (1) an alternative to 'Web 2.0' as a descriptor of the new media environment; (2) referring to a new kind of media studies configured to deal with studying that new environment.

**media conglomerates**   the major media corporations which combine several different activities under a single brand.

**media imperialism**   (also called **cultural imperialism**) the argument that rich and powerful countries (or 'military industrial complexes'), especially the US, dominate poorer ones through control of globalised media industries. Generally adapted now to refer to the role of corporations rather than nation states.

**methodology**   set of philosophical beliefs about an object of research involving the production of methods for that research.

**mid-market**   in classifications of media texts (especially newspapers), the middle position between **tabloid** and **quality**.

**MMS**   Multimedia Messaging System, the protocol for sending sound and moving images via mobile phones.

**mode of address**   the way a text 'speaks' to its audiences and, it is often argued, thereby 'positions' them – as young, old, respected or not, etc.

**model**   in social sciences, a way of imagining how a system might work.

**monopoly**   any market situation where one seller controls prices and the supply of product. In the UK a 25 per cent share will attract the interest of the Office of Fair Trading (OFT) and the Competition Commission.

**moral panic**   term for a widespread public panic around a perceived 'crisis', often involving the overreaction of certain kinds of news media, and accompanying calls that 'something must be done', leading to pressure for legislation, 'stiffer penalties', etc.

**multimedia**   referring to several traditionally separate media being used together, e.g. sound, image and text on computers.

**narration**   the process of telling a story, the selection and organisation of the events for a particular audience.

**narrative**   specialist term referring to the 'telling' of a sequence of events organised into a story. This shapes the events, characters, arrangement of time, etc. in very particular ways so as to invite particular positions towards the 'story' on the part of audiences.

**narrowcasting**   term which contrasts itself with 'broadcasting' to draw attention to the assumed fragmentation of audiences addressed by much television now.

**negotiated**   in audience theory, the idea that a meaning is arrived at as a result of a process of give and take between the reader's assumptions and the 'preferred meaning' offered by the text.

**neoliberalism**   term describing a socio-economic combination of privatisation and deregulation and an accompanying ideological celebration of 'free trade' and 'free markets'.

**news agencies**   organisations, such as Reuters, which gather news stories and sell them to broadcasters and newspaper publishers.

**news values**   a set of widely recognised but rarely explicitly stated criteria used to select and prioritise news stories for publication. Now seen as a broad if rather reductionist guide, needing to be partly updated, especially to take account of 24-hour news and interactive media.

**niche**   very small but highly profitable markets which can sometimes support specialist advertising-led media products.

**ontology**   a philosophical area involved in asking what we take to be real, and what is knowable.

**planned obsolescence**   also 'built-in obsolescence', term to describe the ways in which manufacturers deliberately 'build into' certain products (especially cars) features that prevent them lasting for as long as they could, thus encouraging (otherwise unnecessary) repeated acts of purchase.

**plot**   defined in relation to '**story**' as those events in a narrative which are presented to an audience directly. Others may be ignored because they are so routine (going to the bathroom) or 'hidden' to produce suspense.

**podcast**   a form of broadcasting in which a radio programme or any audio recording (usually containing a speech component) is stored as an MP3 file and can be downloaded (possibly automatically by subscription) and played by listeners at a convenient time on any MP3 player.

**political economy**   study of the social relations, particularly power relations, that together constitute the production, distribution and consumption of resources.

**polysemic**   literally 'many-signed', a text in which there are several possible meanings depending on the ways its constituent signs are read. Often now abandoned in favour of the position that audience or user activity, as part of meaning production, means that no sign can have, securely, only one meaning.

**post-feminism**   position which argues that the condition of women 'after' the successes of the 1960s and 1970s waves of feminist struggles means that they can take for granted respect and equality and enjoy ironic pleasures and playfulness around traditional 'femininity'.

**postmodernism**   complex term used with several meanings, usually involving self-reflexive contemporary culture and media or, more widely, a set of attitudes to the contemporary world.

**preferred reading** (from Hall's encoding/decoding theory of audience readings): the most likely reading of a text by audiences, given the operation of power structures and dominant values both in the institution producing the text and in audiences. Hall argues it always struggles with other possible meanings.

**privatisation** process by which services or utilities in the public sector are transferred to private ownership.

**product placement** an unofficial form of advertising in which branded products feature prominently in films, etc.

**propaganda** any media text which seeks openly to persuade an audience of the validity of particular beliefs or actions. Term is sometimes applied to 'black propaganda' which is not open about its intentions, e.g. in wartime.

**prosumer** term used, in both business and some media studies accounts of the impact of Web 2.0, to emphasise the activity of 'consumers' or users of interactive media. They are said to become a mixture of producers and consumers, hence 'prosumers'.

**public service** a service provided with a prime aim of meeting perceived social needs, rather than private profit. In broadcasting can be a requirement of a licence granted to private sector companies.

**public service broadcasting** (**PSB**) regulated broadcasting which has 'providing a public service' as a primary aim.

**public sphere** a model of a part of social life in which disinterested, rational and open public conversation about social and political matters can be safely held, and thereby form the basis for democratic governance. Coined in 1962 (translated 1989) by Jürgen Habermas (1929–) it now needs updating, though remains a powerful ideal for many forms of media.

**publisher broadcaster** a broadcaster which commissions all programming from other companies rather than making them itself. Channel 4 was the first UK broadcaster to do this.

**qualitative research** research based on exploring the qualities of 'texts', defined broadly to include transcriptions of discussion groups, interviews, etc. as well as individual films, articles, games set-ups and so on.

**quantitative analysis** partly defined by being amenable to statistical analysis, which qualitative research is not, generally. Both qualitative and quantitative methods benefit from working together, rather than being seen as antagonistic.

**racism**   the stigmatising of difference along the lines of 'racial' characteristics in order to justify advantage or abuse of power, whether economic, political, cultural or psychological. See **ethnic (n. ethnicity)**.

**'reality TV'**   form of factual television on UK screens from about 1989. Now used loosely of television which is largely unscripted, making substantial use of ordinary people, and mixing information and entertainment forms.

**red-top**   UK term for a 'downmarket' **tabloid** newspaper (as distinct from 'midmarket' tabloids and compacts, argued to be less sensationalist).

**referent**   in semiotics, the 'real world' object to which the sign or signifier refers.

**regulation**   the process of monitoring and to an extent controlling the activities of industries. Some media industries regulate themselves and others are regulated by bodies set up by legislation.

**reification**   in Marxist theory, a process whereby products and larger social processes, all made by people, are treated as though they have an almost magical reality and logic of their own, as though 'the market' is almost a real 'thing'. Used, along with **commodity fetishism**, in thinking about ideology as a 'masking' of actual social relations.

**re-mediation**   the entry of one (usually older) media form into another, usually argued as occurring in the early years of a new medium (e.g. early cinema used and adapted theatrical forms).

**repertoire of elements**   the fluid system of conventions and expectations associated with genre texts.

**replicability**   unambiguity of research findings such that different researchers at different times would interpret the evidence in exactly the same way.

**restricted narration**   refers to how information about narrative events and characters is distributed – withheld or supplied for the sake of the story.

**retro-sexism**   recent term to describe the ways that older subordinate positions for women (as 'sex objects', as lower earning than men, more confined to the domestic sphere, etc.) can be discerned beneath the apparent irony and playfulness of 'laddish' and 'ladette' cultures, arguments about the 'empowerment' involved in pole dancing, etc.

**romance**  a genre in which the narrative centres on intimate personal relationships, usually related to love, sex and marriage, and often focused on a woman.

**samples**  (1) in digital audio production, sounds or sequence of sounds 'captured' by a computer for use in future productions; (2) carefully selected groups of people chosen in audience research to represent larger populations.

**script**  (1) dialogue and production directions for a radio, film or television production; (2) more broadly, shared expectations about what is likely to happen in certain contexts, based on media knowledge, and also what is desirable, and undesirable, in terms of 'outcomes'. These are often derived from repeated fictional shapes, e.g. expecting 'the happy ending'.

**semiotics/semiology**  the study of sign systems.

**share**  'The share of total weekly viewing for each channel.' BARB definition, http://www.barb.co.uk.

**shooting ratio**  the ratio between the total amount of footage filmed and the amount actually used in a final edited film or TV production.

**sign/signified/signifier**  the sign, in semiotics, is divided into the signifier, or physical form taken by the sign, and the signified, which is the concept it stands in for.

**SMS**  (Short Message Service) see **text**.

**social media**  'Any tool or service that uses the internet to facilitate conversations.' See http://www.briansolis.com/2010/01/defining-social-media-the-saga-continues for fuller discussion.

**social psychology**  the study of human behaviour.

**soft money**  film industry term for funding that derives from various forms of public revenue support such as tax breaks, grants, etc. (by implication commerical funding is 'hard').

**sousveillance**  term which dramatises the difference between 'top-down' and 'from-below' surveillance. Involves recording or watching 'from below', or within, an event (e.g. a demo) by one of the participants instead of the expected 'outside' or official camera crew.

**spin**   activities of press or PR officers (also called 'spin doctors') employed to put a positive 'spin' or angle on stories about their employer or client. The term suggests an unjustifiable degree of intervention in the construction of news, though could be read more sympathetically as, also, a necessary part of any communication.

**standardisation**   can signify 'sameness' but can also denote the maintenance of standards, in the sense of quality.

**stereotypes, stereotyping**   originally a term from printing, literally a 'solid' block of metal type; then, a representation of a type of person, without fine detail.

**story**   all of the events in a narrative, those presented directly to an audience and those which might be inferred – compare with **plot**.

**structuralism**   an approach to critical analysis which emphasises universal structures underlying the surface differences and apparent randomness of cultures, stories, media texts, etc.

**subliminal advertising**   kind of advertising associated with hypnosis. Said to work by flashing barely perceptible messages to audiences in between frames of a film or television advertisements. The idea still fascinates, though it is now discredited.

**symbolic**   used in semiotics of a sign (usually visual) which has come to stand for a particular set of qualities or values, e.g. the 'Stars and Stripes' for the US; see **arbitrary signifiers**, **iconic** and **indexical**.

**synergy**   the combined marketing of 'products' or commodities (including people) across different media and other products, which are often owned by the same corporation such that the total effect is greater than the sum of the different parts.

**tabloid**   the size of a newsprint page, half that of the 'broadsheet'; by extension: sensationalist media form (television and radio as well as the press). Many 'broadsheet' papers are now 'tabloid' size, so in the UK the term 'red-top' often substitutes for 'tabloid'.

**technological determinism**   the idea that technology in itself determines human perception and social changes, rather than itself being socially shaped, from first ideas of what seems feasible, to matters of design, the funding of production, marketing, uses, and consequences, foreseen and unforeseen.

**text**   (1) any system of signs which can be 'read' – a poster, photograph, haircut, etc; (2) text message: short written message sent via use of a service on most mobile phones (see **SMS**). Verb: to text. Often uses a specialised, abbreviated language.

**thick** specialist use of this word, denoting research which combines different approaches, especially in the social sciences, to explain not just forms of human behaviour, but also their contexts and histories.

**tipping point** term for the way that momentum for social change, or appetite for a product, gradually builds up, until a point is reached where the momentum is suddenly unstoppable.

**top-slicing** taking a share of a revenue or income, currently debated around funding of **public service broadcasting (PSB)** in the UK.

**triangulation** a practice in geometry, which determines the location of a point by measuring *angles* to it from other known points, rather than measuring distance directly. The metaphor is often used for the practice of combining of research methods.

**uses and gratifications model** 'active' model of audience behaviour, emphasising the uses to which audiences put even the most unlikely texts.

**USP** unique selling proposition, term used in brand advertising for the supposedly unique quality of products which advertisers seek to communicate to potential buyers.

**verisimilitude** quality of seeming like what is taken to be the real world of a particular text.

**vertical integration** business activity involving one company having acquired another situated elsewhere in their particular production and distribution process. Often used to describe production, distribution and exhibition in the Hollywood 'studio' system.

**vox pop** from the Latin *vox populi* or 'voice of the people', used now of news interviews with men and women on the street, using their own words, though heavily edited by the news programme.

**voyeurism** the pleasure of looking while unseen; has been used in thinking about (assumed) male pleasure in the ways cinema, advertising, etc. construct women as 'objects of the [male] gaze'.

**Web 2.0** term used to suggest a new stage of internet development and usage arriving with 'always on' portable and interactive media, making direct communication easy and attractive, and meaning users often expect sites to offer opportunities for feedback, etc. See also **Media 2.0**.

# Index

This index lists page references to four different kinds of information: key terms, media organisations, people and titles of films, radio and television programmes etc. It isn't exhaustive but, used in conjunction with the Glossary, should help you find out what you want. Definitions (either in the chapter or in the Glossary) will sometimes be signalled by **bold numbers,** illustrations by *italic numbers* and margin entries by (m).

# Introduction to Film Studies

## Fourth Edition

### Edited by Jill Nelmes

'**This fourth edition is even more comprehensive and accessible than previous editions. It addresses new generations of students, asks new questions of film studies and rises to the radical challenge of answering those questions superbly well.**'

Pat Brereton, *Dublin City University*

*Introduction to Film Studies* is a comprehensive leading textbook for students of cinema. This completely revised and updated fourth edition guides students through the key issues and concepts in film studies, traces the historical development of film and introduces some of the world's key national cinemas.

A range of theories and theorists are presented and each chapter is written by a subject specialist, including three new authors, with a wide range of films analysed and discussed. It is lavishly illustrated with film stills and production shots, many of them in colour. It is essential reading for any introductory student of film, media studies or the visual arts worldwide.

### Key features

- full coverage of important topics for introductory level
- in-depth discussion of the contemporary film industry
- six new chapters
- new case studies include *Bamboozled*, *Wild Strawberries*, *Run Lola Run*, *Grey Gardens*, *Grizzly Man*, *Boys Don't Cry*, *Love Actually*, and many others
- marginal key terms, notes and cross-referencing
- suggestions for further reading, further viewing and a comprehensive glossary and bibliography
- website resources at http://cw.routledge.com/textbooks/9780415409285/

ISBN 13: 978–0–415–40929–2 (hbk)
ISBN 13: 978–0-415–40928–5 (pbk)

Available at all good bookshops
For ordering and further information please visit:
www.routledge.com

# An Introduction to Television Studies

## Second Edition

### *Jonathan Bignell*

**'A wonderfully ambitious and clear introduction to television studies for the undergraduate reader.'**
Gill Branston, *University of Cardiff* and co-author of *The Media Student's Book*

In this comprehensive textbook, newly updated for its second edition, Jonathan Bignell provides students with a framework for understanding the key concepts and main approaches to television studies, including audience research, television history and broadcasting policy, and the analytical study of individual programmes.

**Features for the second edition include:**

- a glossary of key terms
- key terms defined in margins
- suggestions for further reading at the end of each chapter
- activities for use in class or as assignments
- new and updated case studies discussing advertisements such as the Guinness 'Surfer' ad, approaches to news reporting, television scheduling, and programmes such as *Big Brother* and *Wife Swap*.

Individual chapters address: studying television, television histories, television cultures, television texts and narratives, television and genre, television production, postmodern television, television realities, television representation, television you can't see, shaping audiences, television in everyday life.

ISBN 13: 978–0–415–41917–8 (hbk)
ISBN 13: 978–0–415–41918–5 (pbk)

Available at all good bookshops
For ordering and further information please visit:
www.routledge.com

# New Media: A Critical Introduction

## Second Edition

*Martin Lister, Jon Dovey, Seth Giddings, Iain Grant and Kieran Kelly*

**'Far more than simply an upgrade or update, this second edition . . . should be required reading for anyone interested in this all-important, but much-mythologised, subject.'**

Julian Petley, *Brunel University*

*New Media: A Critical Introduction* is a comprehensive introduction to the culture, history, technologies and theories of new media. Written especially for students, the book considers the ways in which 'new media' really are new, assesses the claims that a media and technological revolution has taken place and formulates new ways for media studies to respond to new technologies.

Substantially updated from the first edition to cover recent theoretical developments, approaches and significant technological developments, this is the best and by far the most comprehensive textbook available on this exciting and expanding subject.

**Key features:**

- Fully immersive companion website www.newmediaintro.com including new international case studies, extra resources and multimedia features
- New chapters and new case studies on a wealth of material including wikis and Web 2.0, videogames, music as new media, and many, many more
- Packed with pedagogical features to make the text more accessible, easier to use for students and simpler to teach from. These include: • a user's guide • marginal notes • case studies • glossary of terms • an expanded and annotated bibliography to help with further study

ISBN 13: 978–0–415–43160–6 (hbk)
ISBN 13: 978–0–415–43161–3 (pbk)
ISBN 13: 978–0–203–88482–9 (ebk)

Available at all good bookshops
For ordering and further information please visit:
www.routledge.com

# Power Without Responsibility

## Seventh Edition

### *James Curran and Jean Seaton*

'A lucid, engaging account of how Britain's media is developing –
and it is now bang up to date. I couldn't put it down.'
Maggie Brown, *Channel 4 historian and* The Guardian *media writer*

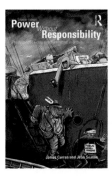

*Power Without Responsibility* is a classic introduction to the history, sociology, theory
and politics of the media in Britain.

Hailed by the Times Higher Education Supplement as the 'seminal media text', and
translated into Arabic, Chinese and other foreign languages, it is an essential guide
for media students and critical media consumers alike.

The new edition has been substantially revised to bring it right up to date with developments in the media
industry, new media technologies and changes in the political and academic debates surrounding the media.
In this new edition, the authors consider:

- the impact of the internet
- the failure of interactive TV
- media and Britishness
- new media and global understanding
- journalism in crisis
- BBC and broadcasting at the beginning of the 21st Century

Assessing the media at a time of profound change, the authors set out the democratic choices for media
reform.

ISBN 13: 978–0–415–46698–1 (hbk)
ISBN 13: 978–0–415–46699–8 (pbk)
ISBN 13: 978–0–203–87140–9 (ebk)

Available at all good bookshops
For ordering and further information please visit:
www.routledge.com

# WHAT MEDIA CLASSES REALLY WANT TO DISCUSS

## A Student Guide

**Greg M. Smith**, *Georgia State University, USA*

You probably already have a clear idea of what a 'discussion guide for students' is: a series of not-very-interesting questions at the end of a textbook chapter. Instead of triggering thought-provoking class discussion, all too often these guides are time-consuming and ineffective.

This is not that kind of discussion guide.

*What Media Classes Really Want To Discuss* focuses on topics that introductory textbooks generally ignore, although they are prominent in students' minds. Using approachable prose, this book will give students a more precise critical language to discuss 'common sense' phenomena about media.

The book acknowledges that students begin introductory film and television courses thinking they already know a great deal about the subject. *What Media Classes Really Want To Discuss* provides students with a solid starting point for discussing their assumptions critically and encourages the reader to argue with the book, furthering the 'discussion' on media in everyday life and in the classroom.

August 2010:
Pbk: 978-0-415-77812-1
Hbk: 978-0-415-77811-4
ebk: 978-0-203-84642-1